England's Landscape
The South West

NORTH EAST

NORTH WEST

WEST MIDLANDS

EAST MIDLANDS

EAST ANGLIA

WEST

SOUTH EAST

SOUTH WEST

Collins

England's Landscape
The South West

Edited by Roger J P Kain

Catherine Brace
Mark Brayshay
Bruce Coleman
David Harvey
Robert A Higham
Roger J P Kain
Mark Overton
Stephen Rippon
Bruce Webb

Series Editor Neil Cossons

ENGLISH HERITAGE

First published in 2006 by Collins, an imprint of
HarperCollins*Publishers*
77–85 Fulham Palace Road, London W6 8JB

www.collins.co.uk

10 9 8 7 6 5 4 3 2
10 09 08 07

Copyright in the text © the individual authors 2006

Images (except as otherwise shown) © Crown copyright. NMR or © English Heritage. Application for the reproduction of images should be made to the National Monuments Record. Every effort has been made to trace the copyright holders and we apologise in advance for any unintentional omissions, which we would be pleased to correct in any subsequent edition of this book.

ISBN 10 – 0 00 715572 7
ISBN 13 – 9 78 0 00 715572 9

British Library Cataloguing in Publication Data
A CIP catalogue record for this book is available from the British Library.

All rights reserved
No part of this publication may be reproduced or transmitted in any form or by any means, electronic or mechanical, including photocopying, recording or any information storage or retrieval system, without permission in writing from the publisher.

The authors hereby assert their moral right to be identified as the authors of this work and the publisher undertakes to observe such assertion and to impose the same condition on its licencees.

Map on previous page:
The regions: the red lines bound the general area covered by each volume.

Publisher & Commissioning Editor Myles Archibald
Production Director Graham Cook
Edited by Rowan Whimster
Designed by D & N Publishing, Hungerford, Berkshire
Indexed by Sheila Seacroft

Printed in Italy by LEGO SpA, Vicenza

ACKNOWLEDGEMENTS

SERIES EDITOR
Sir Neil Cossons OBE
Chairman, English Heritage
President, Royal Geographical Society
The series editor would like to acknowledge the contribution of the following people:

EDITORIAL BOARD:
Professor David Cannadine
Queen Elizabeth the Queen Mother Professor of British History, University of London

Professor Barry Cunliffe
Professor of European Archaeology, University of Oxford

Professor Richard Lawton
Professor Emeritus, Department of Geography, University of Liverpool

Professor Brian K Roberts
Professor Emeritus, Department of Geography, University of Durham

ENGLISH HERITAGE EXECUTIVE EDITORS:
Dr Paul Barnwell, *Head of Medieval and Later Rural Research*
Dr Martin Cherry, *Former Chief Buildings Historian*
Humphrey Welfare, *Northern Territory Director*
Graham Fairclough, *Head of Characterisation*

ENGLISH HERITAGE PROJECT MANAGERS:
Val Horsler, *former Head of Publishing*
Adele Campbell, *Commercial Publishing Manager*

All new ground and air photography was taken specifically for this series. Thanks to: Damian Grady, Senior Investigator of English Heritage Aerial Survey and Investigation Team, and to the photographic and dark-room teams in Swindon; Steve Cole, Head of Photography, and the staff of the English Heritage Photography team. Archive material from the National Monuments Record was researched by the Enquiry and Research Services teams led by Alyson Rogers (Buildings) and Lindsay Jones (Archaeology/Air Photos). Graphics lists were managed by John Vallender and Bernard Thomason. Graphics were produced under the management of Rob Read of 3's Company (Consultancy) Ltd by John Hodgson and Rob Read. All other images were researched by Jo Walton and Julia Harris-Voss.

Contents

Acknowledgements   8

Foreword   *Neil Cossons*   9

1 The Personality of the South West   *Roger Kain*   11
   A Landscape Described, Dissected and Conceived   12

PART I: LAND AND PEOPLE

2 The Environmental Setting of
   Human Occupation   *Bruce Webb* 15
   Geological Foundations   16
   Landform Development   22
   Climatic Conditions   30
   Soils and Vegetation   33
   Environmental Hazards   37
   Conclusions   40

3 Landscapes of Pre-Medieval Occupation   *Stephen Rippon*   41
   The Distinctive Landscapes of the South-west Peninsula   41
   The Chronological Framework   43
   Landscapes of Hunter-gatherers and the Early Impact of
      Human Communities on the Environment   45
   Landscapes of the Earliest Agriculturalists and Their Ancestors   46
   Landscapes of the First Sedentary Farmers   51
   Landscapes of Stratified Societies   55
   The Romano-British to Medieval Transition: Continuity
      in the Rural Landscape and Resource Exploitation   61
   The Creation of the Historic Landscape   63
   The Distinctiveness of the South West   65

4 People and Livelihoods: Agents of
   Landscape Change   *Bruce Coleman* 67
   The Medieval Period   68
   The Early-Modern South West   70
   19th and 20th Centuries   71

CONTENTS

PART II: LANDSCAPES DISSECTED

5 ***Faith, Church and Landscape***   *David Harvey*   75
    The South West in a National Context   75
    The Medieval Legacy: Sites, Fabric and Reformation   77
    Dissent and Nonconformity: Reform and Renovation   81
    Faith, Church and Landscape: Today and Tomorrow   85

6 ***Landscapes of Defence, Security and Status***   *Robert A Higham*   89
    The Changing Military Context   89
    Regional Themes   90
    Devon *Burhs*   93
    New Town Defences   95
    Castle Building from the Norman Conquest   97
    Coastal Defences   103
    Landscape Themes: a Summary   108

7 ***Farming, Fishing and Rural Settlements***   *Mark Overton*   109
    Settlement Expansion and Contraction from
       Medieval Times to the 19th Century   110
    The South West in the International Economy 1850–1939   119
    A New Rural England   125
    Changing Agriculture, Changing Landscapes   130

8 ***Landscapes of Industry***   *Mark Brayshay*   131
    Landscapes of the Farming and Fishing Industries   131
    Landscapes of the Textile Industries   136
    Landscapes of Metal Mining   139
    Slate and Stone Quarrying   148
    Engineering and Foundries   150
    Landscapes of Shipbuilding and Ship-repairing   150
    Landscapes of New Industry   152
    Moving On   153

9 ***Urban Landscapes***   *Mark Brayshay*   155
    Roman Exeter   157
    The Saxon *Burhs*   158
    Post-conquest and Medieval Towns   160
    Early Modern and Renaissance Urban Landscapes   164
    Industry, Trade and the Urban Landscape   172
    Natural Disasters, Warfare and the Urban Landscape   174
    Recreation, Tourism and the Urban Landscape   179
    Urban Landscapes and Encounters with Modernity   182
    Truro, Plymouth and Exeter   183

10 ***Landscapes of Transport***   *Mark Brayshay*   185
    Roads, Tracks and Footpaths   185
    Canal Landscapes   191
    Railway Landscapes   196

Coastal Transport Landscapes	202
Landscapes of Air Transport	204
Transport and Landscape	206

PART III: LANDSCAPES AS SYMBOL AND INSPIRATION

11 Landscape as Heritage and a Recreational Resource — *David Harvey* — 207
- Heritage Defined in the Here and Now — 209
- The Social Context of Heritage in the South West — 210
- Scale, Identity and the Use of Heritage in the South West — 214
- A South-west Heritage Landscape? Dissonance and Opportunity — 215
- Landscapes of Industrial Heritage in the South West — 217
- Landscapes of Rural Heritage in the South West — 219
- Landscapes of Tourism — 222
- Heritage Inertia and the Question of Development — 225
- Cornish Heritage: Distinction and Resistance — 226
- Heritage Futures in the South West — 228

12 Landscapes and Senses of Place — *Catherine Brace* — 229
- Discovering the South West — 230
- Literary Landscapes of the South West — 234
- Envisioning Landscapes — 239
- A Unified Sense of Place for the South West? — 243

Bibliography — 247

Index — 250

Picture Credits — 256

ACKNOWLEDGEMENTS

Chapter 3 (Stephen Rippon)

I would like to thank all the archaeologists and historians with whom I have discussed the landscape of south-west England over the past few years, including Harold Fox, Henrietta Quinnell who kindly allowed access to the unpublished report on Trethurgy Round, and Frances Griffith who gave permission for the reproduction of Figs 3.2 and 3.13. I am extremely grateful to Chris Caseldine, Frances Griffith, Peter Herring, Henrietta Quinnell and Rob Wilson-North for commenting on a first draft of this chapter, though all opinions expressed are my own responsibility.

Chapter 6 (Robert A Higham)

I would like to thank Oliver Creighton for discussion of this chapter and for commenting on a draft of its text. My thanks are also due to Adam Wainwright for supplementing my own knowledge with his recent work on Powderham, whose 18th-century development he has now explored as part of a PhD thesis (Exeter University). I am grateful to Andrew Saunders for sharing his thoughts on early Launceston prior to their final publication. Invaluable help has been received, over the many years I have been exploring this subject, from the staffs of the county record offices and the county sites and monuments records in Devon and Cornwall, as well as from the West Country Studies Library in Exeter. Collaboration from colleagues in Devon (Exeter Archaeology) and Cornwall (Historic Environment Service and Cornwall Archaeological Unit) has also been much appreciated. Permission for reproduction of Fig 6.5 was given by Stewart Brown and for Fig 6.9 by Peter Herring, to both of whom I am grateful. Many details in the text of this chapter were drawn from specialist publications, which have not been cited here, but to whose authors I am much indebted.

Foreword

The landscape of England evokes intense passion and profound emotion. This most loved of places, the inspiration for generations of writers, poets and artists, it is at once both the source of the nation's infatuation and the setting for grievous misunderstanding. For people who visit, the view of England offers some of their most lasting images. For exiles abroad the memory of the English landscape sustains their beliefs and desire for a homecoming.

But for those who live in England the obsession is double edged. On the one hand we cherish the unchanging atmosphere of a familiar place, and on the other make impossible demands of it, believing that it will always accommodate, always forgive. Only in the last half century or so have we started to recognise the extreme fragility of all that we value in the English landscape, to appreciate that it is not only the metaphor for who we are as a people but that it represents one of our most vivid contributions to a wider culture. At last we are beginning to realise that a deeper understanding of its subtle appeal and elusive character is the key to a thoughtful approach to its future.

The unique character of England's landscape derives from many things. But nowhere is the impact of human intervention absent. If geology and topography set the scene, it is the implacable persistence of generations who since the end of the Ice Age have sought to live in and off this place that has created the singular qualities of the landscape we have today. Not, of course, that the landscape before people was in any sense a static thing; on the contrary, the environment untouched by mankind was and is a dynamic and constantly changing synthesis. Every layer of that complex progression can still be found somewhere, making its own peculiar contribution to the distinctiveness of today's England. It is a compelling narrative. Through this series of regional studies our distinguished contributors – as authors and editors – have distilled something of what has created today's England, in order to decode that narrative.

Unique is an overused term. But it has a special resonance for the landscape of England, both urban and rural. What we hope readers of this series will begin to feel is the nature of the qualities that define the English landscape. Much of that landscape has of course been inherited from cultures overseas as conquest and migration brought here peoples who have progressively occupied and settled Britain. They created what might be called our shared landscapes, defined as much by what links them to the wider world as through any intrinsically native characteristics. The peoples whose common bonds stretched along the Atlantic seaboard have left a legacy in Cornwall more akin to parts of north-west France or Spain than to anywhere else in England. There are Roman roads and cities and medieval field systems that have their closest parallels in the European plains from whence they derived. Great abbeys and monasteries reflected in their art and architecture, their commerce and industry, a culture whose momentum lay outside these islands. And when disaster came it was a pan-European epidemic, the Black Death, that took away between a third and a half of the people. England's are not the only deserted medieval villages.

FOREWORD

And yet, paradoxically, much of what today we would recognise as the quintessential England is only some two or three centuries old. Parliamentary enclosure, especially of the English lowlands, was itself a reaction to an even greater economic force – industrialisation, and the urbanisation that went with it. It has given us a rural landscape that epitomises the essence of Englishness in the minds of many. The fields and hedgerows surrounding the nucleated villages of the pre-existing medieval landscape are of course quite new when set against the timescale of human occupation. Indeed, when the first railways came through there remained, here and there, open fields where the rows of new hawthorn hedges were still feeble whips scribing lines across a thousand years of feudal landscape.

As Britain emerged to become the world's first industrial nation its astonishing transformation was at its most visible in the landscape, something new, indigenous and without precedent. It fuelled the debate on the picturesque and the sublime and was a source of wonder to those who visited from overseas. But in its urban and industrial excesses it soon came to be detested, by aesthetes, social commentators and a burgeoning class opposed to the horrors of industrial capitalism. What was perhaps the most decisive contribution of Britain to the human race provoked a powerful counteraction reflected in the writings of Ruskin, Morris, Octavia Hill and the Webbs. It was this anguish that a century ago energised the spirit of conservation in a growing band of people determined to capture what was left of the pre-industrial rural scene.

Today the landscape of England is, as ever, undergoing immense change. But, unlike the centuries just past, that change once again draws its energy and inspiration from forces overseas. A new form of global economy, North American in flavour, concept and style carries all before it. The implications for the long term future of the landscape and the people who live in it are difficult to predict. The out-of-town shopping mall, the great encampments of distribution warehouses crouching like so many armadillos across the rural shires, the growth of exurbia – that mixed-use land between city and country that owes nothing to either – are all manifestations of these new economic forces. Like the changes that have gone before they have become the subject of intense debate and the source of worrying uncertainty. But what is clear is that a deeper understanding of the landscape, in all its manifestations, offers a means of managing change in a conscious and thoughtful manner.

This was the inspiration that led to this new regional landscape series. To understand the language of landscape, to be able to interpret the way in which people make places, offers insights and enjoyment beyond the ordinary. It enables us to experience that most neglected of human emotions, a sense of place. These books set out to reveal the values that underwrite our sense of place, by offering an insight into how the landscape of England came to be the way it is. If understanding is the key to valuing and valuing is the key to caring then these books may help to ensure that we can understand and enjoy the best of what we have and that when we make our own contribution to change it will not only reinforce that essential distinctiveness but improve the quality of life of those who live there.

Neil Cossons

1

The Personality of the South West

ROGER J P KAIN

In 1954 south-west England was characterised by Arthur Davies, then professor of geography at Exeter University, as 'a peninsula surrounded on three sides by the sea'. His tautological description still brings a smile to some faces, but it does serve to stress that there are few places in the region where human activities are unaffected by the interplay of land and sea. The South West is also a peripheral region of Britain and part of its landscape character and development stems from that peripherality. In an earlier work, *The Shell Book of English Villages* (1980), I wrote that the scenery of south-west England is one of its most valuable assets (it boasts two National Parks and 11 Areas of Outstanding Natural Beauty) and the scenic splendour of the varied coastline is undoubtedly a key attraction for tourists. Much of inland Devon and Cornwall, particularly the inland plateaux of north-east Cornwall and north Devon, is nevertheless a rather monotonous landscape, neither wild and picturesque wilderness like the moors, nor with the intimate pastoral variety of east Devon or the South Hams. Travelling by vehicle along byways in parts of Devon can also be very tedious, incarcerated as one is in a sunken lane with hedgebanks rising up above, more like a corridor than an open road and offering only tantalising glimpses of the landscape through gateways. Any suggestion of boredom, though, is dispelled where the plateaux meet the sea in thrilling coastal scenery.

The influence of the sea is felt inland as well as on the coast, not least for the moderating effect that it has on the climate. Winter rarely lasts long and spring arrives early. 'Mild' is an oft-used adjective in tourist guides; St Mawes on the tip of the Roseland peninsula in Cornwall claims to be the warmest wintering place in the British Isles. By contrast, parts of the north coast are open to the full force of Atlantic gales and at about 600m on Dartmoor, blizzards have been known to drift snow to the level of upstairs windows – the scientific classification of much of the South West as part of Britain's Highland Zone (*see* Chapter 2) is well earned.

Within the peninsula, the facts of geology, relief and settlement history interact to produce diversity within an overall unity; as varied a range of landscapes, in fact, as is to be found within a similar small compass anywhere in England. The appearance of the present landscape is a product of a complicated interaction between the facts of its physical environment and the history of its human occupation. This duality is reflected in microcosm in most of the landscape components identified in Part II of this book, but none better than in the case of south-west England's villages (Chapter 7). Part of their character stems from the physical environment, notably the nature of their sites and local building materials, while their arrangement and style are deeply rooted in local human tradition, custom and culture. Many coastal settlement sites are restricted in size with harbour buildings squeezed in at the bottom, cottages piled up tier upon tier up the cliff sides and then a church like a beacon on top (*see* Chapter 5). Other villages are set in protective hollows where houses cluster tightly around a church. Yet others are tributary to a defensive castle (*see* Chapter 6). The range is infinite. And the South West displays some of the oldest continuously occupied landscapes in England: as Stephen Rippon notes in Chapter 3, in West Penwith, at the far western end of Cornwall, the present-day landscape of irregular, stone-walled fields appears to perpetuate a settlement continuity from late prehistoric and Romano-British periods. Yet the South West also contains icons of late 20th-century design: the Tamar Road Bridge, the Eden Project, the UK Met Office, and Cornish wind farms (*see* Chapters 8, 9 and 10).

A LANDSCAPE DESCRIBED, DISSECTED AND CONCEIVED

The first part of this book, headed 'Land and People', contains three chapters. In Chapter 2, Bruce Webb begins our journey of discovery by exploring the physical environment that forms the natural canvas for the human landscape that is constructed upon it. The archaeological legacies – the deep past in the present – are reviewed by Stephen Rippon in Chapter 3, which discusses settlement, economy and people and reveals, *inter alia*, that a great number of present-day settlement sites in the South West are heirs of foundations which pre-date the Middle Ages. The connections between people, their ways of life, and landscape are close. People are the engines of landscape change and development and in Chapter 4, Bruce Coleman takes on the issue of population numbers from the medieval period through to the present day.

The second part of the book is headed 'Landscapes Dissected' and is the largest part in terms of length. These chapters identify the principal landscape components and review their contribution to the present landscapes of south-west England. In Chapter 5 David Harvey reviews not only the obvious contribution of the established Anglican Church in the form of the many hundreds of parish churches and the great cathedrals of Exeter and Truro, but also landscapes associated with dissent in the 18th and 19th centuries and the 'new age' faiths of today. Robert Higham in Chapter 6 explores fortified sites and their impact on south-west England landscapes through an analysis of themes of defence, security and status. Mark Overton in Chapter 7 justly claims that the variety of rural settlement patterns and associated agricultural activity is greater in the South West than in any other region of similar size in England. As Prince Charles wrote in his Foreword to the *Historical Atlas of South-West England*, for many people, including himself, the South West is the quintessence of rural England, synonymous with holidays and an idyllic countryside and coastline. It is all too easy to forget that the region's landscapes of today owe much to industrial activity in the past; relics of earlier industrial activity, particularly associated with textiles and metal mining, are widespread across Devon and Cornwall and, as Mark Brayshay says in Chapter 8, 'past mining, quarrying and manufacturing activities have not only shaped and dramatically altered large swathes of the south-west countryside and added hugely to its diversity and interest, but also defined and constructed an identity for the entire peninsula'. Though rural in character in the popular mind, the South West also possesses a surprisingly large and diverse range of towns – it was one of the most urbanised regions of England in the late medieval period.

The subsequent evolution of south-west England's townscapes reflects in large measure the experience of England as a whole, but as Mark Brayshay reveals in Chapter 9, national trends have found particular local expression and have given the region's towns their own special personality and character. No comparable region of England possesses the amount, density and complexity of route networks as does the South West. No county has as high a ratio of roads to land area as Cornwall, nor probably does any region come close to rivalling the intricate web of footpaths, bridleways and byways of south-west England, now increasingly valued as key recreational resources. Mark Brayshay in Chapter 10 reviews the contribution of these rights of way to the landscape of south-west England in conjunction with those of canals, railways, and sea and air transport.

Having dissected the landscape in Part II, the two contributors to Part III demonstrate that landscape is not an objective, scientific reality but in fact a construct of our minds. What we like, what we cherish and what we consider disposable are all products of our own and our collective senses of place. Above all, what we consider to be heritage is socially created. Heritage purports to be about the past but, as David Harvey states in Chapter 11, 'in reality its value and meaning lie entirely within the present'. The creation of heritage by labelling a landscape as such always involves a process of human decision-making in the present. And seeing a landscape always involves having an imaginative response to it which, as Catherine Brace comments in Chapter 12, 'helps explain why different people have such different responses to places and landscapes', a fact which makes it impossible for us, the authors of this book on the landscapes of south-west England, to convey a message to you the reader in the way that, say, an engineering textbook can unerringly explain the workings of a machine.

This book is about the landscapes of south-west England as they are today. To understand the present, however, part at least of our explanation has to be made with reference to the past layout of farms and fields, of individual buildings, hamlets, villages, towns and cities, of roads, tracks and paths, railways, ports, airports and the myriad components that make up English landscapes. We also need to know something of the drivers of change because an overwhelming proportion of the landscape's components are not, and never have been, consciously 'designed' but are instead the end products of the interplay of social, political, economic and technical processes – processes perhaps best encapsulated by the notion of the 'vernacular'. Some landscape elements are, of course, designed – the streets and squares of a town inspired by classical tenets of urban design, or the gardens and parks constructed to adorn great country houses are two obvious examples. In both architecture and landscape design, taste has ebbed and flowed a number of times in human history between the formal and symmetrical (classical) and the informal, naturalistic and romantic (Gothic). If we are to understand the visual character of the present cultural landscape, we must first understand these tides of taste, which are in turn related to wider changes in the socio-political attitudes, aesthetic tastes, aspirations and ideals of societies at different times in the past. But the overall aim of this book is to explain and interpret what we see around us today in south-west England – to draw attention to relicts from the past in the present.

But we will not be able to explain everything by reference to what was done by people in the past. Much of the 'character' or identity of the landscape is instead bequeathed from the natural environment of rocks, landforms, soils, vegetation and climate. The physical environment, while not determining the outcomes of human activity, is a canvas on which the built environment is constructed – which is why this book begins with Bruce Webb's survey of the physical environment. As he points out, the physical environment is far from static but is subject to dynamic change; nor are human interactions with it stable through time. The environment provides people with a range of opportunities, risks and hazards, the perceptions of which are culturally determined. Further, we need to know about the human processes of the very recent as well as the more distant past to explain the totality of the contemporary landscape. For example, it is not possible to understand the agricultural land-use pattern of today – why particular crops are grown or particular agricultural activities undertaken – by reference only to the physical environment, or to the traditions of the past. We need also to be aware of the effects of the current political regime of agricultural support through the European Union and the interplay of supply and demand economics. Likewise, we may be able to say quite a lot about why the form of the present cultural landscape is as it is by reference to what was constructed in the past, but what of the people who now populate that landscape, maintain it, cherish it, change it, replace it? As David Harvey points out so effectively in Chapter 11, the notion of an historical landscape 'heritage' is as much about the needs of the present as the past in its own right. Nor can landscape be thought of as an objective scientific fact. Catherine Brace reviews the work of cultural geographers who show how personal is an individual's sense of place – some senses might be shared between individuals, but others are contested. Further, 'a sense of place is not innate, it is not something we are born with and it is not something we automatically absorb when we visit a place'. By reviewing the ways in which landscape is represented in poetry, literature and painting she shows how these imagined landscapes contribute to a popular understanding of place and identity.

In 1999, the *Historical Atlas of South-West England* was published and I concluded its Introduction by saying that the *Atlas* invites the whole region to look back to its past as it also looked to its future at what was then the eve of a new millennium. I think that same philosophy applies to this book, though the constituency of readers is probably a wider one, the focus of subject matter is narrower being purely on landscape, while the time depth covered is undoubtedly greater, spanning from geological time to the present day. We invite you to look at the 'past in the present' of south-west England landscapes as presented to you in the following chapters. You will each come to these chapters with your own set of landscape attitudes and landscape experiences. In turn, you will each take from the text and images of these chapters different things; what we as authors hope is that every reader leaves with a positive experience.

PART I
LAND AND PEOPLE

2

The Environmental Setting of Human Occupation

BRUCE WEBB

The south-west peninsula lies mainly to the west of a line running between the Exe and Tees estuaries and therefore traditionally has been considered a part of highland rather than lowland Britain. Certainly, south-west England has features typical of the Highland Zone, being underlain in large part by old, hard and impervious rock types and having prominent upland areas in Dartmoor, Exmoor and Bodmin Moor. However, the region also includes landscapes, particularly along its eastern margins, that have been fashioned from younger, less resistant and sometimes permeable strata, and that therefore have closer affinities with the scarp and vale topography and lowland plains common to much of southern and eastern England. Diversity of physical environment within a relatively small geographical area is, in fact, a distinguishing characteristic of south-west England. The peninsula does not extend more than 200km along its north-east to south-west axis, and at no point is its width from north to south greater than 120km. Yet within these confines there is a wide range of environmental conditions typified, for example, by the often-quoted observation that the climate of the English Riviera around Torquay can sustain plants more at home in a subtropical environment, while vegetation on the summits of Dartmoor, just a few kilometres inland, is sub-alpine in character.

A further distinctive feature of south-west England is that its landscapes are seen as being old or 'inherited' in the parlance of scientists specialising in the development of landforms. The present physical geography of the peninsula has evolved over a period of at least 65 million years, and elements contributed from different parts of this time-span can still be deciphered in the landscape we see today. Despite claims to the contrary, including some based on recent research from Exmoor, the majority view is that south-west England was not extensively glaciated during the cold phases of the last 2 million years, when ice sheets covered large areas of Britain. Absence of significant glacial erosion and deposition helps to explain why features formed in geologically distant times have survived in the South West, and the region is unique in Britain in lying within the upland zone but being largely unglaciated.

South-west England also derives its distinctiveness from its peninsular character. The ratio of coastline length to land area for Devon and Cornwall is higher than in many other parts of Britain, and the influence of the sea is not only apparent in a wide range of coastal landscapes, including spectacular cliffs, major estuaries and numerous small bays and coves, but also makes itself felt in other aspects of the physical environment. In particular, the climate of the South West is regarded traditionally as mild, equable, moist and soft because of the ameliorating maritime influence.

THE ENVIRONMENTAL SETTING OF HUMAN OCCUPATION

OPPOSITE PAGE:
Fig. 2.1 The geology of south-west England*. The map shows the distribution of rocks of different age in the peninsula and highlights the occurrence of the major granite masses, which have been intruded into the older sedimentaries of Devonian and Carboniferous age. It is also clear that rocks of younger age are confined largely to the east of the region. (Taken from Kain and Ravenhill 1999)*

The environmental backcloth to human occupation in south-west England is, therefore, both diverse and distinctive. A full appreciation of the environmental setting must embrace the geological evolution and landform development that occurred over long aeons before the arrival of Palaeolithic and later peoples. Climate, soils and vegetation also need to be considered, however, as dimensions of landscape that have an important bearing on human activity, alongside the hazards to life and property sometimes posed by the environment of the peninsula. Nor should we lose sight of the fact that the ability of people to utilise and to exploit the landscapes of the South West has changed greatly over time, and that human activity itself has also left a mark on many components of the peninsula's physical geography. The environmental backdrop to south-west England is a complex composite of rocks, relief, climate and ecosystems, which poses both opportunities and threats to human occupation past, present and future. Although often interrelated and interacting, the major physical characteristics of the region will be discussed individually and in turn.

GEOLOGICAL FOUNDATIONS

Geology exerts a fundamental influence on the physical landscape through lithology (the nature of rocks), structure (the way they have been deformed) and tectonics (the effects of earth movements). It also affects significantly the human landscape, for example through the materials that are available for building and the opportunities provided for extractive industries. The rocks underlying south-west England are very diverse in terms of age and type (Fig. 2.1), but they can be classified broadly into three groups. These comprise: the older sedimentaries of Devonian and Carboniferous age found in much of Cornwall, south and central Devon and Exmoor; the igneous rocks underlying Dartmoor, Bodmin Moor, St Austell Moor, Carnmenellis, Land's End and the Isles of Scilly; and the younger sedimentary rocks of Permian and later periods that outcrop in east Devon. This simple tripartite classification belies the complex geological development of Cornubia (the term sometimes used by geologists to describe Cornwall and Devon), which can be traced back 500 million years. At that time, south-west England was part of the Gondwana supercontinent and lay 70 degrees south of the equator at a latitude within the present-day Antarctic Circle. Subsequent geological evolution of the region has seen a gradual northward movement and a history of episodic joining of continents and opening of ocean basins associated with plate tectonics – the mechanism by which the more rigid outer layers of the earth are moved.

The oldest rocks exposed in the peninsula, which can be dated with certainty, were formed during the Devonian Period (417–354 million years ago) and were deposited in a marine basin lying on the southern margin of a large continental massif. This Old Red Sandstone continent was formed by an earlier phase of mountain building (Caledonian), extended northwards from Wales to Scotland and beyond, and experienced tropical desert conditions with little cover of land plants. At times during the Devonian Period, sandstones originating in coastal plains and deltas were laid down in north Devon as a consequence of increased erosion and sedimentation in central and south Wales. At other times, the coastline extended further north and marine shales and limestones were deposited. In south Devon, the Devonian strata are largely composed of marine sediments, although sea depth varied during the period. Clear shallow conditions promoted the development of coral reefs and the formation of the massive limestones now exposed around Torquay (Fig. 2.2) and Plymouth. Rocks produced by submarine volcanic activity are also found in the Devonian sequences of south Devon, while strata of this age in Cornwall reveal deposition in a number of sedimentary basins and environments ranging from near shore,

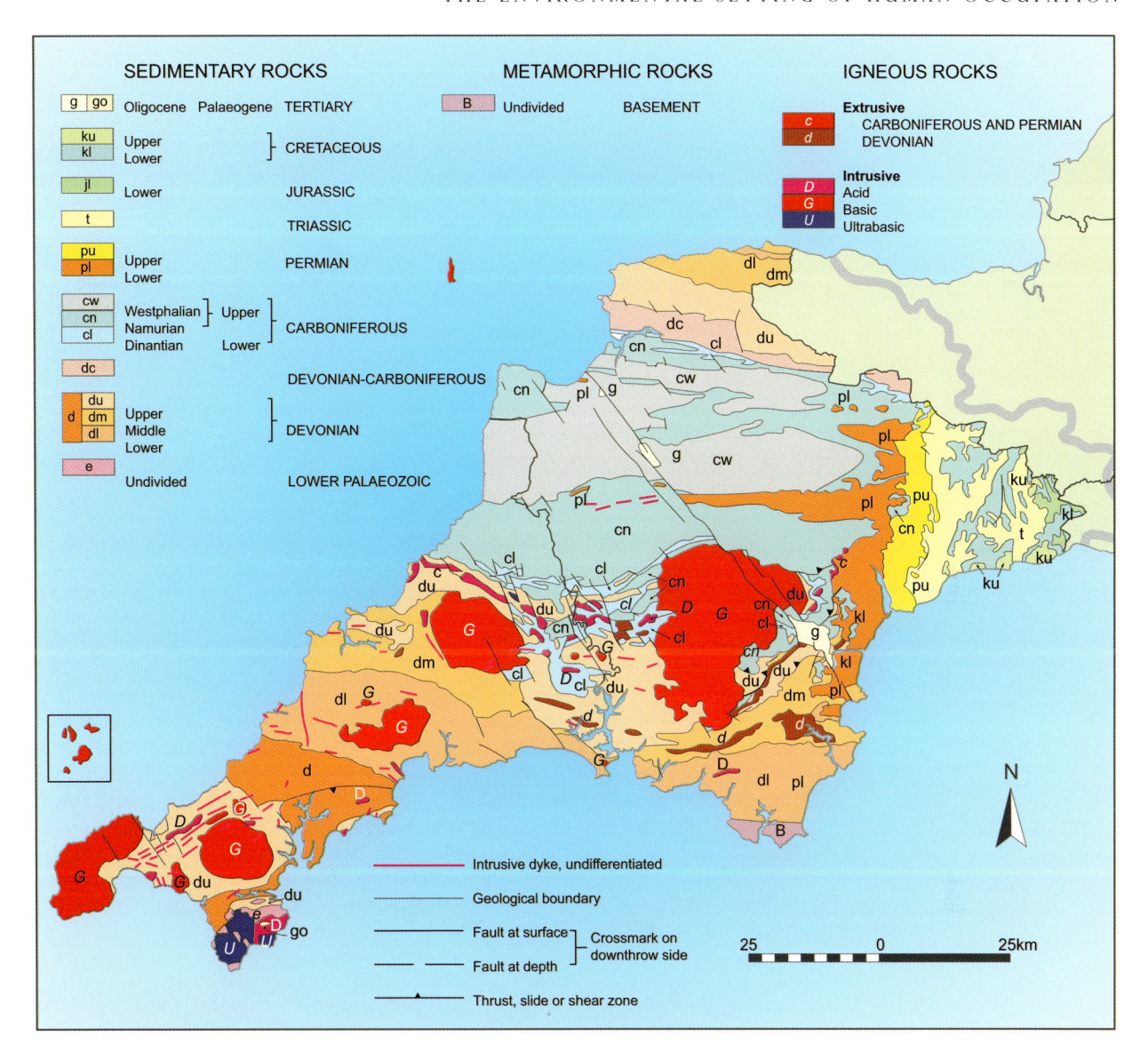

THE ENVIRONMENTAL SETTING OF HUMAN OCCUPATION

Fig. 2.2 Limestones of Middle Devonian age exposed at Berry Head, Torbay. They were formed under tropical and shallow clear-sea conditions at a time when south Devon lay in equatorial latitudes. The environment would have been not dissimilar to the coral reefs of tropical environments today, although primitive calcareous sponges were important components of the ancient biogenic banks that were built up.

through continental shelf to deeper ocean. During Devonian times, the Rheic (Rhenohercynian) Ocean to the south of Cornubia began to close and deformation associated with the Variscan Orogeny (a mountain building period) was initiated. In this process, a slice of oceanic crust was detached and displaced to form what are today the distinctive basic igneous rocks of the Lizard complex.

Sedimentation and volcanic activity in the marine trough continued as the Carboniferous (354–290 million years ago) succeeded the Devonian Period in Cornubia. Evidence from shales, thin limestones and cherts suggests the presence of very deep water during early Carboniferous times. However, thick sequences of mudstones and turbidite sandstones (laid down by sediment-rich currents moving down the submarine slope at the edge of the continental mass) characterise the Culm Measures that formed later in this period, when the northward advancing front of Variscan deformation caused uplift and shallowing on the southern flanks of the marine trough. Coal seams characteristic of the Carboniferous strata in South Wales were not formed in south-west England, although small pockets of sooty deposits, known as 'culm' or 'col', do occur.

The Variscan Orogeny culminated in the late Carboniferous by which time the Rheic Ocean had closed and the accumulated Devonian and Carboniferous strata had been subjected to major compression that generated complex folding and thrusting with a predominantly west–east axis to these structures (Fig. 2.3). Frictional heating associated with plate movements and tectonic thickening caused crustal melting, which led to the intrusion of granite from below in the form of a major batholith (a large body of once-molten material) beneath south-west England, some 290 to 270 million years ago and after the main pulse of the orogeny. The individual granite bodies (plutons) exposed today are linked at depth to this mass, which is about 300km long and 35km wide and extends from east of Dartmoor to west of the Isles of Scilly, and has a total volume of approximately 68,000cu km. Intrusion of the Cornubian granite altered the surrounding country rocks forming metamorphic aureoles, which are the zones changed by the heat of the intrusion and which range in width from less than 1km to more than 7km around the individual plutons. Genesis of the granite was also associated with the formation of a rich variety of metalliferous ore deposits, which have a long history of human exploitation in south-west England. Many of these metal deposits have a hydrothermal origin and resulted from the movement

Fig. 2.3 Folded strata at Hartland Quay, north Devon. The sandstones and subordinate shales of the Upper Carboniferous Crackington Formation have been deformed into a series of upright fold structures exposed in the cliffs. This happened during a period of mountain building caused by movements of tectonic plates and collisions of ancient continental masses that culminated in the late Carboniferous and early Permian periods.

of hot aqueous fluids in the crust as the granite masses cooled. Hydrothermal alteration of granite minerals during the final stages of cooling, together with the effects of subsequent weathering, also formed economically viable deposits of kaolin, locally known as china clay, which are extracted in the St Austell area (Fig. 2.4) and at Lee Moor on Dartmoor. It should be noted that mineralisation in the peninsula is complex and not all of the deposits, including the lead and iron ores of Exmoor, can be related in a simple way to granite intrusion. Increased pressures and temperatures associated with Variscan mountain building also caused low-grade (relatively less intensive) regional metamorphism of the Devonian and Carboniferous rocks, often involving conversion of mudstones to slates. Higher-grade (relatively more intensive) metamorphism occurred more locally in the Start Point area of Devon where schists, which are more coarsely grained rocks than slates, were formed through alteration of sedimentary and volcanic rocks.

Fig. 2.4 China clay quarrying near St Austell, Cornwall. The alteration of feldspar minerals in granite by a complex suite of processes that have operated over many millions of years since the intrusion of the granite masses has formed significant deposits of kaolinite-rich material which has been commercially exploited in parts of Devon and Cornwall. The latter county produced more than 2.5 million tonnes of china clay in the mid-1990s, much of which was exported for use in the paper industries of Germany and Scandinavia.

Significant uplift occurred at the end of the Variscan Orogeny so that at the start of the Permian Period (290–248 million years ago) a mountain chain, at least 3,000m high, lay across Cornubia. At this time, south-west England was part of the Pangean supercontinent, which was drifting slowly northward of the equatorial region and experiencing severe erosion under a hot desert climate. Flash flooding swept material down to the surrounding lowlands, building alluvial fans across sand and gravel plains that also contained playa lakes (periodically inundated features in dryland areas) and dunefields. Under these subtropical arid conditions, iron compounds were weathered to red oxide, which gave a distinctive red coloration to the breccias, conglomerates, sandstones and mudstones formed during this period. Volcanic activity during Permian times produced lavas in the Exeter, Crediton and Tiverton areas and also in parts of Cornwall. Red bed sedimentation continued into the Triassic Period (248–206 million years ago), and a conglomerate of quartzite pebbles originating in western France was laid down by a major river system to form what is now the Budleigh Salterton Pebble Beds. In Triassic times, Cornubia lay 15–20 degrees north of the equator, equivalent to the present-day latitude of West Africa or the Caribbean, and experienced a seasonal, and possibly monsoonal, rainfall regime. The term New Red Sandstone is given to the sequence of distinctive red bed sediments (Fig. 2.5) that was laid down between the late Carboniferous and late Triassic; these sediments now remain largely in south and east Devon but are also preserved in fault-bounded basins that extend the outcrop to the west, especially beyond Crediton and to a lesser extent Tiverton. Major faulting along the lines of the Bristol and English channels and in the Celtic Sea during the Triassic Period separated Cornubia from other upland areas of north-west Europe and established the broad outlines of the peninsula that we observe today.

Most of Devon and Cornwall remained a landmass during the marine transgression that marked the end of the Triassic and beginning of the succeeding Jurassic Period (206–142 million years ago). However, Lower Liassic

THE ENVIRONMENTAL SETTING OF HUMAN OCCUPATION

Fig. 2.5 Littleham Mudstone exposed in the cliffs to the west of Budleigh Salterton, east Devon. Red rocks of Permian and Triassic age form a very distinctive element of the coastal scenery in the eastern part of the peninsula. The red coloration is the result of post-depositional oxidation of iron compounds in sediments that were laid down in arid environments and were derived from rapid erosion of the Variscan mountain chain. The New Red Sandstone rocks include materials that range from being coarse to fine grained. The latter may be especially prone to instability, and the cliffs cut in the Littleham Mudstone are subject to a variety of mass movements that causes local cliff-top recession in the order of 1–2m per year.

shales and distinctive fossiliferous limestones were laid down as shelf-sea deposits in the easternmost part of Devon and along what is now the present coast of west Somerset, although the Jurassic succession is much more extensively exposed in Dorset. At the beginning of the Cretaceous Period (142–65 million years ago), Cornubia had been uplifted and was linked to the Irish landmass. About 105 million years ago the sea returned and the sandy Gault and Upper Greensand successions, which presently cap the Haldon Hills and much of the higher ground in east Devon, were laid down in a shallow marine environment. Although this sea inundated large areas of south-west England, it is likely that Dartmoor, Exmoor and the other uplands remained as islands. However, the sea deepened later in the Cretaceous Period leading to deposition of limestones and eventually the chalk. It is thought that chalk at one time covered much, if not all, of the peninsula but uplift and erosion during the Tertiary Period (65–1.8 million years ago, including the Palaeocene, Eocene, Oligocene, Miocene and Pliocene Epochs) removed these deposits completely from Cornwall and from most of Devon, except for a few pockets along the east Devon coast, as at Beer.

Igneous activity returned to Devon during the Tertiary Period when a granite intrusion created Lundy, which may also have been a centre of dyke swarms (large numbers of fingers or sheets of igneous material) similar to those being formed in Scotland and other parts of Britain at the same time. At the beginning of the Tertiary, Cornubia lay at a latitude of about 40°N and experienced a climate that was tropical or subtropical. The few deposits that survive from the period were laid down predominantly in a terrestrial environment and include residual flint gravels on the Haldon Hills and in the area around Sidmouth. These were derived from subtropical deep weathering and erosion of the former chalk overlayer during the Palaeocene (65–56 million years ago) and were then redistributed by Eocene and later fluvial activity. Significant accumulations of Tertiary clay, sand and lignite (material intermediate between coal and peat) are found in the Bovey and Petrockstowe basins along the line of the Sticklepath fault complex, which extends from Torbay to Bideford Bay. Movements along this major structure can be related to the opening of the Atlantic during Eocene (56–34 million years ago) times and the distant effects of the Alpine Orogeny during the Oligocene (34–24 million years ago). The resulting subsidence in the case of the Bovey Basin led to the accumulation in subtropical river and lake environments of sediments more than 1,200m thick. Small outcrops of later Tertiary deposits in Cornwall provide evidence of wind-blown and slope deposition under a Mediterranean climate during the Miocene (24–5 million years ago) in the case of the St Agnes Formation, and a shallow marine incursion during the Pliocene (5–1.8 million years ago), at the end of the Tertiary Period, in the case of the St Erth Beds. The final period of earth history, the Quaternary Period (1.8 million years ago to the present and including the Pleistocene and Holocene Epochs), was marked in south-west England, as elsewhere in Britain, by major oscillations in climate and sea level. The impact of the Quaternary Period on the peninsula is discussed later in relation to landform development.

BUILDING STONES

The geological diversity of south-west England has furnished a great range of different types of stone for building. In Cornwall, for example, a very varied suite of intrusive igneous rocks has provided many different building and decorative stones, which have been extensively exploited for local and export use. One of the best-known examples is the dark green Cataclews Stone, which is technically a hydrous alkali dolerite and has been worked since medieval times from a quarry on the coast to the west of Padstow to provide material used in churches and mansions. Granite has featured prominently in traditional constructions, which makes the peninsula unique among English provinces (Fig. 2.6). The use of this material is not confined to vernacular building, as is evident from some of the great houses in the region such as Lanhydrock, as well as from a large number of medieval parish churches. The most widely found and versatile stone for building is slate, but it varies in quality. In terms of lightness, durability and imperviousness to rain, slates from Delabole in north Cornwall are highly regarded. In Devon, but less so in Cornwall, limestones have also been used for building. Cretaceous shelly limestones from Beer provide a high-quality freestone that has been used within and beyond the south-west region, whereas the Devonian limestones from south Devon are easily recognisable by their colours and veining when seen in walls and other structures. Various sandstones have been employed in the construction of a range of buildings in the South West. For instance, Cretaceous Salcombe Regis sandstone graces Exeter Cathedral, while Carboniferous sandstones are commonly found in more humble farmhouses and outbuildings of mid-Devon. The use of New Red Sandstones, often in conjunction with Permian breccias (rocks made up of angular fragments set in a consolidated finer matrix) and volcanic lavas, has given rise to very distinctive buildings in Exeter and elsewhere (Fig. 2.7). Less commonly occurring rocks, such as the hornblendes, serpentines and gabbros of the Lizard, have been used locally in south-west England and lend idiosyncratic colours and textures to the resulting buildings. Cob, which is made on site from local clay, gravel, straw and water and is not tied to a particular geology, is a very distinctive building material, especially in Devon. Local clay deposits have also supported small brickworks in the peninsula.

ABOVE: **Fig. 2.6 Sanders Farmhouse, Lettaford, North Bovey, Dartmoor**. *An example of the use of granite blocks, some large and squared, in the construction of a Dartmoor longhouse.*

Fig. 2.7 The frontage of the Royal Albert Memorial Museum and Art Gallery, Exeter. *The building is constructed out of many different local stones including purple volcanic lava, dark red breccia, lighter red sandstone, and grey limestone.*

THE ENVIRONMENTAL SETTING OF HUMAN OCCUPATION

LANDFORM DEVELOPMENT

Fig. 2.8 The topography and major geomorphological features of south-west England. *The map shows the distribution of the major upland areas within the peninsula, the main elements of the drainage pattern and the occurrence of alluvial deposits in the river valleys. Locations of submerged peat deposits around the coast are indicated, and the inset map indicates the major groups of planation surfaces and highlights contrasts in coastal morphology around the peninsula. (Based largely on maps by K J Gregory, in Barlow 1969, and including information from C J Caseldine, in Kain and Ravenhill 1999)*

The relief of south-west England broadly reflects contrasts in the underlying geology (Fig. 2.8). The resistant granite intrusions, for example, give rise to upland areas that decline in height in a westward direction from Dartmoor, which has a peak at High Willhays of 621m, to the Land's End area, where the high ground of White Downs only just exceeds 250m. The Devonian rocks of Exmoor also form a conspicuous upland rising to almost 520m at Dunkery Beacon. In this case, the elevated nature may be more strongly related to uplift during mid-Tertiary (post-Oligocene) times of a fault-defined block, which is now high Exmoor, than to significantly greater erosional resistance of the underlying strata. While contrasts in rock type may dictate details of landform, such as in the distinctive break of slope angle that occurs in many east Devon valleys between the Triassic Mercia Mudstones and the Cretaceous Upper Greensand in the lower and upper parts of the slope profile (Fig. 2.9), there are also instances where differences in rock resistance are not clearly expressed in the landscape.

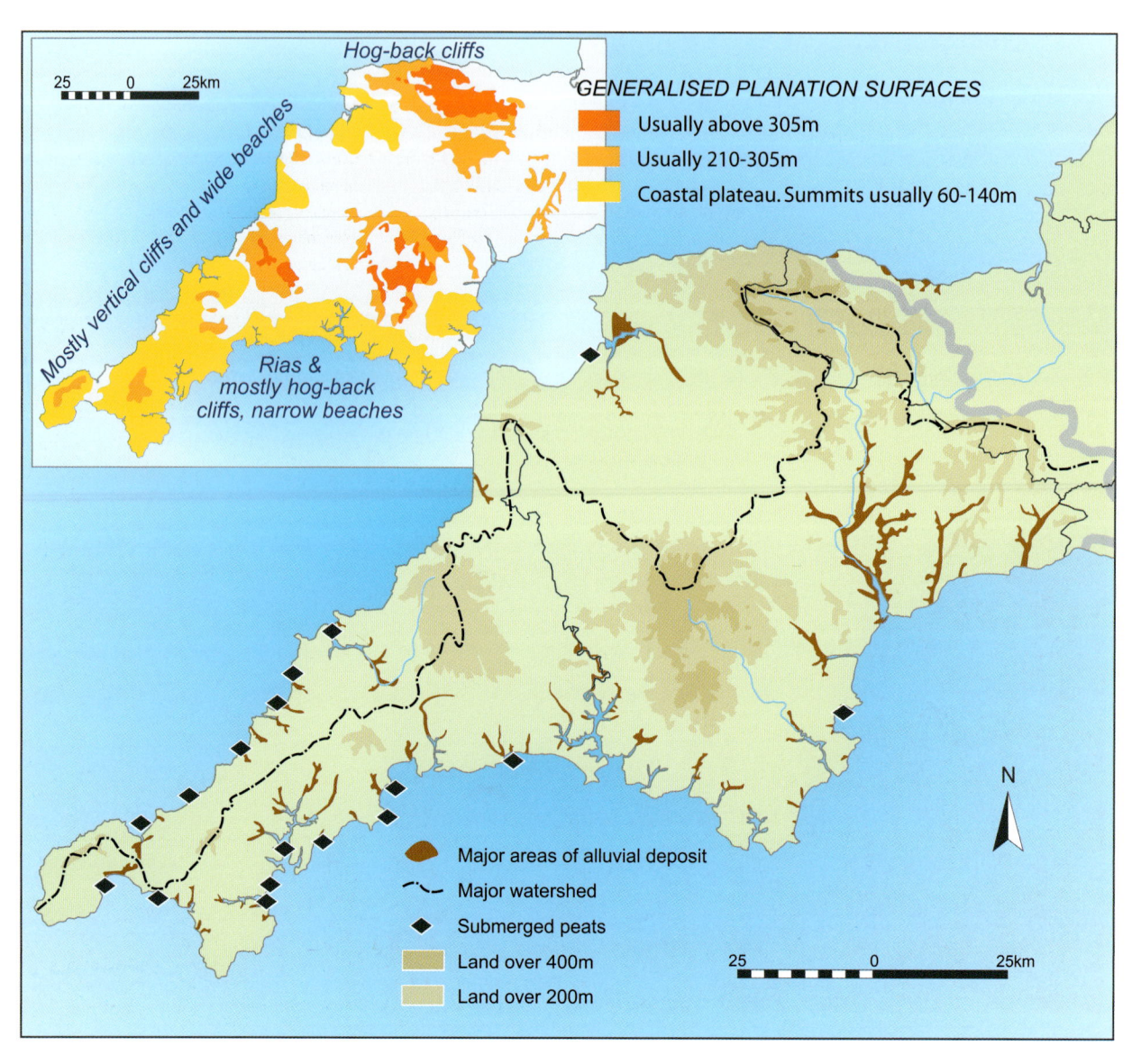

Fig. 2.9 Buckton Hill near Sidmouth, east Devon. *Typical 'whale-backed' topography created by the difference in rock resistance between the Cretaceous Upper Greensand Formation that caps the hill and the Triassic Sidmouth Formation (Mercia Mudstone Group) that underlies the lower slopes. A distinct break in slope angle occurs at the junction between these rock units.*

For example, it is surprising to find that the coastal feature of Morte Bay in north Devon has been eroded largely in resistant sandstones but the surrounding headlands are formed in slates, normally deemed to be weaker rock types.

Planation surfaces (low relief features formed by erosion), which cut across underlying rock types and structures, are features of the south-west England landscape that have long attracted attention (Fig. 2.10). They have been recognised at elevations above 210m, where summits on the high ground of Dartmoor, Exmoor, Bodmin Moor and east Devon are relatively level, and distinct surfaces have also been identified with the height ranges 230–290m and 300–410m (*see* Fig. 2.8). Extensive surfaces of low relief have also been recognised at elevations below 210m, including the coastal zone of south Devon and much of Cornwall, where the landscape is plateau-like and a well-defined bench with a back at approximately 130m has been identified. These features have been the subject of much debate as to how many exist, their age and mode of formation, and what relationship they have with the drainage pattern.

Fig. 2.10 View from Cox Tor across the high moorland area of Dartmoor. *The skyline indicates the low relief character, which is typical of many parts of the uplands in south-west England and is thought to represent remnants of once more extensive planation surfaces formed by erosion most probably during the Tertiary.*

23

Fig. 2.11 The Punchbowl, Winsford Hill, Exmoor. *This feature has been interpreted as being formed by local glacial action. Analysis of the materials at the margin of the bowl and in the valley below has suggested occupation by ice in two cold phases of the Pleistocene. However, a glacial genesis is contested, and the general consensus is that the south-west peninsula was not extensively glaciated in the Ice Ages.*

Fig. 2.12 Great Staple Tor, Dartmoor. *Such residual upstanding rock masses are very characteristic of the granite uplands in south-west England, but also can be found on other rock types. Different hypotheses have been advanced to explain tor formation but the origin of these features is related to weathering controlled by the spacing of joints (fractures) in the granite and stripping away of material under periglacial conditions during the Pleistocene. The large granite blocks on the slopes below the tor are known locally as clitter.*

Although arguments have been advanced that some of these surfaces have been exhumed from beneath a previous cover of Triassic or Cretaceous rocks, the majority view is that they were formed by processes operating during the Tertiary Period. However, some authors have advocated a marine origin, while others have suggested formation by subaerial (land-based) agencies, and there has been much debate as to which surfaces originated in the early Tertiary and which were formed later in this period. The most recent view is that these features may not represent many different planation levels but rather one complex erosion surface that developed under tropical and subtropical conditions during the early Tertiary through processes analogous to those which occur in present tropical landscapes. On granite rocks especially, it is thought that late Cretaceous and early Tertiary chemical weathering contributed to significant kaolinisation. There is evidence of uplift in the region during the late Miocene, and differential movements in the mid- and late Tertiary may account for the appearance of erosion surfaces at different levels in the present landscape.

A downward trend in global mean temperatures throughout the Tertiary developed into the cold phases of the Pleistocene Epoch, which are known commonly as the Ice Ages and commenced about 2 million years ago. During the Pleistocene, climate oscillated between conditions that were as warm as or slightly warmer than today and much longer phases of cooler climate or periods of severe cold, when ice sheets extended southward over the British Isles. Although the last three major cold stages of the Pleistocene generated such ice sheets, there is little evidence that the peninsula was ever overridden by glacial ice. Restricted exposures of glacial till have been recorded in the Fremington–Hele area of north Devon, on the Isles of Scilly and possibly at Trebetherick Point in Cornwall, while giant erratics, comprising far-travelled boulders of rocks exotic to the peninsula, are found scattered around the coasts of south-west England. It is thought that an ice sheet may have impinged at one time along the north coast of the peninsula, although dating of this event is not certain and other mechanisms, such as delivery by icebergs carved from glacier ice lying much further north, have been proposed to account for some of the erratic blocks. There is evidence of a former small glacial cirque (an open hollow which is bounded by an arcuate cliffed headwall) on Exmoor (Fig. 2.11), but other clear examples of glacial landforms are lacking.

In contrast, there is abundant evidence that south-west England experienced periglacial (near glacial) conditions during the cold phases of the Pleistocene, which caused significant landform development and modification. During these periods, the climate would have been arctic in character, the ground would have been permanently frozen at depth and mechanical breakdown of rocks through the action of frost shattering would have been very active. Formation of the tors on Dartmoor (Fig. 2.12) and elsewhere owes much to periglacial stripping of weathered

THE ENVIRONMENTAL SETTING OF HUMAN OCCUPATION

material to leave residual masses of bare bedrock crowning hilltops or projecting above steep valley sides. Erosion brought about by a combination of frost shattering, snowmelt and other processes in periglacial conditions has formed distinctive staircases of bedrock benches on particular rock types, such as at Cox Tor on Dartmoor, and led to numerous hollows, dells and related features throughout Devon and Cornwall. Depositional periglacial features include the relict clitter spreads of coarse granite blocks found on many Dartmoor slopes (Fig. 2.12) and sometimes arranged into distinct patterned ground in the form of stone stripes, circles and polygons. Almost ubiquitous on the slopes of south-west England are deposits of head, comprising frost-shattered angular blocks and stones set in a finer-grained earthy matrix. These unconsolidated materials were laid down in the cold phases of the Pleistocene by gelifluction – a process whereby summer melting of frozen ground near to the surface saturated the regolith (the layer of weathered material above solid rock) and caused slow downslope movement of the sediment mass. The mantle of head varies greatly in thickness, but in some coastal sections, for example between Prawle and Salcombe in south Devon, the deposits form thick aprons more than 30m deep. Inland, cold periods were marked by significant accumulations of periglacial debris in the valley floors. These were dissected by river action in the warmer phases with the resulting formation of a suite of river terraces, such as those found in the Axe valley.

The growth of major ice sheets in the Pleistocene cold phases locked up significant amounts of the world's water. At the height of the last glacial period, approximately 20,000 years ago, sea levels around the peninsula may have been as much as 120m lower than those of today, and south-west England would have formed part of the Eurasian continental landmass. Evidence of former lower sea levels is found in a number of buried and submerged cliffs and associated shore platforms, such as a feature recorded off Plymouth and in Start Bay, which has its base some 40m below present Ordnance Datum (OD), is 10m high and is fronted by a gently sloping, smooth platform. Many estuaries in south-west England, including those of the Taw–Torridge (Fig. 2.13), Tamar, Erme, Dart,

Fig. 2.13 Taw–Torridge Estuary, north Devon. Such features reflect changing sea levels in the Quaternary. In cold phases, sea level would have dropped and the river valleys would have extended beyond the present-day coastline and are preserved today as buried channels offshore that are filled with sediments. During the warmer phases, including the last 10,000 years, sea level rose and flooded the lower parts of the river valleys to form estuaries. The shingle barrier of the Westward Ho! pebble ridge is visible on the south side of the estuary mouth, while the extensive sand dunes of Braunton Burrows occur on the north side.

Fig. 2.14 Raised beach, Pendower, Gerrans Bay, Cornwall. The reddy brown deposit of pebbles and cobbles lying on a wave-cut platform eroded across the blue-grey contorted rocks of the Devonian Pendower Formation at heights up to 4.4m above present sea-level represent an ancient beach. This would have been laid down when the sea was at a higher level during a warm phase of the Pleistocene, most probably around 125,000 years ago. The lighter brown material higher in the cliffs is head, a deposit formed during cold stages of the Plesistocene when arctic conditions prevailed.

OPPOSITE PAGE:

Fig. 2.15 The Isles of Scilly. This granite archipelago, lying almost 50km from Land's End, is the result of sea level rise during historical times. The individual islands we see today formed in the 13th century, and sea-level in this area is continuing to rise by approximately 4mm per year.

Teign and Exe rivers, have evidence of buried channels that were graded to lower sea levels. In contrast, the melting of ice sheets during the warmer interglacial periods caused a recovery of sea level to heights around present Ordnance Datum or greater, which has led to the formation of ancient marine features that can be observed today at or above present sea level. These include 'staircases' of several shore platforms, especially in the height range 0–20m OD, and the occurrence of raised beach deposits, which in places are overlain by fossil sand dunes. Exposures of raised beaches are common around the coasts of the peninsula, including excellent examples between Saunton Down and Baggy Point in north Devon, around Torbay and at Pendower in Gerrans Bay, Cornwall (Fig. 2.14). The sequence of oscillating sea levels during the Pleistocene, which some authors believe were superimposed on a general declining trend, means that features such as the ancient and modern shore platforms we observe today are likely to have been fashioned by marine processes working at a particular elevation at a number of different times, rather than on a single occasion, in the Pleistocene.

Landform development during the Holocene (the last 10,000 years) has been relatively minor. Melting of the ice sheets at the end of the last cold phase in the Pleistocene caused a rapid rise of sea level from minus 40m to minus 20m OD in the first 2,000 years of the Holocene, but Britain did not become an island until about 6,500 years ago and stable sea level close to present Ordnance Datum has only existed for about three millennia. A more recent, but slower, rise of sea level led to flooding of the central low-lying area of the Isles of Scilly in the 13th century to form separate islands (Fig. 2.15). Submerged forests seen today around the coasts of the peninsula during exceptionally low tides or as the result of storm erosion (*see* Fig. 2.8), represent the effects of post-glacial increases in

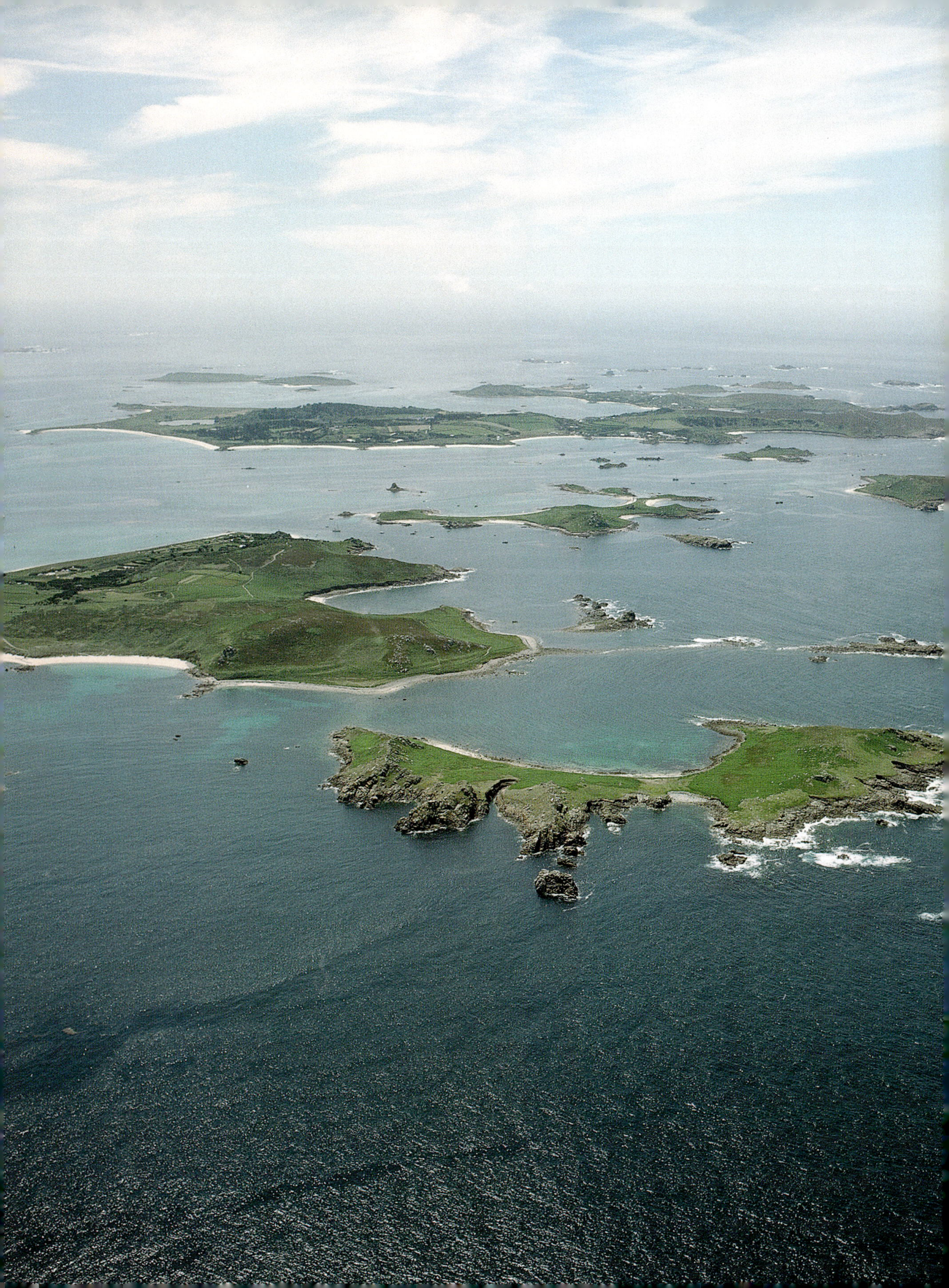

THE ENVIRONMENTAL SETTING OF HUMAN OCCUPATION

Fig. 2.16 Kingsbridge estuary, south Devon. *This feature is a textbook example of a ria or drowned river network, where sea-level rise during the Holocene has formed a tree-like inlet of the sea which extends for considerable distances inland from the estuary mouth at Salcombe.*

Fig. 2.17 Dawlish Warren, south Devon. *This sand spit across the mouth of the Exe estuary was formed by material being pushed onshore during the post-glacial rise in sea level. The feature is complex with four main components comprising outer sand hills and a tract of semi-fixed dunes, a central depression representing a former tidal inlet, a second ridge of stabilised sand over clay, which is now a golf course, and a strip of salt marsh on the inner side of the Warren. The spit has undergone continuing evolution of its form, and the distal (unattached) end is particularly susceptible to change and has suffered breaching and detachment in the past.*

sea level. Woodland became engulfed by peat as water tables rose and then was submerged as the sea encroached on to the land. Holocene drowning of the lower courses of river valleys resulted in inlets known as rias (Fig. 2.16), which are a distinctive element of the coastline in the south of the peninsula. Rising sea levels also swept considerable material from offshore to contribute to the striking features of coastal deposition seen in south-west England today, such as the spit at Dawlish Warren (Fig. 2.17). Loe Pool in Cornwall and Slapton Ley in Devon (Fig. 2.18) represent freshwater lakes formed by the landward movement of shingle barriers that were in place at least 3,000 years ago. There is evidence from Start Bay and the Exe estuary that the major sandspits and shingle bars of south-west England may be a temporary legacy of the effects of the post-glacial (Flandrian) marine transgression rather than features that are in equilibrium with present coastal processes.

While natural processes of erosion and deposition have continued to modify landforms during the Holocene, especially along coasts, this epoch has also been marked by the emergence of human activity as a geomorphological agent. Dredging of significant amounts of shingle offshore from South

Hallsands in the period between 1897 and 1900 to provide material for an extension to the naval dockyard at Devonport, for example, occasioned irreversible and highly damaging coastal erosion. In contrast, several phases of mining activity in west Cornwall have generated distinctive coastal deposits in St Austell Bay. Inland, the effects of reworking of alluvial deposits by the process of tin streaming, dating back to at least the 12th century, has led to gulleying and the disruption of many valley floors on Dartmoor, while more generally the effects of ploughing from later prehistoric times onwards has encouraged accelerated erosion of hillslopes and alluviation of river valleys. Development of urban areas and impoundment of rivers by major reservoirs have altered water flows, sediment loads and channel morphology in the rivers of south-west England, while in spoil heaps from china-clay workings – in the case of those near St Austell sometimes referred to as the 'Cornish Alps' (Fig. 2.19) – and in major embankments and cuttings engineered to facilitate road and rail transport, we see features that may be regarded as anthropogenic landforms.

ABOVE: **Fig. 2.18 Slapton Ley, south Devon.** *This freshwater lake, which is the largest in south-west England, was formed when shingle was pushed onshore by rising sea levels in the Holocene and trapped small streams draining to the coast. The Ley is subject to change due to infilling by sediment and continuing movement of the shingle barrier. Some predictions suggest further sea-level rise caused by global warming may destroy the barrier and the Ley within as little as 50 years.*

Fig. 2.19 Kaolin waste tips, Indian Queens, Cornwall. *The waste products of china clay mining (for every tonne of clay extracted, 9 tonnes of mineral waste is produced) have created an artificial topography of grey-white 'mountains' of spoil. However, there are programmes of tree planting, landscape restoration and heathland creation to offset the environmental impact of this industry.*

THE ENVIRONMENTAL SETTING OF HUMAN OCCUPATION

CLIMATIC CONDITIONS

The climate of south-west England reflects the general setting of the British Isles in the track of the mid-latitude westerlies and its marginal position between the Atlantic and continental Europe. It is further moderated by the more specific regional influences of a southerly latitude, the westward projection of the peninsula into the ocean, and the considerable variation of height across Devon and Cornwall. Maritime air masses dominate the weather of the South West and influence the patterns and gradients of climatological variables across the region. On average, the peninsula has a climate that is mild and warm compared with many other parts of England and Wales, and that is marked by relatively modest annual and diurnal fluctuations in temperature. The average length of the growing season exceeds 325 days along the northern and southern coasts of Cornwall but falls to less than 175 days on the highest ground of Dartmoor (Fig. 2.20). Meteorological Office statistics for the period 1971–2000 highlight contrasts between the uplands and the coastal fringe in terms of average maximum and minimum temperatures and the occurrence of air frost. At Princetown, the annual average maximum and minimum temperatures are 3.0 and 2.6°C lower than those recorded at Teignmouth, while air frost occurs at least five times more frequently at the former compared with the latter station (Fig. 2.20). The declining effect of the moderating maritime influence on temperature is also apparent when comparing statistics from St Mawgan with those from stations situated further

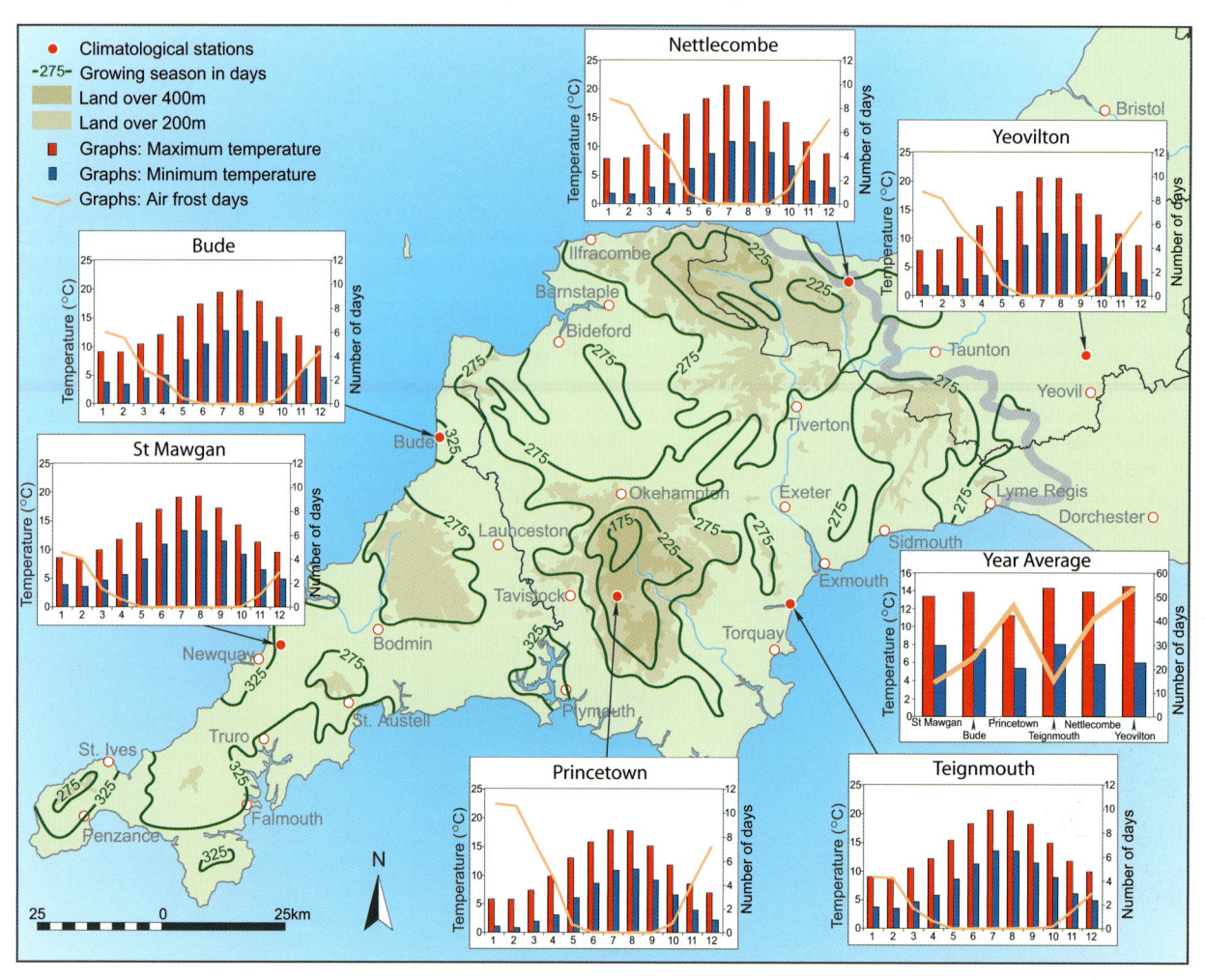

Fig. 2.20 Temperature conditions in south-west England. The map shows the average length of the growing season in the region, based on data collected in the period 1941–70, linked to elevation and to longitudinal position. Met Office data on maximum and minimum temperatures and on the occurrence of air frost in the period 1971–2000 are plotted for selected climatological stations. (The main map is derived from Kain and Ravenhill 1999 and graphs for individual stations have been plotted from data available on the Met Office website, http://www.met-office.gov.uk/index.html)

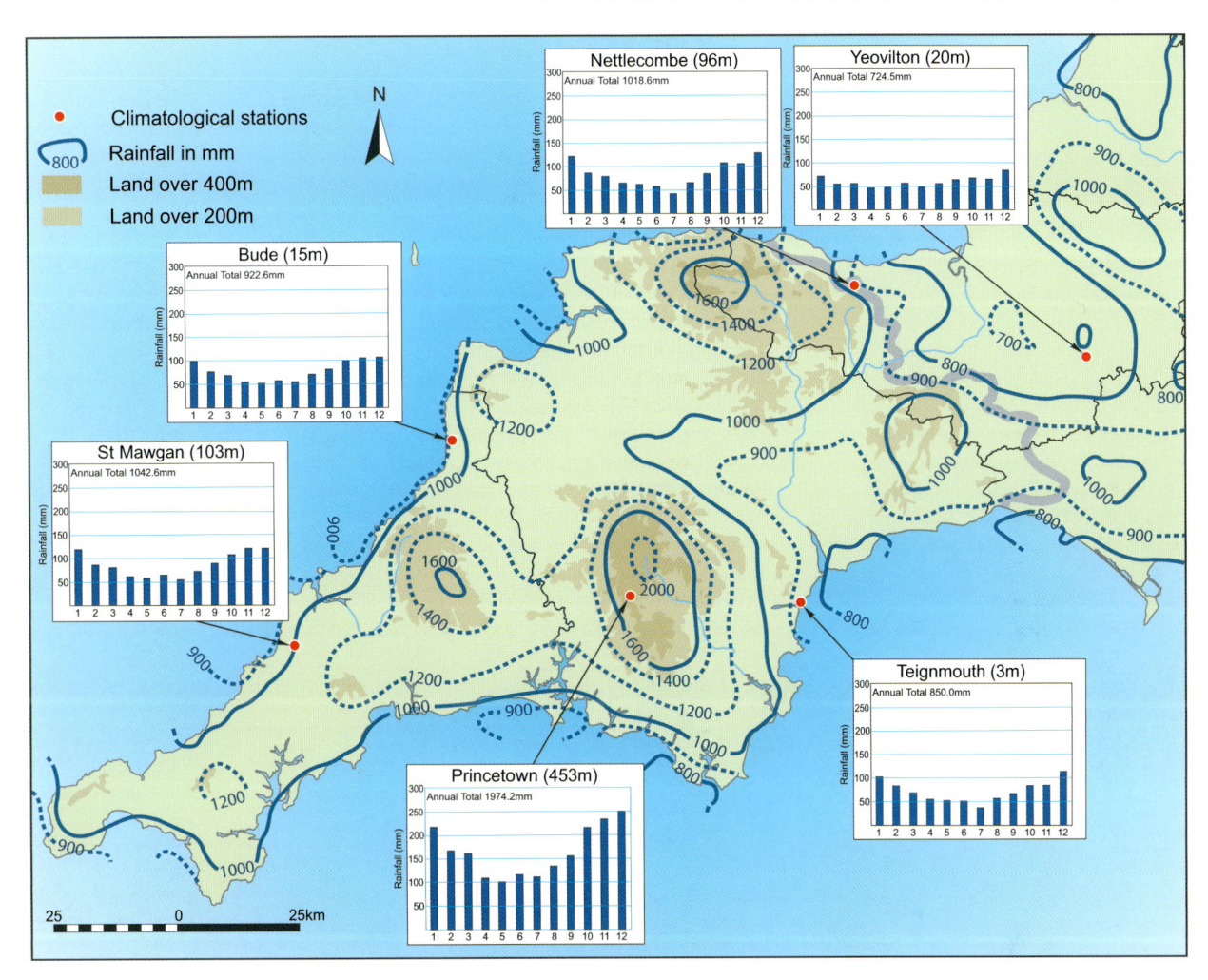

THE ENVIRONMENTAL SETTING OF HUMAN OCCUPATION

east and north within the peninsula. The difference between the peak in maximum temperature, which occurs either in July or August, and the trough in minimum temperature, which is recorded in either January or February, is only 15.6°C at St Mawgan but rises to 16.3°C at Bude and to 17.1, 18.9 and 20.4°C at Teignmouth, Nettlecombe and Yeovilton, respectively.

South-west England is one of Britain's wetter provinces with much of the area to the west of the Exe valley receiving a mean annual-rainfall total greater than 1,000mm (Fig. 2.21). Precipitation receipt is closely related to topography, and the average annual catch exceeds 2,000mm on the highest parts of Dartmoor but falls below 800mm in the lowlands around the Exe estuary, which are in the rain shadow of Dartmoor, Exmoor and the east Devon uplands. Recent Met Office statistics from climatological stations in the region show that significant rainfall occurs in all months, although there is a clear winter peak with a maximum commonly, but not always, in December (Fig. 2.21). Although snowfall is often thought to be more common in eastern England, Met Office data for the period 1961–90 reveal that parts of Exmoor and Dartmoor experience an average of 20 days in winter when snow is falling, which is greater than large tracts of East Anglia. The high moor of Dartmoor is also characterised by an average annual number of days with hail (more than 40 in the 1961–90 period) that is as high as anywhere in Britain and reflects the instability in cold polar maritime air that has travelled over a large expanse of warmer ocean and is forced to rise over the high ground of the South West.

Fig. 2.21 Rainfall in south-west England. The map shows the distribution of mean annual rainfall across the peninsula for the period 1961–90 and highlights a close relationship between rainfall receipt and elevation. Data on annual total and monthly amounts of precipitation in the period 1971–2000 are plotted for selected climatological stations. (Graphs for individual stations have been plotted from data available on the Met Office website, http://www.met-office.gov.uk/index.html)

THE ENVIRONMENTAL SETTING OF HUMAN OCCUPATION

Away from the uplands, snow and hail falls are much less frequent, and the relatively mild climate also ensures that snow lies for significantly fewer days in the South West compared with eastern England.

Cornwall and Devon are among the sunnier counties of England, and around the coasts of the peninsula the mean average daily sunshine totals exceed 4.5 hours. Increased cloudiness associated with the major upland areas reduces these annual average values to fewer than 4 hours per day. Visibility is affected not only by cloud but also by radiation fogs and sea fogs. The former are caused by intense night-time cooling of moist air and occur particularly in the valleys and hollows of inland areas, while the latter are generated along the coast by the passage of moist air over water at a cooler temperature. Data from the Isles of Scilly and Exeter Airport suggest that sea fogs dominate at the former location in summer but radiation fogs often account for reduced visibility at Exeter Airport in winter. The peninsula commonly experiences windy conditions that disperse fog and improve visibility. Wind speeds tend to be greatest near to the coasts, and especially in the far west of the region, but they also are higher in areas of greater elevation.

It is apparent from geological and geomorphological evidence that south-west England has been subject to marked fluctuations of climate through time. Much attention has been given in recent years to the occurrence of global warming during the 20th century and especially over the period since 1970. In Britain, a tendency to wetter winters and drier summers accompanying rising temperatures also has been observed. By historical standards, the decade 1991–2000 was exceptionally warm, and a comparison of Met Office statistics for the 1961–90 and 1971–2000 observation periods at six climatological stations

Fig. 2.22 Recent changes in the air temperature regime of south-west England. The graphs show the difference between annual average and monthly mean maximum and minimum air temperatures recorded at selected Met Office climatological stations in the periods 1961–90 and 1971–2000. (Based on data available on the Met Office website, http://www.metoffice.gov.uk/index.html)

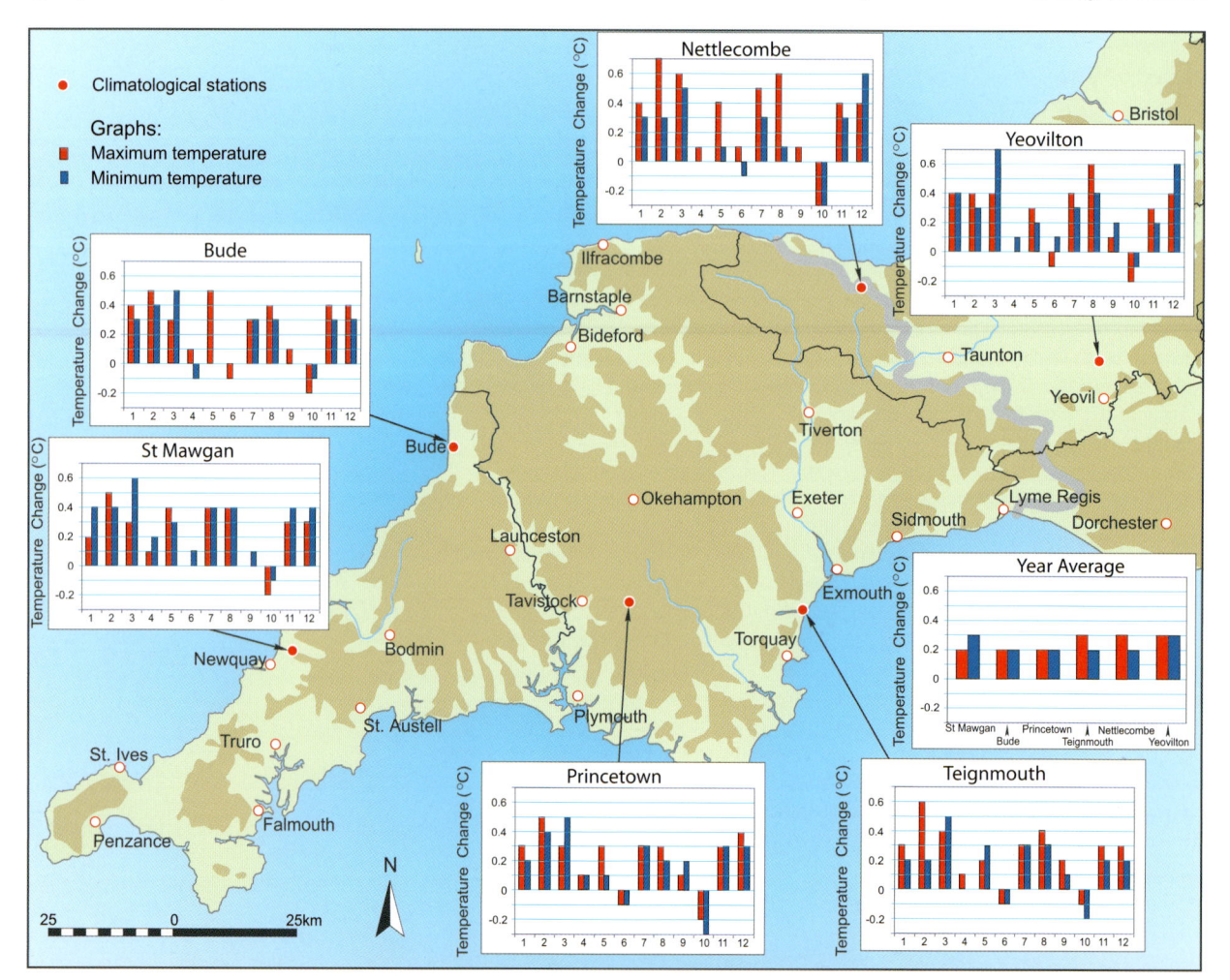

in the peninsula suggests increases in maximum and minimum temperatures of 0.2 to 0.3°C when averaged over the year, but larger changes when individual months are considered (Fig. 2.22). The majority view is that recent global warming can be attributed, in some measure, to increased emissions of greenhouse gases by human activity. Considerable efforts have been made to predict how climate may change during the present century depending on different scenarios (low to high) of greenhouse gas emissions and concentrations for the years ahead. In the case of south-west England, projections for the 2080s suggest, even under low-emission scenarios, that annual average temperatures will be 1.5–2°C higher than in the 1961–90 reference period, and summer (June to August) temperatures will be 2–2.5°C higher in the west of the peninsula and 2.5–3°C greater in the east. Under the scenario of high emissions, annual mean and summer mean temperatures in the South West may be 3.5–4 and 4.5–5°C higher by the 2080s. The modelling for this date also suggests an increase in winter (December to February) rainfall of 10 to 25 per cent but a decrease in summer precipitation of 10 to more than 50 per cent, depending on which scenario is employed. Other changes predicted for the peninsula by the 2080s under a high-emission scenario include a marked decrease (40 per cent) in snowfall, a substantial decrease in summer cloud cover (by more than 16 per cent in the east of the region) and an increase in winter wind speed (5 to 7 per cent).

SOILS AND VEGETATION

Soils strongly reflect the parent materials from which they are derived but their development is also influenced by many factors in addition to geology, including the time available for formation, climatic conditions, topographic and hydrological factors (such as elevation, aspect and drainage), biotic activity and the impact of human modification. It is not surprising, therefore, that soil types show marked local and complex variations across south-west England. However, a generalised distribution of soils for the region (Fig. 2.23) shows raw peat soils, which are permanently waterlogged and have an organic layer more than 0.4m thick, are found on the high ground of Dartmoor due to the wet and cold conditions. Seasonally waterlogged gleys (sticky clay soils) occur on the high ground of Exmoor and display characteristic mottling in the profile as well as a humose or peaty topsoil. Other types of surface-water gleys that are slowly permeable and subject to seasonal waterlogging are typical of the softer shales of the Culm Measures of mid-Devon, the Tertiary deposits of the Bovey Basin and the Liassic clays in the far east of the peninsula. Groundwater gleys occur in the alluvial lowlands of the Exe Valley, and here the seasonal waterlogging is due to a shallow fluctuating groundwater table. The type of soils known as podzols, which are typified by a bleached upper horizon and the accumulation of aluminium, iron and organic matter lower in the profile, owe their formation to percolation and leaching by acidic waters and are found in many upland environments of the peninsula. Brown podzolic soils, which are moderately deep, well drained and stony, are typical of eastern Dartmoor and the Land's End and Carnmenellis granite outcrops. Stagnopodzols, which have a peaty topsoil, are found in western Dartmoor, on the granite uplands of Bodmin and St Austell and also in the Lizard peninsula. Brown soils underlie much of south-west England and characteristically are well or moderately well drained, have an altered, usually brownish, subsurface horizon, and extend to more than 0.3m in depth. Brown earths occur over large areas of Devonian and Carboniferous rocks in Devon and Cornwall, while members of this major group that have significant clay accumulation in the subsurface are associated with Permian and Triassic mudstones and clays. Often, these soils are reddened by the presence of the iron mineral haematite and lend a very distinctive colour to the 'red Devon'

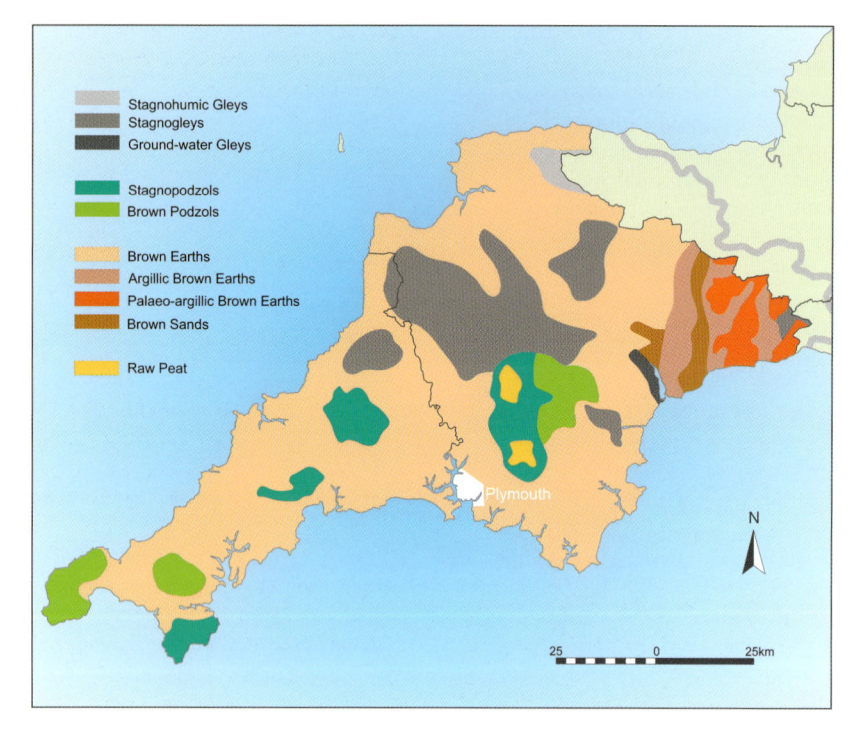

Fig. 2.23 Major soil types in south-west England. *The map shows the general distribution of dominant soil groups across the peninsula and highlights that soil type is not only related to geology but also is influenced by other factors such as topography and climate. (Based on Burnham* et al. *1980)*

agricultural landscapes in the east of the region. Brown sands are developed over the sandstones and gravels of the Permian and Triassic deposits, while a variant of brown soils, which comprises deep loams over clayey horizons and reflects the influence of weathering in warm periods before the last ice advance, is found on the upland plateaux of east Devon. The effects of the Pleistocene legacy on soil characteristics are seen in the enhanced silt content of soils on the Lizard and elsewhere because they are formed over loess, which is a windborne silty drift derived from extensive spreads of glaciofluvial deposits in north-west Europe, especially at the end of the last glaciation.

Human impact on the soils of south-west England has been extensive, and major alterations in soil-forming conditions have taken place since the prehistoric period as a consequence of increasing occupation and utilisation of the landscape. The amelioration in climate and increased chemical weathering at the beginning of the Holocene promoted the development of a vegetation cover and resulted in the establishment of largely mixed deciduous woodland over almost all of the peninsula. The associated soils would have been relatively rich in nutrients, even in areas underlain by parent materials deficient in bases, such as calcium and magnesium, and would have been reasonably free draining. Transition to blanket bog and the formation of peat began approximately 8,000 years ago when Mesolithic communities started to burn woodland margins in order to assist the hunting of game. Through a process of increasing deforestation and exposure, peat was able to spread on Dartmoor, Exmoor and Bodmin Moor during a number of stages up to and including the later part of the 1st millennium BC. Removal of woodland in lowland areas of Devon and Cornwall has also caused changes in soil profiles that have been reinforced by centuries of farming and the practices of ploughing, draining, marling and the application of lime and fertilisers. The rapidity and completeness with which the human hand may alter soil profiles in the peninsula is evident from two examples. On Exmoor, it has been shown that reclamation of podzols and gleys in the 19th century has led within 130 years to the formation of a new surface horizon with brown earth characteristics, while in parts of west Cornwall manuring of land with sea sand, seaweed and other organic material has obliterated relationships with natural soil-forming factors and generated thick man-made soils.

Like the soils that support it, the vegetation of south-west England has evolved throughout the post-glacial period under the twin influences of climatic change and human modification. By 9,000 years ago, the arctic vegetation of the late glacial had been replaced by a woodland cover that was initially birch and pine but was replaced by hazel and oak, and some elm in lower areas, with the advent of a warmer and drier climate. Evidence from Bodmin Moor suggests that oak, birch and hazel probably only colonised the more sheltered sites in upland areas. In the early Holocene the woodland vegetation may have been affected by natural fire but later there is evidence of burning by Mesolithic

THE ENVIRONMENTAL SETTING OF HUMAN OCCUPATION

communities, which in the north of Dartmoor, for example, led to the transformation of primary hazel-dominated woodland, through secondary woodland and upland grassland, to blanket bog within the course of a single millennium. Human impact in removing and changing vegetation has continued to the present day so that now we see a pattern of semi-natural plant communities interspersed with large swathes of agricultural land. A diversity of topography, geology and climate has resulted in the region having a rich and interesting flora. Plants with oceanic southern origins, an Atlantic distribution and northern and montane affinities can all be found within the peninsula. Distinctive plant communities occur in the upland bogs, the east Devon heaths (Fig. 2.24) and coastal landslips (Fig. 2.25), the salt marshes

Fig. 2.24 Heathland vegetation on Woodbury Common, east Devon. Lowland heath and conifers are well developed in east Devon on areas underlain, for example, by the Budleigh Salterton Pebble Beds formation. The vegetation communities are dominated by low-growing heather, shrubs and gorse, but are also sensitive to variations in drainage conditions.

BELOW: *Fig. 2.25 The Hooken landslip near Beer Head, east Devon.* This feature was caused by collapse of the Chalk in the upper part of the cliff following liquefaction in the underlying Upper Greensand formation. The resulting complex sequence of rotational movement has generated an area of undercliff (a complex of ridges and troughs between inland and sea cliffs), which has a distinctive vegetation comprising a dense scrub of privet, dogwood and other lime-loving plants.

THE ENVIRONMENTAL SETTING OF HUMAN OCCUPATION

Fig. 2.26 Dartmoor habitats. *The figure shows the variety of different plant communities and a generalised distribution of habitats in the Dartmoor landscape. (Based on the Dartmoor National Park Authority Fact Sheet on Wildlife and Habitats, http://www.dartmoor-npa.gov.uk/lab-habitats.pdf)*

HABITAT	PLANT COMMUNITY
Blanket and valley bogs	Sphagnum mosses, cotton grass and purple moor grass in blanket bogs, valley bogs more varied
Heather moorland	Dominated by ling, but bell heather, bilberry and western gorse in drier areas, and crossleaved heather and purple moor grass in wetter zones
Grassland	Main grasses are bents and fescues, forming close cropped mat with some flowers, but often contain gorse and invaded by bracken on drier slopes
Woodland	Broadleaf valley and upland woodland dominated by oak, with occasional hazel and rowan, and abundant ferns, mosses and lichens. Conifer plantations mainly Sitka or Norway spruce.
Rhôs pasture	Wide range of wetland plants, and often associated with wet woodland and scrub
Tors, rocks, walls	Lichens, mosses, ferns and flowers.

BELOW: ***Fig. 2.27 Wistman's Wood, Dartmoor***. *This is an example of a small remnant of oak woodland surviving in clitter on west- or south-west-facing slopes and renowned for trees with an extraordinary spreading and gnarled habit and a luxuriant bryophyte cover. Traditionally, these survivals have been thought to be natural remnants of an ancient more extensive woodland cover, and maybe the ancestors of the original forest cover that developed during the climatic amelioration of the Holocene. However, there is some evidence that such woodland was planted in association with tin mining activities in historical times.*

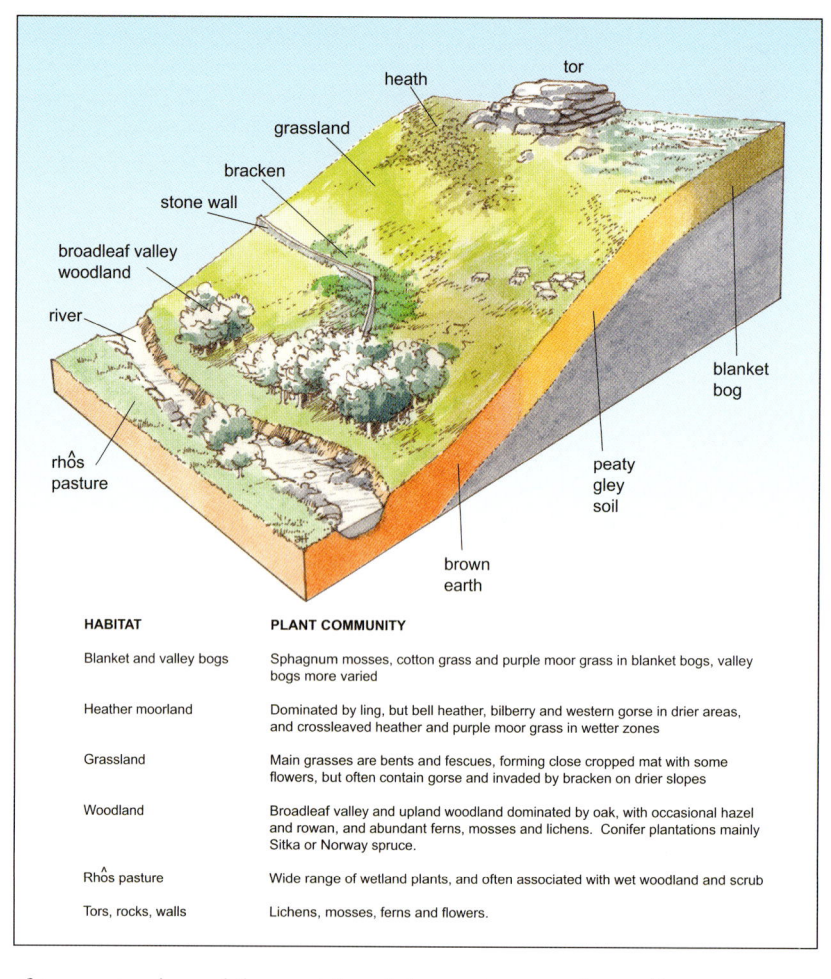

of many estuaries and the coastal sand dune systems, such as at Braunton Burrows in north Devon. The Dartmoor landscape is made up of a series of distinctive habitats (Fig. 2.26), including ancient woodlands such as Wistman's Wood (Fig. 2.27), thought by some to represent remnants of the forest that spread across the South West at the beginning of the Holocene. Human exploitation of the landscape for agriculture and other activities, even in the present technological era, depends on the limitations imposed by soil, wetness, climate and topography. Land capability maps, which classify land from grade 1 (no limitations for agriculture) to grade 7 (extremely severe limitations), reveal that land with moderate limitations (grade 3) caused by climatic conditions is most common across the peninsula (Fig. 2.28). Land capability is better on the lighter soils in the east of the region, but is worse in large tracts of mid-Devon underlain by the Culm

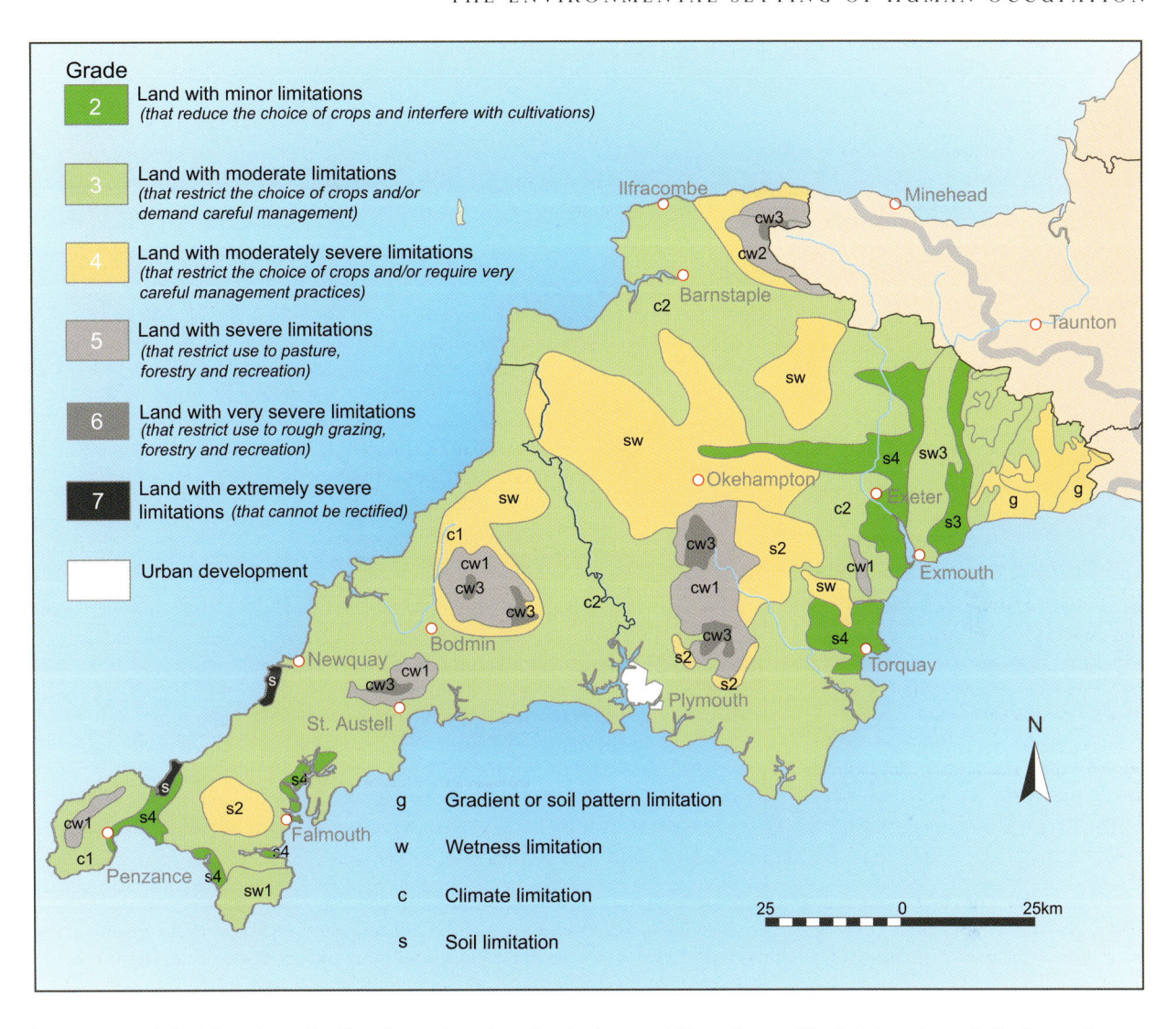

THE ENVIRONMENTAL SETTING OF HUMAN OCCUPATION

Fig. 2.28 Land capability in south-west England. The map shows how the potential for the use of land in agriculture varies across the peninsula. While a number of factors, including the nature of the soil, impose local limitations, climate acts more regionally to reduce land capability. (Based on a map by C J Caseldine, in Kain and Ravenhill, 1999, and on the 1:1,000,000 scale Land Use Capability map of England and Wales published by the National Soils Resources Institute, Cranfield University, Silsoe)

Measures and their heavier soils. Significant deterioration in the capability of land to sustain agriculture occurs in the upland moors of the peninsula, while contamination of land by mine waste has rendered some areas in west Cornwall unrectifiable.

ENVIRONMENTAL HAZARDS

While the landscapes of south-west England have been exploited for human benefit, they also pose some threats and difficulties to the population of the region. In the context of geological and geomorphological hazards, the peninsula experiences moderately active and low magnitude earthquakes, which occasionally cause public alarm but very little damage. More serious is slope instability in the form of landslides, rockfalls and ground subsidence. A survey in the mid-1980s identified 109 landslides along the coastline of Devon and Cornwall and 374 landslides at inland locations within Devon. The latter included numerous features in the Carboniferous Crackington Formation to the west of Exeter, a number of landslides in the dissected uplands of east Devon where Cretaceous Upper Greensand overlies clays and marls of Triassic and

THE ENVIRONMENTAL SETTING OF HUMAN OCCUPATION

Liassic age, and a major concentration of failures in north Devon generated by the August 1952 storm over Exmoor. Along the coast, massive and complex landslides occur from Sidmouth to Lyme Regis and beyond, but cliffs to the west of Budleigh Salterton (*see* Fig. 2.5) and in harder rocks between Boscastle and the Taw Estuary are also susceptible to failure. Marine erosion at the base of cliffs around the coast of the peninsula is an ongoing and common process that, without engineering interventions, often leads to rockfalls and many other types of instability. This results in cliff retreat and loss of land and property to the sea. Ground subsidence with damage to shallow foundations is a particular problem in Torbay, especially through the development of solution cavities in the Devonian limestone and the occurrence of unconsolidated sandy silt soils that have formed over Permian breccias and are susceptible to loss of strength on wetting. One of the most serious natural geological hazards arises from radon, a radioactive gas, that is produced by the decay of uranium and thorium in underlying rocks, especially granites, and seeps into buildings where it is thought to be a health hazard. The National Radiological Protection Board has estimated that the inhabitants of 12 per cent of the homes in Devon and Cornwall receive an annual radiation dose from radon and its decay products that is above the recommended level.

Weather, as well as geology, can also prove hazardous to the inhabitants of south-west England. Severe blizzards affect the region from time to time, such as those recorded in January 1881, March 1891, December 1927 and February 1963 when very heavy snowfall and drifting on Dartmoor, and other areas, caused severe disruption to communications. Freak weather may also afflict the peninsula. One of the most notorious incidents occurred on 21 October 1638 when a tornado accompanied by ball lightning struck the church of Widecombe-in-the Moor on Dartmoor during a service, and the resulting structural damage caused death and injury among members of the congregation. Exceptionally heavy or prolonged rainfall with resulting serious flooding is also a hazard experienced in south-west England. One of the three heaviest falls of rain in a 24-hour period to be recorded in Britain occurred over Exmoor on 15 August 1952 and led to the Lynmouth flood disaster. It is estimated that more than 200mm of rain fell in intense thunderstorms on ground that was already saturated by unusually wet conditions in the first half of the month. Runoff from the steep slopes into the tributaries of the River Lyn draining towards the Bristol Channel was rapid and river levels rose exceptionally fast. Trees blown down in gales during the previous March were swept into the watercourses and formed temporary dams when they collected behind narrow bridges and other obstructions. Failure of these 'dams' generated a series of storm surges that increased the velocity and peak of the resulting flood wave, which destroyed nearly 40 buildings and led to the deaths of 34 people on its arrival in Lynmouth during the night of 15/16 August. There is evidence of an earlier episode of destructive flooding at Lynmouth in 1796, and torrential summer downpours have caused bad floods in other parts of the region including the Camelford area of Cornwall, which was affected in July 1847, August 1950 and June 1957. Persistent heavy rain during the autumn of 1960, when over two-thirds of the average annual rainfall fell between 27 September and 5 December, led to serious flooding in east Devon. Major floods inundated Exeter (Fig. 2.29), Exmouth, Crediton and other settlements in October, and further flooding occurred in Exeter during early December, these events prompting the design and construction of the city's flood-relief scheme. Problems of flooding have continued to afflict the region in more recent years, with villages such as Polperro and Boscastle in Cornwall and Harbertonford in Devon suffering serious and sometimes repeated incidents. In the flash flood that struck Boscastle on 16 August 2004, for example, some 2 million tonnes of water flowed through the village damaging or destroying 70 properties,

Fig. 2.29 Flooding in Exeter. *Very heavy and prolonged rains during the autumn and early winter of 1960 led to a number of major floods in Exeter, which particularly affected the St Thomas area of the city and where residents had to be evacuated by boat.*

sweeping away more than 70 cars and necessitating the evacuation of 100 people (Fig. 2.30). While the evidence for an increased incidence of flooding in recent times due to the effects of global warming is equivocal, future trends towards greater winter rainfall may exacerbate this hazard.

Coastal flooding can also pose a threat to the peninsula – for example, there is sedimentological evidence that a tidal wave, generated by the Lisbon earthquake in 1755, inundated parts of the Isles of Scilly. The future may bring an increased threat of coastal flooding in south-west England, as a consequence of rising sea levels in a warmer world caused through thermal expansion of the oceans and increased melting of ice at present locked up in glaciers and in the world's ice sheets. These effects, coupled with the continued subsidence of the peninsula in response to the retreat of the ice sheet from the rest of Britain at the end of the Pleistocene, are predicted by the 2080s to cause an increase of 160–760mm in mean sea levels above those recorded in the period 1961–90.

Fig. 2.30 Flooding in Boscastle.
The event of 16 August 2004, in which more than 200mm of rain fell in a 24-hour period and peak rainfall intensities exceeded 300mm per hour, is a recent example of the summer storms that from time to time generate very serious flash flooding in south-west England. On this occasion, the efforts of helicopter rescue services prevented any loss of life in the incident.

CONCLUSIONS

South-west England has some spectacular and highly distinctive landscapes. Few people could fail to be moved by the rugged beauty of the tors and boulder-strewn slopes of the Dartmoor upland or fail to recognise in the colour and contour afforded by underlying granite and its erosional history a landscape that is very different from other parts of upland Britain. Just a few kilometres to the north, however, the upland scene is replaced by the monotony of the mid-Devon plateau, while a short distance to the east, a change in soil colour announces arrival in the lowlands of 'red Devon'. These differences emphasise the great diversity of the landscape in the South West, which is not only evident between major sub-regions of the peninsula but is also apparent over quite small areas – witness, for example, the strong contrasts between the majestic cliffs of the north Cornish coastline and the more subdued drowned inlets of the Fal and the Helford rivers, less than 20km to the south. To the themes of distinctiveness and diversity must be added dynamism, since the landscape of the South West, although in some respects old and ancient, is far from static. Many of the elements perhaps more directly important to human occupation, including the climate, soils and vegetation, have changed remarkably over the span of a relatively few millennia and have provided an evolving backdrop to the human history of the peninsula. However, the pattern and progress of human activity, which is the subject of the remainder of this volume, has itself not only modulated and modified many of the physical processes at work in the region, but also occasioned significant alterations of the natural environment. In south-west England, the interactions and interdependencies of environment and human occupation that began in the Palaeolithic Period continue to be no less relevant or influential in the 21st century AD.

FURTHER READING

Invaluable sources of information on the physical geography of the peninsula are provided by Shorter *et al.* 1969 and Barlow (ed.) 1969, especially chapters 3, 4 and 8.

Excellent syntheses of environmental conditions and the use of building materials in the region are to be found in Kain and Ravenhill (eds) 1999.

Detailed and definitive descriptions of the region's geological development are provided by Selwood *et al.* (eds) 1998 (for Cornwall) and Durrance *et al.* (eds), in press for 2007 (for Devon).

The *Classic Landform Guides* published by the Geographical Association for the north Devon Coast by Peter Keene (1996) and for the south Devon Coast by Derek Mottershead (1996) explain a range of landscape features, while a definitive account of the Quaternary landforms of the peninsula is given in Campbell *et al.* 1998.

A modern synthesis of the region's climate is given by Parry 1997, 47–66.

The standard reference work on soils of the region is Findlay *et al.* 1984. Useful summary information on soils and other aspects of the physical geography of Exmoor is to be found in Binding 1995.

The National Park websites (http://www.dartmoor-npa.gov.uk/, http://www.exmoor-nationalpark.gov.uk/) have a range of educational resources on environmental characteristics.

3

Landscapes of Pre-Medieval Occupation

STEPHEN RIPPON

THE DISTINCTIVE LANDSCAPES OF THE SOUTH-WEST PENINSULA

The South West is well known for its wealth of archaeological sites, most notably on the granite uplands of Dartmoor, Bodmin Moor and West Penwith, but the focus of this chapter is not individual monuments but rather the whole landscape and in particular how prehistoric, Romano-British and early medieval communities shaped the character of the present countryside. Chronologically this chapter begins at the end of the ice age and finishes a century or so before the Norman Conquest, by which time many of the essential characteristics of today's 'historic landscape' had come into being – a settlement pattern typically of small hamlets and isolated farmsteads, the network of winding sunken lanes, the complex systems of small fields enclosed by high hedgebanks, and the legacies from the extraction of a wide range of mineral resources.

The eastern boundary of the South West is a fundamental and long-lasting division in the cultural and physical landscape, which runs approximately along the watersheds of the Quantock and Blackdown hills to the west of the rivers Parrett and Axe (Fig. 3.1). It encompasses the whole of the medieval counties of Devon and Cornwall along with the western part of Somerset, including Exmoor. This boundary divides the tribal areas of the Iron Age and Romano-British Dumnonii in the west and the Durotriges in the east, but also marks a fundamental division in the character of the cultural landscape of southern Britain as a whole in being the westerly limit of extensive Romanisation and a countryside characterised by nucleated villages and open fields in the medieval and post-medieval period. The special character of south-west England's landscape has an antiquity that goes back over two millennia.

A number of distinctive features of the region's archaeological research have greatly influenced the extent to which we understand its landscape history. Topographically, the landscape is dominated by a series of uplands of which those formed of granite have given rise to abundant, well-preserved relict landscapes due to the freely available loose stone boulders used for the construction of field walls and buildings. The other major upland, Exmoor, comprises mostly sandstones, slates and grits, and the lack of good quality stone results in a range of less visually impressive monuments, the extent of which has only recently been fully appreciated. Despite the excellent preservation of this upland archaeology, the long history of fieldwork on Dartmoor, and recent surveys on Bodmin Moor and Exmoor, the amount of recent excavation in south-west England's uplands is in fact surprisingly limited.

LANDSCAPES OF PRE-MEDIEVAL OCCUPATION

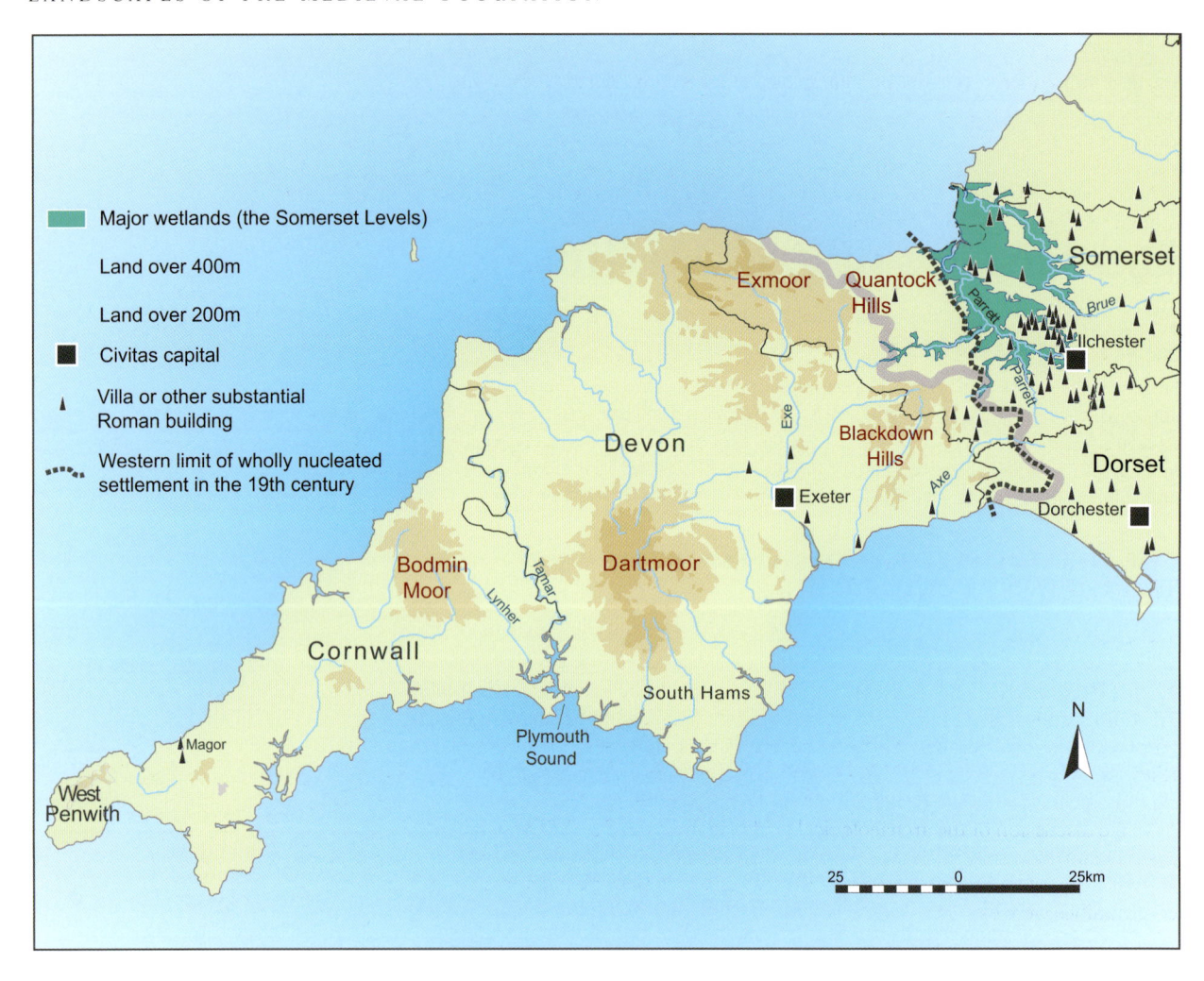

Fig. 3.1 The south-west peninsula. Distribution of villas and other substantial romanised buildings, and the western limit of wholly nucleated settlement patterns in the 19th century, following the work of Roberts and Wrathmell 2000.

Fig. 3.2 Raddon, Stockleigh Pomeroy, central Devon (SS 885031). The crop marks of this Early Neolithic causewayed enclosure and Iron Age hillfort, which was re-occupied in the early medieval period, have only been visible through aerial photography for a few weeks every few years. Following a geophysical survey, the site was excavated in advance of road construction. Without the use of radiocarbon dating the aceramic early medieval phase would probably not have been recognised.

In the lowlands past sites and landscapes are, in contrast, more difficult to locate as subsequent extensive ploughing has flattened most earthworks, while often heavy soils and a modern predominance of pastoral farming makes the extent of crop marks visible from the air relatively limited compared to regions such as Wessex. There has, however, been a long tradition of opportunistic surface collection, which has revealed large numbers of prehistoric flint scatters, though the region's often acidic soils, and a genuine scarcity of pottery used on many later prehistoric to early medieval rural settlements, means that sites of these periods are rarely located through fieldwalking. A transformation in our understanding of south-west England's lowland landscape started in the mid-1980s with the initiation of regular aerial photography that revealed a previously unsuspected density of crop-mark sites (Fig. 3.2 and *see also* Fig. 3.13), while large-scale geophysical survey is also starting to have an impact. Compared to some other parts of Britain there have been relatively few large-scale rescue excavations, though a number of linear developments such as road constructions and pipelines are now providing valuable cross-sections across the landscape and are once again revealing a hitherto unsuspected range and density of sites.

THE CHRONOLOGICAL FRAMEWORK

The chronological framework of the South West is based upon the traditional artefact-based terminology used by British prehistorians – for example the Middle Bronze Age – and these discrete cultural periods are summarised in Table 3.1. Distribution maps for sites from most of these periods can be found in the *Historical Atlas of South-West England* and *The Field Archaeology of Exmoor* (*see* Riley and Wilson-North 2001). All the dates referred to here are based on calibrated/calendar years (eg 3rd millennium BC; *c*. AD 55/60).

While discussion of the archaeological evidence from the South West is based upon the discrete cultural periods listed in Table 1, this chapter is structured around five broader phases defined by the way in which post-glacial human communities were exploiting, modifying and managing landscape:

- Landscapes of hunter-gatherers (Mesolithic: 10th to 5th millennium BC): development of post-glacial climax vegetation (mixed deciduous woodland) exploited by mobile hunter-gatherer groups who may have modified the landscape slightly through the use of fire to open up woodland clearings around the forest margins.

- Landscapes of the earliest agriculturalists and their ancestors (Neolithic/Early Bronze Age: 4th to mid-2nd millennium BC): initial significant clearance of woodland creating a moderately open landscape used for agriculture and hunting-gathering by semi-sedentary, socially stratified communities who laid claim to territories through the construction of ceremonial and burial monuments and the creation of ancestors.

- Landscapes of the first sedentary farmers (Middle/?Late Bronze Age: mid-2nd to ?early 1st millennium BC): emergence of sedentary communities living in stable settlements (both open and enclosed) often associated with small-scale field systems, with large-scale enclosure of the upland margins of Dartmoor. Continued use of some barrow cemeteries but relatively few archaeologically visible signs of social stratification. Possible decrease in the intensity of landscape exploitation in the Late Bronze Age.

- Landscapes of a stratified society (Iron Age, Romano-British and earliest early medieval periods: mid-1st millennium BC to mid/late 1st millennium AD):

TABLE 3.1 THE CULTURAL PERIODS OF THE SOUTH WEST

(AFTER GENT AND QUINNELL 1999 (EARLY NEOLITHIC); HOLBROOK 2001 (ROMANO-BRITISH); NEEDHAM AND PEARCE 1999 (BRONZE AGE METALWORK); QUINNELL 1986, 1994; ROBERTS 1999 (PALAEOLITHIC/MESOLITHIC); AND WATTS AND QUINNELL 2001.

PERIOD	DATES (CALENDAR/CALIBRATED)	DISTINGUISHING FEATURES
Early Mesolithic	10th to 9th millennium BC	Flint axe-heads and microlith points.
Late Mesolithic	8th to 5th millennium BC	Range of diagnostic microliths.
Early Neolithic	4th millennium BC	Early Neolithic south-western style pottery including gabbroic wares.
Late Neolithic	3rd millennium BC	Relatively little diagnostic material including a handful of sites associated with Grooved Ware and Peterborough Ware.
Early Bronze Age	late 3rd to mid 2nd millennium BC	Beakers, Collared-Urn and early Trevisker/Biconical Urn related pottery assemblages. Harlyn (2500–2000 BC, associated with beakers); Trenovissick (2000–1700 BC) and Plymstock phases of metalwork (1700–1600/1500 BC) corresponding to the Wessex I/II phases in Britain generally.
Middle Bronze Age	mid 2nd millennium BC	Trevisker-style pottery, regional variants of Deverel-Rimbury, and Biconical Urns. Chagford (1600/1500 to 1400 BC) and Taunton phases of metalwork (1400–1200 BC).
Late Bronze Age	late 2nd millennium to 7th century BC	Late use of Trevisker-style pottery? Post-Trevisker wares; ? Late Bronze Age Plain wares. Worth (1200–1100 BC), Dainton (1100–950 BC), Stogursey (950–750 BC) and Mount Batten (750–650 BC) phases of metalwork (corresponding to the Wilburton, Ewart Park and Llyn Fawr phases in Britain generally).
Early Iron Age	8th to 5th centuries BC	Early Iron Age shouldered jars (scarce)
Middle Iron Age	4th to 1st centuries BC	South-Western Decorated Wares, eg Devon/Cornish versions of 'Glastonbury Ware'.
Late Iron Age	1st century BC to c. AD 50	Cordoned Ware in Cornwall, some Durotrigian Ware and continuation of SW Decorated Ware in Devon.
Romano-British	c. AD 50 to early 5th century	Mostly locally produced pottery (notably handmade South Devon ware and gabbroic wares in Cornwall), with some imported pottery from the more 'Romanised' parts of Britain and the continent.
Early Medieval	early 5th to 11th century	Mostly aceramic, with 5th to 7th century pottery imported from the Mediterranean on high status sites.

renewed expansion and intensification in landscape exploitation, and the emergence of a new pattern of hierarchical and predominantly enclosed settlement, with a significant number of heavily defended sites, sometimes associated with small-scale field systems. The Roman 'interlude' saw relatively few significant changes in the countryside though the intensity of mineral extraction (including tin and iron) may have increased. Possible decrease in the intensity of landscape exploitation in the very highest uplands in the early medieval period.

- The 'historic landscape' (later early medieval period and later: mid/late 1st millennium AD to present): the late prehistoric, Romano-British and early medieval landscape characterised by enclosed settlements is replaced with the scatter of small hamlets and network of winding lanes associated with the near-continuous fieldscape of today's 'historic landscape'.

LANDSCAPES OF HUNTER-GATHERERS AND THE EARLY IMPACT OF HUMAN COMMUNITIES ON THE ENVIRONMENT

Ice sheets appear never to have reached the South West, and with sea level perhaps 120m below that of today, what is now the south-west peninsula was part of continental Eurasia (*see* Chapter 2). During the glacial maximums this was a frozen land with shattered rock outcrops, gradually eroding hillsides and a coastline that stretched far out to the west, and it was probably only in the interglacial periods that human communities ventured into the region. A scatter of unstratified lithic artefacts testifies to a human presence during these warmer phases though only in the rock shelters at Kent's Cavern and Tornewton (both near Torquay, Devon) and the riverine terrace gravels at Broom in the Axe valley (in Devon), are these in anything close to a stratified context.

Britain was abandoned during the coldest parts of the last Ice Age (the Devensian), but as the climate warmed in about 9500 BC, the vegetation changed from tundra and cold steppe grassland with some herbaceous and shrub cover, through birch-pine woodland to a closed canopy of mixed deciduous forest dominated by oak, elm, lime and hazel that by about 7600 BC blanketed all but the very highest uplands and low-lying alder-dominated floodplains. Sea level was around minus 40 metres below modern Ordnance Datum, and although the basic form of the peninsula was evident, the actual coastline was between 2 and 10 km beyond that of today. This was the landscape that was reoccupied by hunter-gatherer communities of the Mesolithic. The numerous scatters of Mesolithic flints tend to concentrate in river valleys, the coastal zone and the upland fringes above 250m. The coastal zone would have been a prime location for hunting and gathering, providing a rich source of food, along with flint and chert, as reflected in the coastal camps at Westward Ho! in west Devon and at Porlock and the nearby hilltop site at Hawkcombe Head in west Somerset. The overall distribution of Mesolithic findspots, and the inclusion of beach flint and marine shells in assemblages at sites such as Three Holes Cave in the Dart valley, Devon, suggest that river valleys provided the main travel routes within the interior.

It was during the later Mesolithic that human communities first started to have an impact upon the landscape through their use of fire to open up the sedge-dominated peat bogs in the Exe valley floodplain (*c.* 6500 BC), and woodland clearings on and around Dartmoor (*c.* 6200 BC) and possibly Bodmin Moor (*c.* 4700 BC). This firing may represent an attempt to improve hunting by maintaining and improving grazing land, making the location of herds more predictable. On Dartmoor this localised opening up of the landscape may have initiated what became a marked deterioration of the soils in these areas, changing what were reasonably free-draining brown earths to acidic peats.

LANDSCAPES OF THE EARLIEST AGRICULTURALISTS AND THEIR ANCESTORS

The 4th millennium BC saw a profound change in the way that human communities perceived and exploited the landscape, though it must be remembered that parts of the Neolithic/Bronze Age coastal zone are now below sea level and/or have been eroded away. It was during the Neolithic that woodland was cleared, followed by the grazing of domestic livestock and cultivation of cereals in the more open landscape. Monuments, many with links to the rituals associated with death, burial and the 'rites of passage' between the worlds of the living and the dead, were constructed while new types of artefact (notably pottery and ground stone axes) reflect the exploitation of a wider range of natural resources. The origins and significance of this 'Neolithic package' are much debated, and those complex arguments are beyond the scope of this chapter: the key theme here is the growing intensity with which the landscape was exploited both materially and in social interaction.

Early Neolithic clearance of the landscape

The distribution of Late Mesolithic and Early Neolithic flints is broadly similar, suggesting that woodland clearance focused on those coastal, river valley and upland margins that had already started to be opened up through the use of fire in the Mesolithic or in places where the fringes of the surviving woodland cover were easiest to open up. This first phase of substantial woodland clearance, associated with a decline in elm, is dated to about 3500 BC in the Exe valley and around the fringes of Exmoor, and was followed by a pronounced increase in grassland and the first appearance of cereal pollen including rye and oat/wheat. On Dartmoor the palaeoenvironmental record for the Neolithic is poor, but the evidence suggests that some woodland was cleared, followed by grazing to maintain this open landscape. On Bodmin Moor the dating is similarly unclear and though the first appearance of pasture at Rough Tor dates to mid-4th millennium BC, on East Moor the earliest clearance dates to mid-3rd millennium BC; there is no evidence for arable cultivation. The higher parts of Exmoor appear to have remained substantially wooded and although the elm decline occurred in about 3500 BC it was quickly replaced by birch, willow, alder or heathland; there is little indication of grazing and similarly no evidence for the cultivation of cereals.

Settlements and resource exploitation

During the Early Neolithic, notable concentrations of archaeologically detectable activity in eastern Devon – both domestic and potentially ritual – tend to occur on a handful of hilltop sites (eg Haldon Hill and Hazard Hill), some of which are associated with interrupted ditches, the so-called 'causewayed enclosures' known at Hembury, High Peak and Raddon Hill (Fig. 3.2). In Cornwall and west Devon so-called 'tor enclosures', such as Carn Brea and Helman Tor, may represent a regional variation that extends this pattern of Early Neolithic hilltop enclosures into the upland fringes (Fig. 3.3). The communities who used these hilltop sites were part of exchange networks that extended across the South West, and which reflect a growing intensity with which a range of landscape resources was being exploited. 'Gabbroic' pottery, made on the Lizard peninsula in south Cornwall, is found throughout the South West even comprising as much as 10 per cent of the ceramics at sites such as Haldon and Hazard Hill in eastern Devon. Vessels of this fabric have even been found as far east as Hambledon Hill, Maiden Castle and Windmill Hill in Wessex. A number of igneous rocks in Cornwall were also used to manufacture polished axes that reached Devon and beyond.

LANDSCAPES OF PRE-MEDIEVAL OCCUPATION

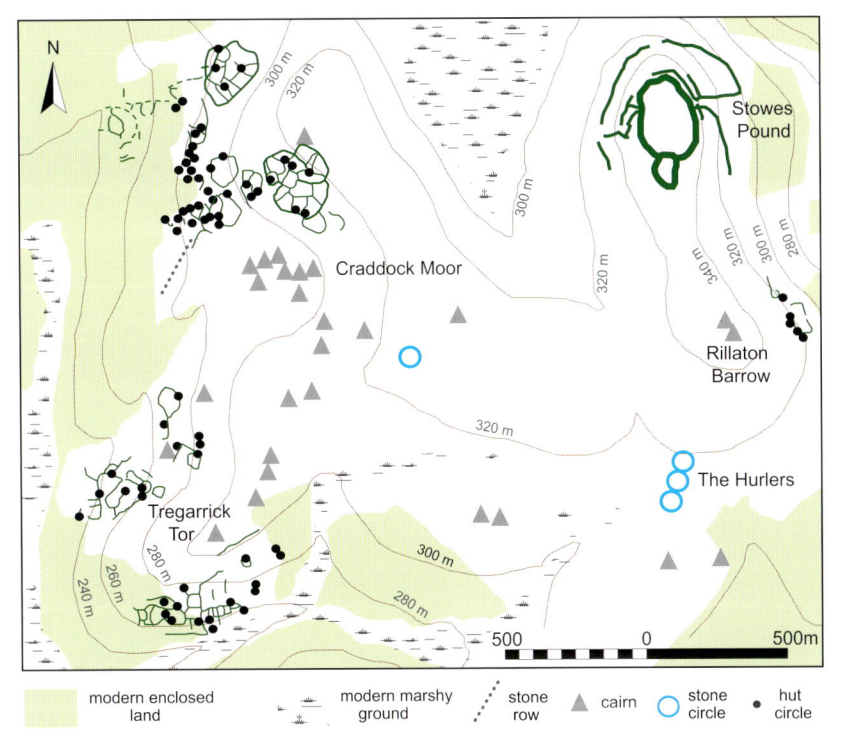

Fig. 3.3 The Craddock Moor complex, St Cleer parish, Bodmin Moor (SX 2571). The probable Early Neolithic 'tor enclosure' at Stowes Pound looks out over a complex of probable Early Bronze Age ritual monuments that are spread across the flatter interfluvial area of Craddock Moor (including the Hurlers triple stone circle, and the Rillaton Barrow: see Fig. 3.5). In contrast, the probably Middle Bronze Age settlements and 'accretive' field systems occupy the west/south-west facing valley sides.

Fig. 3.4 Trethevy Quoit, St Cleer parish, on the south-east fringes of Bodmin Moor (SX259688). Early Neolithic 'Penwith-type' chambered tombs such as this probably sit alongside 'long cairns/mounds' and 'oblong ditches' as south-west England's variants of the long barrows and cairns found in Wessex. In a landscape of probably transient settlement and hunting camps, sites such as these would have provided a monumental permanence within the landscape and a link with the community's ancestors and their territory.

Little is known about the ordinary settlement pattern of the Neolithic (or indeed the Early Bronze Age), and the few flint scatters that have been excavated produced little evidence of structural features. There has been much debate regarding the relative significance of cultivated cereals and the gathering of natural food plants during the Neolithic. In addition to the evidence for cereal pollen in lowland sequences in the South West (*see* above), charred cereals (predominantly wheat with a little barley) have also been recovered from a number of sites such as Hembury and Raddon, though there is also evidence for the continued gathering of natural foodstuffs such as hazelnuts, sloes, crab apple and bramble, thus indicating a very mixed economy.

The creation of landscapes of ancestors

Within this landscape of semi-mobile communities, the burial of the dead and a respect for the ancestors encouraged the construction of a range of ritual monuments that could have provided 'monumental permanence' and simultaneously served as territorial markers (Fig. 3.4). Some of these monuments form part of the suite seen further east in Wessex, such as south-west England's single 'cursus' at Nether Exe in Devon, but there are also more local types, notably 'long cairns/mounds' and 'oblong ditches', which might be the region's equivalent of ditched earthen long barrows of central southern Britain. The recent identification of many of these sites as crop marks in the lowlands of Devon helps to balance the distribution of megalithic monuments that concentrate around the peripheries of the granite uplands, though the impression remains that the extent of monument construction in the South West, both in terms of their scale and relative numbers, was less impressive than in Wessex.

There are several clusters of monuments that reflect the long-term significance awarded to certain locations, such as the hilltop causewayed enclosure at Raddon that overlooks a cursus and oblong ditch at Nether Exe, close to the confluence of the rivers Culm and Exe (Fig. 3.2). On the granite moors, monuments similarly appear to have been located with reference to significant features of the natural landscape. These were clearly special places of long-lasting significance in the landscape associated with the concept of 'ancestors'. They were not, however, exclusively 'ritual landscapes' and areas set aside purely for the dead: as in Wessex, fieldwalking in the lowlands has revealed scatters of lithic artefacts spread amongst the ceremonial monuments. Activity at the ritual complexes could also have been intermittent, with long-term folk memory periodically drawing communities back to these special areas and allowing monuments to be embellished from time to time.

Fig. 3.5 The Hurlers, St Cleer parish, Bodmin Moor (SX 258714). One of three, adjacent, probable Early Bronze Age stone circles, looking towards one of many abandoned 19th-century tin mines at Minions (see Fig 3.3 for a plan). The extent to which the wealth of this region – as reflected in the gold cup, Camerton-Snowshill-type bronze dagger, and possible faience glass beads from the nearby Rillaton barrow – was derived from the exploitation of tin is unclear.

The Late Neolithic

The Late Neolithic is poorly evidenced in the South West, though it appears to have seen something of a change in how the landscape was exploited. On Bodmin Moor, and possibly Dartmoor, there are signs of a regeneration of hazel-dominated scrub and a decrease in the intensity of grazing in about the mid-3rd millennium BC, a phenomenon seen elsewhere in Britain at the end of the Early Neolithic. Archaeologically this discontinuity is also reflected in the abandonment of hilltop sites in the South West, though monuments of the cursus and long barrow type may have continued in use, as was the case elsewhere in southern England. Late Neolithic pottery of the Grooved Ware and Peterborough Ware traditions has only been found on a handful of sites, and although flint scatters are more numerous, the South West contains few examples of the distinctive monument types that characterise the Late Neolithic elsewhere in England: just four henges have been identified, of which one – the Stripple Stones on Bodmin Moor – contains a stone circle. Stone circles are common on all the uplands of the South West and while their clear association with barrows and cairns shows that they were used during the Early Bronze Age (Figs 3.3 and 3.5), this does not preclude their having Late Neolithic

LANDSCAPES OF PRE-MEDIEVAL OCCUPATION

Fig. 3.6 Drizzlecombe complex, Sheepstor parish, south-east Dartmoor (SX 592671). A probable Early Bronze Age ceremonial complex comprising three stone rows, including a 4.3m-high standing stone, with a terminal cairn and 'Giant's Basin' cairn (behind the standing stone) in close association, looking across the Plym valley.

origins. The same is possibly the case for some stone rows (lines of standing stones with presumably some ritual purpose) (Fig. 3.6). Overall, though, the Late Neolithic landscape is poorly visible in the South West of today.

The Early Bronze Age: a further opening up of the landscape

Although the initial felling of woodland in some parts of the South West occurred at the start of the Neolithic, in many areas it was only during the Early Bronze Age that large-scale, permanent clearances were made and the landscape started to be permanently opened up. In the lowlands of the Exe valley the palaeoenvironmental record suggests that the final decline of elm, a further clearance of woodland and an expansion in open grassland and cereals occurred in about 2100 BC. The higher uplands of Exmoor were also probably cleared, and the open landscape maintained through grazing. Most valleys probably still retained substantial areas of woodland but some clearance is recorded both here and on the higher uplands around 1900 BC. Increased alluviation in the Exe valley from about this time may also have resulted from clearance around the upland fringe. Palaeoenvironmental evidence shows there was also an intensification of grazing and some arable cultivation on the uplands of Bodmin Moor, and although there is very little pollen evidence from Dartmoor for this period, the fact that its Middle Bronze Age reaves (field boundaries) were built in a landscape already cleared of woodland suggests that the flatter interfluvial areas were extensively cleared of woodland and that this open landscape was maintained through grazing.

Landscapes of ceremony

In places this increasingly open landscape was characterised by a suite of ceremonial monuments that show a marked tendency to occur in clusters, often in places of long-lasting importance – for example the Class II henge and extensive spread of ring ditches (circular ditches that probably once surrounded earthen barrows) close to the Early Neolithic 'oblong ditches' at Bow near

49

Crediton. A number of megalithic tombs contain Bronze Age burials, such as a cremation at Tregiffian in Penwith, suggesting they similarly had a long-term significance as the houses of ancestors. On the granite uplands of Penwith, Bodmin Moor and Dartmoor, most stone circles, along with the stone rows and cairns with which they are often associated, probably date to the Early Bronze Age. They typically lie on the flatter interfluvial areas, away from what were probably still wooded valleys and steeper slopes (*see* Figs 3.3 and 3.5). Recent work on Exmoor has shown that a similar range of monuments exists there, though on a more diminutive scale due to the lack of good stone: if similar monuments had existed in the lowlands they will not have survived subsequent ploughing, though a notable exception is the Yelland stone row that now lies in the intertidal zone of the Torridge estuary and which was preserved by the encroachment of wetland conditions.

During the Bronze Age there was a significant shift from collective communal burial, which was typical of the Neolithic, to individual interment and such earthen round barrows and stone-built cairns occur right across the South West, including areas such as the Culm Measures of west and north Devon that currently show relatively little sign of earlier occupation. Though a number of unusually large barrows are known, none has yet produced evidence for a Neolithic date, and the majority of excavated barrows are Early Bronze Age. These landscapes of the dead appear to have been abandoned around the mid-2nd millennium BC, though at Leskernick on Bodmin Moor some Middle Bronze Age field banks appear to have been robbed in order to build funerary cairns. The construction and use of barrows also continued, at least to a limited extent, on Exmoor, where radiocarbon dates from a ring cairn at Shallowmead and a round barrow in the small Bratton Down cemetery date to the late 2nd millennium BC.

As with some earlier ceremonial complexes, the location of these mainly Early Bronze Age barrows sometimes shows important relationships to the physical landscape. In some areas they concentrate in areas of the greatest agricultural potential (for example, in the Exe valley) or with access to coastal resources (as in north Cornwall), suggesting that they were relatively central to the community's territory. Others occupy hilltop and watershed locations that may have represented the margins or boundaries of a territory – for instance along watersheds. The deliberate siting of cairns around natural tors on the granite uplands, and the close relationship between Early Bronze Age monument complexes and natural landmarks generally, is in stark contrast to the 'terrain-oblivious' Dartmoor reaves (*see* below) and suggests a very different set of social values and perceptions of the landscape.

The exploitation of tin during the Bronze Age

Tin has always been a scarce commodity in western Europe although the extent to which it was exploited in the South West during the earlier part of the Bronze Age, and indeed later, is unclear. While tin lodes occur on and around all the granite uplands of the South West and their hinterlands, tin ore is most likely to have been obtained in the prehistoric period from the extensive alluvial stream deposits. Any evidence for digging for tin will probably have been destroyed by later activity, though there have been a number of 18th and 19th-century finds of Bronze Age and later artefacts from stream deposits in Cornwall that suggest they were indeed being exploited. Considering the extent to which other local resources were being exploited – for example, china clay in the production of faience beads, and aplite for quern stones, at Shaugh Moor – the evidence for smelting is extremely scarce. This might suggest that an elite controlled production, though it must be remembered that the amount of excavation carried out to modern standards is fairly limited.

LANDSCAPES OF THE FIRST SEDENTARY FARMERS

While there appears to have been an increase in the area and intensity of landscape exploitation during the Early Bronze Age, there remains little indication of permanent or long-lived settlements. By contrast, the Middle Bronze Age saw the appearance of permanent settlements across the lowlands, often associated with small field systems, while the upland fringes of Dartmoor were transformed through the creation of extensive, and sometimes carefully planned, systems of fields: the every-day practice of agricultural subsistence now comes to dominate the landscape. These Middle Bronze Age landscapes spread across the lowlands and the flatter interfluvial areas of the uplands that had already been cleared of woodland, while further forest clearance, particularly around the upland margins, points to a further expansion in settlement.

The upland landscape

Probably the most famous example of a Middle Bronze Age landscape in the South West is that of the Dartmoor reaves (Fig. 3.7). These remarkably extensive blocks of carefully planned field boundaries were constructed around 1700/1600 BC in a landscape where woodland was probably restricted to the valley sides, and in which soils, although acidic, had no peat, no iron pan and lacked significant leaching. Ditches, which formed part of the Middle Bronze Age field systems, were filled with silt, not peat, and there is good evidence for active soil fauna, from earthworms to moles. The reave systems may represent the formalisation of existing arrangements within a social territory, or the appropriation by individual communities of once-open land. The central moorland of Dartmoor, above the terminal reaves, remained open and comprised acid grassland that Andrew Fleming has suggested may have been grazed through intercommoning (the communal grazing of open land), as it was during the medieval period and later. Palaeoenvironmental evidence along with the lack of lynchetting and large amounts of clitter (loose stone boulders) in many fields, suggests that the predominant land use within the reave systems was good quality grassland (not moorland as today) with very limited cereal cultivation.

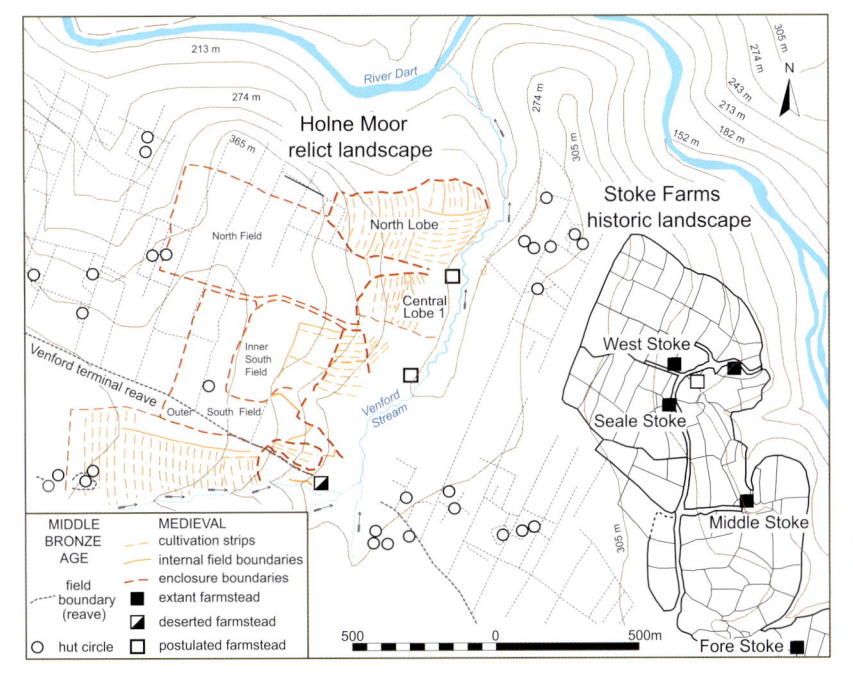

Fig. 3.7 Holne Moor, Dartmoor (SX 6771). The carefully planned 'coaxial' Middle Bronze Age reave system, ending at the 'Venford terminal reave', overlain by an abandoned medieval landscape on the western slopes of the Venford Stream and the still-occupied landscape at Stoke. Stoke is recorded in Domesday Book, though the farmsteads to the west are undocumented: both medieval communities re-used parts of the reave system when laying out their field boundaries (based on the work of S Gerrard, A Fleming and the author).

Fig. 3.8 Grimspound, Manaton parish, eastern Dartmoor (SX 701809), looking south from Hookney Tor. This undated enclosure, containing a series of small 'shieling'-type huts, lies outside the Middle Bronze Age reave system, on the edge of the high open moor at the head of the West Weburn Valley. As there is no associated field system the community here was presumably engaged in pastoralism, possibly seasonally. This site, like many elements of the pre-reave ceremonial landscapes, has a dialogue with the natural landscape: its entrance faces south-east towards Hambledon Tor, and as one looks through the entrance one sees Hookney Tor above.

Some stone-built reaves are known to have had timber predecessors that leave no trace above ground, but it is not known whether these timber boundaries were in fact more extensive than the reaves and only partly rebuilt in stone. What is clear, however, is that large areas of occupied landscape were not structured around stone-built reave systems. Some areas were characterised by simple enclosures without any evidence for field systems (for example, Grimspound: Fig. 3.8), while elsewhere settlements consisted of scatters of round-houses, some associated with a single ovoid field enclosure, or linked by a stone wall or bank that enclosed areas which could serve as cultivation plots and paddocks for livestock at different times of year, with open pasture beyond (Fig. 3.9 and *see* Figs 3.3 and 3.10 for analogous landscapes on Bodmin Moor). In places these formed relatively extensive irregular field systems, which appear to have grown in a piecemeal fashion, comparable to the contemporary 'aggregate' celtic field systems on the Wessex downland.

On the granite moors of Cornwall the flatter interfluvial areas were also largely clear of woodland by the mid-2nd millennium BC, though further clearance is

Fig. 3.9 Merrivale, Dartmoor (SX 556749). Typical Middle Bronze Age hut circle in an open settlement. Dartmoor is famous for its coaxial reave systems (see Fig. 3.7), but large areas were occupied by open settlements, often with small accretive field systems (for example Fig. 3.3). The extent of such unenclosed settlement in lowland areas (without such durable building stone) is unclear.

recorded at Rough Tor. It was in this context of a largely open landscape that, as on Dartmoor, the Cornish uplands came to be occupied by settlements and field systems. While certain examples of the latter do have a coaxial layout, there is nothing on the scale of the Dartmoor reaves; most of the settlements and field systems are similar to the irregular and aggregate field systems of Dartmoor (Figs 3.3 and 3.10). Exmoor has more limited remains of comparable landscapes that are undated. At Codsend Moor, however, the fields appear to pre-date the formation of peat in the late 1st millennium BC; the pollen sequence from Hoar Moor, immediately adjacent to another of the relict field systems, shows a marked period of clearance with an expansion in grazing and possibly some cereal cultivation in about 1700/1600 BC.

The lowland landscape

In places the Dartmoor reaves may have extended some way into the surrounding lowlands (Fig. 3.11), though in most areas the Middle Bronze Age landscape typically comprised several round-houses, sometimes with ancillary buildings, associated with small regular rectangular fields. Palaeoenvironmental evidence, and the possible presence of raised four-post granary structures, suggest some cereal cultivation with a notable increase in the diversity of crops that now include emmer, spelt and bread wheat, barley, peas and flax, although wild foodstuffs such as hazelnuts and sloes were still being gathered. While broadly 'coaxial' (based on a series of long, parallel boundaries) in their layout,

Fig. 3.10 Rough Tor, St Breward parish, north-east Bodmin Moor. Middle Bronze Age settlement and 'accretive' field system looking south-east towards the probable Early Neolithic 'tor enclosure' on Rough Tor (from SX 137820).

Fig. 3.11 Bittaford, on the southern fringes of Dartmoor, looking south-east from Western Beacon (SX 657574) into the South Hams. Andrew Fleming has suggested that the regularity in the historic landscape here results from the re-use of Middle Bronze Age coaxial reave systems.

these lowland Middle Bronze Age field systems were on a relatively small scale, spreading over no more than a few hundred metres, and are in no way comparable in scale to the contemporary Dartmoor reaves.

The problem of the Late Bronze Age and the apparent abandonment of the uplands

Just as the Late Neolithic is poorly represented in the South West, so is the Late Bronze Age. The palaeoenvironmental record is poor and relatively few archaeological sites have been recognised. Across the region most settlements occupied by communities using Trevisker-style pottery appear to have been abandoned, a process that at Trethellen Farm Jacqueline Nowakowski suggests represented a process of deliberate 'closing down'. Due to the relative scarcity of pottery in use at the time, only a few settlements have been identified, but these include both open and enclosed examples, which appear to be closer in character to the Middle Bronze Age tradition as opposed to the succeeding Iron Age landscape dominated by a hierarchy of more heavily defended settlements.

In common with other parts of Britain, south-west England's uplands appear at first sight to have been abandoned at this time. Traditionally, it has been argued that this was due to a climatic deterioration, which made farming in these areas increasingly difficult, though some scholars have more recently argued that in the north of Britain pollen sequences in fact show continued occupation and cultivation of the uplands during the 1st millennium BC, and that archaeological evidence for their abandonment is ambiguous and poorly dated. So what was happening in the South West? The limited excavations to date suggest that the Dartmoor reaves were abandoned between about 1400 and 1200 BC; only a few sites show evidence for Late Bronze Age or Early Iron Age occupation and there is just one known Middle to Late Iron Age settlement, at Gold Park on Shapley Common, alongside a handful of other findspots. On Bodmin Moor, peat started to form around abandoned Middle Bronze Age round-houses at Stannon Down before the walls had time to collapse, and the only site to have produced Iron Age pottery is at Garrow Tor, where a Bronze Age house was re-used, perhaps by transhumants (seasonal graziers). On Exmoor there has been no excavation of the relict field systems and their associated hut circles so no comment can be made on the date of their abandonment.

The key question is whether this *apparent* scarcity of evidence for Late Bronze Age and Iron Age settlement reflects the *actual* desertion of the uplands, or whether it is a product of differential *site visibility*: were the moors deserted altogether, or was there simply a change in the nature and location of land use? It is possible, for example, that there was a shift in the form of settlements, from stone-built houses and enclosures that remain highly visible in the archaeological landscape, to less easily recognised open settlements and timber buildings: this was the case at Gold Park and Shaugh Moor but is unlikely to have been a widespread phenomenon, as throughout the lowlands of the South West there is a marked trend *towards* enclosed settlement at this time (*see* below). Indeed, while the palaeoenvironmental record for this period is frustratingly poor it does suggest that south-west England's uplands saw a decrease in the intensity of human activity. Dartmoor appears to have seen the spread of ericaceous heath and some woodland regeneration, while on Bodmin Moor the Rough Tor sequences show a regeneration of hazel-alder woodland in the late 2nd millennium BC. On Exmoor, by contrast, there appears to have been continuity in land use.

Overall, therefore, the results from survey, excavation and radiocarbon dating suggest that south-west England's uplands saw a decrease in the density of settlement, including the abandonment of the Dartmoor reaves, but that some grazing must have continued, which prevented large-scale woodland regeneration. It is tempting to see some link between these vast areas of upland pasture and the adjacent Iron Age hillforts that were subsequently well placed around all the upland–lowland interfaces, though this category of site has seen so little excavation that their period of construction and occupation, and the part they played in the wider landscape, remains uncertain. It is also unclear whether this apparent decrease in human activity in the uplands was due to climatic deterioration. It is certainly true that the upland moors of today have severe or very severe limitations for agriculture due to their climate: for example, 2,000mm of rainfall on Dartmoor is approximately double, and the average growing season of 175 days just half, of that in the surrounding lowlands (*see* Chapter 2). Any worsening of the climate would make these areas even more inhospitable, although there is little independent evidence for a climatic deterioration in the South West during the 1st millennium BC. On Bodmin Moor and Exmoor, acid grassland and cotton grass did develop in this period, though podsolisation, the spread of heather and the growth of peat bogs, both there and on Dartmoor, was a process that had started long before the Late Bronze Age. Overall, this decrease in the intensity of settlement on the uplands was probably a cultural phenomenon, and may simply represent the retreat of settlement from areas that inherently were less suited to agriculture: without high population pressure the 'experiment' of intensive upland settlement had not proved worthwhile.

LANDSCAPES OF STRATIFIED SOCIETIES

Though the Late Bronze Age landscape is poorly understood, the late 2nd and early 1st millennia BC do appear to witness a discontinuity in the landscape, most obvious in the uplands but also reflected in the emergence of a new pattern of settlement in the lowlands. Middle to Late Bronze Age settlements across the South West show relatively little outward sign of social stratification, and while some were latterly enclosed with encircling banks, these were on a modest scale. By the Iron Age this changed with the emergence of a new pattern of predominantly enclosed settlement, ranging from well-defended hillforts through to small, enclosed farmsteads. Palaeoenvironmental evidence suggests an increasingly open landscape with further clearance where woodland remained, most notably around the uplands. There was some cereal cultivation, though in most areas the extent to which this involved more than very localised field systems is unclear. This landscape of enclosed settlements spread up to the upland fringes but not beyond, although the open landscape of the higher moors was presumably maintained through grazing. Although hillforts and the more strongly defended enclosed settlements were abandoned by the late 1st century AD, Romano-British society continued to show signs of stratification, with an elite living in the *civitas* capital at Exeter and a scatter of villas and other settlements in its hinterland also exhibiting some degree of Romanisation. In the early Roman period at least, the army also probably had a role in exploiting the region's rich mineral resources. For most of the population, however, life probably carried on much as before with few signs of any significant change in the overall character of the landscape. This pattern of broad continuity is also seen after the Roman period ended, when the increasing numbers of palaeoenvironmental sequences register very little change in land use: in many respects the early to mid-1st millennium AD saw a continuation in the patterns of landscape exploitation that were established during the Iron Age a thousand years before.

The landscape of enclosed settlement

Hillforts and coastal promontory forts (locally known as 'cliff castles') are found throughout the South West, though compared to their neighbours in Wessex they are relatively small, lightly defended, contain comparatively small round-houses,

Fig. 3.12 Bats Castle, Dunster, Somerset (SS 987421). An Iron Age hillfort with a typical hilltop location on the eastern fringes of Exmoor.

and demonstrate a complete absence of grain storage pits (Fig. 3.12). The function of these sites is likely to have varied in time and space, though where excavation has been undertaken, evidence for domestic occupation has usually been found. What dating evidence there is suggests a slow but poorly understood development that starts in the Early Iron Age, as in the case of the palisaded enclosure that pre-dates the hillfort at Raddon. Late 2nd millennium radiocarbon dates from a large hilltop enclosure at Liskeard in Cornwall may, however, parallel a Late Bronze Age trend towards defended hilltop settlement seen further east in Wessex. There is little evidence for the occupation of hillforts after the end of the Iron Age.

Fig. 3.13 South Hams, southern Devon. Crop mark of a rectangular enclosure of a type dated elsewhere to the Iron Age/Romano-British period. Note the lack of evidence for an associated field system.

Lower down the Iron Age settlement scale there is a range of enclosures that can be distinguished from hillforts by their relatively small size, hillslope (not hilltop) location, and the modest scale of their banks and ditches (Figs 3.13 and 3.14). The most substantial of these sites – termed 'multiple enclosures' – have several circuits of widely spaced banks and ditches, defining an internal area of some 0.2 to 1.6ha, which appear to have been constructed from around the 4th or 3rd centuries BC and were mostly abandoned by the 1st century AD. A majority of identified Middle Iron Age to Romano-British settlements, however, were enclosed by simple univallate, non-defensive ditches and banks that enclosed internal areas of between 0.1 and 1.0ha and show some regional variation in their morphology. In lowland eastern, central and south Devon there is a predominance of rectangular and square forms (Fig. 3.13), while in Cornwall and west Devon a greater proportion are oval or circular (hence the local term 'rounds'), though with some rectilinear examples. In north and west Devon and around Exmoor there is greater variety but a predominance of ovoid forms which are termed 'hillslope enclosures' (Fig. 3.14). Excavated examples show that collectively these all form a distinctive class of enclosed settlements – what in medieval terminology would be called farmsteads and small hamlets – that characterised south-west England's landscape from the Middle Iron Age through to the early medieval period (5th and maybe 6th centuries), although no individual sites appear to have been occupied for the whole of this period. Some, however, may be earlier or later: south-west England's tradition of enclosed settlement, albeit with relatively insubstantial banks, goes back to the Middle

Fig. 3.14 Sweetworthy, Luccombe, Somerset *(SS 890424). A small cluster of particularly well-preserved hillslope enclosures on a spur between Aller Combe (background) and Aller Water. The larger enclosure, 70m in diameter (on the left), appears to overlie an earlier one that is 40m across; two other enclosures of a similar size lie to the south-west (right on the photograph) and each contains the platform of a single round-house. Note the lack of evidence for associated field systems even on the unenclosed moorland.*

Bronze Age – the hillslope enclosure at Higher Holworthy in Parracombe has now revealed Middle Bronze Age pottery – while another example, at Dunkeswell on the Blackdown Hills, turned out by contrast to belong to the 12th to 14th centuries AD.

In areas where preservation conditions and visibility are good (as both earthworks and crop marks), the density of enclosures can be as high as two or three per square kilometre, though excavated examples suggest that such sites were not all contemporary. It is also possible that we are aware of only part of the settlement pattern of this period as the extent of open settlements in the Iron Age and Romano-British periods is unclear. The Middle Iron Age open settlements at Long Range and Langland Lane in east Devon, for example, were discovered during road construction and were not identifiable on air photographs, and the relative scarcity of datable material culture on rural settlements of this period that have been excavated shows that such sites would be difficult to locate through fieldwalking.

Agricultural expansion during the Middle to Late Iron Age and Romano-British periods

There are few palaeoenvironmental sequences for the Iron Age and early Roman periods in the lowlands, though at Bow in central Devon the landscape was already virtually cleared of woodland by around the 3rd century BC, apart from small patches of alder carr on the wetter areas, and some oak/hazel woodland presumably restricted to the steeper hillsides. Elsewhere the Middle Iron Age (5th to 3rd centuries BC) may have seen some expansion of agriculture: south of Exmoor, at Hares Down, alder woodland was cleared from the valley bottom and replaced with grassland, while in the southern fringes of Exmoor there is also evidence for woodland clearance. On Bodmin Moor, there was a major clearance phase at Rough Tor. What woodland remained in the South West by this time was probably managed with increasing intensity.

This expansion and intensification of land use appears to have continued into the Late Iron Age and Early Romano-British periods: at Hares Down there is a further decline in alder, followed by a general episode of woodland clearance; higher up the moorland fringe at Moles Chamber there was a dramatic woodland clearance around the start of the Roman period. On Dartmoor the palaeoenvironmental record for this period is poor, but cultivation terraces on Wotter Common date to the Middle to Late Iron Age, when there was also some increase in the intensity of land use at Tor Royal. At Sourton Down the main phase of woodland clearance also dates to this period, and interpolation between radiocarbon dates suggests that an intensification of land use at Merrivale may date to the Roman period. On Bodmin Moor there was further woodland clearance and an increase in herb-rich meadows during the Roman period at Rough Tor and Tresellern Marsh.

Though great care has to be taken when converting radiocarbon dates to calendar years, a number of episodes when the intensity with which the landscape was exploited increased could date to the later Romano-British period. On Exmoor, a marked episode of woodland clearance coupled with evidence for cultivation at Codsend and Hoar Moors is dated to around the 3rd to 4th centuries AD, while at Lobbs Bog to the south there was a marked decline in alder at about this time. In the lowlands of eastern Devon there was similarly a marked phase of woodland clearance from the valley at Aller Farm in Stockland and an increase in the indicators of pastoralism around the 3rd century AD. This possible later Roman intensification in Devon may be paralleled to the east in Somerset and Dorset where the 3rd to 4th centuries saw considerable agricultural wealth and innovation, as reflected in wetland reclamation, investment in villas (also seen at Holcombe in east Devon) and urban prosperity.

The impact of conquest and the extent of Romanisation

During the mid-1st century AD the south-west peninsula was drawn into the Roman world. The Second Legion established its base at *Isca Dumnoniorum* (modern Exeter) around AD 55, and a number of small forts were located across the South West, but most notably in and around the lowlands of central and eastern Devon. This military occupation ceased in about AD 80 and the legionary fortress at Exeter went on to become the *civitas* capital of the Dumnonii, equipped with the normal range of civic amenities including a basilica and public baths. The extent of Romanisation elsewhere in the South West is, however, surprisingly limited. Features so characteristic of the landscape of Roman Britain further east, such as small towns and Romano-Celtic temples, are entirely absent from the peninsula, and although a few small villas are known in the far east of Devon, these all lie to the east of the Blackdown Hills and so may fall within the territory of the Durotriges (as the pottery from sites such as Seaton certainly suggests). A number of villas and other 'Romanised' settlements in the hinterland of Exeter possess simple stone or timber buildings that show Roman elements to their design – for example, the three-roomed timber building with veranda at Topsham – although even here the native tradition of round-houses continued into the 3rd century, as at Pomeroy Wood near Honiton.

Beyond this central lowland zone, however, the only example of a Romanised site is the villa at Magor near Camborne in the far west of Cornwall. This is a curious structure and Malcolm Todd has been tempted to see it as the residence of an official, perhaps from the procurator's office. Large amounts of 1st to 2nd-century Roman material culture have also been recovered from the multiple-enclosures at St Mawgan-in-Pydar and Carvossa, which presumably represent communities that had a greater engagement with the rest of Roman Britain. Other signs of Romanisation are scarce indeed, for example fragments of Roman tile from Barnstaple, Totnes and Plymouth, all of them on navigable rivers or estuaries, and while very small amounts of imported Roman pottery and coins have been recovered from a number of rural farmsteads across the South West, mass-produced pottery, notably south-east Dorset Black Burnished Ware, does not show up in significant amounts further west than Exeter.

Patterns of land use

It is difficult to establish the relative importance of arable and pastoral farming through palaeoeconomic evidence, though cereals were clearly being grown and in east Devon this was on a sufficiently large scale to require raised granaries and corn driers. The region has very poor faunal assemblages, due to its acidic soils, though Edward Maltby has shown that as far as the material from Exeter reflects the composition of livestock in the surrounding landscape, then it appears that cattle predominated followed by sheep and pigs in roughly equal numbers. Livestock were driven to Exeter on the hoof, and a number of town houses had farmyards or stockyards suggesting they were either the urban residences of native rural landowners, or perhaps grazier-butchers.

It is notable that most Iron Age and Romano-British settlement enclosures in western Somerset, Devon and eastern Cornwall visible as both earthworks and crop marks do not *appear* to have been associated with field systems (Figs 3.13 and 3.14). Although Middle Bronze Age to Romano-British ditched field systems have been recorded in the east of Devon and parts of Cornwall, it may be that field systems have not survived elsewhere because they consisted simply of a bank, as was the case on the limestone hills south of Newton Abbot, which have produced Iron Age and Romano-British material. Like the lynchetted field system at Beer Head, these would not survive prolonged ploughing. It is also possible that although substantial enclosure ditches show up as crop marks on aerial photographs, lesser field boundary ditches do not.

In the far west of Cornwall the situation is rather different, with extensive areas of lynchetted late prehistoric and Romano-British field systems forming the basis of the modern landscape, even in this relatively exposed coastal location. Considering the extent to which the archaeology and landscape of this area differs from the rest of the region from the Neolithic onwards, however, west Cornwall's near-continuous late prehistoric and Romano-British fieldscape cannot be taken as an analogy for the whole of the South West.

Resource exploitation and external contact

Throughout the later prehistoric, Romano-British and early medieval periods, communities in the South West developed links with other parts of southern Britain, the near continent and even the Mediterranean. Several coastal islands and promontories appear to have been particularly significant as 'ports of trade', notably Mount Batten, in Plymouth Sound (Fig. 3.15), and probably St Michael's Mount off the south coast of Cornwall. Significant quantities of late Roman material have also been recovered from Tintagel, in addition to large amounts of 5th and 6th-century pottery imported from the Mediterranean. The basis of this trade is unclear though the region's richest resource was potentially tin. The documentary evidence is unreliable before the 1st century BC, although thereafter we have clear documentary references to the trading of tin from the South West. A number of vessels made of tin discovered in stream deposits suggest exploitation was widespread, and although ingots have been found on several settlements, evidence for smelting is as yet limited. The large number of late Roman coin hoards from south-west England's stream deposits, the expansion of the pewter industry both here and around Bath, and elevated tin levels in the Erme valley south of Dartmoor, suggest an increase in production just as the Roman Empire's major tin mines in Spain were becoming exhausted.

Archaeological evidence has also been forthcoming for the exploitation of other metals in the South West. At Duckpool, near Morwenstow, on the north coast of Cornwall a series of possibly industrial-scale hearths was used for working lead, pewter (a tin alloy) and possibly copper alloy (along with extracting dye from dog whelks). Metal-working debris from Exeter includes evidence for 'cupellation' (the separation of silver from base metals such as copper) from the late occupation of the legionary fortress (c. AD 69–75), and for 'parting' (the separation of silver and gold) from a 2nd-century roadside ditch. Tin is an essential component of pewter (an alloy with lead), and stone moulds for producing pewter bowls have been found in the far west of Cornwall. Lead does occur in the South West, at Newlyn in west Cornwall and most notably at Combe Martin in north Devon, and although evidence for its exploitation in the pre-medieval period is lacking, the possibility of Roman working cannot be ruled out.

Fig. 3.15 Plymouth Sound looking south-west from Hawks Tor *(SX 554625), Shaugh Prior parish, in south-west Dartmoor. The south-west peninsula is some 200km long and at most just 120km wide: no point in Devon is more than 40km from the coast, while in Cornwall the figure is little more than 25km. Throughout the region's history (and prehistory) many of its natural resources have been traded further afield, and the numerous natural harbours, such as Plymouth Sound, have played host to 'ports of trade' such as the Iron Age and Romano-British site at Mount Batten.*

The main focus of the Romano-British pewter industry in the later 3rd to 4th century was in the hinterland of Bath close to the major lead source on Mendip. The involvement of the army in extracting Mendip lead is well known, and the evidence from Exeter suggests that the military authorities may similarly have been involved in exploiting south-west England's rich mineral resources. The fort at Nanstallon, occupied between about AD 55 and AD 80, is in a region rich in minerals just to the west of Bodmin Moor, and the discovery of silver-rich slag on a crucible fragment, together with iron-working debris, hints at the army's involvement in exploiting these resources. Two fortlets on the north coast of Devon, at Martinhoe and Old Burrow (occupied between c. AD 50 and AD 75), would have maintained a view across the Bristol Channel, and together with forts at Axminster, Hembury, Cullompton, Tiverton, Clayhanger, Rainsbury and Wiveliscombe they may testify to an interest in both Exmoor and the Blackdown Hills, where recent work has shown that iron was both mined and smelted. On Exmoor, the character of the early Roman pottery assemblages at Brayford and Sherracombe Ford (Fig. 3.16) is very similar to that of the legionary phase at Exeter, while trial excavations of a quarry pit adjacent to a furnace and dump of slag at Upottery on the Blackdown Hills produced a pottery assemblage of military character dating to the late 1st century.

One resource that does not appear to have been extensively exploited in this period was salt, obtainable by boiling sea water. Just two sites are known from south-west Cornwall: at Trebarveth (occupied around the 2nd to 4th centuries AD) and Carngoon Bank (3rd to possibly 5th or 6th centuries).

Fig. 3.16 Sherracombe Ford, Brayford, western Exmoor, looking north up the valley towards the high moorland (SS 719366). Excavations have recently shown that this well-preserved site was used for smelting and working iron during the Roman period. The pottery assemblage from here, and other sites, suggests military involvement in the exploitation of iron on both Exmoor and the Blackdown Hills.

THE ROMANO-BRITISH TO MEDIEVAL TRANSITION: CONTINUITY IN THE RURAL LANDSCAPE AND RESOURCE EXPLOITATION

Just as the archaeologically visible, and highly distinctive, landscapes of the Early Neolithic, Middle Bronze Age and Iron Age/Romano-British periods are separated by less visible Late Neolithic and Late Bronze Age 'discontinuities', so the landscape of late 'prehistory' is separated from the 'historic landscape' of today by what remains a 'dark age'. The lack of material culture makes the early medieval landscape of the South West extremely difficult to locate let alone understand, although the increasing use of radiocarbon dating, palaeoenvironmental analysis and the distribution of Mediterranean imports suggests three indications of early post-Roman continuity. First, the tradition of enclosed settlement continued into at least the 6th century, though this included some reoccupation of hilltop sites; second, there was no significant change in the patterns of land use in the lowlands and upland fringe; and third, there was continuing external contact and exchange with traders from the Mediterranean at coastal sites, perhaps involving tin.

Very little is known about settlement patterns and field systems after the 4th century as a lack of distinctive coins and ceramics in Devon makes it difficult to know when the more Romanised sites were abandoned. Within Britain generally, the collapse of the market-based economy will have had the greatest impact in areas that 'bought into' the Roman economy, so the more localised economies of the South West would have been relatively unaffected. Though some decline in settlement is seen in the 4th century – a feature common to large areas of late Roman Britain – a number of rural settlements in the South West certainly continued to be occupied into the 5th and even the 6th centuries. A number of hilltop sites were also reoccupied (*see* Fig. 3.2), but these sites are a world apart from the massive defences of South Cadbury and Cadbury Congresbury in Somerset. Rather than representing an example of 'refortification', they are perhaps better seen as reflecting a continuation of the Romano-British tradition of enclosed settlement, as they are of a similar scale to the contemporary ovoid lowland enclosure at Hayes Farm near Exeter.

The reoccupation of hilltop sites suggests some changes in landscape and society during the 5th century, but a growing body of palaeoenvironmental evidence strongly suggests broad continuity in what remained an open lowland landscape. Only on the higher moors is there some evidence for a decrease in the intensity of human activity. On Exmoor there was a decline in arable and grassland, and an increase in heather and possibly woodland on the highest uplands around the 5th century, while on Dartmoor there are hints at Merrivale and Tor Royal of a slight decrease in the intensity of human activity. On Bodmin Moor, there was continuity in land use at Rough Tor North, but possibly slight regeneration at Tresellern Marsh and Rough Tor South. These uplands, however, lay beyond the main areas of settlement, and as early medieval place-names suggest, they were probably used for transhumant grazing; a decrease in the intensity of their exploitation need not therefore suggest a widespread dislocation in the landscape. In short, the overriding theme in the agrarian landscape between the late Roman period and at least the 6th to 7th centuries is one of continuity.

During the early medieval period we get the first evidence for ownership and control of land and resources through the medium of inscribed memorial stones, which occur across Cornwall and west Devon, with two outliers on Exmoor. Perhaps the clearest reflection of a stratified society is the distribution of late 5th- and 6th-century pottery imported from the Mediterranean. By far the greatest concentration has been found at the rocky coastal promontory at Tintagel in north Cornwall, which can best be interpreted as a 'royal citadel'. Other such sites may well exist: St Michael's Mount is certainly a contender. The importation of this pottery suggests that communities in the South West had something of value to exchange, and there are documentary references to English traders taking tin (presumably Cornish) to the continent from the 7th century. A number of finds in Cornwall prove that tin was being worked in the early medieval period. At Praa Sands four ingots were found eroding from a 7th to 9th-century intertidal peat, while a number of early medieval artefacts have been recovered from tin stream deposits, such as an oak shovel from Boscarne, near Bodmin. Actual evidence of tin smelting is, as ever, scarce though the Romano-British site at Duckpool (*see* above) was certainly occupied from around the 8th century, and the apparent hiatus between the mid-4th and 7th centuries may simply reflect the limited nature of the excavations. Radiocarbon dates from both Exmoor and the Blackdown Hills have shown that iron production continued well into the post-Roman period.

A number of coastal sites have been interpreted as trading sites or beach markets, such as Bantham, immediately south of Dartmoor, where ephemeral traces of occupation associated with late Roman and early medieval Mediterranean imported pottery have been recovered from a coastal dune complex to the north of a rectilinear enclosure of late Roman date. A similar 'port of trade' potentially lies at Mothecombe (in south Devon) from which imported pottery has also been found, while a collection of 40 tin ingots has been recovered from the adjacent Erme estuary which, though undated, are of an Iron Age to early medieval type. It is noticeable that together with Tintagel and St Michael's Mount, those sites that appear to have seen contact with the external world are located on open coasts, rather than up sheltered estuaries, which perhaps reinforces the impression that these are 'ports of trade' on the relatively 'neutral territory' of the coastal fringes of Dumnonia.

Overall, therefore, it seems that while there were some socio-economic dislocations in the early medieval landscape, and a decrease in the intensity with which the highest uplands were exploited, the overall theme was – as might be expected in an area that was never that heavily Romanised – one of continuity.

THE CREATION OF THE HISTORIC LANDSCAPE

In West Penwith, at the far western end of Cornwall, the present pattern of small, irregular, strongly lynchetted, stone-walled fields appears to perpetuate that of the late prehistoric and Romano-British periods, and at a number of locations this early origin for the historic landscape has been established through excavation and the stratigraphic relationship with late prehistoric/Romano-British settlements. It is tempting to argue that here the present hamlets and farmsteads, so closely integrated with the field boundary pattern, represent elements of the prehistoric settlement pattern that have continued to be occupied, making this one of the oldest areas of 'historic landscape' in the country. West Penwith, however, appears to be unique in this respect within the South West. In a number of places the Dartmoor reaves were incorporated into medieval field systems (*see* Fig. 3.11) but this does not imply their continued use, but simply the re-use of still visible, but long-derelict, features. These are in fact landscapes of discontinuity and this appears to have been the dominant theme in most, if not all, areas beyond West Penwith.

Though the early medieval landscape is poorly understood, rather like that of the late Bronze Age, the mid-1st millennium AD appears to represent a discontinuity, from which emerged the countryside of today. The origins of today's historic landscape are obscure, but by the time that we have good archaeological and documentary evidence for the character of medieval agriculture and landscape in the South West (around the mid-14th century) it already had certain key features including a dispersed settlement pattern characterised by unenclosed small hamlets and isolated farmsteads, which were connected by networks of tracks and sunken lanes. These settlements were surrounded by a mixture of enclosed fields held in severalty (individual ownership) and small-scale subdivided or 'open' field systems (managed in a communal fashion), that were separated by unenclosed common land on the higher ground (Fig. 3.17).

Fig. 3.17 Countisbury, Exmoor (SS 747497), from the south. The 'historic landscape' – the present pattern of settlements, fields and roads – appears to have emerged towards the end of the 1st millennium AD, replacing the Iron-Age/Romano-British/early medieval landscape characterised by enclosed settlements, though the process through which this occurred remains ill-understood.

Fig. 3.18 Natsley in Brayford, north Devon *(SS 699381), looking south-west from the hillfort at Shouldsbury Castle across west Devon. This oval-shaped intake of land is typical of settlements on the fringes of Exmoor that palaeoenvironmental evidence suggests were colonised around the 10th century* AD, *while the field-boundary pattern is of a type suggestive of the regionally distinctive system of agriculture known as 'convertible husbandry'.*

A crucial contrast with the enclosed farmsteads and small, localised field systems of the late prehistoric and Romano-British periods, is that by the high Middle Ages most of the lowlands of the South West were covered by a near-continuous fieldscape. This supported a regionally distinctive system of mixed agriculture – known as convertible or ley husbandry – first documented in the 14th century within which the majority of fields (closes or parcels of open fields) were subject to alternating grain and grass crops, often with a short period of cultivation (two to three years) followed by a long grass ley of six to eight years (*see* Chapter 7). The origins of this system of agriculture, and the landscape that supported it, are not documented but palaeoenvironmental research is increasingly pointing to a date in the late 1st millennium AD.

The creation of the near-continuous fieldscape and system of convertible husbandry that so characterised the historic landscape of the South West appears to have been associated with a transformation of the settlement pattern (Fig. 3.18). In and around Exmoor, for example, the deserted medieval hamlets immediately adjacent to hillslope enclosures at Bagley and Sweetworthy, first identified by Mick Aston and cited as possible examples of continuity, are in fact unique: the landscapes of Iron Age/Romano-British enclosed settlements, in places certainly occupied into the 6th and 7th centuries, are unrelated to the historic landscape of unenclosed medieval hamlets and farmsteads and their road and field-systems. Oliver Padel has shown that habitative place-names in Cornwall, notably *tre-* (farmstead, hamlet, estate) and *bod-* (dwelling), were being used by the 8th century, but none of these settlements is located within an earlier enclosure making it unlikely that these medieval hamlets represent prehistoric or Romano-British settlements that simply continued to be occupied. Aerial photography and geophysical survey are similarly confirming that beyond West Penwith the field systems associated with Iron Age and Romano-British enclosed settlements are unrelated to the medieval pattern.

The earliest unequivocal evidence for the present 'historic landscape', and the tenurial structure within which it was created, comes in the form of 8th- to 11th-century charters, which record a pattern of substantial estates across the South West that around the 10th century were in the course of fragmenting. The ten 8th- to 9th-century charters record estates with an average hidage of 13.5 hides, in contrast to the 10th-century average of 4 hides (though in places larger estates may have survived in the form of the extensive composite manors recorded in Domesday, such as the 44 hides of Pawton). An earlier pattern of extensive territories in Cornwall may be mirrored by the six medieval hundreds forming estates of a similar structure to the Welsh *cantref*, each with its own administrative centre of *llys*.

So how far back can we trace this landscape of medieval hamlets and farmsteads? Landmarks in the boundary clauses of some charters (mostly 10th and 11th century) make frequent reference to roads and fords, suggesting a landscape with a well-established framework of communications that still survives to this day, while the Cornish habitative place-names were certainly being created by the 8th century (*see* above). Unfortunately archaeology has little to add to this. Most excavated medieval settlements are in secondary locations such as the uplands and heavy clays of the Culm Measures, which may account for their lack of pre-13th-century pottery. Even if sites can be excavated in the primary settlement regions, however, the lack of pre-11th-century pottery would make dating their origins difficult, and though radiocarbon dating the earliest stratigraphic horizons may have some potential, these deposits may not have survived the subsequent occupation of a site.

This early medieval period remains, therefore, a frustrating one. It clearly saw the genesis of the historic landscape across much of the South West (beyond those areas of western Cornwall where prehistoric landscapes appear to have remained in use), but there remains a gap between the latest dates (*c.* 5th to 6th centuries) for the use of the late prehistoric/Romano-British landscape characterised by enclosed settlements, and the date when pollen sequences suggest that the medieval pattern was emerging (*c.* 7th to 8th centuries). This was a turbulent period with some immigration from Wales/Ireland and emigration from the South West to Brittany. The eastern part of the kingdom of Dumnonia (modern Devon) was absorbed by the West Saxon kingdom of Wessex from the late 7th century – the minster church at Exeter was founded by 690 and probably in 670 – though the 'West Welsh' of Cornwall retained their independence until the 9th century. The relationship between these political upheavals and the emergence of the historic landscape is, however, unclear.

THE DISTINCTIVENESS OF THE SOUTH WEST

The south-west peninsula forms one of the most distinctive and discrete parts of the English landscape, bounded to the east by the watersheds of the Blackdown and Quantock hills. Today, and more particularly in the medieval period, this was the boundary between landscapes of nucleated villages and open fields to the east, and areas characterised by more dispersed settlement patterns to the west. In earlier times the line of the Blackdown–Quantock hills also marked the eastern limit of evidence for early Anglo-Saxon settlement, acculturation and exchange networks as reflected in burials and artefacts; the same line marks the western limit of extensive Romanisation. So when did this regional identity emerge?

The initiation of systematic woodland clearance and the incorporation of agriculture into subsistence regimes (on whatever scale) occurred more or less simultaneously across southern Britain during the Early Neolithic, as did the adoption of a suite of ceremonial monuments that has similarities in both the South West and in Wessex with the 'tor-enclosures' of Cornwall and west Devon, perhaps representing a topographically driven local variant of the causewayed enclosures that occur as far west as central Devon. 'Long cairns/mounds' and 'oblong ditches' may represent another local variation, in this case earthen long barrows. The exchange networks that led to gabbroic pottery and Cornish stone axes reaching as far as Wessex similarly reflect integration as opposed to isolation. In the Late Neolithic/Early Bronze Age, however, the local distinctiveness of the South West develops, with a scarcity of henges and an abundance of stone rows. Parallels can be drawn between the landscapes of Middle Bronze Age communities in the South West and Wessex, though by the Iron Age regional divergence was once again becoming marked, notably in the character of the settlement pattern. Even within the peninsula, there were significant local variations in landscape character. Although the Iron Age tradition of enclosed farmsteads extended into the far west of Cornwall, this area developed its own distinctive settlement pattern with a continuation of open settlement and the emergence of a tradition of stone-walled courtyard houses, which usually occurred in isolation or small clusters, occupied from the 2nd century AD through to the early medieval period. The far west of Cornwall appears to have missed a major landscape upheaval sometime between the 6th and 8th centuries, when the Iron Age and Romano-British landscape of enclosed settlements and small localised field systems was replaced with the medieval pattern of small hamlets set within a near-continuous fieldscape. This regionally distinctive landscape may from the start have been associated with the equally distinctive form of convertible-husbandry-based agriculture in which fields were ploughed for several years and laid down to grass for a period of around six years. This suggests that the Midlands and western Wessex were not the only part of England to see a major landscape transformation in the late 1st millennium AD: the creation of villages never occurred in the South West, not because this was a region that was remote from the centre of landscape innovation, but because it had already developed in its own distinctive way of organising agrarian production.

FURTHER READING

The most comprehensive overview of the archaeology of south-west England remains Todd 1987; in addition there are the special issues of *Cornish Archaeology* 25 (1986) and *Proceedings of the Devon Archaeological Society* 52 (1994). The most recent distribution maps of sites, with a brief period-by-period commentary, can be found in Kain and Ravenhill (eds) 1999.

For Bodmin Moor *see* Johnson and Rose 1994. For Dartmoor *see* Fleming 1988; Gerrard 1997; and Balaam *et al.* 1982. For Exmoor *see* Riley and Wilson-North 2001. For West Penwith there is no published overview but *see* Herring 1993, 1994.

On palaeoenvironmental evidence *see* Fyfe and Rippon 2004.

The exploitation of tin is discussed by Gerrard 2000. For iron working in the Blackdown Hills *see* Griffith and Weddell 1996.

The origin of south-west England's historic landscape is discussed further in Rose and Preston-Jones 1995 and Rippon 2004. The early medieval charters for the South West are discussed in Hooke 1994, while the early medieval inscribed stones are discussed in Thomas 1994. For place-names *see* Padel 1985.

4

People and Livelihoods: Agents of Landscape Change

BRUCE COLEMAN

The connections between people, their ways of life and landscape are close. Human populations have left their mark through the utilisation and appropriation of the land by means involving both construction and destruction. Human settlement has changed the landscape and increasingly so as population has grown. The present-day landscape thus provides a record of human existence over history – in the South West as elsewhere. For much of that history the great majority of people were concerned primarily with survival and subsistence and the land they settled provided the means through various forms of exploitation of natural resources. Though agriculture long remained the primary activity, the nature of the South West meant that mineral extraction, the sea and industrial employments also provided livelihoods as the peninsula was developed beyond a crude subsistence economy.

The nature of the peninsula, including its geology, climate and coastline, has both permitted and limited the growth of population and shaped the nature of economic activity. It has ensured that the demography of the South West has sometimes differed significantly from that of much of the rest of England. Only in relatively recent times have most people derived their livelihoods from occupations little or not at all related to the terrain they occupy. Even then housing, employment, recreation and other social activities have shaped the environment. Despite the popular modern image of Devon and Cornwall as representing a natural or 'unspoilt' landscape in contrast to more populous and built-up environments elsewhere, much of the region's landscape has been shaped by the needs and pressures of its population over several millennia.

Chapter 3 has reviewed settlement and population in south-west England to around the end of the first millennium AD; this chapter opens in the 11th century, and specifically with the evidence of Domesday Book (1086). Its discussion of the population history of the South West will be light on the kinds of statistics modern demographers expect. Only in the 19th century did the recording of social statistics come to permit much precision of quantification or analysis. For earlier periods there is only partial and incomplete information, which leaves estimates of population to educated guesswork. For much of the period of human habitation we are reliant on indirect evidence – of settlement and land utilisation, for example – to help us identify trends and orders of magnitude. The same is true of comparisons between south-west England and other parts of England. Much of what follows is impressionistic, but its implications for landscape formation and change remain crucial.

THE MEDIEVAL PERIOD

The conquering Normans who moved into the South West after 1066 had only a minor demographic impact in the region. Norman feudal lords replaced the Saxon landholders and brought a small service class with them, but there was no large-scale immigration. In landscape terms the most dramatic change was the construction of a number of castles, which symbolised military occupation as well as stronger royal control (*see* Chapter 6), but the region experienced no widespread 'wasting' of the kind that devastated northern England. The needs of the new regime led to the first systematic collection of information on England's counties in the shape of the Domesday Book of 1086. Though a survey of landholding rather than a census, it did enumerate elements of the population. For Devon, Domesday recorded 17,308 inhabitants of rural manors and 845 burgesses in the five boroughs; for Cornwall it listed a rural population of 5,360 and 68 burgesses in its sole borough, Bodmin. From these figures most historians assume a population approaching 70,000 for Devon and around 25,000 for Cornwall. Domesday may have under-recorded inhabitants in areas of sparse and dispersed settlement and particularly in Cornwall (it ignored the Isles of Scilly completely). Modern estimates based on Domesday suggest a population for the whole of England approaching 2 million, of which the South West accounted for about 5–6 per cent.

The South West as a whole was more thinly populated than most of southern and midland England, but it contained sharp contrasts in densities (Fig. 4.1). The moors and uplands were barely populated (except by seasonal transhumance), there were vast areas of 'waste' not even recorded by Domesday, and there were numerous isolated settlements with only handfuls of inhabitants. Both counties, however, had sub-regions of heavy population density – in each case significantly eastern rather than western. They included Cornwall's eastern borders, the river basins of the Exe, Taw and Torridge in Devon and the coastal strip from the Teign to the South Hams. The most populous manors often bore Saxon names, had concentrated settlement and lay in fertile and largely arable areas. Devon's most populous place in Domesday, Crediton, an episcopal manor and the site of a minster, recorded 407 people and 185 plough-teams. Cornwall's largest manor, Pawton, listed 86 people and 43 teams. Such concentrations reflected agricultural prosperity and particularly arable fertility.

Fig. 4.1 Population distributions at the time of the Norman Conquest.

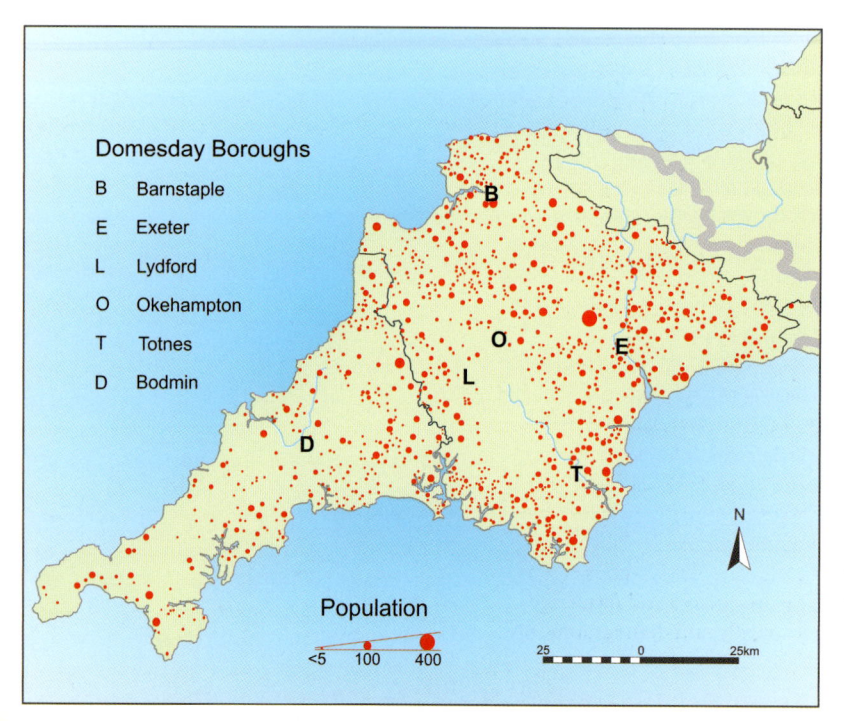

That Domesday listed only six boroughs in the South West indicated the limited significance of its urban sector, even presuming the importance for trade of estuarine ports like Exeter, Totnes and Barnstaple. Counties to the east were better planted with boroughs: Dorset (much smaller than Devon) with five, Somerset with nine, Wiltshire with ten. Exeter, designated a city, accounted for over half the burgesses recorded in Devon, and probably had a population of 2,000 or more. Totnes may have had 500–600 inhabitants, Barnstaple, Lydford, Okehampton (the last an emerging borough effectively created by the new Norman castle) and Cornwall's sole borough of Bodmin perhaps 300–350 each. Such a modest urban sector could have only a marginal influence upon population movement within or into the region. Over the period between Domesday and the arrival of the Black Death in 1348 the population of England (and indeed most of Europe) increased dramatically. England's may have more than doubled. The South West shared in this growth and probably had more than 200,000 inhabitants by the early 14th century. The economic expansion associated with this growth had important consequences for the region's landscape. The causes of the surge of population are uncertain, though the 'Little Optimum' period of climatic warming during the early medieval period was a factor. Marginal land became more viable and there was considerable expansion of land use and settlement in the South West as population increased.

Towns were clearly a far more significant element in the region by 1348 than they had been in 1086. Exeter now had a population approaching 4,000. The lay subsidy of 1334 assessed it at £366, ranking it 27th in England, but it put Plymouth ahead at £400 and 23rd. The six boroughs of Devon and Cornwall in 1086 had now grown to 57, though some would never be serious towns. Their relative sparseness towards the northern coastline reflected the importance of the south coast's continental links. The few successful inland towns usually had associations with tin or cloth, though rising towns like Tavistock, Ashburton and Tiverton also benefited from their promotion by manorial lords and from fertile hinterlands. Urban growth affected the landscape in various ways. The demand for timber and fuel intensified the process of disafforestation. The needs of urban and industrial populations as well as of ships and fleets meant more intensive agriculture and a more settled, cleared and cultivated landscape. The plentiful supply of stone in the region facilitated building or rebuilding in both town and countryside. Many farm and manor houses, as well as churches, date from this period and signify a developing society.

Mortality crises hit England in the 14th century and continued in their impact into the 15th. There are problems in estimating the scale of that mortality and also in explaining it. Some historians identify the classic Malthusian trap – human fertility had outrun the growth of available food supplies and the days of reckoning had come – while others see disease (plague in particular) as to some extent an independent variable. A further issue is how far the general English experience was shared by the South West.

The first mortality shocks occurred between 1315 and 1322 when a sharp climatic deterioration produced a concentration of bad harvests and livestock diseases in a society in which subsistence was now more stretched. Most of England suffered severely, but Devon and Cornwall, particularly the latter, did not and their records show little evidence of unusual mortality. Land was not in short supply, the population was less dependent on agriculture (certainly less on wheat production) than elsewhere, and the more mixed, even semi-industrial, economy was less vulnerable to climatic and agrarian fluctuations. The low levels of taxation of the peninsula reduced the impact of the Crown's wartime exactions. The South West was better placed than much of England by the time the Black Death arrived in 1348. That plague hit the peninsula hard is not in doubt. It arrived first in south-western ports from the continent before moving on to Bristol and London. The diocese of Exeter (which included both counties) was a notable sufferer and its deanery of Kenn, adjacent to Exeter itself, the worst of all for clerical mortality, losing 86 incumbents from 17 parishes between 1349 and 1351. Though lay categories left no comparable records, there were both towns and rural manors that suffered death rates many times the normal. But the worst cases tell us little about the overall impact on the region, nor how its experience related to that of other regions and to national averages. The consensus is that plague (which recurred with another virulent outbreak in the early 1360s) killed about 40 per cent of England's population, taking the previous total of more than 4 million back towards 2.5 million by the 1370s. It tended to take the young, especially men, rather than marginal groups like infants and the aged, and it had a different seasonal pattern from normal mortality. As it hit the productive and fertile age groups hardest, it was highly disruptive both economically and demographically.

The South West probably suffered less than much of England. Plague proved to be more persistent in eastern England than in the West, where more dispersed patterns of settlement lessened the impact. The South West was a series of mini-economies, not all closely linked to other regions and to the continent. Even in the first and worst outbreak in 1348–9, the impact in the region was uneven, western Cornwall suffering badly but eastern Cornwall relatively little. Tin production almost ceased for a few years but recovered almost completely by the 1380s, while the agricultural impact was uneven, some manors finding themselves short of tenants while others experienced no problems. The speed of economic recovery in the South West, given that it could scarcely attract migrants from stricken regions to the east, suggests that its own reserves of population had not been among the worst depleted. Certainly it did not suffer permanent economic damage or dislocation or require major structural transformations. The 14th century was to be followed by a period in which the South West gained – demographically, economically and politically – in relation to much of the rest of England.

England's population declined further for much of the 15th century before stabilising and starting to pick up again to around 2.25–2.75 million by the 1520s. The South West may have fluctuated around 150,000 for some time, though Jonathan Barry estimates some 200,000 in 1569: 142,000 for Devon and 61,000 for Cornwall. The 1377 poll-tax figures had suggested that the overall density of the rural population in Cornwall was now higher than in Devon (excepting Exeter), but both counties had uneven and fluctuating densities within them.

The South West, or at least parts of it, experienced some economic downturn in the mid-15th century, occasioned perhaps by declining yields from alluvial tinning in Cornwall and by the disruption of continental links as the English Crown was pushed out of France. War and coastal raiding from France and Brittany became threats to the southern coastline and its trade. But these were temporary setbacks to the region's longer-term gains. Schofield's comparative analysis of taxation assessments from the 1330s and from the early 16th century shows how much the South West advanced among the English counties. In the 1330s Devon and Cornwall had been ranked 34th and 35th among the 38 counties in terms of assessed wealth per 1,000 acres. By 1515 they were 18th and 27th and, in terms of increase over the period, placed first and third. That Somerset was now ranked the second most prosperous county (and sixth in terms of relative advance) suggests a larger regional factor not exclusive to Devon and Cornwall. Though population distribution did not necessarily match that of wealth, economic buoyancy had demographic consequences. Growth was probably helped by some inward migration, but much of it was locally derived. Parish register evidence from the 16th century onwards indicates that the Devon and Cornwall mortality rates for infants and children were lower than in much of England; this favourable survival rate may have been a factor in the regions's demographic buoyancy in earlier centuries.

THE EARLY-MODERN SOUTH WEST

Between about 1550 and 1650 England experienced a century of rapid population growth, which pushed the total above that achieved before the Black Death. The following century saw another falling-back, not perhaps in aggregate numbers but in growth rate and with a number of minor mortality crises. Again it is not clear how far this phase of relative restraint arose from Malthusian pressures or from the impact of disease. By the mid-17th century England's population exceeded 5 million and by 1750 it approached 6 million. The South West reflected this trend more positively than some other regions and its share of the nation's population was growing for much of the period. It was during these two centuries that the region achieved its greatest importance within the nation. Jonathan Barry estimates that the south-western population of around 200,000 in 1569 grew to nearly 300,000 by 1603 (Devon 207,500 and Cornwall 90,000) and to 325,000 (Devon 227,000 and Cornwall 98,000) by 1660. The last figure represented 6.3 per cent of England's total population.

This period also saw significant redistributions of population (Fig. 4.2). The South West, except perhaps Plymouth, did not attract many immigrants, but there were major transfers within the region, largely as a result of short-wave migration from countryside to town and from agricultural districts to industrial or maritime ones. The growth of Cornwall's population from almost 100,000 in 1660 to around 150,000 in 1760 changed the balance between the east and the west of the county. A 'surplus' population on the eastern border was drawn westwards into the mining districts, though it also contributed to the rapid growth of Plymouth across the Tamar. The county's western half now had a similar population density to the eastern and was increasing faster. Though Devon still had a higher overall density than Cornwall, the difference was slight when major urban areas were excluded. In Devon the old pattern of a more populous and settled eastern half still held. Migration also showed some gender differentiation. Movement to the industrial areas, especially to mining, was predominantly male, that to the towns, with their demand for servants, more female. The rural districts of the peninsula were breeding a demographic surplus for export to elsewhere in the region and, indeed, beyond it. By the early 17th century Devon had a population density more than 10 per cent above the mean for England (admittedly a mean reduced by the sparse population of the northern counties) and could sustain some outward migration. From the late 18th century a dramatic and sustained growth of population took off. Although this was to some extent a European phenomenon, the rate of growth in Britain and, until 1840s, in Ireland would remain well above that of the rest of western Europe.

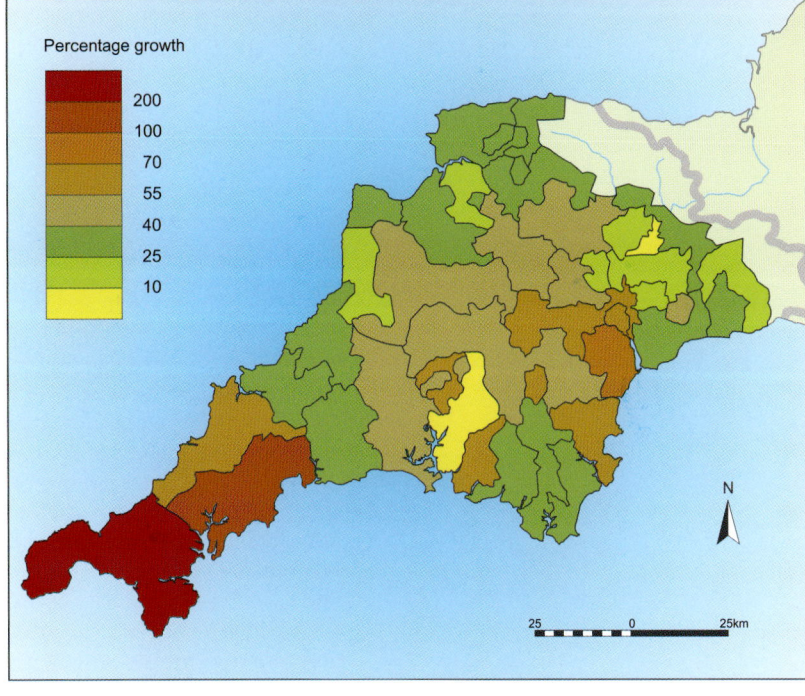

Fig. 4.2 Population growth 1660–1805.

19th AND 20th CENTURIES

The 1811 census (a more reliable count than the pioneering effort in 1801) of England and Wales recorded a population of 10.3 million. Devon (383,000) and Cornwall (221,000) totalled 604,000, or 5.86 per cent of the national total. By 1861 the population of the two counties had reached 953,000, a growth of 57.8 per cent in the half-century, with Cornwall (67 per cent) growing faster than Devon (52.5 per cent). This increase, though rapid by past standards, was slower than that of England and Wales. Over the next 50 years the region's growth-rate fell dramatically behind the national one. The south-west's population of 1.28 million in 1911 represented a growth of only 7.9 per cent since 1861, compared to 79.6 per cent for England and Wales. By 1861 the two counties had only 4.74 per cent of the population of England and Wales; by 1911 just 2.85 per cent. Particular decades pinpoint the change dramatically: between 1811 and 1821 the region's population growth was 15.73 per cent, not far behind the national 17.5 per cent. For the decade 1851 to 1861, the respective figures were 4.25 per cent and 11.7 per cent; between 1871 and 1881 the region actually lost 4.07 per cent of its inhabitants, while the national increase was 14 per cent. In 1811 Devon's population had put it third among the non-metropolitan counties; by 1911 it was fourteenth.

PEOPLE AND LIVELIHOODS: AGENTS OF LANDSCAPE CHANGE

Behind these figures lay a drift into economic decline and marginality. A process of de-industrialisation had begun in the mid-18th century when changes in fashion, intensified competition and shifts in overseas markets hit the Devon woollen industry. The extractive industries had a different profile and went on expanding into the mid-19th century. Western Cornwall had perhaps passed its peak by the 1840s when there was some overseas emigration of miners, but copper extraction in east Cornwall and west Devon continued to provide handsome profits until the 1860s. It was said that some 5,000 miners left Cornwall in 1866 alone. In the 1870s, St Just in Penwith lost nearly one-third of its inhabitants. Tin production continued relatively successfully until the 1890s when it was hit by similar problems. The year 1896 was one of collapse when Cornish tin production halved. By 1929 only 3,000 were employed in Cornish mines, by 1939 fewer than 1,000. The continuing haemorrhage of population from the county – declining in six of the seven census decades from 1861 to 1931 – was one consequence.

Agriculture had its own profile of decline. High wartime demand for the victualling of fleets at Plymouth and Torbay led to expansion and prosperity between 1793 and 1815. After the Battle of Waterloo in 1815 deflation and agricultural depression hit the two counties, though they were less dependent on grain production than much of southern and eastern England. But the most acute agricultural depression came in the century's second half, particularly from the 1870s. Emigration from agricultural Devon, to the colonies and the USA as well as to more prosperous parts of England, became substantial. With diseases hitting Devon's livestock industry, the decade between 1871 and 1881 saw the county as a whole losing population. This depression-related fall in the agricultural population was a feature of the larger south-west region. Somerset, Dorset and Wiltshire all had little population growth in the late 19th century and, in some decades, actual decline as production contracted in the face of cheap imports.

South-west England in economic decline and demographic stagnation (or worse) offered stark contrasts with more buoyant parts of the country, particularly with the industrial centres. The region was becoming peripheral to an advanced industrial economy. Within the South West itself the demographic picture was a mixed one. Infant and child survival rates remained better than in most parts of the country, even as general mortality rates declined slowly in the 19th century. Low population densities and a mild climate gave the region a salubrious image. The large towns (and in terms of mortality the region was fortunate to have few of these) displayed a more mixed picture depending on population densities and water supply, but also on class and income-levels. In Exeter, which suffered from the first cholera epidemic in 1832, the wealthier neighbourhoods had lower mortality rates than the poorer ones, a differential that was not new but which actually increased around the mid-19th century. Only at the end of the century did improved sewerage and water supply start to erode such differentials.

The way in which these processes were reflected in the distribution of population is indicated in Fig. 4.3. In the early census decades of the 19th century Cornwall was still growing faster than Devon, and at the 1841 census it peaked at 39.1 per cent of their combined population. Thereafter its share declined, while Devon's increased (albeit only modestly); by 1961 Cornwall had only 29.4 per cent of the region's inhabitants. Cornwall's mining districts lost population spectacularly

Fig. 4.3 Percentage change in population density 1851–1911.

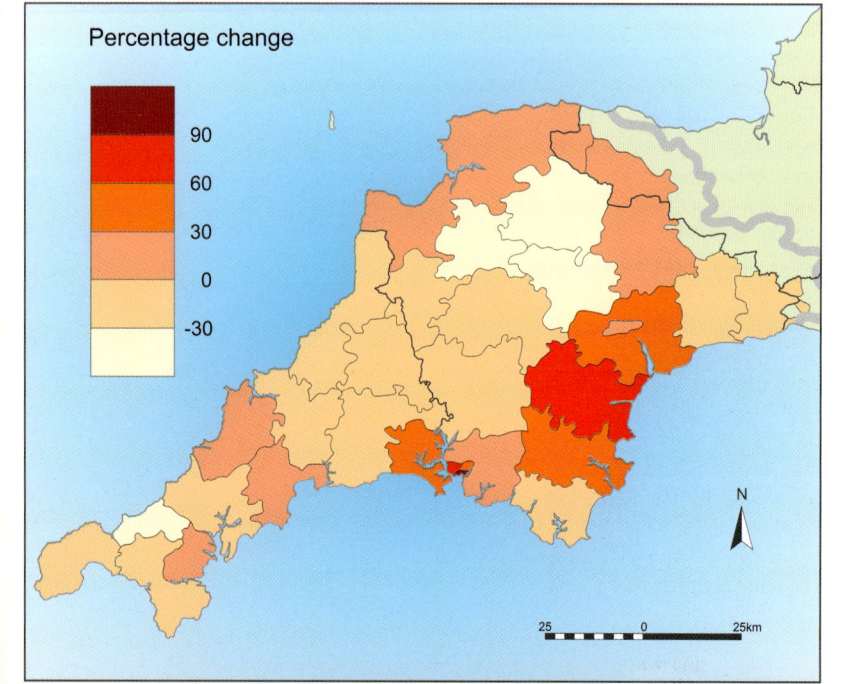

and rapidly; so, more steadily, did much of agricultural Devon, even as other parts of the county continued to expand. The ancient bias towards the southern coastline re-asserted itself as Exeter, Plymouth, Torbay and resort towns sucked in people from rural Devon. This southward shift, less pronounced in Cornwall than in Devon, changed the balance between the rural and the urban districts. Well into the 20th century most rural areas were losing inhabitants, while the major urban centres continued to grow. In 1811 Exeter and the Plymouth conurbation had represented one-ninth of the population of the two counties; by 1911 the proportion was about one-quarter. By 1961 Plymouth, Torbay and Exeter accounted for over half the population of Devon. Still largely rural in area and landscape, the South West had ceased to be predominantly rural in terms of its inhabitants.

This demographic recession involved, in its early decades, large-scale outward migration. The South West was raising people for export. Over the decades this loss of the young and potentially fertile reduced the fertility of the remaining population, particularly in the mining and agricultural districts, and by the early 20th century the South West was no longer producing significant demographic surpluses for migration. An ageing of the region's population was being intensified by the nature of inward migration too. Though Plymouth attracted some young men to naval and industrial employment, much of the migration into the South West was by older and retired people who added little to the region's demographic vitality.

The late 20th century saw a reversal of some of these trends. The population of Devon in 1991 (1.016 million) was 53.4 per cent above the figure for 1901, that of Cornwall (471,000) 46.1 per cent. An acceleration from a position of slow or negative growth had begun in the 1960s. Until then the region's growth rate had been below the national one and Cornwall had lost residents even in the 1950s. But after the census of 1961, growth in the two counties ran ahead of the national figure. Cornwall was now adding to its numbers faster than Devon and achieving rates of growth unseen since the early 19th century. Between 1971 and 1981, for example, the population of England and Wales grew by 0.8 per cent, Devon's by 6.7 per cent and Cornwall's by 13.2 per cent.

Some of the negative factors of the late 19th century had by now worked themselves out of the system. De-industrialisation had almost exhausted itself. Other regions would now suffer from it instead. Agriculture, benefiting from price-support systems both before and after Common Market entry in 1973, was no longer shedding labour as between the 1860s and the 1930s. More urbanised and suburbanised than a century earlier, the region was no longer a byword for rural decline and depopulation. Numbers began to recover in some villages, as wider car-ownership brought extended suburbanisation and enabled people to commute longer distances to work in the towns. Some of the population growth in east Cornwall and west Devon was the result of overspill from Plymouth. Many places saw new housing estates built. Improvements to the peninsula's spinal roads from the 1970s and the construction of the Tamar road bridge integrated the region more effectively and improved links to the counties further to the east. The South West, despite cutbacks in its rail system, became a less isolated and better integrated region.

Retirement patterns have been another factor in making the South West one of England's fastest growing regions. Earlier and better-funded retirement and increasing life expectancy added to the region's numbers as elderly migrants opted for the attractions of climate and coastline and turned some communities into virtual retirement centres, a trend begun in resort towns like Torquay and Sidmouth in the previous century. More than half the residents in some of the east Devon coastal resorts are retired. The region's exploitation of its attractions for holiday-makers fared less well as the seaside holiday began to lose out from the 1960s to cheap overseas package holidays, but later on increased car-ownership and improved roads facilitated tourism and weekending. Newquay became a surfing mecca and one of the region's fastest-growing towns. The environment became one of the peninsula's greatest assets as people gained more leisure, mobility and spending power. One limitation of this economic and demographic gain remained the seasonality of much of the trade. Newquay's permanent population is only one-quarter of the figure in high summer.

The growth in population in the South West in the 20th century was generated almost entirely by net inward migration, a reversal of the pattern of the previous century. Most of that inflow has come from more prosperous and populous regions, the Midlands and particularly the South East, as retired people sell up and realise some of their equity by moving to cheaper property in Devon and Cornwall. The consequently ageing demographic profile depresses the region's potential for natural growth. Though there is some movement into the area by young professional people, it is counter-balanced by the outward migration of many of the region's indigenous educated young towards London and the South-East. The inward flows of the young recruited by the higher education institutions of the Exeter, Plymouth and Falmouth areas – Exeter's population grows by around 10,000 during university terms – are seasonal and temporary in character.

The region's demographic history ends with a renewed buoyancy of population over recent decades, even if the picture is not, as in some earlier periods, one of natural growth through increased fertility and survival rates. The region's future depends partly on the fortunes of the 'grey economy'. The historical experience, however, has been one of constant fluctuations. Though the South West has to some extent reflected the demographic experience of the rest of England, particularly that of a larger western region, there has never been a stable relationship with national developments and trends. As a peripheral region with distinctive features it has sometimes gained and sometimes lost in its share of the national population. Periods of expansion and of recession alike have reflected the performance of the regional economy and its various sectors. This demographic history has both shaped and been shaped by the landscape, most obviously so in respect of mining, agriculture and the coastal economy. The region has been highly diversified economically – both Devon and Cornwall have contained distinctive sub-regional economies – and some parts have flourished while others have decayed. The landscape and its accretions reflect these historical experiences. For a region now so heavily dependent upon tourism and retirement – and, underlying both of these, upon perceptions of the 'quality of life' it offers – the nature of the landscape and the demographic character of the area are likely to remain closely linked.

FURTHER READING

The standard study of Domesday Book population is Darby and Welldon Finn (eds) 1967; *see also* Ravenhill in Kain and Ravenhill (eds) 1999, Chapter 15.

On the early medieval period *see* Miller and Hatcher 1978; and on the late Middle Ages Hatcher 1977. Hatcher takes a largely non-Malthusian position and holds that the South West was hit less hard by plague than much of England.

Barry, in Kain and Ravenhill (eds) 1999, Chapter 16, is an excellent review of the early modern period.

The classic study of English population history from the 16th to the 19th centuries is Wrigley and Schofield 1981. It refers extensively to south-west England.

Specifically on the 19th century *see* Bryant, in Gregory, Shorter and Ravenhill (eds) 1969, 125–42. For a more general discussion of population trends, *see* Gilg, in Kain and Ravenill (eds) 1999, Chapter 17.

The most recent demographic history of the South West is examined in more detail by Gilg, 'Population Changes in the Twentieth Century', in Kain and Ravenhill 1999, 125–135.

PART II
LANDSCAPES DISSECTED

5

Faith, Church and Landscape

DAVID HARVEY

THE SOUTH WEST IN A NATIONAL CONTEXT

Viewed from a national perspective, the ecclesiastical landscape of the South West would, at first sight, seem to fit comfortably within a picture-postcard vision of idyllic rural scenes (Fig. 5.1). It is quite easy to conjure up an image of the landscape of Devon and Cornwall characterised by a particular set of ecclesiastical accoutrements; the solid stone-built tower of a medieval parish church, the age-old yew tree set within an ancient graveyard, even the local anecdotes of obscure saints and eccentric curates and the comfortable 'chocolate-box' village surrounding it all. Certainly the churches of Devon and Cornwall would appear to fit well within this view of a 'national' ecclesiastical landscape. Stockleigh English, for instance, is just one of many hundreds of seemingly 'age-old' local rural parish churches which match this national idyllic vision, as well as making up a valuable resource for tourism in modern Devon and Cornwall (Fig. 5.2). However, just as the vision of a 'national rural life' owes more to the imagination and constructed ideals of more worldly practices, an examination 'beyond the postcards' of Devon and Cornwall reveals a greater complexity and variety of religious landscape than the popular image of quaint parish churches might suggest.

Although the South West does indeed contain physical incarnations of all the images mentioned in the opening paragraph, a deeper examination reveals a distinct pattern within the physical 'religious landscape'. It also possesses a legacy of development that has transformed many aspects of the very fabric of the

Fig. 5.1 Widecombe-in-the-Moor, Devon. *The solid church tower of Widecombe-in-the-Moor, nestling in a deep and comfortably green Dartmoor valley, is surrounded by a solid stone village that seems to cling to it for security.*

75

Fig. 5.2 Stockleigh English, near Cheriton Fitzpaine in mid-Devon. *The appearance of a church, rectory, squire's house and parkland seems synonymous with a certain brand of quintessential Englishness.*

apparent 'medieval' ecclesiastical landscape almost beyond recognition. Although the ideal of a church in every parish was a medieval invention, and almost every rural church throughout Devon and Cornwall was long-established by the 15th century, a great deal of development and change has occurred throughout the subsequent 500 years. In part, this is due to changes that were wrought within the region by the Reformation. Partly, however, it has also been a consequence of processes of urbanisation and industrialisation, which, despite the overwhelmingly 'rural' image of the South West (so carefully nurtured today), have been so crucial to the evolution of our present landscape.

Another common fallacy is to think of the Christian landscape of Devon and Cornwall as being a singular, uniform product of the Anglican establishment. This could not be further from the truth as more than two-thirds of all the religious establishments in Cornwall and Devon are not of the established Anglican church. Indeed, the dissenting traditions of Devon, and the strong adherence to Methodism in Cornwall, qualify as distinguishing features of the region as a whole.

As we enter the new millennium, there is a greater recognition within all modern communities that faith resides in a multitude of forms: from the great organised religions such as Islam, Judaism or Buddhism, to a myriad of alternative faiths that range from New-Ageism to Druidism. While Devon and Cornwall may not be recognised as major centres for many of these other faiths, a survey of the religious landscape of the South West would not be complete without some discussion of their impact. Recent years have similarly witnessed a massive rise in alternative forms of spirituality, particularly in Cornwall, where the form and feeling of the landscape itself has become intertwined with various forms of spiritual reflection.

This chapter will explore these themes, starting with a review of developments associated with the ecclesiastical landscape as it emerged from the medieval period, before turning to the development of newer directions in the landscape of faith in Devon and Cornwall (Fig. 5.3).

FAITH, CHURCH AND LANDSCAPE

Fig. 5.3 Map showing places mentioned in the text.

THE MEDIEVAL LEGACY: SITES, FABRIC AND REFORMATION

Cornwall and Devon have an extraordinarily rich legacy of medieval (and earlier) ecclesiastical patterns and practices that are 'writ large' within the physical landscape. The earliest evidence for post-Roman Christian activity exists in the form of memorial stones, mostly situated in Cornwall, that reveal a close connection between the south-west peninsula and other Celtic Christian regions, most particularly with South Wales. This distinctive Celtic Christian presence in Cornwall was sustained through the rise by the 9th century of ecclesiastical communities at places such as St Buryan, St Keverne, Probus, Padstow and Bodmin. Although the framework of parishes today appears very uniform, the much older patterns and processes that they represent are far from uniform, and make up an enigmatic presence in the supposedly orderly world of landscape division today. In Cornwall, this is clearly demonstrated through the form of ancient parishes; here, several such church communities are recalled in a list of saints' names dating from the 10th century (Fig. 5.4), comprising one of the very earliest pieces of evidence for such ecclesiastical organisation anywhere in Britain.

77

FAITH, CHURCH AND LANDSCAPE

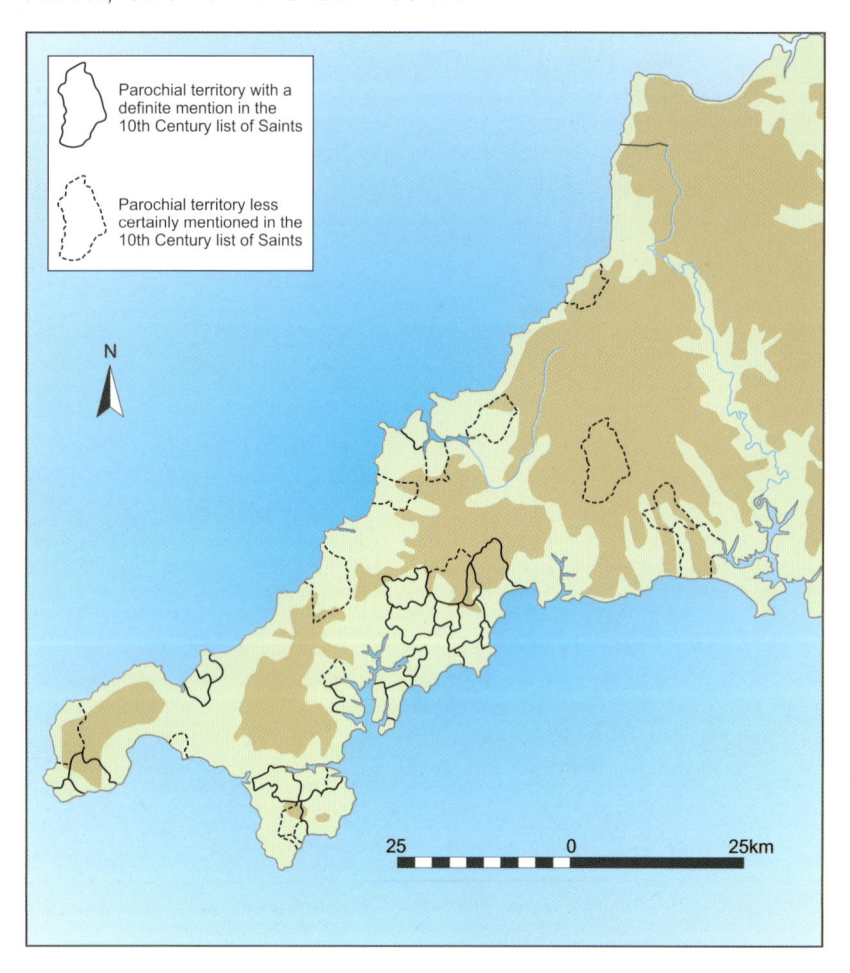

Fig. 5.4 Map showing places associated with a 10th-century list of saints.

Fig. 5.5 Merther Uny, near Helston, Cornwall. Once recognised as a parochial centre in its own right, the ruined chapel site of Merther Uny recalls the martyrdom of St Euny.

In contrast to Cornwall, the expanding influence of the English-centred Church into Devon from around AD 700 has left that county with a legacy of *minster* establishments, still recognisable even today in the large parish units and associated chapels and churches of such places as Crediton and Axminster. Hartland, for instance, appears to have developed as a strongpoint within an early medieval estate that included Welcombe as well as the very large parish of Hartland itself. All in all, the intricate patterns of parish boundaries that weave their way across the countryside, often in an alarmingly awkward fashion and with detached portions, dependent chapelries and split-townships, recalls the memory of local manorial manipulation, hereditary settlement and disputes over tithes, stretching back over many centuries.

The most important and long-lasting legacy of the medieval church landscape lies in the spatial positioning of the religious sites themselves. Closely allied to this geography of church location is the way in which elements of the landscape and its settlements are named; from the 'monkish' overtones of the Meneague region of the Lizard Peninsula, to the many hundreds of village, farm and even field-names that either reflect a local religious establishment's dedication, or which may recall the presence of an otherwise long-forgotten well, shrine or pilgrimage site – for example, the place-name elements such as *lan*, *eglos*, *venton* or *merther/merthyr* that occur at many hundreds of locations in Cornwall (Fig. 5.5).

The situation of ecclesiastical establishments has long been the subject of academic debate, partly because of the presence of some obvious geographical patterns. It is often noted that many churches in the South West are situated away from settlement centres, and particularly so in Cornwall. The church of Tintagel (Fig. 5.6), for instance, is still located well away from the village centre of the same name, while throughout

Cornwall, the epithet of 'churchtown' is still used to describe a distinct hamlet centred around a church within an area otherwise characterised by dispersed settlement (Fig. 5.7).

If the geographical location of ecclesiastical establishments makes a significant contribution to the character of the historic landscape, then the naming of the elements of landscape associated with such locations must also be remembered. In Cornwall, the naming of parishes, settlements and even towns after the saints to whom the local churches are dedicated is itself a significant and

Fig. 5.6 The church of Tintagel from the air. The sub-circular shape of Tintagel churchyard is typical of early ecclesiastical sites in the West Country, as is its separation from the main settlement site.

LEFT: **Fig. 5.7 Morvah Churchtown, west Cornwall.** Reflecting the typical pattern of much of Devon and Cornwall, Morvah Churchtown is the parochial centre in an area of dispersed farming settlements.

79

Fig. 5.8 A road sign. Many Cornish towns and villages are named in honour of obscure, and often local, saints.

Fig. 5.9 The flag of St Piran is increasingly recognised as a symbol of Cornish difference, flying even on Anglican churches.

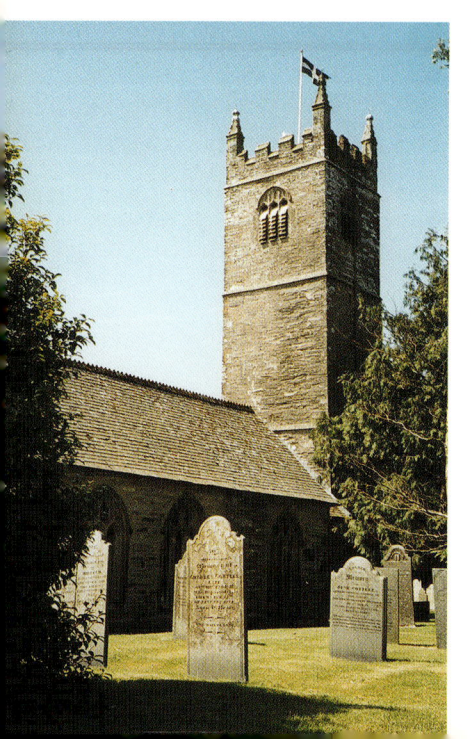

distinct practice – as for example at St Day, St Germans, St Tudy, St Teath and St Mabyn (Fig. 5.8). The vast majority of these names are either of obscure local origin, suggesting a whole geography of local saintly legends, or they are 'inter-Celtic' and commemorate the very real connections that Cornwall held with Brittany, Wales and Ireland during the late 1st millennium AD. An example of the former is St Gwinear, commemorated at Gwinear Churchtown in west Cornwall, and also in a *Life*, written around AD 1300, which tells of Gwinear's martyrdom at the hands of a local warlord and his subsequent journey around the local area, visiting local springs, wells and significant trees, while carrying his head under his arm! A saint with wider inter-Celtic connections is the Breton monk, St Winwaloe (or Tewynnoc), who is commemorated at both Gunwalloe and Landewednack on the Lizard peninsula, as well as at Towednack, Poundstock, Tremaine and possibly St Winnow elsewhere in Cornwall, as well as at East Portlemouth in Devon. As St Guenole, he is also commemorated at Landévennec in Finistére; in Brittany, he is revered as one of the most important saints of the latter part of the 1st millennium AD. Thus it is that the present landscape of church foundations, and one which distinguishes Cornwall from Devon, reflects a complex historical geography of inter-Celtic relationships independent of an English polity and even today represents an important strand of communal feeling of Cornish identity and difference (Fig. 5.9).

Although the legacy of the early medieval church in the landscape of Devon and Cornwall is felt very strongly through themes of location and naming, a considerable amount of its physical fabric also remains in existence in shrines, crosses and holy wells, as well as in actual church buildings. In terms of their surviving architecture, the majority of 'medieval' church buildings in Devon and Cornwall actually date from the 15th and 16th centuries, at the very end of the medieval period, even if they may have been built on much older foundations. Indeed, the ancient circular *lans* (enclosures) that surround many Cornish churches have had a particularly strong and continuing effect on the development of settlements. An excellent example of this is at St Buryan, where the morphology of the village, even today, is very much dictated by the sub-circular early Christian enclosure (Fig. 5.10). In places, the churchyard of St Buryan stands fully 2.4m above the surrounding land, suggesting a very early occupation and long use of the site. Archaeological excavation has also suggested that this churchyard is built on top of an Iron Age 'round', a form of defended farmstead typical of late prehistoric Cornwall.

Although many of the earliest ecclesiastical centres in Cornwall, such as those at St Keverne or St Germans, appear to have developed from 'Celtic Christian' religious communities, formal monasticism in the South West was not very well developed before the Norman Conquest anywhere west of Glastonbury. The increased enthusiasm for the monastic life that occurred throughout the British Isles between the 11th and 13th centuries is nevertheless reflected in the region's material remains; by the time of the Reformation in the 16th century, the number of formal religious communities in Devon and Cornwall had increased from 2 to 36.

While some of these sites have survived in a physical form to the present day, it should always be remembered that their original 'medieval' attributes will have been transformed, both in terms of their physical shape and meaning, over the intervening centuries. In a physical sense, this transformation can be recognised through the wholesale alteration or dismantling of a large number of sites and shrines. For instance, as well as a multitude of lesser chapels, wayside shrines and holy wells, major centres such as Totnes, Barnstaple, Plymouth and Bodmin lost important parts of their ecclesiastical heritage when their religious houses were dissolved during the reign of Henry VIII. Part of Tavistock Abbey ended up, ironically, as a dissenting meeting house when, in the 1690s, the Duke of Bedford granted the hall to a Presbyterian ministry with which he sympathised. Exeter

FAITH, CHURCH AND LANDSCAPE

Fig. 5.10 St Buryan from the air. One of the few such sites to have undergone some excavation, the church site of St Buryan, near Land's End, is demonstrably ancient; its sub-circular *lan* enclosure is at the centre of a 'wheel' of ancient tracks and church paths, many of which are lined with medieval 'Cornish crosses' marking routes to church.

alone lost two friaries, two priories and a large hospital at this time. A large number of pilgrimage centres also either disappeared or were altered. The important pilgrimage destination of St Michael's Mount, for instance, maintained its physical being in the landscape despite undergoing a radical transformation in its purpose and appearance. However, the nearby pilgrimage centre of St Day almost disappeared, with only its name and memory enduring in the ecclesiastical landscape of this part of Cornwall. Thus, although the 'medieval legacy' of ecclesiastical sites in Cornwall and Devon is very rich, it is also a partial one.

The presence of a medieval legacy of the church in the landscape of Devon and Cornwall reflects a distinct geography of location, territorial organisation, naming and survival. A number of elements of this 'medieval geography' have been lost, while the meaning of that which has survived has been transformed by developments over the succeeding 500 years.

DISSENT AND NONCONFORMITY: REFORM AND RENOVATION

The assumption that there was a relatively smooth transition from a uniform Catholic landscape of the early 16th century, to an equally uniform Anglican one less than a century later, should be viewed with suspicion. In reality, the picture was much more complex, depending on whether a particular Anglican parish lay in a rural or urban area, was poor or wealthy, or was loosely or strongly controlled by its patrons. Although there were very few Catholics in the early modern landscape of Devon and Cornwall, increasing numbers of Quakers, Congregationalists, Baptists and Presbyterians all had a considerable impact, especially at a local level. The first Baptist chapel in the region opened in Dartmouth in 1600, and Plymouth had one by the 1620s. In Plymouth, this expression of dissent became a very important component of the city's sense of community – historical events such as the passing by in 1620 of *The Mayflower* (which actually embarked on its journey to America from Southampton, merely stopping off in Plymouth), and the city's adherence to the Parliamentary cause in the Civil War became key moments in Plymouth's religious and community identity and are remembered to this day.

FAITH, CHURCH AND LANDSCAPE

Fig. 5.11 Loughwood Baptist Chapel in Dalwood, between Axminster and Honiton, Devon. In the 17th century, worshippers at this chapel (built in about 1653) risked imprisonment for their faith.

Fig. 5.12 Map of percentage share of Anglican and non-Anglican attendances, as listed in the 1851 religious census.

During the early modern period a majority of the population of Cornwall and Devon continued to adhere to the established Anglican church, whether through genuine enthusiasm, pragmatism or apathy, and the 18th century witnessed the stimulation and development of the notion of national identity linked to a religious landscape of Anglican parochial organisation. Linda Colley has argued that a common investment in Protestantism taught people a new sense of Britishness, in opposition to a Catholic and continental 'other', at a time when national identity was emerging as a central component of self-identification. This easy association between national identity and the established Church has survived the constitutional reforms of the 19th century, and been augmented by a passionate pursuit of a sense of rural idyll that leaves us today with a notion that the 'typical' village church (with its rectory or vicarage attached) is somehow natural and uniformly associated with the 'British' nation. Although Devon and Cornwall have relatively few of these 'typical' villages, the association of national identity with the established Anglican church is still strong, represented in the display of military colours in the more important churches and the flying of the St George cross at many more.

Alongside the old Anglican traditions, the legacy of religious dissent remains equally strong in the landscape of Cornwall and Devon. Even today, the strength of Nonconformity can be seen as one of the region's defining characteristics in comparison to other parts of England. The material remains of the 'old dissent' are not exceptionally numerous, but do have a distinctive geography of their own, with specific concentrations in the urban areas and in the richer farming districts, particularly of east Devon (Fig. 5.11). The most important feature of old dissent, however, and of Quakers and Baptists in particular, is the way in which, as 'gathered' churches, they abandoned the aim of incorporating all the people living in one place into any pretence of a 'national' church. In distinct contrast to the forces of Anglicanism, the rise of dissent meant that the previously fundamental link between a uniform parish structure and a sense of local identity – the parish and its congregation – was broken.

In terms of its impact on the ecclesiastical landscape of the South West, the single most important development of the 18th and 19th century was the spread of Methodism, or the 'new dissent'. By 1851, 737 (67 per cent) of Cornwall's 1,104 places of worship were Methodist and only 265, or 24 per cent Anglican. In Devon, where strands of old dissent remained relatively strong, there were 379 Methodist chapels (about 30 per cent of the total) compared with 549 Anglican churches and 369 other Nonconformist chapels (Fig. 5.12). Further analysis reveals a slightly more complex picture than this simple distinction between Devon and Cornwall suggests. The eastern parts of Devon tended to follow a strongly Anglican direction, but with a substantial minority of old dissent that is mirrored further east in Somerset and Dorset. Central and western Cornwall maintained an exceptionally robust Wesleyan Methodist tradition, while the areas on either side of the

River Tamar contained a relatively strong presence of the Bible Christian wing of the Methodist movement.

The reasons for the remarkable success of Methodism in the South West, and most particularly in Cornwall, are complex and should not be laid at the feet of some innate sense of 'Celtic difference'. Charismatic Methodist leaders worked extremely hard to create and maintain a constituency within the population, and found the regions where mining and fishing dominated the local economy to be particularly fruitful recruiting grounds (Fig. 5.13).

Fig. 5.13 Gwennap Pit, near Redruth, Cornwall. John Wesley preached on 18 occasions between 1762 and 1789 at Gwennap Pit to crowds of up to 20,000 people.

While the facts and figures on the historical strength of Methodism are impressive in themselves, it is the relationship between Methodism and the landscape of Devon and Cornwall that is perhaps the most enduring legacy. That relationship can be viewed from two directions: on one hand, the impact of the topography and the geography of the region on the development and form of religious dissent; on the other, the great impact that Methodism itself has had on the landscape of Devon and, especially, Cornwall. The relative isolation of many communities in the south-west peninsula, particularly while it remained under the control of one very large diocese centred on Exeter, was an important contributing factor to the success of Methodism in this region. Exeter itself has always been viewed as 'ever faithful' to the Anglican cause and it continued to be strongly connected to the centres of Anglican power. The establishment of a bishopric at Truro in 1877 can thus be seen as a means by which the Anglican Church sought to re-establish its authority within this largely dissenting region. Conversely, for the Bible Christians in particular, it was the rural isolation and hamlet life that was crucial to their success in evangelising a type of society into which other forms of religious organisation had failed to penetrate to any great effect.

In terms of the landscape of today, towns such as St Just and Camborne are still physically dominated by their Methodist chapels, which provide a sense of

FAITH, CHURCH AND LANDSCAPE

Fig. 5.14 Methodist chapel in St Just, near Land's End, Cornwall. *Whatever the real numbers of people attending such establishments, Methodist chapels such as this one at St Just physically dominated their towns, and represent a distinctly 'Methodist' landscape legacy.*

personality and identity to their civic integrity (Fig. 5.14). There are scores of wayside chapels throughout Cornwall, each with seating for hundreds of people, which are situated in locations that are today seemingly devoid of much population (Fig. 5.15). This apparent (and very real) over-provision of religious facilities reflects a long history of competition for popular support from scattered settlements, as various Methodist sects struggled to maintain and expand their influence. A consequence of this process of popular petition for support is that the provision of Methodist places of worship in areas such as the western half of Cornwall ignored the older system of established parishes, preferring instead to follow local demographic patterns. While on the face of it much of Cornwall would seem to correspond to an archetypal 'Methodist landscape', the speculative and competitive nature of a great deal of the chapel building should warn us against attaching such a uniform label. The Methodist movement of the 19th century was very far from unified, while the over-capacity of chapels meant that there were always literally thousands of empty seats. While bearing these facts in mind, we should not let them belittle the overwhelming presence of Methodism in western Devon and Cornwall, particularly in the industrial, mining and fishing districts.

Returning to the established Anglican church, the reforms and changes in the 19th century do not display themselves very obviously in the landscape in terms of new churches. This was nevertheless a period of great material investment in the religious provision of all faiths, which involved a massive

Fig. 5.15 A wayside chapel near St Austell, Cornwall. *Passers-by today might wonder where the congregation for isolated chapels such as this one came from. Although built as central points in areas of dispersed settlement to which people came from many miles around, there was also much over-provision of Methodist chapels as various sects competed for the local populace.*

programme of parish church renovation and a small but increasingly noticeable expansion of the Catholic faith in the South West (Fig. 5.16). The Gothic revival of the late 19th century also left its mark, particularly in the urban areas, in the form of such 'landmark' churches as Charles Church in Plymouth, or St Leonard's and St Michael's in Exeter, which were built at this time. Even in rural areas the fashion for church renovation meant that many small 'medieval' churches were altered or sometimes completely rebuilt during the late 19th century. Perhaps the largest alteration to the Anglican landscape of the South West, however, was the break-up of the old Diocese of Exeter and the associated foundation of Truro as a cathedral city.

Fig. 5.16 Exeter Cathedral. *This centre of Anglicanism in the South West has, within a few hundred metres of its doors, Catholic and Baptist churches (in South Street), as well as the Methodist church at The Mint – all built in the 19th century.*

Fig. 5.17 The Methodist chapel at Crows-an-Wra, near St Buryan in Cornwall, *is now a private house.*

FAITH, CHURCH AND LANDSCAPE: TODAY AND TOMORROW

In terms of faith and the modern landscape of Devon and Cornwall, the rich legacies of the past have been augmented by a range of new developments, perhaps more diverse than ever before. Within the Christian faith, many old churches and chapels have been de-consecrated, renovated and put to alternative uses, while in an increasingly secular society many more seem to find their primary meaning in their value to tourism or as architectural heritage. As the 20th century drew to a close, many chapels had been turned into homes (Fig. 5.17) – the New Connexion Chapel in Penzance, for instance, had been

FAITH, CHURCH AND LANDSCAPE

converted into flats, a large chapel in Trewellard renovated as a Meadery restaurant, while the Mount Zion Methodist Chapel of Mousehole is now the private home of a rock star. Even the landscape of practising Christianity in Devon and Cornwall is experiencing change, perhaps best witnessed in the renovation of a stationer's warehouse in Exeter into a distinctly modern evangelical chapel (Fig. 5.18).

Another enduring legacy of faith in the modern landscape of Devon and Cornwall is found in the landscapes of commemoration. As elsewhere in Britain, these are most often found associated with memorials and other sites that honour and remember the dead of two world wars. Although they can also be seen to celebrate a secular idea of nation and community, an element of Christian faith is nearly always strong, nowhere more so than in the carefully preserved ruins of the bombed Charles Church, set within a roundabout in Plymouth (Fig. 5.19). Such war memorials are so ubiquitous that they are rarely remarked upon or seen as being a distinctive part of the south-west's landscape of faith. However, it is their very nature as 'taken-for-granted' elements within the everyday street-scene and at the physical heart of the community that provides them with their legitimacy as central elements within the modern-day landscape of faith.

Non-Christian faiths have always been present in Devon and Cornwall; the Jewish graveyards at Exeter and Penzance are particularly well-known

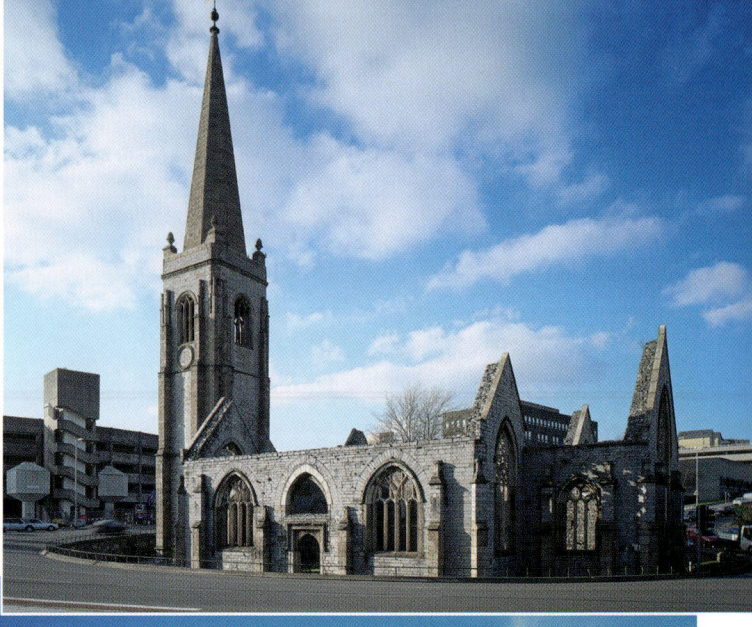

TOP LEFT:
Fig. 5.18 Belmont Chapel, Western Way, Exeter. *The evangelical Belmont Chapel is housed in a converted stationery warehouse.*

TOP RIGHT:
Fig. 5.19 The bombed-out remains of Charles Church in Plymouth commemorate the Blitz.

BOTTOM RIGHT:
Fig. 5.20 Mosque and Islamic Centre, York Road, Exeter.

FAITH, CHURCH AND LANDSCAPE

landmarks. Although other non-Christian organised religions do not yet have a very significant presence in the landscape of Cornwall and Devon, recent years have witnessed a large growth in their number – Exeter now has a large and vibrant Muslim population, while there is a Mahayana Buddhist Centre in Barnstaple (Fig. 5.20).

Finally, a survey of faith in the landscape of Devon and Cornwall would not be complete without mention of the myriad of alternative spiritual and religious practices that are now to be found in the landscapes of the South West. For these groups it is the landscape itself that often lies at the heart of their faith, rather than its expression through 'churches' constructed within that landscape. By definition, these groups are very difficult to categorise, but are perhaps most easily typified by the sentiments expressed within the long-running *Meyn Mamvro* magazine and website (Fig. 5.21). Promoting a blend of Paganism, earth mystery and folklore, such groups have been highly influential within a popular constituency that stretches well beyond what might be imagined as a relatively small core following. The association of particular landscapes and sites – and especially monuments such as menhirs, Iron Age fogous and Bronze Age stone circles – with a sense of 'spirituality' is certainly not a new phenomenon (*see* Chapter 3). However, the idea that such sites are somehow 'magical', are positioned along 'lines of energy', and contain a 'special palpable atmosphere' has certainly become more popularly accepted (rightly or wrongly) by a public that is more and more concerned with 'escaping' the trappings of modern civilisation – even if this is done, mobile phone in hand and car parked on the verge, as part of a weekend break to a Cornish holiday home. The last 30 years, in particular, have witnessed a re-interpretation of many archaeological sites and of the wider landscape itself, the meaning of which has begun to be transformed from one based on scientific enquiry and curiosity to one of 'spiritual well-being' (Figs 5.21–5.23).

Charting the legacies of something as intangible as 'faith' within the landscape of Devon and Cornwall would seem at first sight to be an impossible task. This chapter has explored how elements of faith in all forms may be traced within the landscape, from the development of bounded parochial territories and the naming of places in the landscape, through the foundation of buildings and

Fig. 5.21 **Meyn Mamvro** *publication.*

Fig. 5.22 Rag 'clouties' hanging from trees around a holy well at Sancreed near Penzance in Cornwall.

Fig. 5.23 Men-an-Tol and the 'spiritual' landscape of west Cornwall. *The landscape itself is often seen as conveying a sense of spirituality to many people. A strong 'earth mysteries' tradition in the South West has taken this faith further, attaching significance both to ancient megalithic sites (such as the Men-an-Tol) and to more recent Christian sites such as the chapel at Madron or the holy well at Sancreed (see* Fig. 5.22*).*

monuments that represent a particular religion, to the practice of seeing the very landscape itself as an article of spiritual revelation. Such a survey can only ever be partial, but as this review has shown, people's beliefs have played as significant a part in shaping the environment of the South West as have more obvious features such as its economy and society.

FURTHER READING

Kain and Ravenhill 1999. This landmark publication has several excellent chapters associated with aspects of faith, both within a medieval and post-medieval context. The maps are clear and the text adds a very useful commentary.

Meyn Mamvro. Started in 1986, *Meyn Mamvro*, or 'stones of our motherland', is published three times a year, and is associated with the *Cornish Earth Mysteries Group*. The website (http://www.meynmamvro.co.uk/) has links to a wide variety of sites connected to Paganism, folklore and ancient sites in Cornwall, as well as a number of more general 'environmental' groups.

Olson 1989. This is a scholarly investigation of the nature of Christian sites in Cornwall from before the Norman Conquest.

Orme (ed.) 1991. This is an excellent and easy-to-read survey of the long-term development of Christianity in Devon and Cornwall.

Thomas 1994. As the title suggests, Charles Thomas's book brings to life a highly complex and ambiguous set of mainly archaeological evidence in order to recount important aspects of the story of pre-Conquest Christian experience in the South West.

6

Landscapes of Defence, Security and Status

ROBERT A HIGHAM

THE CHANGING MILITARY CONTEXT

The theme of this chapter is fortified sites built from the late Anglo-Saxon period onwards and the ways in which these often, but not always, relict features continue to influence south-west England's present landscapes and townscapes. Defended sites frequently had more than one purpose and to think of them purely as defences not only limits our view of their function but also our appreciation of their surroundings. In contrast to the Roman and modern periods, the medieval period witnessed governance by kings and princes who lacked the centralised resources of their predecessors and successors. There were no standing armies and few 'systems' of defence. When kings and other powerful people waged war they did so as much in a private capacity as in any 'public' sense. Physical defence was therefore diffused throughout society in this period, whereas earlier and later it was more centrally controlled. This partly explains the proliferation of walled towns and castles, which are such hallmark features of the medieval period: protection was sought by rich individuals and communities and, since their collective efforts also contributed to the wider 'defence of the realm', their ambitions were generally supported by kings, though with suitable restraints on the emergence of over-mighty subjects. But the notion of protection operated at two levels, hence the contrast between 'security' and 'defence' in the title of this chapter. As well as defence against real or potential threats of a truly military nature, communities and individuals needed day-to-day security within a society that, although offering royal law to all free men, offered no equivalent of a modern police force. Thus protection was important at two related, but different levels.

The third element of the title – 'status' – is equally important. It is easy to under-estimate the extent to which defences have been built as much to impress as to protect. Defences displayed two important things simultaneously. First, they showed off the wealth of an individual or community, for the resources needed to build defences were very considerable. Second, they displayed the elevated rank of builder-owners, expressed in their ability to create barriers between themselves and the rest of society. This use of building as social expression runs from early prehistory to the present day, but was particularly marked in medieval times because, for the reasons earlier explained, building of defended sites was a widespread social practice.

In the late 9th century, Vikings threatened southern England and the resulting *burhs* of Alfred and his successors were military establishments as well as centres of royal government. The Normans inherited the shire towns, which had often evolved from the *burhs*, but they added a new phenomenon, the castle, built both in old towns and throughout the countryside. Warfare, as well as political power-bargaining, was heavily oriented to the possession of castles, as defences against threats both internal and external and also for new conquests in Wales and Ireland. The fortification of towns, especially in the south, became more prominent from the 13th century with increased threat of attack from France. In the form of the Hundred Years War, this lasted through the remaining medieval period, and was aggravated by internal dissent in the 15th-century Wars of the Roses.

From the 16th century, with the emergence of stronger, more centralised government, the role of private fortification fell away, as warfare and defence became an exclusively royal matter. Nation-states in their modern sense emerged and military organisation changed. A potential invasion from Spain and France in Henry VIII's reign led to massive expenditure on coastal fortification, with further investment by Elizabeth I against the background of Spanish attack. In the 1640s, the walls of many towns had a final 'hurrah' when besieged either by Royalists or Parliamentarians in the Civil War. Later in the century, the coasts faced a Dutch threat. From the 18th century, the development of regular armies saw the building of permanent garrison establishments for infantry and cavalry. Soon the external threat was once again France, with major defensive activity in the Napoleonic period and again in the mid-19th century. The 20th century, experiencing two world wars and the subsequent Cold War, saw further additions, particularly in coastguard stations, observation posts, pill-boxes and – in response to the latest technology – radar stations and airfields.

Many fragments of our present-day environment can be illuminated through studying defended places from the past thousand years. While archaeological sites are prone to destruction to the point of invisibility, defended sites are often more resilient. This is sometimes because they occupy situations less likely than others to be chosen for subsequent redevelopment, and sometimes because the survival of even fragmentary defences can protect interiors from wholesale destruction. But it is also because defended perimeters continue to emphasise their apparent significance, giving such places a lasting importance in the consciousness of succeeding societies (more so, for example, than the site of an abandoned farm or even a village). Thus, defended places reflect 'the past in the present', capturing popular imagination as well as academic attention.

REGIONAL THEMES

The evidence from the South West reflects national trends while also displaying regional characteristics. These arose from the region's varied geographical and historical experiences, which can be illustrated with reference to general themes and also particular places. Many aspects of south-western history, including matters to do with defence and security, have been affected by the peninsular nature of the region. On the north, the coast is often inhospitable and affords few major points of access, but on the south the opposite is true. Here there are numerous estuaries and inlets whose exploitation since early times has provided so much of the region's maritime experience. We sometimes encounter places that were medieval ports, though their former character is not now obvious: this is because the tin-streaming activities which were crucial to the region's medieval economy also contributed to the silting of rivers, so that places such as Plympton (Devon) and Tregony (Cornwall) were eventually left 'stranded'. It is not surprising that a significant proportion of defended places of all periods were situated near coasts. These include three of the four late Saxon *burhs* (Barnstaple, Totnes, Exeter), several medieval castles (including the above alongside Plympton, Trematon, Tregony, Tintagel), early modern artillery fortifications at Dartmouth, Plymouth and Fowey, and subsequent defences, such as Berry Head (Brixham), along the south coasts of both counties. A recently published map of major concentrations of coastal defences all over the British Isles, picks out Falmouth and Plymouth as south-western defended places of particular significance on a wider front. Though Plymouth was not a port as early as some, from the late medieval period onwards it accumulated trading, dockyard and defensive activities, which gave it not only regional but also national importance.

However, the concept of 'coastal defence' needs careful handling. It is easy to characterise it as defence against seaborne invasion, which sometimes it was. But it also involved provision for the security of coastal activities – trade, fishing and so on – and, increasingly in more recent centuries, protection of major anchorages against the possibility of use by enemy fleets. More modern 'coastal defences' were also protected on the landward side for protection against enemies who might gain a landfall. A final, and important aspect of coastal locations of defended places was simply that, in the pre-modern era, they reflected the enormous role of coastal communications.

The major characteristics of the region's internal geography are the balance of highland and lowland and the broadly north–south orientation of the river valleys. The major uplands of Exmoor, Dartmoor and Bodmin created interruptions in the otherwise accessible landmass which, at least in the medieval period, afforded numerous locations suitable for the building of the high-status defended estate centres that are generally known as castles. Distribution maps of the latter reveal a generous pattern in the lowlands and valleys but far fewer on the higher ground, though sometimes on its fringes, as at Okehampton and Lydford.

As well as being affected by geography, the landscape setting and distribution of fortified sites were also influenced by broad historical trends. In the matter of coastal defence, of course, the two influences conjoin, with on-going seaborne threats from the French, Spanish and Dutch between the 14th and 19th centuries encouraging an accumulation of outward-looking fortifications on the south coast. But this was not simply a defensive matter; places such as Fowey, Plymouth and Dartmouth developed little in the early medieval centuries, but experienced major growth as ports from the 14th century onwards. Military activity in the 12th-century civil war – often involving the building and besieging of castles – lay in an arc across southern England with Devon at its western end. It is likely that some undocumented castle earthworks, numerous in the Taw–Torridge area, represent private fortifications built by landowners involved in that conflict, a conflict which, while having a national dynastic framework, was also worked out through competition at regional and local level.

Also relevant to the theme of defence and security is the rural and urban settlement history of the region. In the late Saxon period, shires in the heart of Wessex had numerous royal *burhs*, but Devon had only four and Cornwall had none. This reflected the late absorption of the region into the West Saxon kingdom, with Cornwall at this stage still regarded as peripheral. It also provided a very low base level of urban activity to support the Norman and later foundation of seigneurial 'new towns' and the enhancement of rural places to market boroughs. Thus, while in most English counties, these new growths were modest in number, in Devon and Cornwall they proliferated because there were so few urban foundations at the outset. Thus many of the region's castles had an urban connection, being associated through lordship with one or more of these numerous new boroughs: in Devon, at Bampton, Plympton, Okehampton and Great Torrington; and in Cornwall, at Launceston, Restormel, Tregony and Week St Mary. It is also notable that, whereas the walled town was a widespread phenomenon in England generally, in Devon and Cornwall the only medieval town to have a walled circuit, apart from the four original Saxon *burhs*, was Launceston, a town developed in association with a castle by the earls of Cornwall. Although some coastal ports eventually had seaward defences in the later medieval period, these did not enclose the towns themselves (though Plymouth was to be enclosed in the 1640s).

LANDSCAPES OF DEFENCE, SECURITY AND STATUS

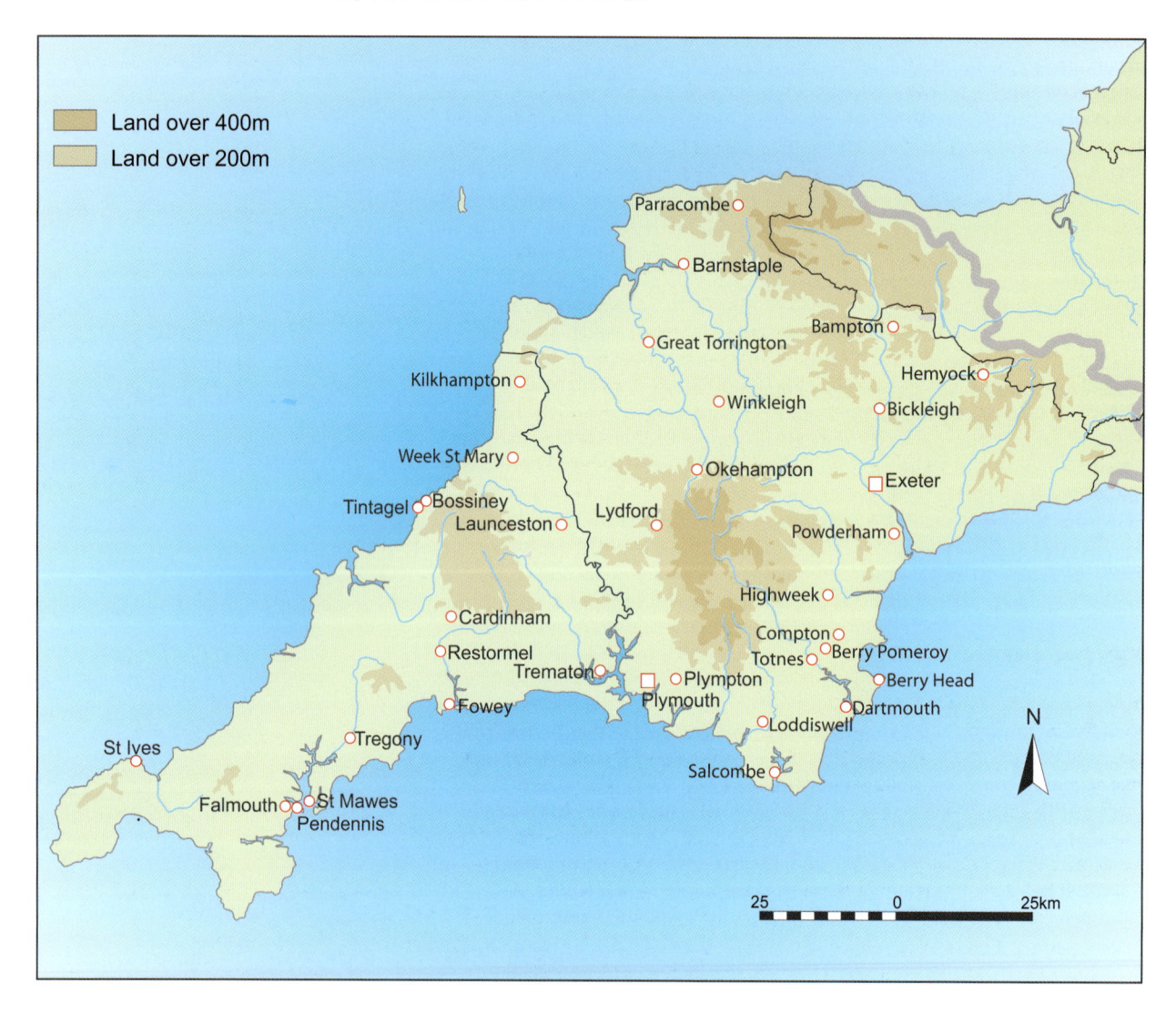

Fig. 6.1 Map showing principal places referred to in the text.

As explained in Chapter 3, the South West is characterised by a dispersed pattern of settlement; nucleated villages are fairly rare and places that appear village-like today are often in practice the successors to small boroughs. Rather, the landscape contained farms and hamlets, parish churches and scattered manor houses. This had a bearing on the locations of medieval seigneurial residences – which in their defended form were castles – because these too might stand in relative isolation rather than as part of a nucleation of settlement. It was once argued that isolation indicated the desertion of settlements that once stood next to such castles. In some cases this may have been so, but it is probably not a general explanation. The overall dispersed settlement pattern, however, does help explain why, at first sight, so many rural castles seem somewhat 'dislocated'.

Against this geographical, historical and settlement background, how do the fortified sites of the South West compare with those of other regions? The answer is that there was much comparability. Thus in terms of defence of estuaries and anchorages against real or potential threats in the Channel, from seaborne Vikings based in northern France through to the Second World War, some of the south-western *burhs*, castles, artillery fortresses and modern installations are simply reflections of wider English phenomena. On the other hand, within these sites there were defended places of national importance, for example at

LANDSCAPES OF DEFENCE, SECURITY AND STATUS

Plymouth, as already mentioned, and notably also at Dartmouth, the late 15th-century artillery tower of which was innovative in its overall concept and the design of its gun ports. The accumulation of coastal defences in Devon and Cornwall, between about 1480 and the 1530s, also meant that the region was at the forefront of coastal defence and already well-provided for when Henry VIII's famous national scheme of building was begun in 1538.

Similarly, in the castle-building centuries, the activities of the land-owning class mirrored the wider national scene. Significant gaps in the south-western picture remain, however, most notably in a lack of data about late Saxon aristocratic (possibly defended?) residences. It is nevertheless known that all the Saxon urban *burhs* received castles under either direct or indirect royal influence and numerous rural estates were given castles by successions of landowners over several centuries. There is no reason to be surprised at their numbers, for few had a significant military role except in their protective potential: they were the high-status estate centres and grand residences of the region's rich and powerful. As elsewhere, their builders sometimes created enduring landscape contexts for them, including hunting parks, markets or seigneurial boroughs, and new or re-founded priories. There was a fashion for circular great towers in the 12th–14th centuries (Trematon, Launceston, Plympton, Totnes, Barnstaple) but this was not exclusively south-western, as these are found elsewhere, in South Wales, for example.

DEVON *BURHS*

Present-day plans of the four Devonian *burhs* owe much to the late Saxon period, when the motivation for enclosure was serious defence as well as to make a major statement of royal status and control. Exeter's walls are of Roman origin and have also some surviving late Saxon work. The slightly irregular streets that overlie the Roman grid were first laid out in the late 9th century but were extended in subsequent centuries. At Totnes, the medieval outline is thought to overlie that of the 10th-century *burh* that succeeded the Alfredian foundation at Halwell. It had a spinal street but limited development of side streets. At Barnstaple, the later medieval perimeter is again presumed to have followed *burghal* lines. In all three, the wider setting was provided not by land but by water: the rivers Exe, Dart and Taw were important points of access for peace-time trade and communication as well as defence against seaborne Viking threat.

Fig. 6.2 Lydford, Devon, a view from the south-west.

Lydford

Lydford (Fig. 6.2) differs in two ways from the region's other *burhs*. First, it lay inland, on the western edge of Dartmoor, situated not to prevent access by invaders from the coast but to protect the western flank of Wessex (there being no *burhs* in what was to become Cornwall) and probably to control and defend administration of the vital resource of tin. The development of the Devonian *burhs* by Alfred reflected not only defensive needs but also greater interest in the region's economic wealth at a time when shires further to the east were facing greater Viking disruption. Exeter, with its new mint, was probably developed as the controlling centre of the tin industry, with Lydford playing an initially subsidiary role – although it had its own mint by the late 10th century. Second, although it was described in Domesday Book as a borough it did not develop into a flourishing later medieval town, but became instead a more specialised centre relating to the administration of the stannary laws and Dartmoor. From the end of the 12th century, the rise of Lydford and Devon's other stannary towns, as well as Cornwall's emergence as a major tin producer, meant that Exeter's earlier control of the industry was lost. But since Lydford's early topography was not obscured by these or later events, it remains one of England's best-surviving *burghal* plans, though representing the smallest category of this type of settlement. In the aerial view in Fig. 6.2, the site is seen from the south-west, with its single main street running up the image. The steep slopes of the promontory on which it stands, partly surrounded by the famous Lydford Gorge, are visible at the bottom of the picture, with the gentler approach to the neck of the promontory at the top. The defences (whose earthworks can just be seen in the right-centre of the image, but which once encircled the whole place) have been shown through excavation to have been considerable in scale, involving both timber and stonework. When established in the late 9th century, this *burh* had attributes of serious defence (it was attacked unsuccessfully in 997 by Vikings, perhaps attracted by its mint) and also offered some security for the surrounding population. It had a crucial association with Dartmoor and particularly the stannary laws in the later medieval period – the stannary prison was here – first under the Norman and Angevin kings, later under the earls and dukes of Cornwall (hence Lydford and Dartmoor's continuing inclusion within the Duchy). From this presence arose the succession of two castle sites, one in the late 11th century of earth and timber (its earthworks are just visible in the bottom left corner of the site), the later one substantially of stone (centre, beyond the church).

The church, though a late medieval structure, is dedicated to St Petrock, an early Celtic saint, and a fragment of post-Roman imported Mediterranean pottery was found in excavation. So it seems likely that the Alfredian *burh* was not the first settlement on the site. Because of its eventual decline, Lydford's internal plan is very clear – a single main street with some narrow side lanes creating a series of 'blocks', which are probably primary features of the *burghal* plan. Elsewhere in the South West, we are accustomed to seeing small medieval boroughs of 13th-century growth that have later declined, producing village-like settlements in the modern landscape. Here, this process has occurred with a town of much earlier origin. It is also notable that use of the space within the primary settlement has not given rise to modern expansion by in-filling: this has occurred outside the original perimeter, to the north.

By the 19th century, the extramural part of the settlement was small and clustered at the road fork outside the defences: its spread is a more modern development. The wider, moorland setting lies beyond the top of the photograph and originally included some 50,000 moorland acres (20,230ha). The Forest of Dartmoor (together with Exmoor created probably by Henry I) was what remained after King John disafforested Devon in 1204. It was either a separate manor or part of Lydford manor as described in medieval sources (technically a 'chase' when not in royal hands after 1239) and this enormous area has constituted Lydford's ecclesiastical parish up until modern times – the later civil parish, around Lydford itself, is far smaller. Despite the antiquity of the road that runs down the spine of the settlement, this is no longer a significant through-route. But it was formerly the crucial road connecting Lydford with its moorland resources. The present main road around the north-west corner of Dartmoor is also of great antiquity, but it developed to connect Okehampton and Tavistock – two new towns of the Norman period whose growth eventually eclipsed Lydford.

Dartmoor's tin production was later overtaken by Cornwall's, contributing significantly to the economic decline of Lydford. In the 19th century the area was bisected by a railway line, whose dismantled course runs across Fig. 6.2. Thus one of England's best-preserved small *burghal* plans now seems rather isolated down a byway from the main roads of its area. But at the junction of the road from Lydford with the Okehampton–Tavistock road, just visible in the extreme top right of our photograph, the pathway which continues on to Dartmoor was still called Moor Gate in the late 19th century – a reminder of Lydford's historic connection with its once mineral-rich hinterland.

NEW TOWN DEFENCES

Among the many new towns in the South West, only one was defended. At Launceston the earls of Cornwall developed a market centre in association with their castle. Here town walls, as elsewhere in England, provided security for a commercial community as well as a symbol of Launceston's status as the earl's borough and of its separateness from rural society. A view from the east reveals Launceston's medieval origins preserved in the modern landscape but surrounded by later growths (Fig. 6.3). What we today call Launceston was a creation of the Norman Conquest. The earlier centre had been at St Stephen's, where there was a house of secular canons and market also called Launceston (*lan-stefan-ton*). St Stephen's is situated north-west of medieval and modern Launceston (which eventually took its name) and lies outside the photograph along the road which leaves the frame upper-right. The castle site, which occupies the centre of the illustration, was founded before 1086 by Robert of Mortain, who chose this valley-spur site for his castle and also established there a new town, called Dunheved. This new complex was a base with both military and economic value, sited near the main land route across the Tamar into Cornwall. To help make it viable, he transferred the market there from St Stephen's, which eventually declined, though it was still a flourishing centre in the 14th century. Robert of Mortain thus created two of the hallmark characteristics of Norman colonisation – a castle and a new town. In the 12th century the collegiate church at St Stephen's was suppressed and the third classic feature of Norman colonisation, a new ecclesiastical presence, appeared in the form of an Augustinian priory. Founded in about 1140 by the bishop of Exeter, this lay between Launceston and St Stephen's. The final medieval component was a suburb called Newport, which had separate legal status as a new town by the late 13th century. Situated outside Launceston in the direction of St Stephen's, it has retained the name and lies off the right of our view.

The photograph covers part of a complex site to which issues of status, security and defence directly relate. Central to the view is the castle and town, established as the centre of Norman administration for Cornwall. Although the administrative centre of

Fig. 6.3 Launceston, Cornwall, *a view from the east.*

the earldom (and later the Duchy) of Cornwall shifted to Restormel/Lostwithiel at the end of the 13th century, Launceston remained the centre of shire business down to the early 19th century. The castle consisted of a massive motte with a large bailey. Excavation has revealed its evolution from a timber-built fortification to a collection of major stone-built defences and residential structures. Prominent in the photograph are the twin structures on the motte top, as well as parts of the bailey walls and a gatehouse visible on the left. Immediately outside the castle, the curving street and house plots reflect the perimeter of the castle's defences.

Below the motte and within the town, the parish church is visible: it existed as a chapel by the late 13th century (but was parochial from 1380) and its building reflected the growth of the urban community and its achievement of independence from existing religious centres. It was extensively rebuilt early in the 16th century. Another major signal of urban self-esteem comes from documentary evidence, from the early 13th century onwards, that the town was walled (its earliest known borough charter is also from this period). Whether it had always been enclosed – perhaps initially in timber – we do not know. But it has been suggested that the primary Norman settlement of the 1070s may have been a single large enclosure, within which the distinction between independently defensible castle and town emerged as occupation and building gradually developed along separate lines. But enclosing the town in stone during the 13th century reflected a national trend towards more clearly defined urban consciousness. According to early modern travellers the walls were in good condition, but they subsequently disappeared, most of the gates being demolished in the early 19th century. The route of the defences can, however, be traced and the South Gate still stands, just visible on the mid-left of the photograph where the north–south internal High Street joins the line of the former town wall. The long curving road which runs from the right edge of the photograph across the lower centre and then back in the castle's direction reflects the course of the defences, the town wall having stood just within this line. Launceston was already outgrowing its defended perimeter in the medieval period: the built-up area on the right-hand extremity of the photograph is successor to a suburb outside the north gate first documented in the 13th century. On the left side of the photograph lies part of the larger built-up area of the modern town. At Launceston, defence in the strictly military sense was probably never an issue – indeed, despite the military circumstances of its foundation at the Norman Conquest, the castle itself never had a defensive life in real terms and its evolution, too, was influenced primarily by matters of status and security.

The final dimension to this castle's landscape context is its relationship with the rural area shown immediately above the castle in the photograph. Here a small valley is occupied by the Kensey, a tributary stream of the River Tamar. The valley contained a very important structure in the medieval manorial economy, a water mill, known as the Castle Mill, first referred to in the late 12th century (but presumably older) and lying immediately below the castle. The valley also contained a deer-park, for whose maintenance there is both documentary record (it is first referred to in the late 13th century but was not necessarily new at that point) and archaeological evidence in the form of deer-bones excavated within the castle. Deer-parks were important resources of the medieval economy, in addition to their role as high-status social environments that could be manipulated for aesthetic effect. When immediately adjacent to a castle or rich house, they afforded pleasant views devoid of the clutter of peasant settlement as well as a facility for the outdoor entertainment of guests. The 13th-century tower on the motte at Launceston has a large window overlooking the park: from this tower the earl, his representatives or guests could survey a fine piece of manipulated landscape whose character was in marked contrast to the busy market town which flanked the castle's other side. The castle stood at the interface of sharply contrasting, but very complementary environments.

LANDSCAPES OF DEFENCE, SECURITY AND STATUS

CASTLE BUILDING FROM THE NORMAN CONQUEST

The most obvious phenomenon of the medieval concern for status, security and defence was the proliferation of castles, beginning at the Norman Conquest and lasting for centuries. This process started with King William's foundation of Exeter Castle in 1068 after his siege of the city. It was drawing to a close around 1500, when the owner of the manor house at Compton (Devon) added a pseudo-defensive façade to its frontage, motivated by a mixture of domestic security and a desire to create a house in the castle tradition of rich rural society.

In our present-day environment, castle sites may be either relict or living; some also had permanent impact on their surroundings. At Exeter, despite the loss of its outer enclosure to encroaching streets, the inner enclosure fossilised the shape of a whole zone of the city. Exeter Castle was a living institution until very recently: the law courts functioned there until late in 2004. Not far away, at Powderham on the Exe estuary, the late 14th-century fortified house built by the junior branch of the Courtenay family is still occupied by their descendants, and thus lives as a castle in a real, social sense.

A majority of castles have become relict features, however, even though some of their associated landscape features are still living. The classic examples are castles with urban connections. Thus, for example, at Okehampton the castle founded in the late 11th century and its adjacent hunting park (enclosed in the early 14th) are both abandoned, whereas the present town, located away from the castle, is the direct descendant of the borough founded by the castle's first lord before 1086 and granted a charter by one of his successors early in the 13th century. These components are mapped in Fig. 6.4, which also shows the location of another relict feature, the original site of a priory that later moved to Forde, now in Dorset. Similar situations apply at Great Torrington, Plympton and Launceston, where castle and town were conjoined, and at High Week the castle earthworks may represent an early manorial centre of the estate on whose edge the borough of Newton Bushel was later founded (in 1246) by the then lord of the manor. Together with the abbot of Torre's adjacent borough of Newton Abbot, it makes up the modern town of that name. At Bampton, Winkleigh and Tregony, castle settlements that were originally medieval boroughs later declined so that while still evident in the landscape they are small and now more rural in character. At Berry Pomeroy, centre of the Pomeroy estates, a dislocated settlement pattern existed, but here with a difference: the borough of Bridgetown (carved from Berry Pomeroy parish) was developed in the 13th century by the Pomeroy lords when their manor house was near the church in Berry but *before* their manor was provided with a castle in the 15th century. In modern times, the borough has lost its separate status and is part of Totnes. Berry Pomeroy Castle, however, was situated within a hunting park established in the early 13th century and with which it made a small seigneurial landscape. This was later enhanced with three meres (probably originally fishponds) in the valley below, from which fine views of the castle, rebuilt in renaissance

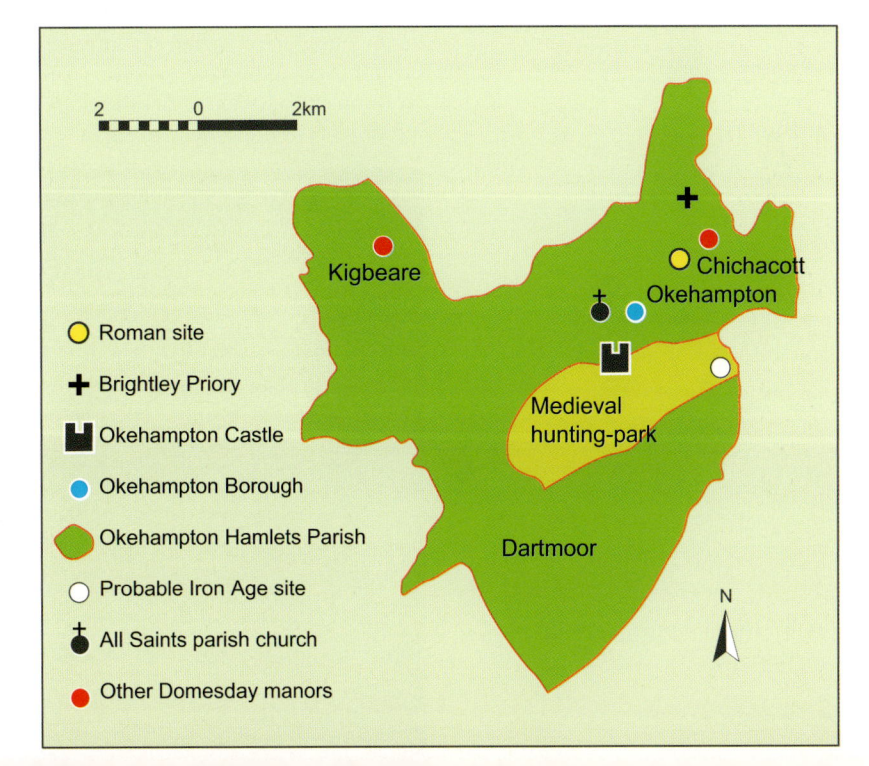

Fig. 6.4 Okehampton, Devon, *main settlement components.*

LANDSCAPES OF DEFENCE, SECURITY AND STATUS

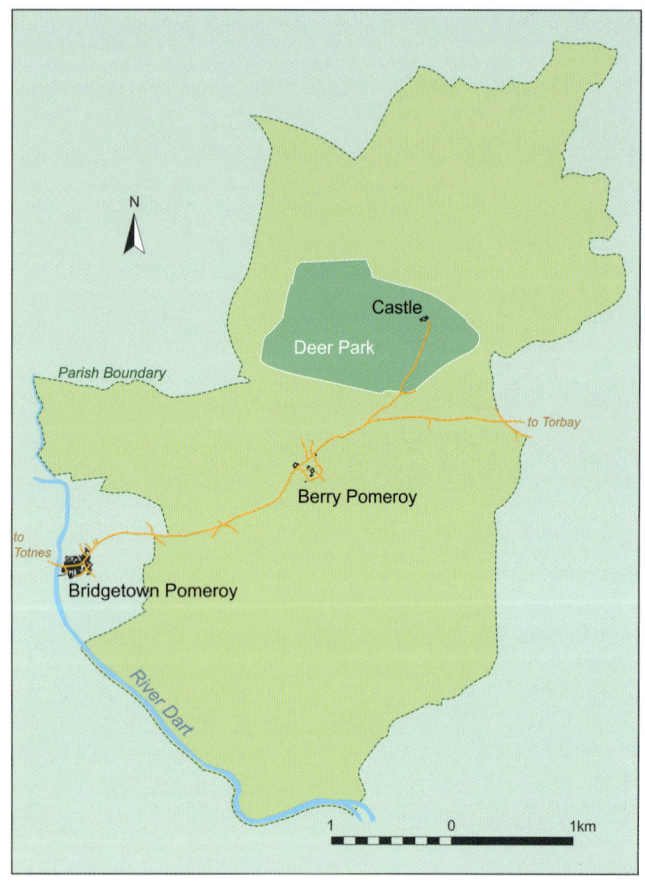

Fig. 6.5 Berry Pomeroy, *Devon, main settlement components.*

architectural style in the 16th and 17th centuries by the Seymours, could be enjoyed. The situation is illustrated in Fig. 6.5 (in which, however, the meres are not shown).

Other places shown on Fig. 6.1 reflect variations in settlement history. In Devon, Hemyock and Bickleigh are contrasting examples of small 14th-century castles set in nucleated and dispersed settlements, respectively. At Loddiswell, the castle either belonged to a medieval settlement that has since disappeared or was always isolated, perhaps for short-lived military use or as a hunting lodge. At Parracombe, the castle overlooks a nucleated settlement which is not really a rural village. Its foundation is obscure and it is an open question whether the castle attracted a settlement, or whether the nucleation was brought about by a much later, unrelated, event.

In Cornwall, the castles at Bossiney and Tintagel may reflect a shift of site between the 12th and early 13th centuries, a process which is paralleled elsewhere in England. At Trematon, the castle stood a mile away from the hamlet which was the rural manorial centre. A market appeared by 1086, presumably the origin of the tiny castle-town which occurs in later documents, and the castle soon had its own park. But it was at nearby Saltash, in the same parish, that a much more successful new town developed during the 12th century, adjacent to the ferry-point across the River Tamar. At Kilkhampton the relationship of the castle's use to the promotion of the village, half a mile away, to a market centre by the 13th century, remains unknown. At Cardinham, the manorial context of the early castle, a mile away from the later manorial centre, is also obscure.

An aerial photograph of Okehampton (Fig. 6.6) shows some of the territory in Fig. 6.4, viewed from the south. Here, the positions of castle, borough and parish church are distinct, a frequent feature of seigneurial landscapes in regions with dispersed settlement patterns. They are clearly visible on the photograph: castle at centre-left; borough at centre-right; church (tower behind trees) at upper-left-centre. This landscape, whose origins lay in the early Norman period, was further developed in about 1300 with the Courtenays' hunting park on the edge of Dartmoor (in the picture foreground).

Fig. 6.6 Okehampton, *Devon, a view from the south.*

98

Another aerial photograph (Fig. 6.7) illustrates Week St Mary, in north-east Cornwall, viewed from the north-east. This was originally a rural settlement whose Norman landlords (named Wyke) built a small castle as their manorial centre and who in the 13th century promoted the existing settlement to the status of a small rural market town with a market place and burgage tenements. The castle is evidence of seigneurial interest and this became the basis of economic investment. In the sub-rectangular field immediately to the right of the church the castle earthworks survive, representing the remains of a low motte that formed the castle's nucleus. Like other declined rural boroughs, the settlement now has more of the character of what would be called a village in other parts of England.

Fig. 6.7 Week St Mary, Cornwall, *a view from the north-east.*

At Restormel in Cornwall, viewed here from the north (Fig. 6.8), a castle was connected administratively and economically with a town which lay some distance away, as at Okehampton. A simplified map of the various components of this castle's landscape (Fig. 6.9) shows particularly clearly the outline of its extensive park, which also included a mill. This map is oriented with north at its top, the reverse of the aerial view.

The castle and first borough of Lostwithiel were founded some time in the 12th century by the Cardinan family – the evidence is a retrospective charter of about 1295 – who were prominent tenants of the earls of Cornwall and took their name from their castle at Caerdinham. The borough was a port at the lowest crossing-point over the River Fowey and at its highest tidal point. From the late 14th century onwards, its activities were limited by progressive silting of the river, but up to that time it had been amongst Cornwall's busiest ports. The river is clearly visible at the top of the photograph, broadening out towards its estuary. The castle, on a valley-sited spur a mile north of the borough, would have provided some security for the economic investment that it represented, as well as a seigneurial residence in an important manor. The borough had a new church (St Bartholemew), a grid of streets, a bridge and a quay on its eastern side. In 1268, Earl Richard of Cornwall, on his acquisition of the castle, added part of his own adjacent manor of Penkneth and made a second borough (which was granted its own charter) adjacent to the first and subsequently known as Penknight. New arrangements for markets and other urban rights were granted. The composite town that emerged, together with its modern growths, is visible in the upper-centre of the photograph.

The status of the place was enhanced when Edmund (earl

Fig. 6.8 Restormel, Cornwall, *a view from the north.*

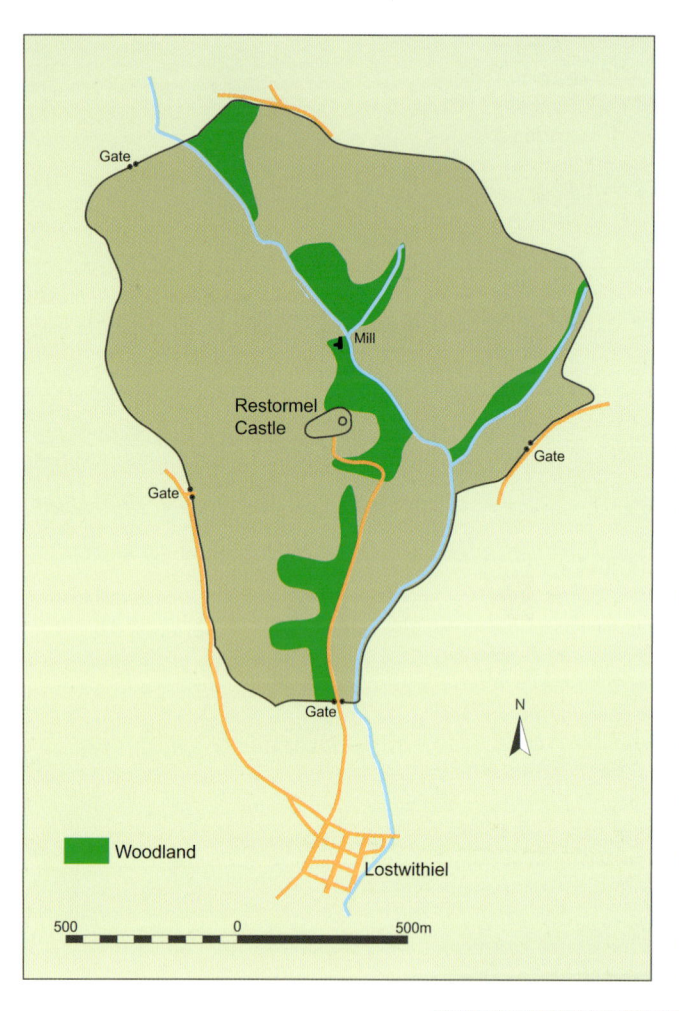

LANDSCAPES OF DEFENCE, SECURITY AND STATUS

1272–99) made Restormel and Lostwithiel his major administrative centre in Cornwall, which it remained under the Duchy, replacing Launceston's earlier functions. Edmund built the administrative block near the quayside and its substantial surviving remains are known, slightly erroneously, as the 'Duchy Palace'. It was particularly important as the centre for the control and taxation of the Cornish tin industry. Lostwithiel and Restormel soon became part of the Duchy of Cornwall, and in 1337, when the Duchy was created for Edward, son of Edward III, the double borough had in excess of 350 burgesses and the castle was described as a sumptuous place with many buildings. The outlines of the town's gridded plan and of its burgage plots are clearly preserved in the present-day layout. The river crossing-point had been bridged by the late 13th century and the present structure is based on a 15th-century replacement. The borough church of St Bartholomew was originally dependent on a rural parochial centre at Lanivery but itself achieved parochial status in the 15th century. It has been suggested that the castle park had been laid out in the mid-12th century with the original castle (whose supposed earlier origins are controversial), although its first documented reference was in 1250. Its perimeter is clearly depicted on the famous map of the southern English coast drawn up for Henry VIII, having been maintained as an economic asset by its later owners. This wooded valley-based park was created around the River Fowey, with the castle at its centre; it may have been deliberately designed so that its original 12th-century aristocratic hunting users were not aware of the 'peasant landscape' of everyday agriculture beyond its upper slopes. If this

ABOVE: ***Fig. 6.9 Restormel, Cornwall**, main settlement components (reverse orientation from Fig. 6.8).*

***Fig. 6.10 Tregony, Cornwall**, a view from the south-west.*

interpretation is correct, it underlines very well how the environs of castles could be manipulated not only for defensive and economic reasons but also to create a social milieu suitable to the high status of their occupants. Restormel's artificially created environment is thus another fascinating example of the phenomenon encountered at Okehampton and discussed above. In so many cases, when castles and parks eventually fell out use and became relict (if prominent) landscape features, the urban foundations to which the castles had given rise became the more permanent and living settlement elements.

Tregony, in Cornwall, viewed here from the south-west (Fig. 6.10), is a declined medieval borough with castle site. Developed by the de Pomeroy family, the borough existed by 1200 and extended from an earlier nucleus around their castle and church, both of which have since been destroyed. It was extended in several stages until it reached St Cuby's church, the original parochial centre (at the top of the picture). Originally a port at the lowest bridging point of the River Fal (lower left quadrant of picture), Tregony declined as the river silted up during the 17th century.

Plympton, south Devon (Fig. 6.11), is the last example of the relationship of castle and new town to be discussed here. The de Redvers lords of Plympton came from Normandy, not with William the Conqueror in 1066 but with Henry I in 1100. Richard de Redvers was enriched with numerous estates that had formerly belonged either to the king or his tenants-in-chief, and from the 1140s, these estates were the basis of the earldom of Devon. Richard de Redvers was also granted the Isle of Wight and lands in Hampshire, for which he developed Carisbrooke Castle as his administrative centre. Richard established two principal manors in Devon as family residences: one an undefended manor house at Tiverton, in the Exe valley, the other a castle at Plympton. At both, there was also significant urban development. This view of Plympton, from the south-east, shows (in the centre of the photograph) the tree-ringed outline of the castle (a large motte and bailey, first referred to in written record in the 1120s) with the parish church immediately east of the motte. The lie of the surrounding streets reflects the castle's outer defences, particularly on the south where a narrow street skirts the castle, forming a back lane to the larger Fore Street that runs parallel to it. Property lines running from both sides of Fore Street probably fossilise burgage tenements of medieval origin. The area between the church and the castle is likely to be an infilled market place. The castle was twice beseiged on behalf of kings, in 1136 (Stephen) and again in 1224 (Henry III). It passed in the 1290s, with all the de Redvers lands, to the Courtenays, who maintained it until the mid-16th century. It was the

Fig. 6.11 Plympton, Devon, *a view from the south-east.*

LANDSCAPES OF DEFENCE, SECURITY AND STATUS

inheritance of the de Redvers wealth, as well as his own family's, which enabled Hugh Courtenay to rebuild Okehampton and transform the house at Tiverton into a castle. He may well have undertaken work at Plympton at the same time.

Although Plympton's charter was not granted until 1194, other documentary records reveal that the borough was in existence by 1130 at the latest. The church adjacent to the castle was first dedicated to St Thomas of Canterbury (re-dedicated to St Maurice in post-medieval times), which may indicate a significant late 12th-century stage in its development, if not origin. There is a strong likelihood that the castle and borough were created from the start in one process of seigneurial investment, with a church emerging as levels of independent urban population and activity became significant. Eventually a small parish (Plympton Erle) was created out of the much larger parish of Plympton St Mary in which the new settlement was situated. The larger unit was a pre-Norman royal estate with a Saxon minster that was re-founded as a priory of Augustinian canons in the early 12th century. The latter lay north-west of the castle-borough, in the upper left of the photograph beyond the modern housing area which occupies its centre. The church visible in the photograph at this point, St Mary's, was originally a chapel built by the priory for parochial use. This point, at the western end of the ridgeway that runs diagonally across the upper right of the photograph, marked the landward limit of Plympton in the medieval period, beyond (from the now-green field in the top left of the photograph) lay the tidal marshes of the Plym estuary. In the medieval period, this tidal creek flowed sufficiently close to the castle-borough to allow access to the River Plym and thence to Plymouth Sound. This connection gave Plympton (a stannary town from the 14th century) some port activity (for the export of slates and tin), and there is an early 13th-century reference to a boat bringing provisions to Plympton Castle from another de Redvers manor at Exminster, on the Exe estuary. As elsewhere in the region, progressive silting eventually killed the maritime link. Thus it is not only the decline of the castle, and eventually the borough, that has altered our perception of the medieval townscape and landscape of Plympton, but also broader topographical change. This phenomenon of the 'castle-town' was observed also at Launceston in Cornwall. But the situations are also significantly different in that whereas at Launceston the town itself was also walled, at Plympton only the castle was defended. The borough was prosperous in its heyday, which lasted down to the 18th century. Later, however, it acquired a character that one commentator has described as 'what one imagines a Gascon *bastide* would have looked like if Gascony had remained English until today'.

It has sometimes been said that Norman castles are more interesting than those of the later medieval period, but the latter have received much academic rehabilitation in recent years. Powderham Castle was established in the 14th century, then transformed on several occasions and its surroundings altered by a succession of owners. In Fig. 6.12 the site is shown from the south-west, set in parkland bounded by the River Exe at the top and its tributary stream, the Kenn, at the bottom, with a hamlet beyond the castle and a small parish church just visible by the estuary edge. It might be supposed that this view reveals a medieval landscape, with castellated house in surroundings deliberately created by its lords and now comprising a collection of relict

Fig. 6.12 Powderham, Devon, *a view from the south-west.*

features. While there are certainly medieval components, what we see is the product of an evolution that stretched down to the 19th century. The manor, including land to the west of the area illustrated, came in 1325 to Hugh Courtenay, son of the lord of Okehampton, as part of the marriage portion of his wife, Margaret, daughter of the Earl of Hereford. After her death in 1390 it was settled on their fourth son, Sir Philip Courtenay. He established the castle and his descendants remained there as a junior Courtenay branch. Their castle was a secure home, which contributed to the defence of the estuary and, from its prominent position, proclaimed their wealth to anyone sailing in the Exe: they had shipping interests as well as landed ones. They survived their senior relatives and this family has remained in continuous occupation at Powderham ever since, the earldom of Devon being revived for them in the early 19th century. Thus in both family and landscape terms, Powderham has remained a 'living' castle down to the present day.

Powderham was attacked in 1455, during the Wars of the Roses, further building work was recorded in 1539 and 1540, and again the site was attacked in 1645, during the Civil War. Major works are documented for 1710–27, the 1750s and 1760s, the 1790s, 1840s and 1860s. These investments resulted in the medieval house being progressively truncated and buried within new structures, its original character being lost in the process but the country house role of the medieval castle being re-enforced. In the first half of the 18th century, the Courtenays embanked the estuary with a new sea wall and road. This reclamation increased the acreage of the northern part of the manor at the expense of salt marshes. Further land-improvement in the 1780s transformed the River Kenn from a broad tidal inlet into a narrower, canalised water-course. The combined effect of these changes was to alter the castle's setting from a maritime one to a more land-locked one. Between about 1765 and 1780, the area around the castle was redesigned as a formal deer-park that stretched from the Kenn northwards to the hamlet of Powderham, and from the reclaimed estuary edge inland to a point west of the castle. Transformation into the castle and landscape depicted in Fig. 6.12 was completed in the 19th century, with new building works, new access southwards to Kenton and the building of the Exeter–Plymouth railway, which completed its isolation from the Exe.

COASTAL DEFENCES

From the late 15th century onwards, a connecting theme for many new fortified places was provided by coastal defence. This had late medieval precedent in the 14th-century works carried out at Plymouth and Dartmouth, and at Fowey and St Ives in the 15th century. But it was from the work at Dartmouth, built at local initiative but with royal financial support between 1481 and 1494, that a new era in south-western defensive traditions sprang. By then there was increasingly a sense that security of the coasts of the region was a matter not just of local concern but of national importance. This emphasis is graphically illustrated by three maps recently published in the *Historical Atlas of South West England* (see Further Reading) depicting defensive works built at various dates between about 1500 and the mid-20th century. From the early 16th century, coastal defence was increasingly a royal rather than local responsibility.

By the early 16th century, additional works had been added to Plymouth and Dartmouth and new ones built at Salcombe and Brixham in Devon and St Michael's Mount and Penryn in Cornwall. Thereafter, there was a more or less continuous history of building at many locations. The total of coastal installations shown on the three published maps runs into dozens. Many of them were small and have no surviving remains. The larger and better-preserved examples, which looked out to sea but often also had landward defences, are important more for

Fig. 6.13 Dartmouth, Devon, *a view from the estuary into the harbour.*

what they tell us about national defence and the evolution of military technology than for any major impact upon settlement or landscape history. Nevertheless, the concept of 'status', so important in the Middle Ages, did not disappear. Just as medieval castles represented the status of their builders within society, the fortifications built by later kings, queens and governments were not only instruments of defence but also symbols of power, intended to impress contemporary foreign rulers with seriousness of intent.

In the Dart estuary and the environs of Dartmouth, south Devon, fortifications were built from the 14th century onwards (Fig. 6.13). Visible are Kingswear Castle (bottom right), Dartmouth Castle (upper centre left) and Bayard's Cove Castle (faintly visible on the Dartmouth shore, centre view). These and others represent concern with securing a major harbour, rather than defence of the town itself and were not castles in the medieval social sense. Dartmouth Castle was an innovative artillery fortification, built between 1481 and 1494, at the interface of medieval and modern defensive traditions. It was connected to the opposite bank of the estuary by a chain system.

The fort at Pendennis on the south Cornish coast (Fig. 6.14) is one of many elements in the scheme of coastal defences organised by Henry VIII. Faced with the prospect of a combined threat from both France and Spain, he undertook massive expenditure on a series of forts stretching from East Anglia to south-west Wales. Pendennis was one of two fortifications guarding the approaches to the deep-water anchorage in the Carrick Roads, the other fort being at St Mawes situated on its eastern side (*see* Fig. 6.1). Pendennis was built in 1540–5 and much extended between 1597 and 1611. This view is taken from the south-east, looking along the narrow peninsula that separates Falmouth Bay (on the left) from what is now Falmouth harbour (at top right). The core of the fort is the circular tower with its surrounding earth-filled wall. A circular form is characteristic of Henry VIII's coastal defences. Pendennis had several levels of gun emplacements and its original design was soon altered by the addition of the governor's lodging. At the extremity of the peninsula, at the bottom of the view, was a small artillery blockhouse also built in the 1540s, providing shoreline strength – neither Pendennis nor St Mawes were themselves on the shoreline. The Elizabethan works, stimulated by the scare of Spanish invasion, took a different form, employing the up-to-date angled bastion at various points on a massive stone-revetted earthwork perimeter. This perimeter, with its wide, dry ditch, is clearly visible in the photograph. Later, earthworks were also built across the neck of the peninsula to provide protection from landward attack. Surviving internal buildings are from about 1800 onwards, the earlier ones having disappeared. The defences of Pendennis were continuously maintained. The fort suffered a prolonged siege in 1646. In the 18th century, further batteries were added beyond the perimeter of the Elizabethan plan, and these were enhanced during the Napoleonic wars. Armament was still in use here in the Second World War.

The contrast with Dartmouth Castle is considerable. Although the latter had moved away from traditional concepts of the medieval castle, in its innovative and large gun ports (and in not being a high-status residential site), it retained some medieval characteristics in its tower and blockhouse shape. And although it was built away from the medieval town, it was built to protect its harbour at the initiative of its townsfolk. At Pendennis, by contrast, the modern world of fortification is clear: it was a purely royal work (reflecting defensive need as well as national status), part of a wider scheme (which medieval fortifications rarely were) and employed new physical forms. It was placed at a forward point to guard the seaward approach to a sensitive area rather than to guard a specific settlement. Indeed, Pendennis and Falmouth are excellent examples with which to illustrate this point, for Falmouth (at the top of the photograph) hardly existed when the fort was first built. The town owed its growth to the efforts of a local family's investment, eventually receiving a royal charter in 1661. The medieval ports situated on the deep inlets from the Carrick Roads were at Truro (which survived), at Tregony (which failed because of silting) and at Penryn (up-shore from Falmouth, and which declined as Falmouth grew). Falmouth's development into a flourishing port owed something to the security of its harbour area provided by the forts at Pendennis and St Mawes. But the fort did not create Falmouth in the sense that some medieval castles created new towns. Their eventual juxtaposition hides a complex narrative, whose first episode lay not in protection of human settlement, but in protection of an important anchorage from use by an attacking fleet.

Thus, as we move through the early modern period, the relationship between defence and landscape remains clear in the sense that fortifications were situated advantageously in relation to topography. The aerial view makes that point abundantly clear in the case of Pendennis. But what changed was the relationship between defence and settlement. The characteristically medieval integration of a social network, drawn from castle, village, scattered hamlet, town and town wall, gave way to a situation in which the military character of fortifications was enhanced, the protection they afforded helped nearby places (whether existing or subsequent) to prosper, but their specifically physical influence on settlement evolution and morphology declined. Thus Pendennis fort is today a relict feature but still well preserved on its sea-girt headland, while Falmouth, beyond, remains a significant port. But their connection is one of juxtaposition rather than integration.

Fig. 6.14 Pendennis, Cornwall, a view from the south-east.

LANDSCAPES OF DEFENCE, SECURITY AND STATUS

Berry Head (Brixham) (Fig. 6.15) is another example of the theme of coastal defence. Here, again, the fortification was aimed not so much at preventing a hostile landing (though it was defensible against attack in the event of this) but more at protecting the anchorage for fleets in Torbay, immediately to its north. In the 16th century, Brixham received an artillery blockhouse during the expansion of coastal defence in Henry VIII's reign when concerns about a French threat were on-going. A gun battery was established at Brixham in 1691, and others were added for the port's defence around 1745 and 1780, including sites on Berry Head. The main military development came, however, in the Revolutionary and Napoleonic Wars, from 1793 onwards, when the Crown purchased the headland. There were several stages of enhancement over the next 20 years but the site was dismantled in 1817 when the wars were concluded. There was also investment in Brixham itself, with a military hospital, store-houses, a pier and an improved quay.

It is these works of about 1800 for which Brixham is well known and their setting is well illustrated in Fig. 6.15. It looks from east to west, along the headland, with Berry Head in the foreground with Brixham beyond, and the view stretching away to Churston Point, with Torbay on the right. Brixham itself is now surrounded by broad modern extensions of its built-up area. Originally it had a long, narrow shape, its harbour settlement connected with the higher-lying rural nucleus of Higher Brixham and the parish church. The long breakwater defines Brixham's outer harbour and the inner harbour, mainly an 18th-century development, is visible beyond with its pier and quays.

The most obvious element visible in the photograph is the stone-revetted earthwork, with angled ends and dry moat, built across the narrow neck of the peninsula to protect the approach to the main battery and the now-disappeared barracks and other structures that lay within. Its parapet had embrasures and platforms for 12-pound guns. At the tip of the headland was the principal Half Moon Battery, whose outline can just be discerned, housing twelve 42-pound guns. Also prominent is the perimeter of the southern fort, built as a forward point of protection for the headland fort, and situated where the coastline broadens out in the mid-left of the photograph. It had emplacements for eight 24-pound guns, as well as barracks and stores. In the corresponding position on the northern coast (though not visible on the photograph) were two further batteries, Castle Battery and Hardy's Head, for 24-pound guns.

While of great military and naval significance, the heavy fortification of this promontory made no lasting contribution to landscape or settlement history in the senses discussed earlier in relation to medieval castles. The forts were built where best located for their specific purpose of guarding the approach to the Torbay anchorages. Their landscape dimension arises from the advantage their builders took of the natural topography, which offered a prominent headland surrounded by high cliffs. But the forts and their garrisons nevertheless constituted an important specialised settlement for a few decades. The small, un-manned lighthouse, established in 1906 on the headland tip above its steep cliffs and

Fig. 6.15 Berry Head, Devon, a view from the east.

LANDSCAPES OF DEFENCE, SECURITY AND STATUS

clearly visible in the photograph, is an on-going reminder of Berry Head's maritime importance.

To conclude this brief coverage of coastal fortified sites, Fig. 6.16 is a vertical aerial view of Plymouth on which the positions of numerous defensive works are marked. This is not a 'real' map of Plymouth's fortifications in any particular period, but a cumulative depiction starting in the later medieval period and ending, for convenience of illustration, in the mid-19th century. Different types and dates of fortification are not distinguished. The general message of the photograph is very clear: that the protection of Plymouth was addressed seriously over many centuries, first as a port (as at Dartmouth and Fowey) but later also as a naval base and dockyard and south-west England's most populous town. Gradually emerging from amalgamation of originally separate settlements, Plymouth developed as a port and military embarkation point by the end of the 13th century. A towered enclosure (of which but one masonry fragment survives) was built by Sutton Pool harbour in the 14th century, beginning a tradition of defence which has continued without break. Nationally famous amongst these works is the 17th-century Citadel, still a prominent feature of Plymouth's waterfront, and many other elements of this fortified maritime palimpsest also survive. Other, once-important structures have, however, disappeared, including

Fig. 6.16 Plymouth, Devon, accumulated fortification around the city, from the 14th century to the 1840s, superimposed on a vertical aerial photograph. *Some simplification has been introduced in locations of dense activity. The dot symbols represent individual defences, from major forts, through blockhouses, to individual gun batteries, with no differentiation of size, date or type. Some dots represent successive works on the same site. The Plymouth town wall of the 1640s (A) and the defences, begun in the 1750s, around Devonport Dockyard (B) are shown as simplified lines, representing the areas encompassed rather than the actual course of the perimeters. The defensive emphasis in this 500-year period, however, was on seaward protection. From the 1850s onwards, much effort was also put into landward works.*

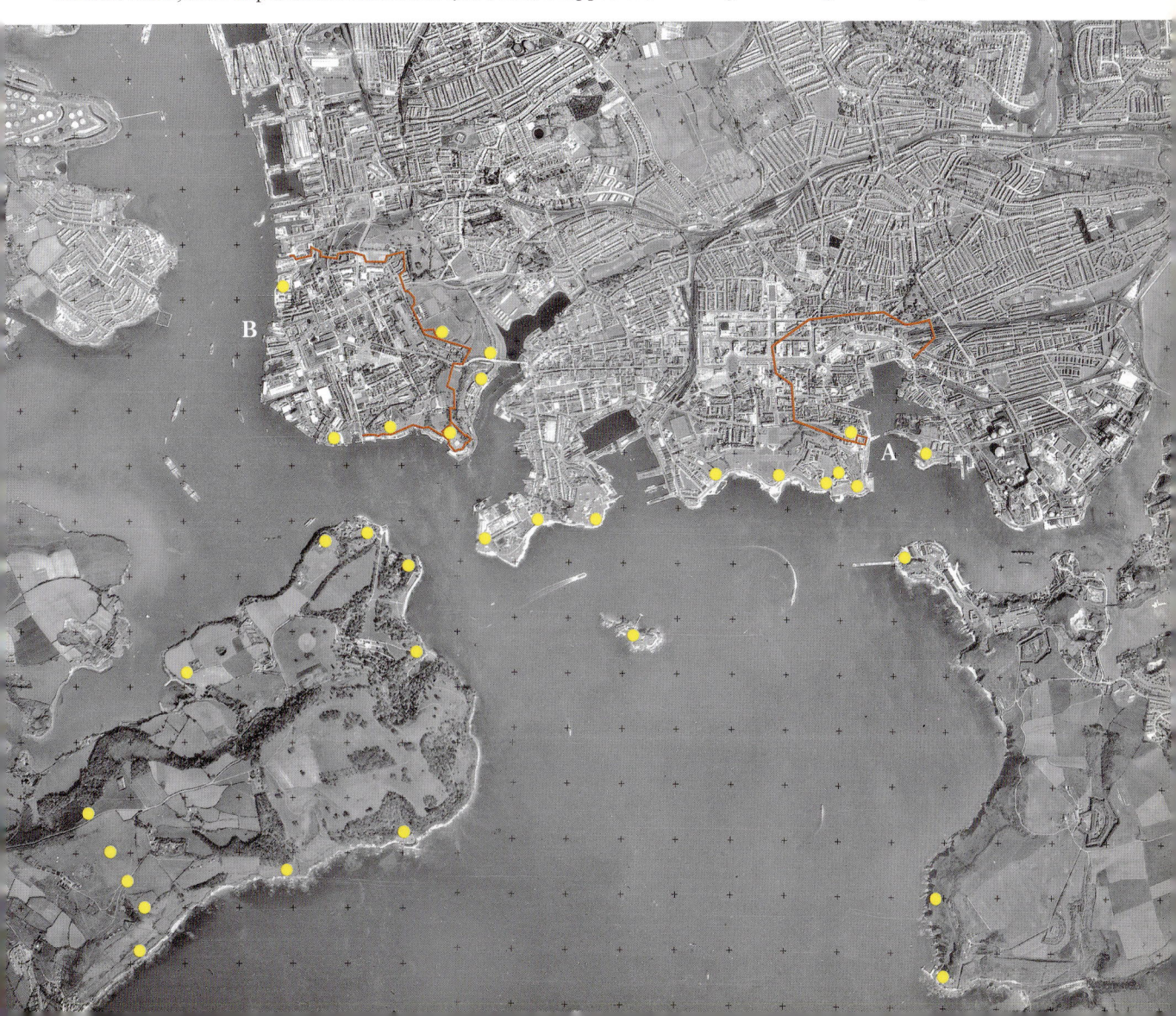

the city walls built in the 1640s. The influence of Plymouth's defensive history upon its townscape has been uneven, sometimes leaving indelible traces but sometimes being more temporary in nature. The maritime environs provided both the necessity and the variety of its defensive history: the anchorage of Plymouth Sound is surrounded by a broken coastline of tidal inlets into which also flow the Tamar and Plym rivers. Up to the mid-19th century, as illustrated here, the emphasis was mainly upon seaward-facing defences. But from the 1850s this was extended northwards to include significant land-facing works.

LANDSCAPE THEMES: A SUMMARY

This chapter has ranged, explicitly and implicitly, over various definitions of landscapes. These have included broad views of geography as well as details of the more immediate surroundings of sites. But attention has also been given to other social, political and military matters: for the landscape approach is not the only way to study defended sites. Indeed, in some cases landscape setting might be a relatively minor attribute, and other themes – for example building design – may be worthy of greater attention. During the 20th century, because of easier access (the motor vehicle) and visibility (the aerial photograph), the archaeological past was increasingly seen to survive not just as individual sites but as connected landscapes, in which relict, historical and modern features co-exist in a contemporary palimpsest.

In looking back over the subject matter of this chapter we can see that all our defended sites are set in landscapes. But it is the medieval castle, whose surroundings were frequently manipulated by their lords, which lend themselves most readily to a landscape appreciation because it is here that the articulation of surrounding human-made elements is most obvious. And it is also within the medieval sites that we can approach landscape most directly in the sense of the artist's view. The open moorland, whose mineral and hunting resources underpinned Lydford's importance, was clearly visible from the Saxon *burh* and later borough: its inhabitants enjoyed a visual connection with their wider landscape. From windows and wall-walks in castles such as Launceston, Restormel and Okehampton, views of adjacent hunting parks could be enjoyed. And, conversely, from within such parks, fine views of the castles themselves could be relished without the encumbrance of intervening rural or urban dwellings. This particular landscape theme began in the context of defended castles, but it was to have a long future in the polite architecture of post-medieval country houses and their landscaped environments. This continuity was no coincidence: castles themselves had often been the country houses of the medieval centuries.

FURTHER READING

Readers wishing to pursue the subject might read some of the following and study appropriate Ordnance Survey maps from the late 19th century onwards. There is also no substitute for visiting the places described here in their landscape settings.

Creighton 2002; reprint 2004.
Duffy *et al.* (eds) 1992.
Griffith 1988.
Higham (ed.) 1987.
Kain and Ravenhill (eds) 1999, especially chapters 19–23, 51 and 52 (by Robert A Higham, Nicholas Orme, Peter Gaunt, Michael Duffy, Mark Blacksell, Harold Fox and Terry Slater, respectively).
Pye and Woodward 1996.
Saunders 1989.
Wilson-North (ed.) 2003.

7

Farming, Fishing and Rural Settlements

MARK OVERTON

The variety of the rural settlement pattern in the South West is greater than for any other area of similar size in England. Figure 7.1 shows a simple threefold classification in which settlement is dominated by nucleated villages, hamlets or

Fig. 7.1 Rural settlement in the South West.

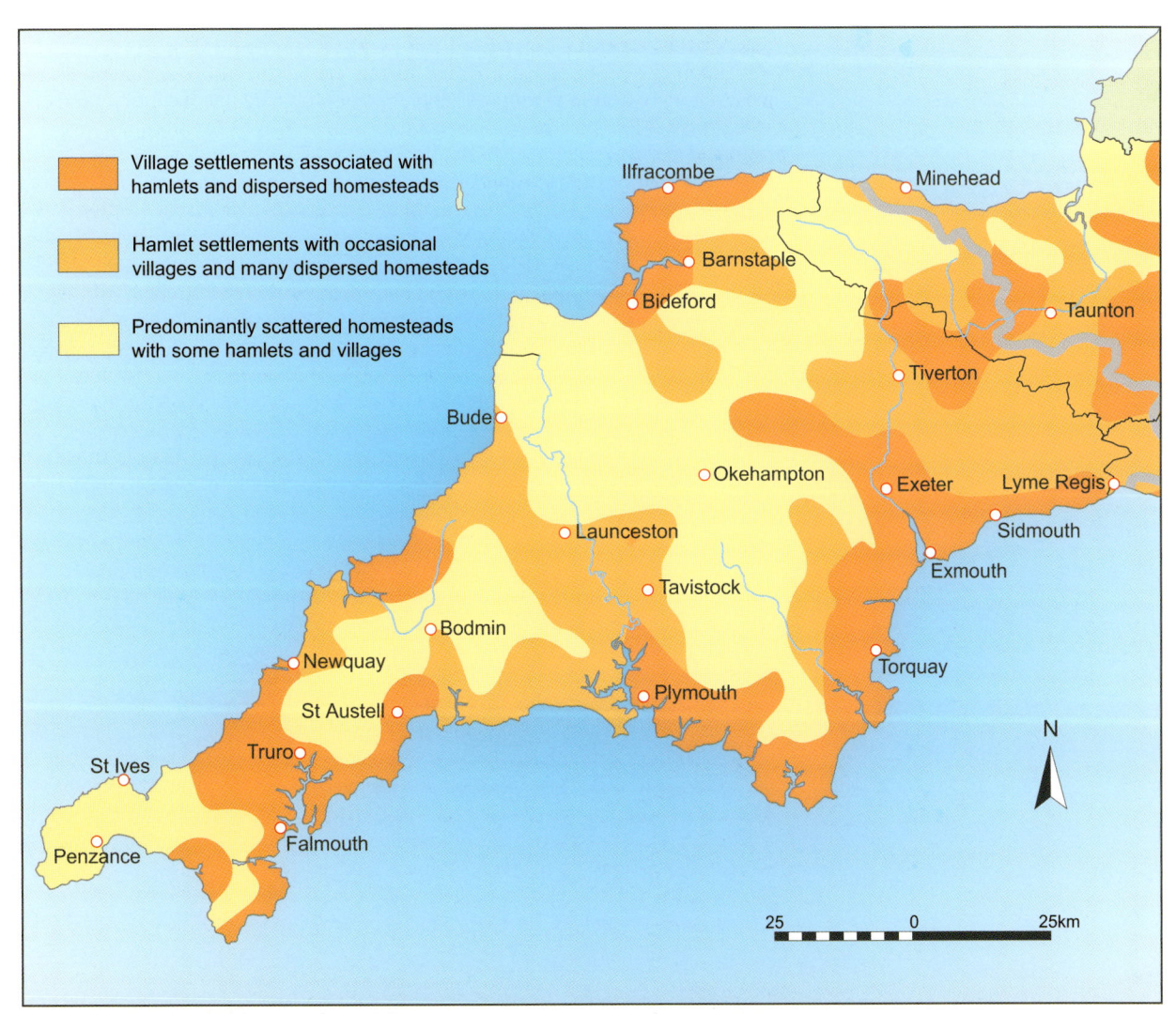

isolated farms. This variety reflects not only the great diversity in soils, topography and climate in the South West, but also the process of colonisation and settlement and the subsequent development of agriculture and field systems. In medieval times farming was mainly for subsistence, so local influences were the most important in shaping agriculture and rural settlement, particularly the size of the local population. By the turn of the 19th century, a national market in many agricultural commodities had come into existence, and rural developments in the South West were subjected to national as well as local influences, particularly developments associated with the 'agricultural revolution', which boosted the efficiency of English agriculture. After 1850 agriculture became increasingly subject to international forces and south-west England's farmers adjusted their farming practices (and their fields, farms and settlements) in response to the pressures of a global market. Free trade eventually led to price falls and depression in the late 19th century, which lingered on until the Second World War. After the war a new rural England came into being; an era of unprecedented growth in the efficiency and productivity of farming and a decline in employment. Overproduction combined with European regulation then contributed to another period of depression in the late 20th century, once again prompting sometimes painful adaptation and diversification in the farming community.

SETTLEMENT EXPANSION AND CONTRACTION FROM MEDIEVAL TIMES TO THE 19TH CENTURY

The first great statistical source in the history of England, the Domesday Book of 1086, records 980 places for Devon and 263 for Cornwall, but this may significantly underestimate the number of separate settlements. It has been estimated that the total number of settlements in Devon was nearer 9,000 and for Cornwall more than 1,500, although these estimates depend on assumptions about the relationship of entries in Domesday to the pattern of settlement on the ground. According to W G Hoskins the number of ploughlands recorded for a manor refers to the number of farms from which rents could be expected. If this is the case, then the pattern of settlement in 1086 was very similar to that of the mid-20th century. Thus many of the farms and villages in the landscape today were in existence at the time of Domesday; and by 1300 – the high-water mark of medieval colonisation – probably most of the farms in existence in the mid-20th century would already have been inhabited.

This is not to say that the same amount of land was under cultivation 700 years ago. In 1086 perhaps half the land of Devon was classed as 'waste', that is uncultivated land, left in a state of almost natural vegetation. As population began to grow in the 13th century, colonisation accelerated, assisted by a charter of 1205 that permitted the 'deforestation' of the whole county (with the exception of Dartmoor and Exmoor). Population pressure in the 13th century saw an expansion of some settlements from a single farm into a hamlet and the reclamation and incorporation of new land into existing farms. Land was colonised on the edges of the high moors, but there was also colonisation and settlement on lower ground: for example by clearing woodland and draining the marshes bordering the lower Exe and Taw. Thus came into being the distinctive south-west English landscapes in which dispersed hamlets co-exist with nucleated villages. Indeed, in many areas of Devon in particular, nucleated villages, hamlets and dispersed farms can all be found within the same tract of country.

There is no doubt that many of the village settlements of medieval times were surrounded by large 'open' fields subdivided into strips, and that the amount of subdivided open field existing in Devon and Cornwall has been underestimated. This is not to say that every village had a regulated common-field system as was

FARMING, FISHING AND RURAL SETTLEMENTS

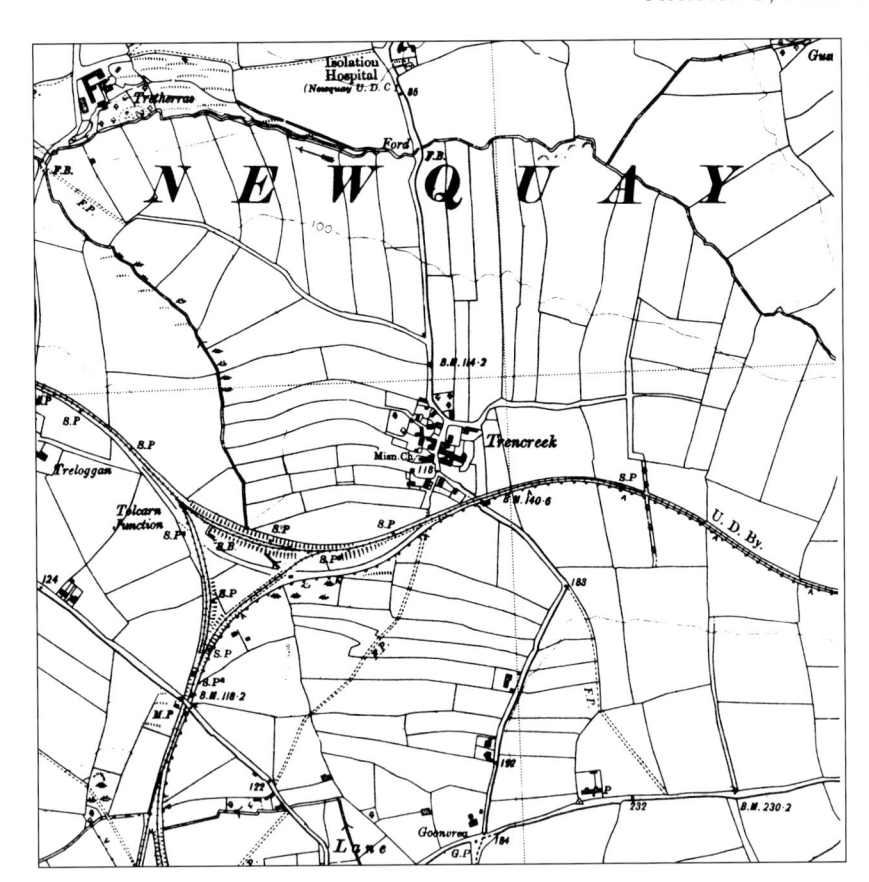

Fig. 7.2 1:10,000 map of the area south-east of Newquay in Cornwall.

normal in the midland counties of England, but it is likely that many villages had arable fields with an individual holding consisting of scattered strips. Strip boundaries are often fossilised in the present-day landscape and can be particularly striking when seen on a 1:10,000 map or from the air. An absence of such boundaries, however, does not necessarily indicate that subdivided strips were not present at some point in the past. Much depends on the circumstances in which the former open field was enclosed. Sometimes areas of former subdivided fields are evident in the present landscape when enclosure resulted in small strip-shaped closes (as in east Devon in medieval times, for example, associated with the establishment of pastoral farming). In other areas, enclosure resulted in larger fields with little suggestion of former strips (for example, enclosure in south Devon in the 16th and 17th centuries). An example of such fossilised strips is shown in Figs 7.2 and 7.3. These fields were part of the field system of the village of Trencreek, now on the eastern edge of the built-up area of Newquay. To the north of the village fossilised strip boundaries are laid out on a north–south axis, and to the south on an east–west axis. To the west of the village the east–west alignment of the original fields is reflected in the orientation of subsequent building development.

Remarkably, the open fields of Braunton in north Devon survive to this day, although not in their original medieval form. The Braunton Great Field is a tract of arable land of about 360 acres (145ha) with no internal hedges, consisting of strips of land (which are the unit of ownership) varying in size from ¾ of an acre (0.3ha) to 6 acres (2.4ha) separated by narrow grass 'baulks'. A document of 1324 refers to the scattered strips and some of the names given to groups of strips are still in use today. Open or subdivided fields existed in a great many forms and it is unwise to infer too much about the operation of a field system, in particular the nature of the property rights to land, without detailed

Fig. 7.3 Aerial view showing fossilised strip boundaries, *just south-east of Newquay in Cornwall.*

documentary evidence. Figure 7.4 gives an impression of how medieval open fields may have looked, but considerable consolidation and enclosure has taken place, so in the medieval period the field system would have been more extensive and many strips would have been narrower. In 1840 for example, 490 strips are mentioned in the Braunton tithe records: this had reduced to about 400 in 1889 and today there are fewer than 200. The Great Field has no statutory protection or historic designation and cannot be classified as an Ancient Monument due to its changing nature. It is particularly vulnerable to the amalgamation of individual strips and the loss of baulks and headstones.

Fig. 7.4 Aerial view of Braunton Great Field in north Devon.

FARMING, FISHING AND RURAL SETTLEMENTS

Another type of field system that was common in the South West was the so-called 'infield-outfield'. The infield was a collection of fields close to the nucleus of the settlement under permanent cultivation, while the outfield consisted of more physically marginal land that was cropped intermittently. Typically, part of the outfield was broken up and cultivated for a few years, before reverting to grass. There was undoubtedly some variation in practice across the South West, but it seems that the outfield waste was cultivated at intervals of between 20 and 40 years. This system was characteristic of areas where pressure of population was low, and where land quality declined away from the centre of the settlement. One example of this is Fig. 7.5, which shows field boundaries in the parish of Towednack on the Penwith peninsula. The infield consists of the small fields close to the settlement, which in medieval times would have been under permanent cultivation. The boundary of the outfield is indicated by the broad sweeping curve.

*Fig. 7.5 **Aerial view of infield-outfield at Amalveor in Towednack** in the Penwith peninsula, Cornwall.*

In 1348 the Black Death arrived in England and within two years between a third and a half of the population had been wiped out. Repeated outbreaks of the plague kept population low until the early 16th century and so it is not surprising that the 14th and 15th centuries saw settlement contraction. Whereas some parts of the country saw the wholesale abandonment of villages, few south-western villages were abandoned because there were comparatively few nucleated villages to start with. But there was considerable settlement contraction as some hamlets shrank in size and others were abandoned. Some regions, such as mid-Devon and the environs of Bodmin Moor, became very sparsely populated, giving the landscape an empty air that it still carries today. Whereas population pressure in the 13th century encouraged the reclamation and cultivation of poor soils on the fringes of Bodmin Moor, they were abandoned as population contracted in the 15th century, and arable cultivation was concentrated on the fertile coastlands. The early medieval arable field systems of two hamlets below Hound Tor on the edge of Dartmoor were abandoned towards the end of the 14th century, as were fields at Venford, although such abandonment was not widespread around Dartmoor (Fig. 7.6).

With the exception of a few isolated examples, the open field of Devon and Cornwall was enclosed before the era of parliamentary enclosure in the 18th and 19th centuries. Indeed, John Hooker, who wrote *A Synopsis Chorographical of*

FARMING, FISHING AND RURAL SETTLEMENTS

Fig. 7.6 Hound Tor *deserted medieval village on Dartmoor, Devon.*

Fig. 7.7 A Devon hedgebank.

Devonshire in the late 16th century, considered 'the most part is enclosed'. Just a little later, Richard Carew described Cornwall as falling 'everywhere from commons to enclosures'. Field boundaries were in part determined by the local landscape and resources, with hedges in the lowlands and stone walls on the moors, but a feature of many Devon field boundaries is the massive hedgebanks, sometimes faced with stone, surmounted by a hedge with trees. As Hooker put it, 'theise growndes for the most part be divided and severed wth mightie greate hedges and dytches' (Fig. 7.7). Cornish hedges are similar, often consisting of two faces of stone containing an earthen or rubble core topped with topsoil and turf.

'Enclosure' is of two kinds. The first, open-field enclosure, was responsible for replacing large subdivided open fields with much smaller, often rectangular, fields, thereby creating ring-fenced farms to replace farms consisting of intermixed arable strips. This kind of enclosure usually saw the removal of common property rights and the establishment of private property entitlements, so that the exclusive rights of ownership of a piece of land also gave exclusive rights of use. The second kind of enclosure was 'reclamation enclosure', that is the physical incorporation of land under a low-intensity agricultural use and its conversion for higher-intensity use. The most common example of this in Devon and Cornwall was the physical enclosure (by hedging or walling) of 'waste' and converting it either to arable or to improved pasture.

While open-field enclosure was almost complete in the South West by the 16th century, reclamation enclosure continued under renewed pressure of population in the century after 1550 and again in the century after 1740. In 1600 perhaps 20 per cent of Devon was under natural vegetation. Most of this was enclosed before 1850, by reclaiming waste adjacent to existing farms and, to a limited extent, by creating new farms. For example, we know from contemporary surveys that Bidwell Farm, in the Devon parish of Thorverton, increased in size from 88 to 105 acres (35 to 43ha) between 1661 and 1800 as new fields were created on the slopes of the Raddon Hills. Some completely new farms were created in the more agriculturally inhospitable upland areas such as the Blackdown Hills. Enclosure of waste continued into the 19th century, and over 10,000 acres (4,000ha) of common and waste were enclosed by parliamentary act in Cornwall between 1775 and 1845 and over 40,000 (16,000ha) in Devon. In particular there was an expansion of farming on the moorland fringes, with 'newtakes' from Dartmoor in the form of large rectangular fields. Many of these 19th-century enclosures have now reverted to moorland or rough grazing.

The most spectacular of all the reclamations in south-west England was on Exmoor. In 1814 the moorland was put up for sale by the Crown and most of it was purchased by John Knight. Subsequently two generations of the Knight family ploughed up uncultivated land, created some 16 new farms and drove new roads across the moor for a period of some 70 years. This created a distinctive landscape of large straight-sided fields with spacious farmhouses surrounded by sycamore and beech windbreaks. They also developed the village of Simonsbath, including its church and post office.

While most English landscapes, including those discussed so far, were but the incidental by-products of economic activity, some distinctive landscapes were consciously designed. From the early 18th century, many landscape parks were constructed around large country houses; as Walpole put it, 'an open country is but a canvass on which a landscape might be designed'. Although the best-known landscape parks lie elsewhere in England, there are good examples in the South West. In Cornwall these include Port Eliot near St Germans, laid out by Repton in 1792–3, and Werrington Park near Launceston, of about 1740. Devon examples include Bicton, extensively developed in both the 18th and 19th centuries, Mamhead, in part developed by Capability Brown, and nearby Ugbrooke Park also developed by Brown (Fig. 7.8). This was laid out for the 4th Baron Clifford in about 1770 and is characteristic of Brown's work, with perimeter woodland along the horizon, and parkland sweeping down to a lake and the house. His idea was to create a landscape composed of water, grass and

Fig. 7.8 Ugbrooke Park in Chudleigh, Devon.

trees, which appeared 'natural', but eliminated the 'false accidents' of nature. Clifford's chaplain, Joseph Reeve, made the point in a poem:

Hence thro' the whole irregularly great,
Nature and Art the wond'rous work complete;
In all so true, so unperceived the skill,
That Nature modified is Nature still.

Our knowledge of the agricultural systems practised in the South West before 1866 is fragmentary, since it was not until then that systematic agricultural statistics were first collected. However, a variety of sources gives us some indication of changing agricultural patterns between the medieval times and the 19th century. Domesday Book records the number of plough teams, which gives an indication of arable farming, as well as an indication of the number of people. The greatest density of arable farming, and the highest population density were found on the rich red soils of east Devon and in the South Hams. By contrast, Cornwall had a very low density of plough teams in 1086, on a par with areas of poor-quality land elsewhere in England, including the Weald and the New Forest. Two centuries after Domesday the evidence from manorial account rolls and tithe records emphasises the importance of rye and oats in arable farming in the South West. There were, however, distinct regional variations: barley and wheat were more common in south Devon, as they were on the lighter soils of the Cornish coastlands, while the extreme east of Devon saw wheat as the predominant crop. Yields were relatively high, since rye and oats were not very demanding crops and were usually grown in rotations with a very long ley. Livestock farming also varied across the two counties in the medieval centuries. South Devon and the Cornish coastlands had an emphasis on dairying, while north and mid-Devon specialised in cattle rearing. Sheep were common across the South West, but in medieval times it seems as though they were small, yielding fleeces with very low weights.

While major ports for coastal and overseas trade were well established in the medieval period, smaller fishing towns and villages began to be established in the 14th and 15th centuries, such as Polperro, Port Isaac and Mevagissey in Cornwall. By the 16th century the Cornish and south Devon coasts were ringed with fishing ports ready to take advantage of the pilchard harvest. The pilchards arrived from Spanish waters in late summer or early autumn and were caught with a seine net. The other main catch in the 16th century was herring, which appeared off the north coast in the autumn. The seasonal nature of the fishery and the hazards associated with other types of fishing meant that most fishing was carried out by farmers as a part-time activity. Since their farms were inland, the buildings that developed on the coast were 'cellar settlements', collections of storage huts along the beach that served as bases for their fishing operations. From the early 16th century, these temporary cellar settlements acquired more permanent residents, although it is likely that most fishermen maintained an interest in another occupation such as farming well into the 18th century. By that time, the fishing grounds extended north to Iceland and across the Atlantic to Newfoundland and New England for cod.

As Fig. 7.9 shows, by 1801 the nature of arable farming in Devon and Cornwall had changed considerably. Rye had almost disappeared and wheat and barley now dominated. In Cornwall (we have insufficient information for Devon) the proportions of wheat and barley were each about 35 per cent and the remaining arable consisted of 20 per cent oats and 5 per cent each of turnips and potatoes. For Cornwall we know that barley had disappeared by 1600, but the reduction in the proportion of oats came after the mid-17th century. There is no obvious explanation as to why the dominant grains changed from relatively low-quality rye and oats to higher-quality wheat and barley. There may have been a gradual change in taste towards wheaten bread and ale or beer made with malted barley

FARMING, FISHING AND RURAL SETTLEMENTS

but we have no clear evidence that this was the case. It is also possible that the production of higher-value crops indicates an increase in inter-regional trade in agricultural products and that at least some of this wheat and barley was being exported from the region. An increase in trade is certainly evident in the livestock sector: although the geography of livestock production appears not to have changed, more cattle reared in the South West were driven to other parts of England, principally the environs of London, to be fattened up for slaughter.

A change in arable cropping was probably accompanied by other improvements, although evidence is fairly sparse. Devon farming had a high reputation, at least with Oliver Cromwell, in the 17th century, and a report on the agriculture of the South West commissioned by the Royal Society in 1664 makes this clear. In Devon the report's author speaks of ley husbandry, land drainage, the extensive use of a wide variety of manures, and soil improvement through the application of sea-sand, lime and marl. However, the arable rotations described in the report for both counties consist of several grain crops taken in succession and cereal yields were not especially high in comparison to other areas. The report also describes a practice called 'beat-burning', 'burn-baking' or 'Denshiring', which continued into the 19th century. Land being reclaimed from waste, or which had been under grass for a considerable time, was stripped of its turf, which was then piled into heaps, allowed to dry and burnt. The ash was then spread over the ground. Beat-burning was a defence against wire-worm and other soil pests and allowed wheat to be grown as the first crop on the reclaimed land. Increasingly, lime was added to the soil at the same time.

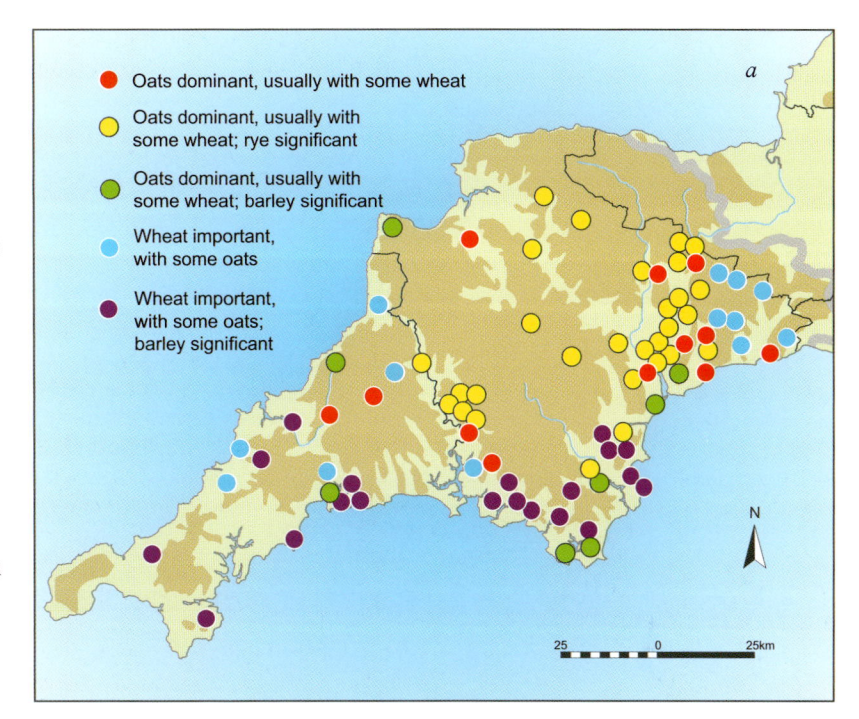

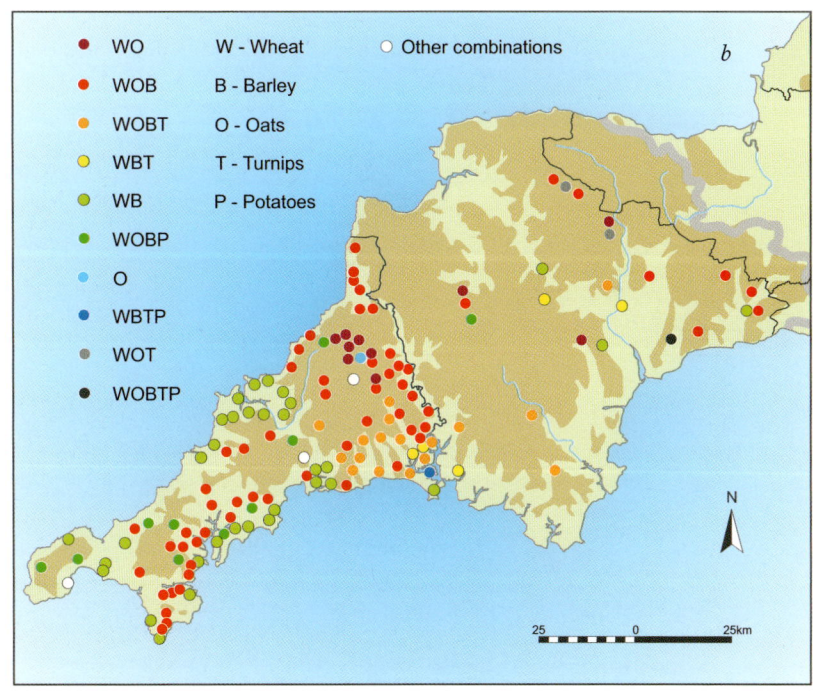

By the 18th century, the pace of agricultural change in the country as a whole was accelerating. Historians continue to debate the timing and nature of the 'agricultural revolution' in England (recent scholarship puts the period of most rapid improvement in the early 19th century) but by 1800 or so, farming in many parts of England was transformed by the integration of turnips and clover into arable rotations, new breeds of cattle, and the removal of common fields by enclosure. It is probably a little unfair to judge the progress of farming in Devon

Fig. 7.9 Medieval crop combinations (a) and crop combinations in 1801 (b).

117

and Cornwall by these criteria, since the arable fields of the two counties had already been enclosed, and their mild climate and long grass-growing season meant that there was less imperative for sowing 'artificial grasses' like clover.

Perhaps this is why contemporary commentators on Devon agriculture such as Charles Vancouver, who published his *General View* of the county's agriculture for the Board of Agriculture in 1808, were not very enthusiastic about the state of the county's farming. Worgan, who wrote the *General View* of Cornwall, thought that 'the adventurous spirit of mining, particularly in the western part of Cornwall, has in some measure withdrawn the industry, attention, and capital from Agriculture', and he later states: 'The general course of crops, in the county of Cornwall, is extremely reprehensible.'

On the other hand another contemporary commentator, William Marshall, regarded some parts of the South West very favourably. He described the 'Vale of Exeter', from the vantage point of Stoke Hill just north of Exeter, in his *Rural Economy of the West of England*, published in 1796, as 'deep rich Vale lands thickly set with Hedgerow Elms, pruned up to poles and rising in close order'. According to Marshall, 'its *happy* Inhabitants' believed it to be, 'the richest finest Country in the world'. This landscape is shown in Fig. 7.10; although now without its standard elms, it is the classic Devon landscape of sunken winding lanes and thatched cob farmhouses.

There is other evidence of agricultural progress, especially in Devon. The 1801 crop returns indicate that in the parish of Diptford in the South Hams, turnips comprised a quarter of the arable acreage (excluding 'artificial grasses'), which was high by the standards of the best 'new husbandry' involving the Norfolk four-course rotation. In other parts of the county the proportions were much lower, and the crop comprised about 10 per cent of cropland on average. Turnips had made some headway into south-east Cornwall (*see* Fig. 7.9) where at least seven parishes had more than 15 per cent of their cropland under turnips, but as with much of Devon it is likely that the 'old Devon course' of three grain crops in succession predominated.

More striking than the appearance of turnips is the intensive cultivation of potatoes in western Cornwall. Although potatoes had been introduced into England in the late 16th century, they did not spread rapidly until the end of the 18th century, when they were to be found in areas of growing population. The extensive cultivation of potatoes was necessary to support the high population densities in the tin- and copper-mining parishes of the west of the peninsula, since in about 1800 an acre of potatoes provided about five times as many calories as an acre of wheat.

Fig. 7.10 Lower Exe valley in Devon, *looking south*.

As Fig. 7.9 shows, the crop appears in a number of crop combinations, reaching more than 25 per cent of cropland in St Just in Penwith.

Although contemporaries castigated arable husbandry, there was general agreement that cattle breeding in Devon had reached a degree of excellence. Indeed no other British county has two native breeds of cattle. This reflects the differences in agriculture between the territory of 'Devon' cattle, in the north of the county, and that of the 'South Devon', found mainly in the South Hams. The Devon was developed by James Quartly from 1776, and then by his son Francis, who ran Great Champson farm from 1793 to 1836. The animals were bred primarily for beef and for traction as oxen. Devons were patronised by the agricultural propagandist Coke of Holkham, and by the 1840s had spread into Cornwall, replacing the original black cattle. The South Devon was recognised as a distinct breed by the end of the 18th century and was valued more for its milk than for its meat. Traditionally it was considered to have been a cross between a Devon and a Guernsey.

THE SOUTH WEST IN THE INTERNATIONAL ECONOMY 1850–1939

The repeal of the Corn Laws in 1846 brought about free trade in agricultural products, and for 20 years or so English farming prospered, during an era known as 'high farming'. In many areas intensive farming systems developed, with high inputs and high outputs, based on the principles of the Norfolk four-course rotation, but now modified and extended to include a wider range of fodder crops. The most intensive systems on the light soils of eastern England included catch crops and were supported by imports of feedstuffs such as oil-cake and fertilisers such as guano. As the century progressed, farming became increasingly mechanised through the use of implements such as seed drills, horse hoes, turnip cutters, threshing machines and mechanical reapers. However, few contemporaries were enthusiastic about Devon farming in the mid-19th century. Small irregular fields, often on steep slopes, were not suitable for the new machines. Yet between the mid-1830s and the mid-1870s there was a remarkable increase in the arable acreage in the South West, due not to an increase in the cultivated area, but to a growth in the cultivation of oats, roots and green crops at the expense of pasture. The 'old Devon course' of three grain crops sown in succession without a fallow crop was in decline, although it still attracted the wrath of contemporary commentators. One of the most striking changes was in mid-Devon, which moved away from a predominantly pastoral regime to become a major arable region.

An important development in the fishing industry during the 19th century was the introduction of trawling to catch fish to be sold fresh. Trawling enabled fish that live close to the seabed (such as cod, plaice, sole and turbot) to be caught with a net. Before that, cod were caught using hooks, which by comparison was highly inefficient. During the 19th century trawling came to dominate the fishing fleets of Brixham and Plymouth. The industry was given a great boost by the arrival of the railway from the mid-century onward since fresh fish could be dispatched to London and the growing cities of the industrial north.

Little change was made to rural settlement in the 19th century. In 1848 a report on Devon agriculture considered that 'A good homestead is rarely to be met with', and many landlords seemed unwilling to invest in their tenants' houses and buildings. Exceptions were the 'model farms' built in the county, as part of a vogue by large landowners for constructing new farms and farm buildings that were both aesthetically pleasing and designed to promote efficient farming. There are 43 documented and recorded examples in Devon and 22 in Cornwall. The best Cornish example is Trebartha Barton, built by the Rodd family who owned most of

Fig. 7.11 Kilworthy model farm near Tavistock, Devon.

the parish of North Hill. An 18th-century example survives on the Killerton estate in Devon, but the most impressive is that at Kilworthy on the Tavistock estate (Fig. 7.11). This model farm formed part of the Duke of Bedford's extensive Devon estates, and in 1851 was rebuilt as a Victorian factory farm, including covered yards and dung pits, and a waterwheel to power barn machinery.

After the 1870s, free trade began to have an adverse effect upon English farming: indeed the last quarter of the 19th century has been referred to as the period of a 'Great Depression' in English agriculture. The main cause of this depression was a fall in agricultural prices. Whereas wheat was sold at an average price of 55 shillings per quarter in the period 1870–4, it had fallen to 28 shillings by 1895–9. Overall, between the late 1870s and the early 1890s the price of wheat fell by 52 per cent, barley by 37 per cent and oats by 34 per cent. Costs did not fall, so many cereal farmers faced a potentially disastrous situation. The fall in prices was in turn caused by a surge of cereal imports, which rose from 1.5 million tonnes in 1870 to almost 3.5 million tonnes by 1900, mostly from the developing prairies in North America, from Argentina and from Russia. Cereals were produced in these areas at much lower cost than in England and under a low-intensity farming system compared with the high-intensity systems in use in England. Technological advance also dramatically reduced the costs of transporting cereals, both within countries through the use of railways, and across the sea in the new screw-driven ships. Although it is difficult to generalise about trends in livestock prices, fat cattle prices fell by 24–30 per cent between the late 1870s and the early 1890s, cheese and butter by 25–33 per cent, sheep by 23 per cent and wool by 40–50 per cent. The price fall was encouraged by the increasing imports of frozen meat and other livestock products from Australia and New Zealand from the 1890s, so that meat imports rose from 5 lbs per head of the population in 1861–5 to 44 lbs in 1906–10. Overall, the proportion of the country's labour force in agriculture fell from 22 per cent in 1850, to 9 per cent in 1900–10 and 6 per cent in 1920–30; agricultural incomes as a proportion of national income fell from 19 per cent in 1870, to 8 per cent in 1900 and 4 per cent around 1930.

The Depression generated two Royal Commissions held during 1880–2 and 1894–7, and it is clear from evidence presented to them that those hardest hit

FARMING, FISHING AND RURAL SETTLEMENTS

were the large cereal farmers of eastern England (and of course their landlords) while the pastoral South West suffered to a much lesser extent. Yet, there were significant changes in both farming and the landscape. The arable area of Devon and Cornwall fell by almost a quarter between 1875 and 1914, while the area under grass rose by 40 per cent (Fig. 7.12). The acreages under wheat and barley fell by 50 per cent and 42 per cent respectively, while the acreage of oats rose by 44 per cent. As Fig. 7.12 shows, the geography of adjustment was uneven. Both west and east Devon demonstrate major contractions in the arable acreage, with a smaller contraction in north Devon, and much lower reductions in arable in Cornwall.

Thus the mainstay of south-west England's farming from 1850 to 1914 was dairying together with sheep and cattle breeding and rearing. The home-fattening of beef increased to supply expanding local markets, and overall the number of cattle, excluding cows and heifers, grew by 60 per cent between 1871 and 1911. Pig production also became a speciality, and by the 1930s Devon and Cornwall accounted for almost 10 per cent of the total pig population of England and Wales. Pig production was strongly associated with dairying, since the pigs were fed on left-over separated milk, and was concentrated particularly in the dairying regions of east Devon and west Cornwall.

Fig. 7.12 Percentage change in arable cultivation in Devon and Cornwall, 1875–1914.

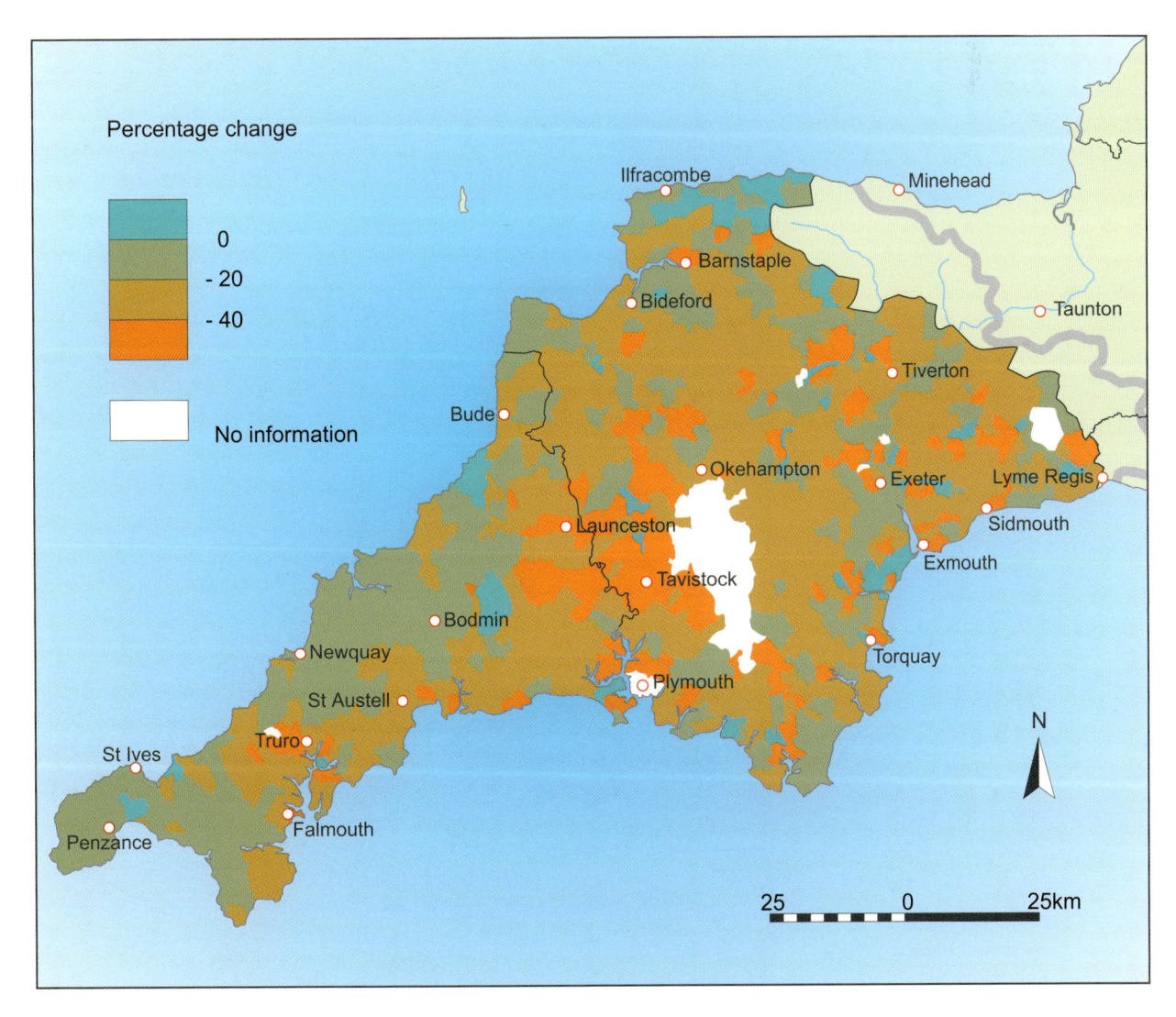

FARMING, FISHING AND RURAL SETTLEMENTS

Fig. 7.13 Market-garden crops in Cornwall.

Diversification of farm production in the face of falling prices and profits took place when farmers could exploit the natural advantages of their farms. In certain areas of the South West these were where good soils and a sheltered position combined with a mild climate to enable early crops to be produced. The key to marketing these crops was the railway, which could speed early vegetable crops to Covent Garden in London and other metropolitan centres. In 1889 the Great Western Railway conveyed 300 tons of strawberries, 4,500 tons of new potatoes and 8,000 tons of broccoli from Devon and Cornwall to large urban centres in the rest of the country. The main areas of market gardening were in: the Tamar valley, which specialised in soft fruit; the Fal estuary; and the Mount's Bay area of western Cornwall, stretching from Mousehole east to Perranuthnoe and north to Hayle (Fig. 7.13). The distinctive landscape between Mousehole and Lamorna Cove consists of tiny fields on the sheltered south and east-facing cliff (Fig. 7.14). These maximised the benefit from low sun angles and were used to cultivate daffodils and potatoes from the late 19th century, taking advantage of the completion of the railway to Penzance. These little fields are now largely abandoned, superseded by the demand for more accessible larger fields that can be cultivated by modern mechanised equipment.

By the 1930s an area east of Gulval was known as the Golden Mile, where vegetables were cultivated continuously. Early potatoes were planted in January

Fig. 7.14 Fields along the coast between Lamorna Cove and Mousehole in Cornwall.

and lifted in June, to be followed by broccoli, which cropped from November to April. There were other small pockets of market-garden production, usually for potatoes, in the hinterland of Plymouth, along the sheltered valleys of the north Devon coast and around Moretonhampstead in mid-Devon.

These agricultural changes were reactions to a changing price environment that was in turn the consequence of free trade initiated by the repeal of the Corn Laws in 1846. The painful adjustments to price falls were temporarily brought to an end as prices soared during the First World War, and in 1917 the government guaranteed cereal prices. After the war, world prices plummeted and there was deep depression in both agriculture and industry. Within this environment protection became politically possible, and from the 1920s onwards, a series of measures was gradually introduced to help the farming community. In 1932 the Wheat Act introduced the deficiency payment, which was the difference between the price at which the farmer sold his product and a notional price set by the government. Also in the early 1930s, Agricultural Marketing Acts reorganised the marketing of milk, potatoes and hops, and the first of these became particularly important for south-west England's farmers, through the establishment in 1933 of the Milk Marketing Board.

Nevertheless, depression continued into the 1930s. By this time most of Devon and Cornwall was dominated by pastoral farming based on permanent grass; in Devon the amount of arable land in the 1930s was roughly a third of what it had been in the 1870s. The depression of the 1920s and 1930s saw a further deterioration in the quality of land in the South West, as in many other parts of the country. A survey of grassland in 1940, for example, saw much of Devon and almost all Cornwall under the poorest quality grassland. Much of the poorer land had become agriculturally sub-marginal and was being abandoned, and farming was now characterised by low inputs and low outputs, sometimes known as 'dog and stick' farming. There was widespread neglect of many essential forms of farm maintenance such as hedging and ditching, and many landowners attempted to survive by cashing in on capital appreciation in other ways. For many, especially in parts of Cornwall, the only profitable crop was of bungalows. With the development of motor traffic in the 1930s, holiday accommodation, often built by speculative builders, developed around Looe, Porthleven, Gwithian, and especially to the north of the Padstow estuary around Polzeath.

The South West is one of England's least wooded areas and at the start of the 20th century only about 3.5 per cent of Cornwall was under woodland, and about 5 per cent in Devon. This reflects the windy environment, especially in Cornwall, but also centuries of felling for boat building and agriculture. Some plantations were created in the 19th century, such as the conifer plantation at Brimpts on Dartmoor, established by the Duchy of Cornwall in 1862, but it was not until the demands of the First World War made further inroads into woodland, and a national concern over its removal led to the establishment of the Forestry Commission in 1919, that there was a real impetus to afforestation. One of the Commission's first initiatives in the South West was the development of Fernworthy Forest on Dartmoor (Fig. 7.15). First planted in 1921 this forest is a good example of a 'commercial forest' as it contains many of the main timber-producing species grown in this country. In 1936 work also began on the nearby reservoir that was designed to provide water for Torbay, and this was completed in 1942.

Changes to farming activity in the South West induced by the Second World War were sudden and dramatic. The agricultural sector of the country as a whole doubled its output during the war and by 1945 was producing about 75 per cent of the country's needs. Much of this was achieved through the 'plough-up' campaign, the object of which was to bring permanent pastures under the plough. The effect of this process in the South West was spectacular. Between June 1939 and June 1943, the arable area of Devon and Cornwall rose by 38 per cent, but the area of tillage by 105 per cent reflecting a fall in the proportion of temporary grass. The acreage of wheat rose by 315 per cent over the period, and there was a fourfold increase in the area under potatoes. Other wartime policies put a strong emphasis on milk production as a health food and this also had a major impact on the farming of the South West.

The consequences of this were that many all-grass farms gave way to farms practising ley husbandry, which integrated grass and arable crops. There was also less distinction in land use, since all farmers were compelled to plough up, irrespective of the nature of their land. Maintenance tasks that had been neglected before the war, such as hedging and ditching and the repair of buildings, were undertaken once again. A shortage of agricultural labour during the war stimulated the adoption of agricultural machinery: in Devon, for example, the number of tractors doubled between June 1942 and June 1944.

Fig. 7.15. Fernworthy reservoir and forestry on Dartmoor.

TABLE 7.1 AGRICULTURAL STATISTICS FOR DEVON AND CORNWALL 1900–2000 (HECTARES FOR CROPS; NUMBERS OF ANIMALS FOR LIVESTOCK)

	1900	1910	1920	1930	1940	1950	1960	1970	1980	1990	2000
Wheat	34,581	28,900	30,051	13,909	17,869	15,433	4,621	8,772	13,118	22,559	33,864
Barley	30,997	29,128	26,554	13,617	18,368	20,597	61,368	72,486	90,949	70,370	51,282
Oats	75,478	75,316	85,692	57,858	75,775	48,473	15,592	14,212	7,448	5,748	6,595
Mixed corn	–	–	23,543	21,843	34,675	62,208	24,237	20,881	6,042	–	–
Potatoes	7,318	6,273	8,554	4,695	8,153	16,706	7,490	5,290	5,275	5,649	4,566
Maize	–	–	–	–	–	–	–	74	1,030	3,411	12,389
Orchards	13,126	13,076	9,968	10,560	10,014	9,264	6,563	1,843	668	519	947
Vegetables	–	–	–	–	3,040	3,852	3,327	4,117	2,619	2,306	2,149
Flowers	–	–	–	–	656	907	1,031	900	516	1,362	2,245
Crops & grass	735,550	737,415	717,692	719,893	708,786	712,223	721,139	716,961	714,692	697,372	659,135
Setaside	–	–	–	–	–	–	–	–	–	2,689	14,085
Cattle	483,711	519,607	496,131	536,788	466,356	722,280	811,454	985,578	1,089,487	1,063,082	977,558
Pigs	184,503	179,559	157,026	226,215	280,289	147,670	373,555	477,039	307,339	268,130	220,180
Sheep	1,246,080	1,330,325	939,041	1,175,007	735,741	986,235	1,598,172	1,651,692	1,969,340	2,638,313	2,425,199
Horses	86,404	93,105	90,687	66,239	19,438	–	–	–	–	–	–

A NEW RURAL ENGLAND

The years of depression were ended after the Second World War by government protection for British farmers. The 1947 Agriculture Act established a framework that guaranteed prices and assured markets for about 80 per cent of the products of British farming. Support from the government also included specific grants and incentives, usually directed at speeding the adoption of new technology. Entry into the European Economic Community in 1973 continued the spirit of the 1947 Act as British farmers continued to enjoy protection. Thus the years from the end of the war until the early 1980s were ones of prosperity for most farmers in the south-west of England as prices were high and markets guaranteed.

Farming readjusted after the war but, taking a longer-term view, the immediate post-war period saw an unprecedented growth in British agricultural output. Over the period 1867–1985 the most rapid growth in output took place between 1946 and 1965, although output continued to grow (at 1.4 per cent per annum) from 1966 to 1985. Nationally, the cereal acreage doubled between the 1930s and the 1980s.

Farmers in the South West responded to the price incentives given by the support structures, as the figures in Table 7.1 demonstrate. These show the area under selected crops (in hectares) and the total numbers of cattle, pigs, sheep and horses in Devon and Cornwall during the 20th century. The total area of crops and grass in the two counties remained roughly constant, although it has fallen since 1980. After 1960 tillage occupied only about 20 per cent of this area and the dominant land use in the South West continued to be pastoral. Within the cereal sector, oats declined dramatically after 1940 to be replaced by barley as the dominant crop, although the barley area had fallen since 1980, while that for wheat was growing. Thus by the early 21st century the area of wheat was more than double what it was in 1950, although still short of its wartime peak. Two recent developments were the increase in the area under maize, which had almost doubled that of oats, and the appearance of 'setaside', land that farmers were paid to leave uncultivated and which amounted to nearly 10 per cent of the area of tillage in 2000.

Before the First World War there were more than 13,000ha of orchards in the South West (mostly in Devon), but under pressure of competition from Europe this shrank to one-twentieth of that size by 1990, although in the subsequent

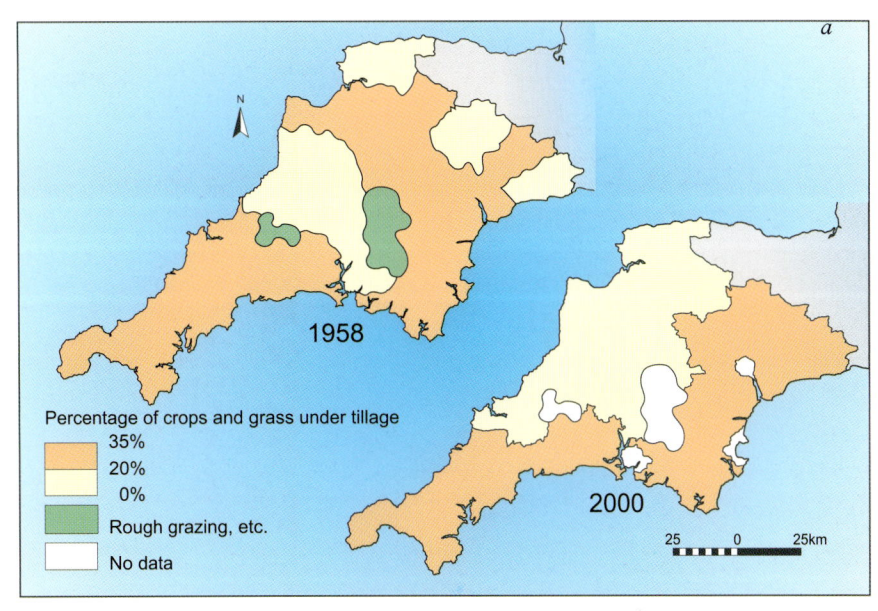

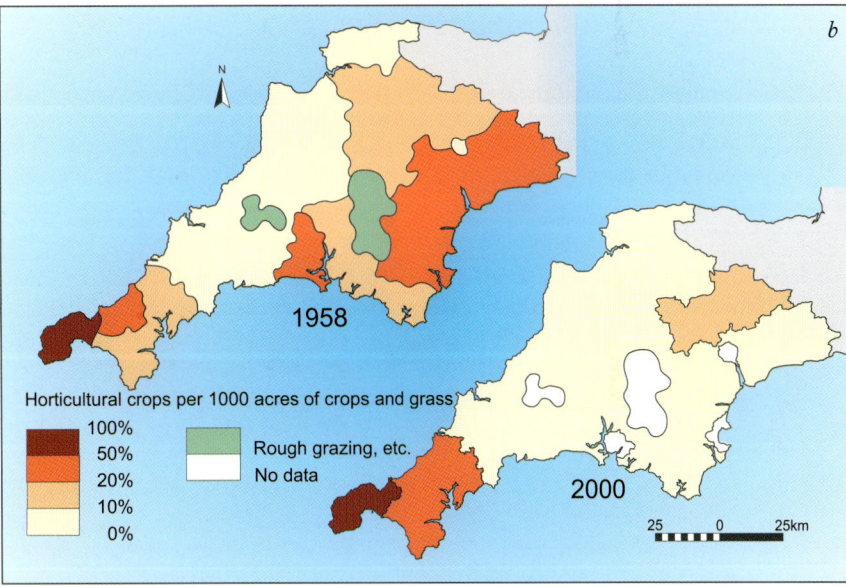

Fig. 7.16 Tillage as a percentage of crops and grass (a), and horticultural crops per 1,000 acres (400ha) of crops and grass (b), 1958 and 2000.

FARMING, FISHING AND RURAL SETTLEMENTS

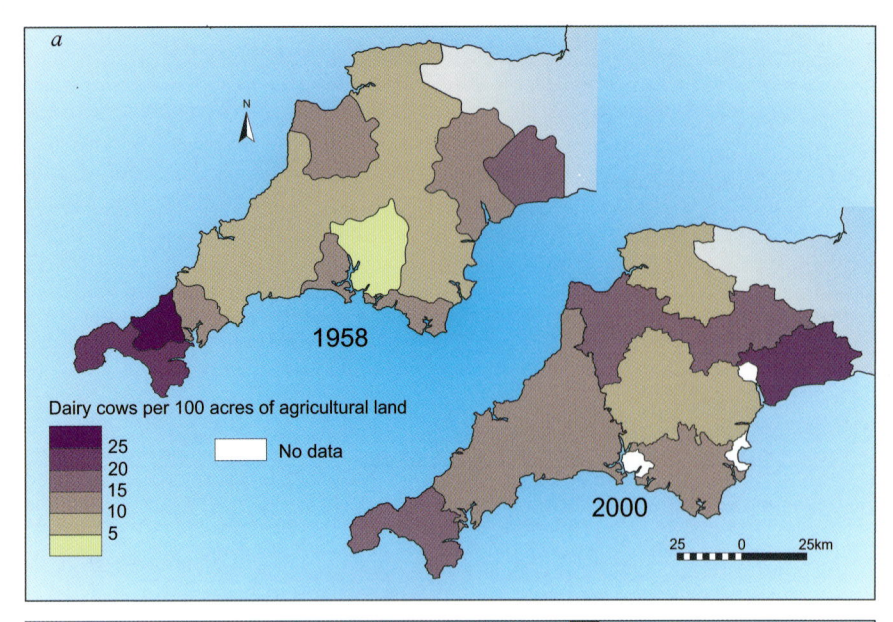

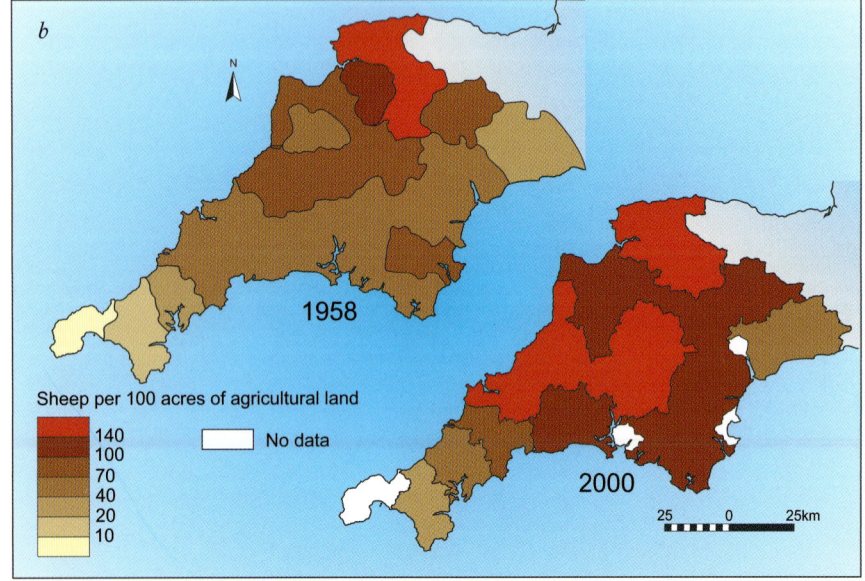

Fig. 7.17 Dairy cows (a) and sheep (b) per 100 acres (40ha) of agricultural land, 1958 and 2000.

decade there was a small increase. The area under vegetables (mostly in Cornwall) rose to a peak in 1970 but by 2000 had fallen to be overtaken by the area devoted to the production of flowers and bulbs. The production of vegetables had been hit by high-quality but cheaper European imports, while a growth in interest in domestic gardening encouraged the production of flowers, bulbs and nursery stock. The numbers of cattle for both beef and dairy rose post-war, but have remained roughly constant for the last 30 years. The rise in the number of sheep continued, with some 2.5 million animals in 2000.

Figures 7.16 and 7.17 show the geography of this changing land use, comparing the pattern in 1958 with that of 2000. The slight reduction in tillage between the two dates occurred on the more marginal soils of north Devon and north Cornwall, while there was an increase in the proportion of tillage in parts of east Devon. The decline in horticultural crops is shown dramatically in Fig. 7.16b. Cultivation of these crops is now concentrated in the far west of Cornwall, whereas in the 1950s there were significant pockets of horticultural crops in the Tamar valley and in east Devon. The number of cattle in the South West grew to some extent after the 1950s, but as Fig. 7.17a shows, the distribution of dairying had become more uniform across Devon and Cornwall, with a decline in the far south-west of Cornwall, and an increase in north and mid Devon. Finally, Fig. 7.17b shows how the considerable increase in the sheep population remained fairly uniform across Devon (with the exception of east Devon) and west Cornwall.

From the 1970s onwards, real farm incomes were on a generally downward path, mainly because of the strength of the pound against European currencies. Real incomes doubled between 1990 and 1995, but they fell by 70 per cent between 1995 and 2000, although by the early years of the 21st century they were rising once again. As in previous periods of falling incomes or 'depression', farmers had to diversify their activities. Whereas in the late 19th century they adjusted the purely agricultural elements of their farm enterprise, diversification in the early 21st century took wider forms. There was, for example, a growth in agricultural contracting as well as increased on-farm processing and sales of produce, which in 2003 were reported on nearly 27 per cent of diversified holdings. This 'added-value' type of enterprise had become a major growth area over the previous ten years. The market for speciality products in particular

FARMING, FISHING AND RURAL SETTLEMENTS

experienced rapid growth through the success of groups such as 'Taste of the West' that created important food links between producers and processors, and generated ancillary employment.

Agricultural intensification led in the past to the loss of some traditional features such as hedges, orchards, woodlands and semi-natural grasslands. Many hedgerow trees were lost in the 1970s through Dutch elm disease. Field amalgamation and hedgerow removal in particular weakened the structure of the traditional rural landscape of some of south-west England's most intensively farmed areas. Although hedgerow removal has become less of a problem, a lack of appropriate hedgerow management has resulted in continued loss. As a result, erosion of the once-strong field-enclosure pattern remains ongoing, albeit at a lesser rate.

The area of the South West under forestry increased sharply from 1980 (Fig. 7.18). The national survey of woodland trees undertaken by the Forestry Commission and completed in 2000, showed that in Devon about 10 per cent of the land area was under woodland of 0.8ha or more, an increase of 12,600ha or a rise from 8 per cent of land area between 1980 and 1997. Moreover, 60 per cent of this was broadleaved woodland, a rise of 45 per cent, while the proportion under conifers was 25 per cent, and that under mixed woodland 13 per cent. For Cornwall, 7.5 per cent of the land area was under

Fig. 7.18 Woodland of more than 2 acres (0.8ha) in Devon and Cornwall, 2002.

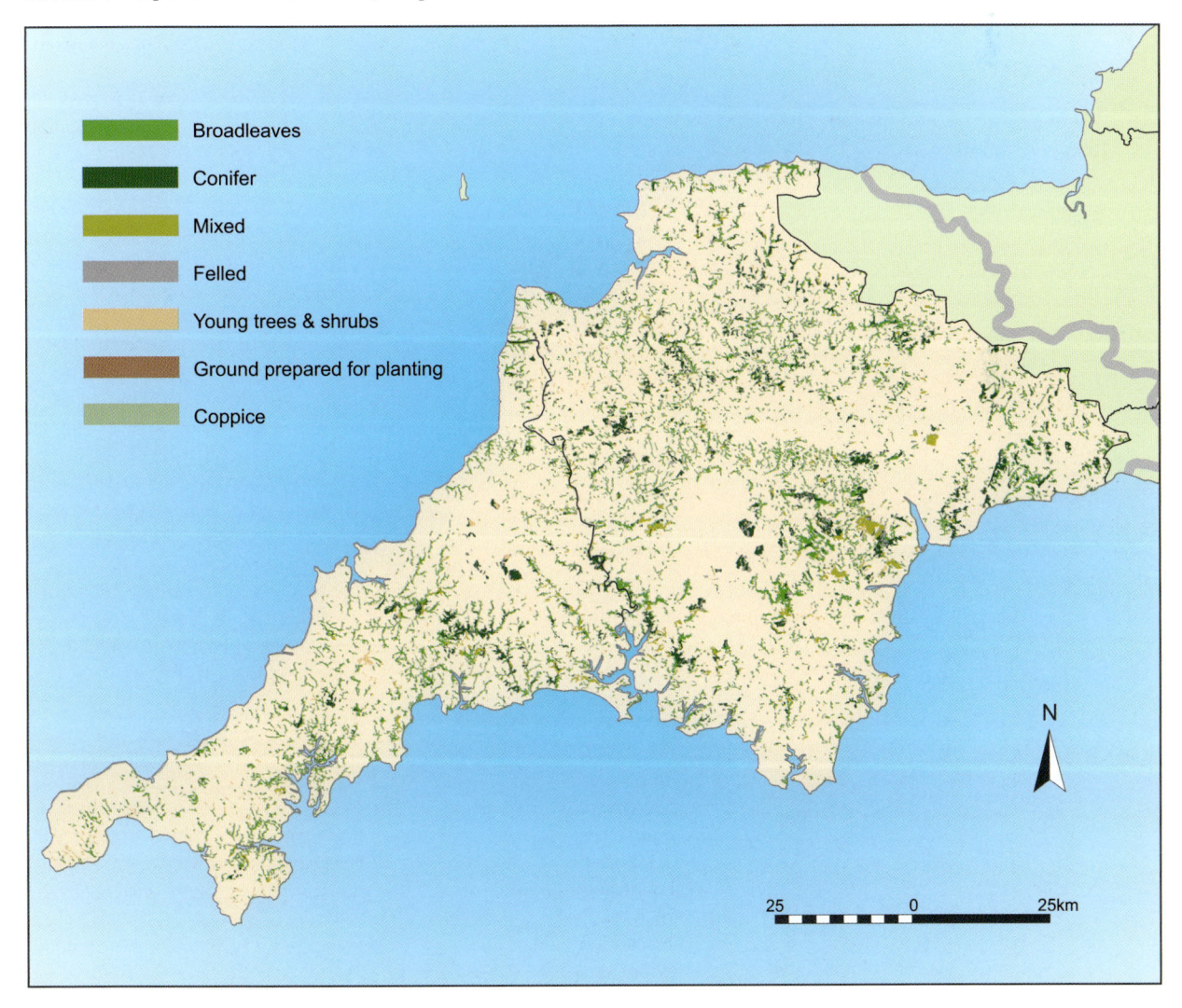

FARMING, FISHING AND RURAL SETTLEMENTS

woodland of more than 0.8ha and 66 per cent of this was broadleaved, with mixed woodland comprising 10 per cent and conifers 19 per cent. Woodland cover increased by 8,500ha from 5 per cent of the county in 1980 and the area of broadleaved woodland increased by 68 per cent.

Figure 7.19 shows another example of woodland and reservoir land use on a marginal upland area. In 1946 nearly 74 per cent of Bodmin Moor was classified as 'moorland, roughland and wetland', but by 1992 this had fallen to 53 per cent. Although the area of improved farmland increased in response to government and then European Community assistance, the proportion of land under forestry increased from 0.3 per cent in 1946 to 6 per cent in 1992. The majority of this afforestation was for conifers and mostly took place in the 1970s, marking a direct transfer of land use from moorland to forestry.

During the 20th century, south-west England's fishing suffered a long period of depression that lasted from the end of the First World War until the 1970s. The Brixham trawler fleet failed to adopt steam or motor propulsion and south-west England's fleet as a whole was the victim of competition from boats from the east-coast ports. Reorganisation and reinvestment in the late 1960s arrested decline. As Fig. 7.20 shows, by 1990 Newlyn and Brixham were the

Fig. 7.19 Colliford reservoir and woodland at Smallacombe Downs on Bodmin Moor, Cornwall.

FARMING, FISHING AND RURAL SETTLEMENTS

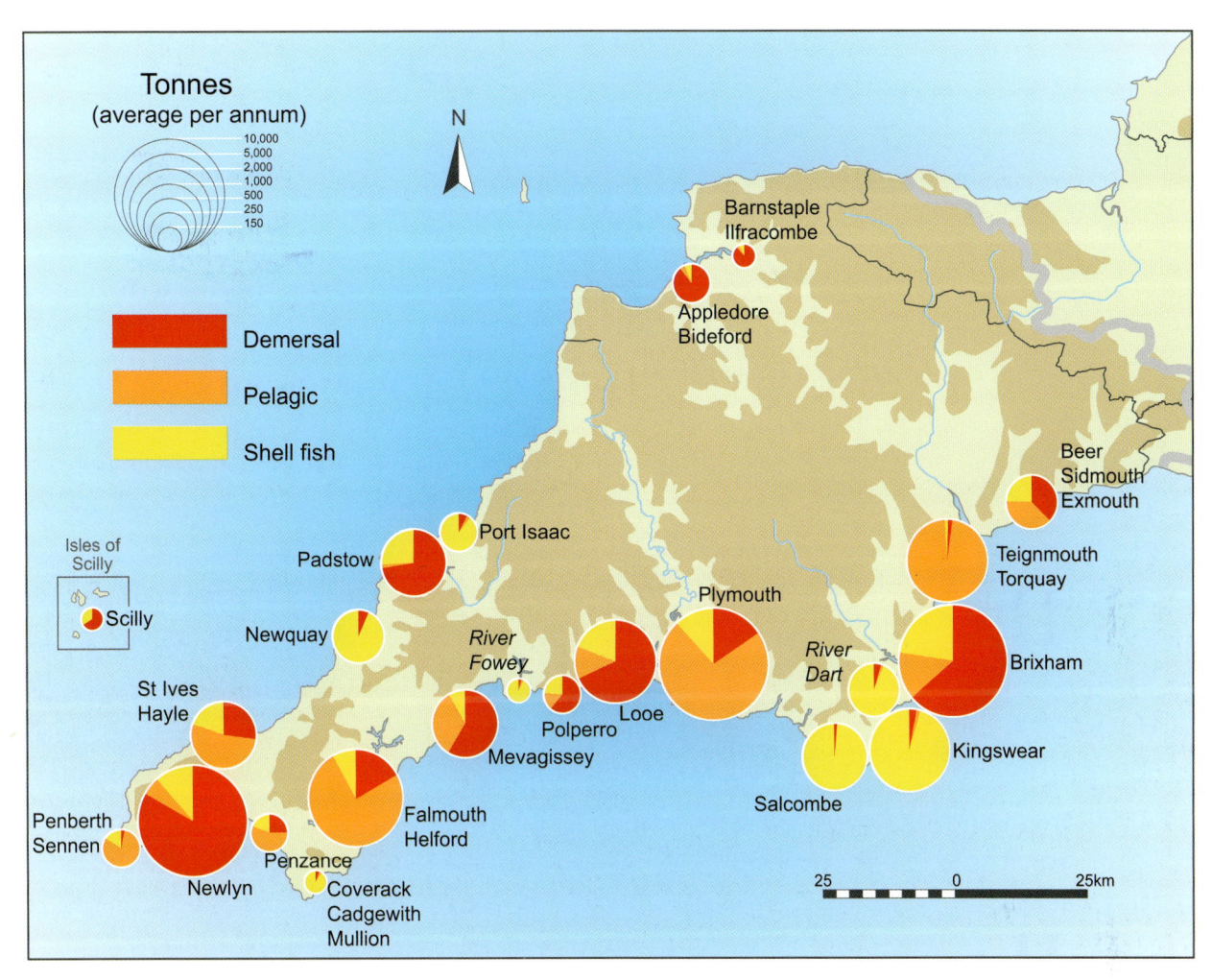

leading centres of a revived industry, taking mainly flatfish. Plymouth, Teignmouth and Torquay were responsible for the major catches of pelagic fish – principally mackerel, although in Cornwall, Falmouth and Helford were significant in the pilchard fishery.

The most important changes to rural settlement in the 20th century were those that reflected the decline in agricultural employment. At the end of the 20th century only about 6 per cent of the Cornish workforce was involved in farming and some 4 per cent of the Devon workforce. In many parts of the South West, therefore, the majority of those living in rural areas were not working on the land but were either employed locally in some other occupation or were commuting to an urban centre. The most valuable parts of many small farms had become the farmhouse and barns. As farms were amalgamated, their farmhouses were sold and no longer occupied by farmers, while barns were converted into residential units (Fig. 7.21). In some cases farm buildings have been turned into

Fig. 7.20 Fish landed at ports in the South West, 1986–90.

Fig. 7.21 Barn conversion in progress in Cornwall.

FARMING, FISHING AND RURAL SETTLEMENTS

Fig. 7.22 Holiday camps north-east of Perranporth, Cornwall.

commercial units for just about any non-agricultural use. Some of these uses are for leisure and tourism, and a few farms in the South West have become little more than museums and collections of fairground rides. In other areas, new rural settlements are of chalets and caravans that form holiday camps or parks (Fig. 7.22).

CHANGING AGRICULTURE, CHANGING LANDSCAPES

Although the rural landscape of the South West is an old one, with many of its features established by the time of Domesday Book over a millennium ago, it is still developing and adapting to ever-changing economic conditions. Periods of agricultural prosperity brought investment, reclamation and often the expansion of settlement. On the other hand, agricultural depression brought retrenchment in conventional farming matched by diversification and novelty. Prosperity and depression are themselves the result of the relative movements of farmers' prices and costs. In medieval times the pressure of population pushed prices up, but also had a direct effect in forcing cultivation and settlement on to new land. By the turn of the 20th century, the 'agricultural revolution' had a relatively limited effect in the South West, although farmers successfully adapted their farming to new agricultural conditions. From the late 19th century, a global market operating under free trade subjected British farmers to competition, which prompted a depression that lasted until the Second World War. After the war, the free trade inaugurated with the repeal of the Corn Laws was replaced by a regime of price support and regulation that created a new prosperity. For various reasons this structure gave less support to farmers during the 1980s and 1990s and by the early 21st century south-west England's farmers were once again facing retrenchment in conventional farming and searching for forms of diversification that would lead to their salvation.

FURTHER READING

Balchin 1983.
Countryside Agency 1999.
Grigg 1989.
Herring 1998.
Hoskins 1952.
Hoskins 1954.
Landscape Design Associates 1996.
Overton 1996.

8

Landscapes of Industry

MARK BRAYSHAY

The relics of past industrial activity are widespread across Devon and Cornwall. They serve as haunting, evocative memorials to generations of men and women whose work has contributed so much to the creation of this region's extraordinary landscapes. Industrial archaeology today contributes far more to the scenery of south-west England than the enterprises that still thrive. As in other English regions, much of Devon and Cornwall's traditional industry has lost its vitality and quietly died. However, the processes of decay began rather earlier in this region than elsewhere and industrial decline in the South West has been a drawn-out, sometimes painful, experience. Past mining, quarrying and manufacturing activities have not only shaped and dramatically altered large swathes of the south-west countryside and added hugely to its diversity and interest, but also defined and constructed an identity and character for the entire peninsula. In a real sense, therefore, the industrial landscapes of Devon and Cornwall are central to this region's narrative and they are the embodiment of its spirit.

LANDSCAPES OF THE FARMING AND FISHING INDUSTRIES

The oldest industries in both Devon and Cornwall are farming and fishing. Food and drink manufacturing, the businesses that traditionally supplied the needs of farmers, and those that depended on particular farm-produced raw materials, all played an important part in shaping the South West's relict landscapes of industry. Water-powered mills for grinding grain were once common everywhere in the region. In the post-medieval centuries much was achieved in Devon and Cornwall to enhance the efficiency of waterwheels and to advance the technology. For example, the Dutch-born hydraulic engineer, Cornelius Vermuyden, well known for his work on the drainage of the Fens in eastern England, came to Falmouth in 1672 to advise on the construction of a leat to power the town's corn mill in Swanpool Street. Almost a century later, John Smeaton, famous for building a lighthouse for the Eddystone Reef, south of Plymouth, adjusted the design of waterwheels so that the 'buckets' filled fully to the brim causing the wheel to turn faster. He also improved the escape of water via the tailrace to minimise the check on the wheel's speed. Building and maintaining mills required the skills of millwrights and the products of sawmills and foundries. The 1893 edition of Kelly's *Directory* lists 19 millwrights in Devon, 24 iron founders and 21 sawing, planing and moulding mills. When viewing the remains of an old mill building and its associated structures, it is thus important to remember that it was once at the centre of a large web of related enterprises and activities that each contributed to the overall operation of the local economic system.

LANDSCAPES OF INDUSTRY

OPPOSITE PAGE:

Fig. 8.1 Cadgwith, The Lizard, Cornwall, *showing the former 'pilchard cellars' above the beach, where the fish were pressed, salted and packed. One of these, next to the Cadgwith Cove Inn (on the right of the picture), is now the Old Cellars Restaurant. Each week several tonnes of crab are still landed in Cadgwith as well as catches of lobster, mackerel, monkfish, shark and mullet.*

Moving from the makers to the users of mills, William White's 1870 *Directory of Devonshire* lists no fewer than 456 millers, while the 1873 edition of Kelly's *Directory of Cornwall* includes 313. A dramatic decline occurred after the First World War and closures continued throughout the 20th century. Only a few survive today. In Devon, Bridge Mill at Bridgerule near Holsworthy, the Otterton Mill near Budleigh Salterton and the refurbished Totnes Town Mill are examples of more or less intact 18th- and 19th-century flour mills. The 18th-century mill at Cotehele in St Dominick, which worked commercially until 1964, has been restored by the National Trust. Other examples in Cornwall include Trewey Water Mill at Zennor, Trevillett Mill near Tintagel and Melinsey Mill at Veryan, near Truro.

Modern demand for organic foods has stimulated the restoration of some old flour mills for commercial production. Indeed, the premium prices that can be secured for locally grown produce of all kinds has prompted a revival in Devon and Cornwall food-processing industries. These vigorously promote their county name as a major selling point. More small and medium-sized food and drink producers existed in the South West in the early years of the 21st century than in any other English region. A notable sector is the production of cream, ice cream and cheeses. While some creameries, such as Rodda's of Scorrier, have existed since the 19th century, a number of new dairy firms have been established in the past 20 years. Some developed as small businesses attached to farms that grew to factory scale as their products achieved recognition and secured substantial markets. This was the case at Higher Langage Farm in Plympton. Another example is the Taw Valley Creamery in North Tawton. Although owned by Glanbia plc as one of their four British creameries, in 2005 Taw Valley employed 125 people and was one of Europe's largest cheese-making firms.

Small breweries and cider-making plants benefited from this growing interest in high-quality, local produce. While closures have occurred, several new brewing businesses were formed during the decade up to 2005. The largest, however, is still the St Austell Brewery, which was established in 1851 and in 2005 employed a workforce of over 900 in its Tregonissey Lane premises. Easily the region's oldest brewery, the Blue Anchor in Helston has existed since the 15th century. One of the most recent, the Ales of Scilly Brewery, was founded in 2001 at Higher Trenoweth, near St Mary's in the Isles of Scilly. In all there are more than 30 working breweries in Devon and Cornwall, the majority of them very small enterprises, of which several operate in association with just one particular inn. In 2005 there were 29 cider makers in Devon and another six in Cornwall. The famous Inch's cider makers at Winkleigh closed in 1998, but the premises were later revived to operate as the Winkleigh Cider Company. Wine making in Devon and Cornwall has expanded markedly since the early 1990s and a number of successful vineyards came into production. The valleys of the Dart and the Camel provide particularly favourable conditions. Near Totnes, the Sharpham and Beenleigh wineries have become well known, while the 8,000 vines on the Camel Valley estate near Bodmin can, in a good year, produce up to 15,000 bottles of quality wine.

Fish preserving was once a major south-west industry, particularly in Cornwall, where the pilchard catch supported employment in numerous 'fish cellars' in the county's fishing ports. The fish were packed in casks, layered with salt. During the inter-war years, this ancient industry dwindled away and only the buildings survive, occasionally as ruins, but usually put to other uses (Fig. 8.1).

As a key ingredient in mortar, lime had been a requirement in the building industry for centuries. From the mid-16th century, however, demand grew dramatically for supplies of lime to dress agricultural land. Although Tudor farmers regarded it as a miracle fertiliser, the effect of liming was to neutralise soil acidity thereby enabling the mobilisation of essential plant nutrients contained in animal manure. Limestone quarried at Aberthaw in Glamorgan was

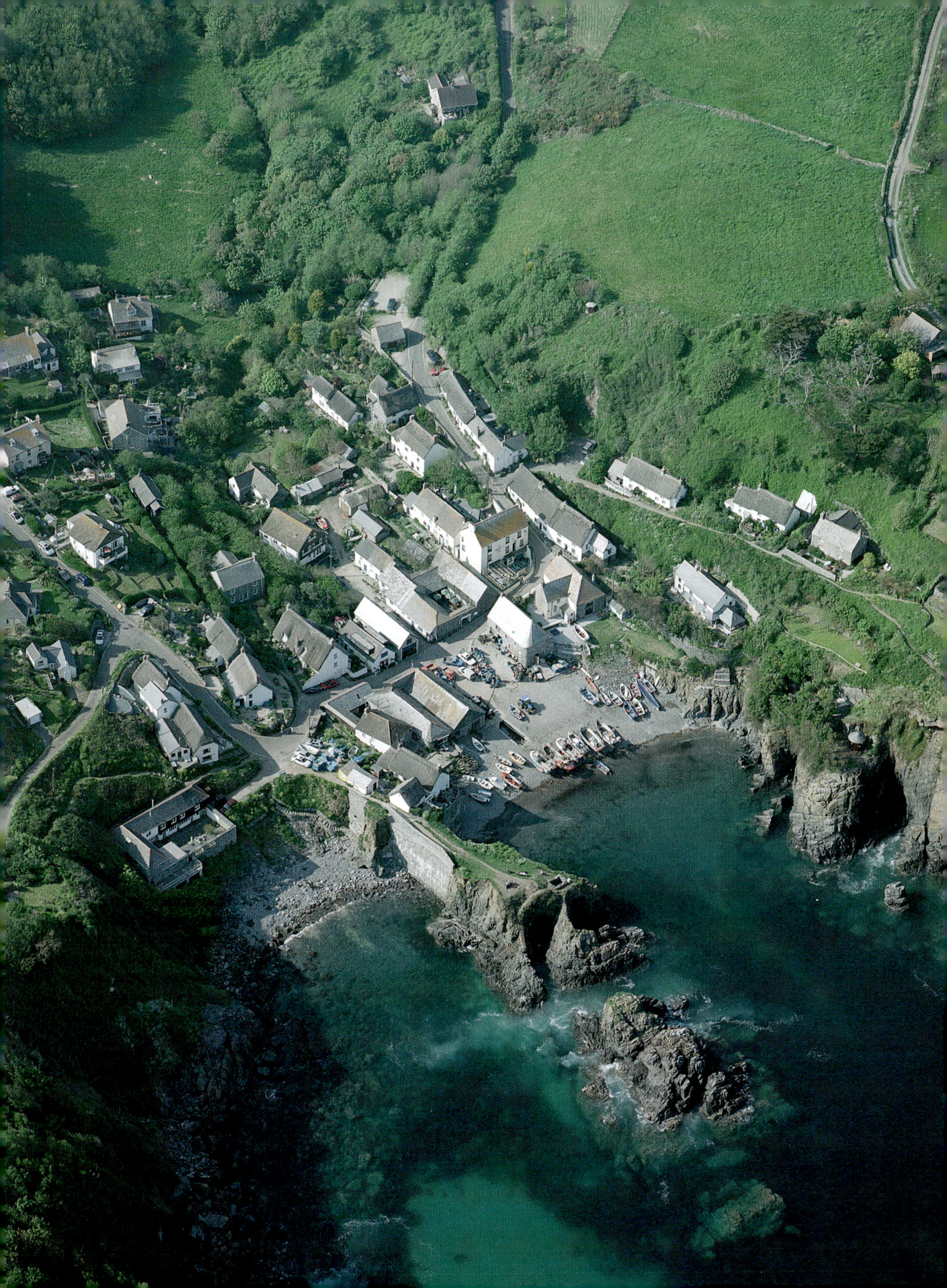

LANDSCAPES OF INDUSTRY

imported together with coal from South Wales. Because of the relatively high cost of transporting these ingredients, kilns were usually erected near to coasts or rivers (Fig. 8.2). Once burned, limestone becomes quicklime. This rather nasty, unstable substance was spread on the land where contact with moisture converted it into the rather more benign 'slaked lime'. Most of the oldest kilns occur in east Devon. Until the late 18th century, calcareous sea-sand was used instead of lime in the acid-soil areas of Cornwall and west Devon; most of the lime kilns in the area from the Tamar valley westwards were thus built only after 1750 (Fig. 8.3). By the mid-19th century, however, as other chemical fertilisers were introduced, the use of lime declined and the kilns fell out of use. Very few were constructed after 1840. The ruined shells of scores of these small, stoutly built industrial structures remain in the Devon and Cornwall landscape.

OPPOSITE PAGE:

Fig. 8.2 Lime burning, leather tanning, fulling, and papermaking in Devon and Cornwall, c. 1500–1800.

Fig. 8.3 Lime kilns, Morwellham Quay, on the River Tamar in Devon. Interest has grown in the industrial archaeology of lime burning in Devon and Cornwall and this and a few other sites have been the subject of restoration projects to make them accessible for heritage tourists. Good examples include Bampton and Tuckenhay in Devon.

Other industries connected with the needs of agriculture also thrived in Devon and Cornwall. For example, many small foundries produced edge tools like those made by the remarkable Finch Foundry at Sticklepath on the northern side of Dartmoor, which was originally a cloth mill but was converted in 1814. Making paring hooks, hammers, picks, shovels, hay knives, axes and hoes, the business survived until 1960, and is now a working museum (Fig. 8.4). In the 19th century, there were also small brass and iron foundries engaged in making and repairing agricultural tools in Calstock, Wadebridge, Saltash, St Agnes, Launceston and Penryn. In addition, the skills of local blacksmiths were in great demand in a region where farming and mining were key activities. At least 800 smithies were at work in the region in the 1890s. Today, many disused or converted forges survive as an indication of this once widespread and ubiquitous craft.

Leather tanning and dressing, and the manufacture of leather goods, have

Fig. 8.4 Finch Foundry at Sticklepath, near Okehampton in Devon, showing the two unique 'trip' hammers and the shears, all worked by a single waterwheel.

LANDSCAPES OF INDUSTRY

been important south-west industries in the past. A region of rich pastures supporting large numbers of sheep and cattle provided plentiful quantities of hides, and tanneries certainly existed in Devon by the early 1500s. Oak bark and lime were also required and, by the 18th century, local supplies were augmented by imports. Heavy leather, for which the hides were spread with a lime-and-manure mix, and then soaked for at least six months in a solution of oak bark and water, was used to make boots, shoes and saddles. Dressed leather, made by smoking and oiling a skin and then soaking it in a solution of water and alum for two or three weeks, provided the material for making gloves, clothes and bags. Gloves were made throughout Devon and Cornwall by the 17th century, but specialist centres developed for the making of boots and shoes. In the early 18th century, for example, Daniel Defoe commented on the sale of boots, shoes, gloves, purses and breeches in Liskeard market and on the shoe sales he saw in Redruth. By then, Exeter, Plymouth and Tavistock had all become centres of the leather trade, but the industry was otherwise widely dispersed across the region until Victorian times (see Fig. 8.2).

Water-powered vat mills in which paper was made by hand began to be built in the South West from the 1630s – Exeter's first paper mill was established in 1638. Favoured locations such as the Exe and Culm valleys offered an abundance of clean water and the industry thus developed in Crediton, Cullompton, Colyton and Moretonhampstead. The Plymouth area was another zone of concentration. Only one mill was ever founded in north Devon, at Barnstaple in 1746 (see Fig. 8.2). By the beginning of the 19th century, 37 of England's 434 paper mills were located in Devon and Cornwall. Tradition and local skills have meant that quality papermaking has survived in Devon into the 21st century, albeit on a considerably reduced scale, at locations such as the Devon Valley Mill near Exeter, where paper has been produced continuously since 1767 (Fig. 8.5).

Fig. 8.5 The Devon Valley Mill at Hele near Exeter, where hand-made paper was first made in 1767.

LANDSCAPES OF THE TEXTILE INDUSTRIES

Between the Tudor and the Georgian eras, the South West was one of England's foremost regions for the production of woollen cloth. During the 16th century, local sheep flocks supplied the region's demand for fleeces. At that time, they mostly yielded a short staple that was used to make a coarse fabric known as kersey. Spinning and weaving were common throughout the South West. Once the 12-yard (10.9m) lengths of material left the loom, they were taken to fulling or tucking mills where water-powered hammers 'thickened' the fabric, thereby flattening it and concealing the weave to give it a smooth appearance and feel. After fulling, cloths were stretched out to dry on tenterhooks in rackfields. Even when all the physical evidence of these processes has disappeared from the landscape, their former existence is sometimes still preserved in local Devonian and Cornish place-names.

LANDSCAPES OF INDUSTRY

Fulling mills were established in Devon by the 13th century, but later became widespread in the South West, especially between 1500 and 1800. Locations where a plentiful supply of fast-flowing water was available were favoured (*see* Fig. 8.2). The region's poorest fleeces were produced in west Devon and Cornwall (Cornish 'hair') and used to make south-west England's traditional rougher woollen cloths, known as Tavistocks or straits. But it was from the sale of kerseys that the region grew rich. Peter Blundell made a fortune marketing Tiverton kerseys in London, and used some of his wealth in 1599 to endow the town's famous school. Other wealthy Tudor merchants, such as John Lane in Cullompton and John Greenway in Tiverton, spent generously on the embellishment of their parish churches. Clothiers in Ashburton, Buckfastleigh, Totnes, Truro and Falmouth also prospered. Exeter was by far the region's largest centre for the cloth trade, however, and the city's powerful Guild of Weavers, Tuckers and Shearmen ran their industry from Tuckers' Hall in Fore Street (Fig. 8.6). The ordinary folk who made and finished the cloth did not share in this wealth. Spinners, dyers, weavers and those who laboured in the fulling mills of the South West were skilled men and women, but their rates of pay were generally low and their standard of living was poor. Real prosperity was confined largely to those who ran the industry, owned its plant and marketed its products.

By 1600, growth in manufacturing had outstripped the supply of home-grown wool and increasing quantities of fleeces from Ireland were imported via Barnstaple, Bideford and Padstow. These produced longer 'combed' or worsted yarn, which in part enabled the development of serge manufacture in Devon. Serge combined short-staple 'woollen' thread as the weft, with a longer 'worsted' warp to produce a light, hard-wearing cloth that quickly found a large European market. Although straits and kerseys were still produced in the South West, it was the introduction of these 'new draperies' in Devon that led to a huge 17th and early 18th-century expansion in the industry, which may be gauged by noting the rapid growth in the quantity of serge shipped from Exeter. In the 1660s, some 10,000 pieces were exported each year. By 1686, the number had risen to 114,000, leaping in 1710 to 365,000. By then Exeter was handling a quarter of all English cloth exports and the trade sustained the city's rising and conspicuous phase of prosperity in the later Stuart era.

After 1714, there was a downturn in south-west England's cloth trade as competition from East Anglia and Yorkshire clothiers and a reduction in foreign demand began to exert an impact. In 1777, Devon nevertheless secured a monopoly to supply 390,000 serge pieces each year to the East India Company. This business yielded only slender margins, however, and in any case masked south-west England's continuing loss of ordinary market share both at home and in Europe. When the East India Company contract ended in 1833, the region's serge industry entered its final phase of decline. As the 19th century progressed,

Fig. 8.6 Tuckers' Hall, Fore Street, Exeter, was the fullers' guild chapel, built shortly after 1471. It survives as a tangible legacy of Exeter's national prominence in the medieval wool trade. Secularised at the Reformation and divided into an upper and lower hall, the building was 'restored' by the Victorians, who installed the round-headed windows.

LANDSCAPES OF INDUSTRY

woollen mills closed one by one and only a handful remained at the start of the 1900s. However, Coldharbour Mill in Uffculme, in part still powered by water and steam, survived until 1981 after two centuries of spinning worsted and woollen yarn. A year later, the mill reopened as an industrial heritage museum (Fig. 8.7). Although textiles are still produced in places such as Tiverton and Dartington, south-west England's cloth industry has virtually died out. Some former mill buildings remain. Though it was used as a grist mill in the years before its closure in 1938, a good example is Tuck Mill in Payhembury. A woollen-mill building and some 18th-century weavers' cottages may also be seen in Culmstock.

In 1755, Thomas Whitty developed luxury carpet manufacture in Axminster as a specialist offshoot of the woollen industry. At first Whitty's carpets were based on the designs of those imported from Turkey, but a more eclectic range of patterns was gradually used. One of the finest surviving examples was woven in Whitty's factory in 1770, to a design by Robert Adam, for the saloon of Lord Boringdon's Saltram House. It cost £126 and echoes the neo-classical decoration and colour scheme that Adam devised for the saloon's ceiling (Fig. 8.8). According to the factory's usual practice, when the Saltram order was finished, the bells of St Mary the Virgin in Axminster were rung and the carpet was carried to the church to be blessed. Whitty's business became insolvent, however, and in 1836 carpet making transferred to Wilton in Wiltshire. Harry Dutfield of Kidderminster revived manufacture in Axminster in 1937 and his factory building still survives in the town. By 1950, Dutfield's company had acquired Berry's Woollen Mill in Buckfastleigh as a spinning and dyeing plant capable of supplying yarn to the Axminster complex, and both factories continue to operate. Today, the Axminster factory covers some 5ha and each year produces almost a million square metres of carpet (Fig. 8.9).

From the 16th century until the 19th, fine hand-made lace, produced on a domestic scale by skilled female workers, was a speciality of the east Devon towns of Honiton and Ottery St Mary. By the 1600s, the craft had spread to Colyton, Beer, Seaton, Sidbury and Sidmouth. At the end of the 17th century, an estimated 4,500 people were engaged in pillow or bobbin lace-making and the activity flourished until John Heathcoat established his machine-made lace factory in Tiverton in 1815. Heathcoat brought his business and workforce from Loughborough in Leicestershire to escape the attentions of Luddites and took over the 18th-century West Exe woollen mill as the base for the mechanised production of nets and lace fabrics. Though no longer engaged in lace making, the mill still produces textiles and Heathcoat's

Fig. 8.7 Coldharbour Mills at Uffculme in Devon is still partly powered by water and steam. Originally built in 1799 by Thomas Fox to spin woollen and, later, worsted yarns, this survives as a heritage tourism attraction and an important example of Georgian industrial architecture, industry and enterprise. The complex includes a restored 1821 High Breast Shot waterwheel and a 1910 Pollit & Wigzell 300hp steam engine.

Fig. 8.8 The Saloon, Saltram House, Devon, designed by Robert Adam. The carpet, woven in Axminster to Adam's design, was made in 1770. Note also the corner candelabra made in Matthew Boulton's foundry in 1772, and the suite of furniture made by Thomas Chippendale in 1771–2.

LANDSCAPES OF INDUSTRY

ABOVE: **Fig. 8.9 The building in Silver Street, Axminster, Devon**, *associated with the town's historic carpet-making.*

LEFT: **Fig. 8.10 Heathcoat's, Tiverton, Devon.** *The original factory buildings are on the right of the picture.*

striking contribution to the townscape of Tiverton's West Exe district remains clear (Fig. 8.10). He provided a school and a considerable quantity of workers' housing, and in 1876 the company built an employees' institute.

LANDSCAPES OF METAL MINING

Devon and Cornwall are rich in minerals. Extraction of tin from deposits associated with the granite of Dartmoor has the longest recorded history. While tin also occurs in the metamorphic rocks that encircle the moorland granite and predominate in the Tamar valley, copper ore is more important in those zones. Considerable quantities of arsenic occur in association with the Tamar valley metal lodes and these were commercially exploited and processed in the 19th century for use in paint and dyes, as well as for glass manufacture and in the chemical and pharmaceutical industries. Tin and copper were often encountered in the same mine in Cornwall, though the richest copper reserves were in the Camborne–Redruth and Caradon districts. The silver lead ores that occur in the Coombe Martin area of north Devon, in the Bere peninsula between the Tamar and Tavy in the west of the county and on the southern fringes of Dartmoor have also been commercially exploited in the past. There has also been lead mining on a limited scale in the Teign valley, while manganese deposits have been

LANDSCAPES OF INDUSTRY

Fig. 8.11 Tin-streaming landscape at Black Tor, Dartmoor. *The widespread scale of the tinners' activities has left few moorland valleys completely unchanged. Remains of blowing houses can be seen at the edge of the stream. At such sites, small waterwheels were used to power stamping machinery, which crushed tin ore to a powder, and also to operate the bellows that provided a forced draught of air for a smelting furnace. Water for the wheel was brought in by diverting the stream above the site into a leat. After smelting, ingots of tin metal weighing 100–200lb (45–91kg) were taken to one of the four 'coinage' towns of Chagford, Ashburton, Plympton and Tavistock for assaying (checking the content) and payment of tax to the Exchequer.*

commercially worked in the area of Upton Pyne and Newton St Cyres, to the north-west of Exeter. Small quantities of iron have been extracted on Dartmoor, for example at Haytor, Shaugh Prior, Boringdon, Meavy and Ilsington. Iron has also been worked in St Agnes and St Austell in Cornwall, and North Molton and Milton Abbot parishes in Devon. Wolfram (tungsten) has been extracted at Hemerdon Ball in Plympton and, though never exploited, deposits of uranium exist at Kingswood in Buckfastleigh.

Because bronze is an alloy of copper and tin, it is possible that Dartmoor tin deposits were exploited 4,000 years ago in the Bronze Age, but there is very little reliable landscape evidence of any prehistoric working. Much more is known, however, about the moor's tin industry in medieval times. For example, records indicate that tin deposits were being worked near the River Plym at Brisworthy in Dartmoor's Sheepstor parish in 1168. Dartmoor's tin output peaked in 1525 when 252 tons were produced. The metal had a wide range of uses, most prominently as a component of pewter (an alloy of tin and lead), which was used for making plates, bowls, drinking vessels and cutlery.

Tin ore, or cassiterite, is found in lodes (narrow bands) in Dartmoor granite. Where the lodes reach the surface, they are naturally eroded and collect as alluvial deposits in the streams and rivers that drain the moor's high ground. Medieval and early-modern tinners extracted cassiterite from alluvial deposits in a process known as streaming. Artificially diverted streams were created to wash out alluvial deposits, the running water separating the heavier ore from other material. Dartmoor valleys where tinners once worked are easily recognised. They have been broadened, their sides have been steepened and their floors contain rubble mounds, walls and channels through which today's streams meander. Such was the widespread scale of the activities of the tinners that few Dartmoor valleys can be considered wholly natural features (Fig. 8.11).

Tin ore was collected and processed near to the moorland streamworks. This involved crushing the material, originally using mortar stones but by later medieval times through the use of small stamping mills powered by waterwheels. Before being smelted, the pulverised ore was further refined by washing out impurities. As early as the 15th century, smelting plants known as blowing houses were becoming common. In these, waterwheels powered bellows that produced a blast of air to raise the temperature of the fire, thereby producing fast, effective smelting. Molten tin was ladled into mould stones to form ingots that were then transported to one of the moor's four stannary towns (Chagford, Ashburton, Tavistock or Plympton) to be checked, weighed, hallmarked and taxed. The physical remains of all these processes survive in abundance on Dartmoor (Fig. 8.12).

After its boom years in the early 16th century, the Dartmoor tin industry declined. There was a brief revival in the early 18th century followed by another lull that lasted until the late 1700s when deep-mining technologies encouraged a

OPPOSITE PAGE:

Fig. 8.12 Field remains of Dartmoor's tin industry.

LANDSCAPES OF INDUSTRY

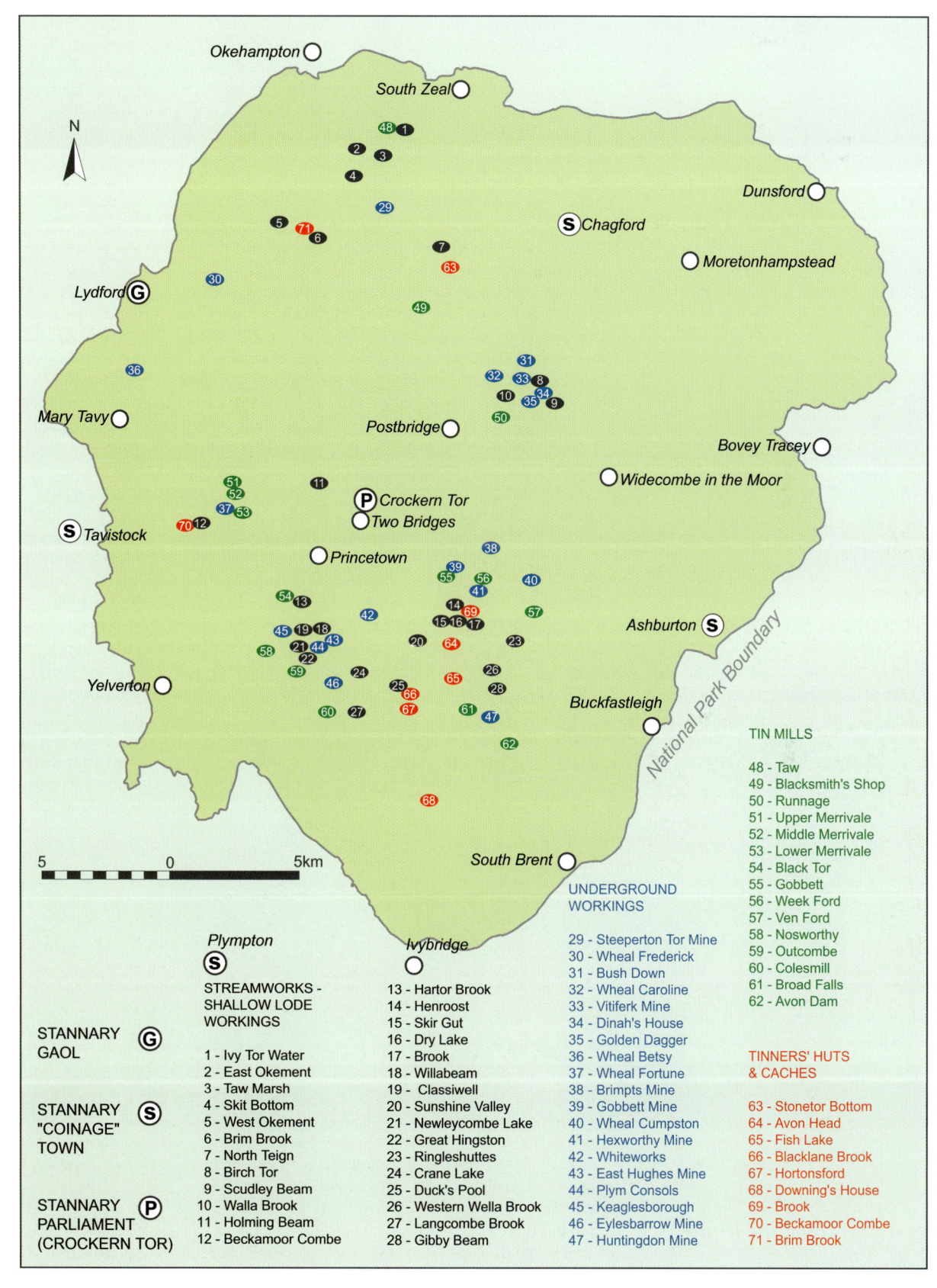

TIN MILLS

48 - Taw
49 - Blacksmith's Shop
50 - Runnage
51 - Upper Merrivale
52 - Middle Merrivale
53 - Lower Merrivale
54 - Black Tor
55 - Gobbett
56 - Week Ford
57 - Ven Ford
58 - Nosworthy
59 - Outcombe
60 - Colesmill
61 - Broad Falls
62 - Avon Dam

TINNERS' HUTS & CACHES

63 - Stonetor Bottom
64 - Avon Head
65 - Fish Lake
66 - Blacklane Brook
67 - Hortonsford
68 - Downing's House
69 - Brook
70 - Beckamoor Combe
71 - Brim Brook

STANNARY GAOL (G)

STANNARY "COINAGE" TOWN (S)

STANNARY PARLIAMENT (P) (CROCKERN TOR)

STREAMWORKS - SHALLOW LODE WORKINGS

1 - Ivy Tor Water
2 - East Okement
3 - Taw Marsh
4 - Skit Bottom
5 - West Okement
6 - Brim Brook
7 - North Teign
8 - Birch Tor
9 - Scudley Beam
10 - Walla Brook
11 - Holming Beam
12 - Beckamoor Combe
13 - Hartor Brook
14 - Henroost
15 - Skir Gut
16 - Dry Lake
17 - Brook
18 - Willabeam
19 - Classiwell
20 - Sunshine Valley
21 - Newleycombe Lake
22 - Great Hingston
23 - Ringleshuttes
24 - Crane Lake
25 - Duck's Pool
26 - Western Wella Brook
27 - Langcombe Brook
28 - Gibby Beam

UNDERGROUND WORKINGS

29 - Steeperton Tor Mine
30 - Wheal Frederick
31 - Bush Down
32 - Wheal Caroline
33 - Vitiferk Mine
34 - Dinah's House
35 - Golden Dagger
36 - Wheal Betsy
37 - Wheal Fortune
38 - Brimpts Mine
39 - Gobbett Mine
40 - Wheal Cumpston
41 - Hexworthy Mine
42 - Whiteworks
43 - East Hughes Mine
44 - Plym Consols
45 - Keaglesborough
46 - Eylesbarrow Mine
47 - Huntingdon Mine

141

LANDSCAPES OF INDUSTRY

significant return to the moor to extract tin from well below the surface. At least 100 mine sites on Dartmoor and its immediate boundary were worked in the period between about 1770 and 1940. Most of these were located in the metamorphic aureole zone that surrounds the granite of the high moorland. Where possible, tin was obtained by cutting adits into the hillsides, but shafts were also sunk. Among the deepest of the mines on the moorland granite, at around 128m, were those at Vitifer and Golden Dagger. Other notable deep mines in the granite zone include Eylesbarrow, Birch Tor, East Vitifer, Whiteworks and Hexworthy. Eylesbarrow is also the last place where tin smelting on Dartmoor was carried out. Quantities of tin ore continued to be sent to South Wales for use in the tin-plate industry until the late 1930s, but the scale of output was by then very small.

Although small-scale tin streaming had occurred in Cornwall for many centuries, the start of underground mining in the early Tudor period marks a turning point in the county's industrial history. Throughout the reign of Elizabeth I, however, annual output was never much above 450 tons and substantial growth was further delayed by the Civil War until the late 17th century. But by the 1670s, notwithstanding some years of lower production, well over 1,000 tons of tin were being produced annually; by the 1740s, 1,700 tons were on average being sent each year for coinage. From the 1690s, there was in addition a rapid development of copper mining. Within a decade, more than 2,000 tons of copper ore were being raised each year. This period thus witnessed the beginnings of Cornwall's industrial revolution.

Copper was Cornwall's supreme product, but for just 150 years. Substantial expansion occurred in the 19th century; in 1844, spectacularly rich deposits were discovered in Devon at Blanchdown Woods near Tavistock. The development of these lodes, in places up to 12m thick, for a time made Devon Great Consols the world's leading producer and the richest copper mine in the South West. The combined copper output of Cornwall and west Devon reached a peak in 1856 when 209,000 tons were raised. Within a few years, however, extensive discoveries in South Australia, Michigan, Chile and Cuba caused the

Fig. 8.13 Devon and Cornwall tin and copper production.

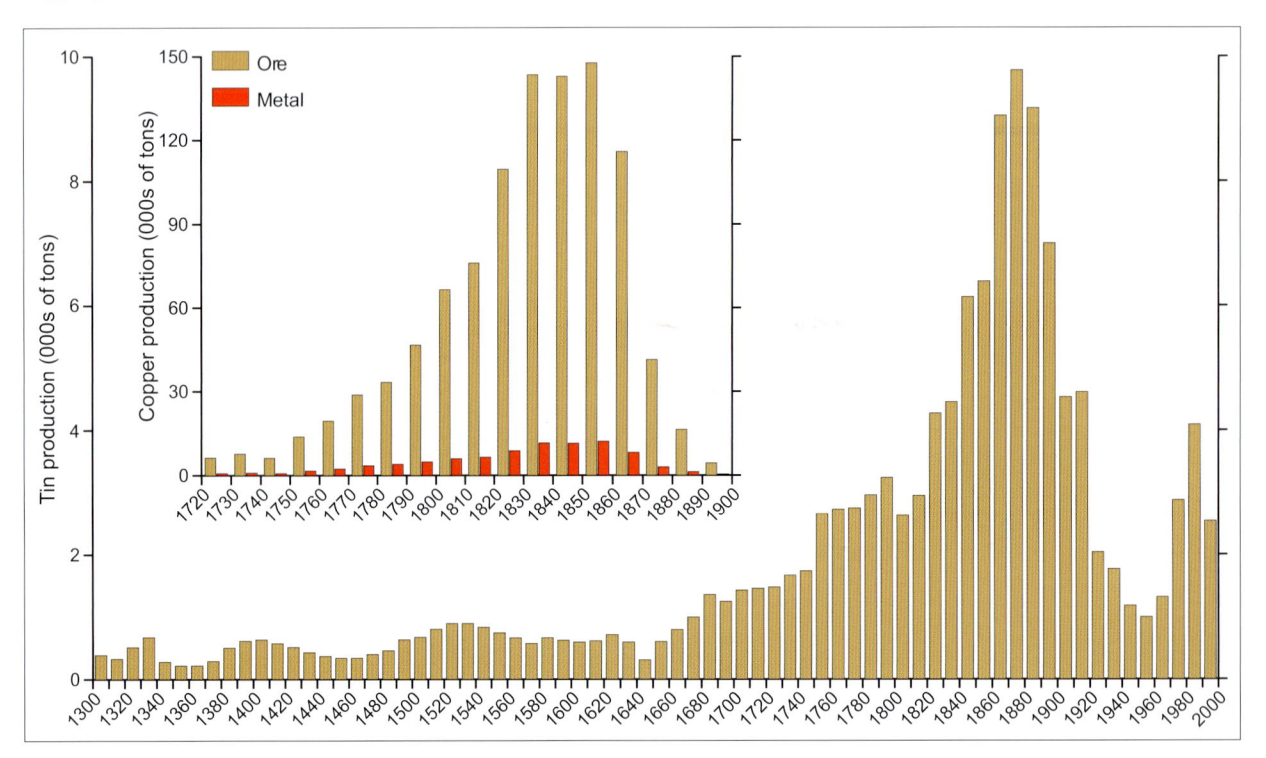

LANDSCAPES OF INDUSTRY

price to fall and south-west England's copper mines crashed in 1866. Though a few mines limped on until the 1890s, the era of the South West as a 'copper kingdom' had ended (Fig. 8.13).

Fig. 8.14 Geevor tin mine, St Just, Cornwall. *A general view of the headframe from the south-east.*

BELOW: ***Fig. 8.15 South Crofty tin mine, Cornwall.*** *Robinson's shaft and engine house from the south-west.*

Reserves of tin continued to be worked in Cornwall, sometimes deep below the unprofitable copper lodes. Competition from cheaper foreign tin reserves and the difficulty of extracting the ore at great depth in the old mines of Cornwall caused a sharp decline in the industry at the beginning of the 20th century. Although output slumped to a low level in the 1950s, there was thereafter a modest revival and hopes were entertained that the industry might thrive once again. This optimism ultimately proved unfounded and, after struggling desperately for survival, Cornwall's last surviving mines, Geevor and South Crofty, finally succumbed. Geevor in Pendeen has already re-established itself as a visitor attraction and plans for a similar enterprise at South Crofty are being devised (Figs 8.14 and 8.15). At the time of writing, the mining heritage of Cornwall and west Devon is being considered for World Heritage status.

The landscape signature of metal mining in both Devon and Cornwall has proved almost indelible. The remains on the surface provide only a

ABOVE: **Fig. 8.16 Underground workings at South Crofty tin mine, Cornwall**. An abandoned drive.

ABOVE RIGHT: **Fig. 8.17 South Crofty tin mine, Cornwall**. Rock drilling.

scant guide, however, to the vast extent of the abandoned underground labyrinth of workings, often still hazardous and liable to collapse, or to flood and pollute the region's streams. This hidden geography of subterranean shafts and levels represents another aspect of south-west England's remarkable mining legacy (Figs 8.16 and 8.17). On the surface, the rapid adoption of steam power to pump out water and raise ore has bequeathed a striking visible legacy of 18th- and 19th-century engine houses and associated chimney-stacks. Like giant stumps in a petrified forest, Cornwall's old mine engine houses have become iconic landscape elements. Some have been repaired and conserved as visitor attractions with their restored Boulton and Watt steam engines once again in operational order. The engine houses at East Pool in Redruth and Levant in St Just in Penwith are National Trust properties (Fig. 8.18). Underground workings at Geevor, the Levant Mine and its neighbour, Botallack, extend far out beneath the sea and the ruined engine houses for the Crowns section of the latter perch precariously on the cliff edge, indicating the positions of the shafts down which miners descended and through which ore was raised (Fig. 8.19).

Fig. 8.18 The Levant tin mine, Cornwall, engine houses restored by the National Trust. The restored building houses a beam 'whim' or winding engine built in 1840 by Harveys of Hayle to raise ore 278 fathoms (508m) to the surface. The adjacent building housed an engine used to pump water from the mine.

A dozen intensively mined districts may be identified in Cornwall and west Devon (Fig. 8.20). Amalgamations, name changes and imprecise records make it almost impossible to construct a complete list of the mines that have been worked in these areas. However, as Figs 8.21, 8.22 and 8.23 show, there are areas of the South West where the landscapes of mining are overwhelmingly dominant. About 90 mines have existed in the Camborne–Redruth district,

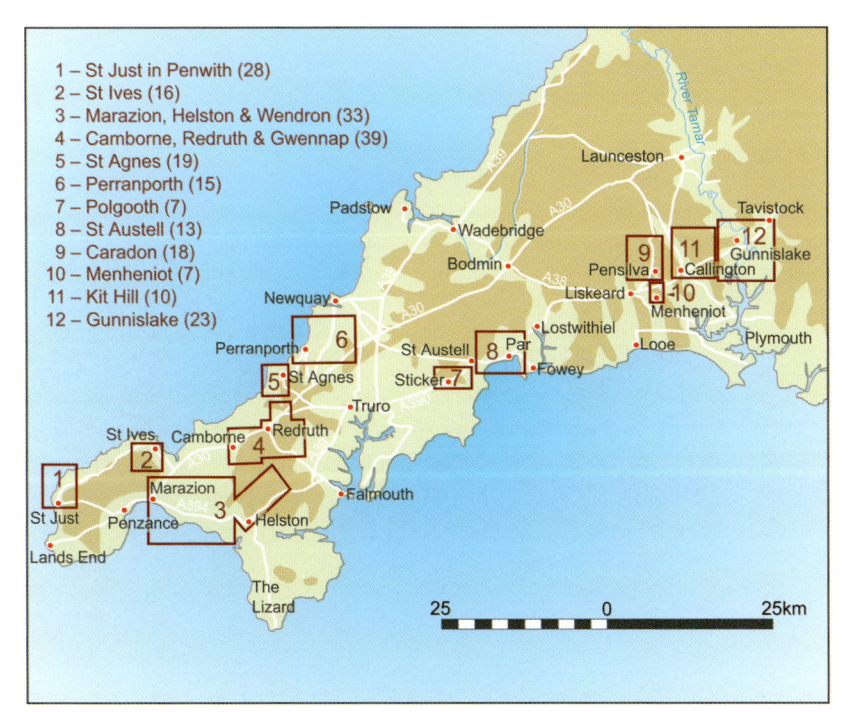

Fig. 8.19 Botallack Mine, Cornwall.
These engine houses of the Crowns section were restored and made accessible by the Carn Brea Mining Society in 1985. The larger, lower house, built before 1835, had a 30-inch (0.76m) pumping engine with a chimney-stack placed inside the building to save space. The other engine house was built in 1862 and had an enclosed winder for the diagonal shaft that descended 1,360 feet (414m) below sea level. Operations ceased here in March 1895 when the price of tin plummeted. Overall, between 1860 and 1895, this section of Botallack produced well over £1 million worth of copper, tin and arsenic. Parts of Botallack were reworked between 1907 and 1914 for arsenic.

1 – St Just in Penwith (28)
2 – St Ives (16)
3 – Marazion, Helston & Wendron (33)
4 – Camborne, Redruth & Gwennap (39)
5 – St Agnes (19)
6 – Perranporth (15)
7 – Polgooth (7)
8 – St Austell (13)
9 – Caradon (18)
10 – Menheniot (7)
11 – Kit Hill (10)
12 – Gunnislake (23)

Fig. 8.20 Major mining districts of the far South West. *The number of mines in each area is given in parentheses.*

145

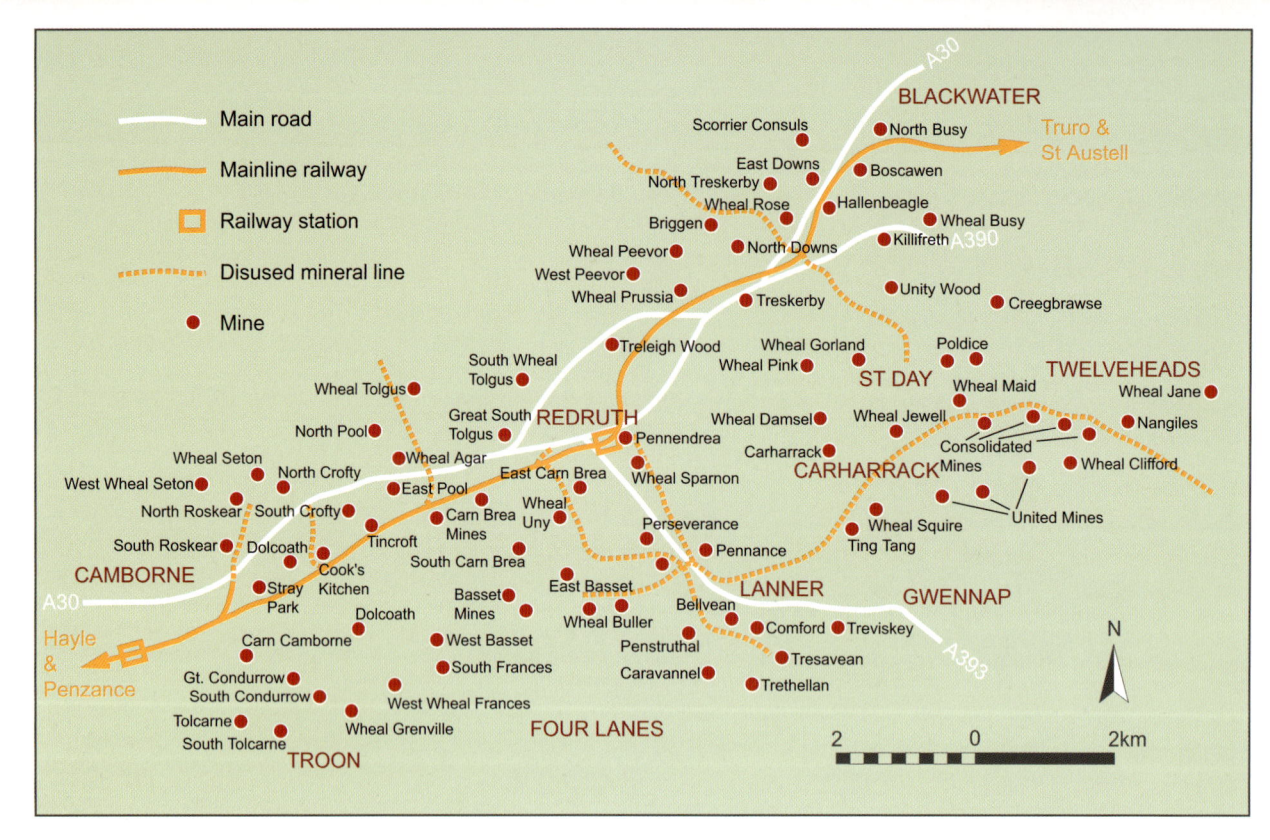

Fig. 8.21 *Mines of the Redruth, Camborne and Gwennap district.*

Fig. 8.22 *Mines of the St Just district.*

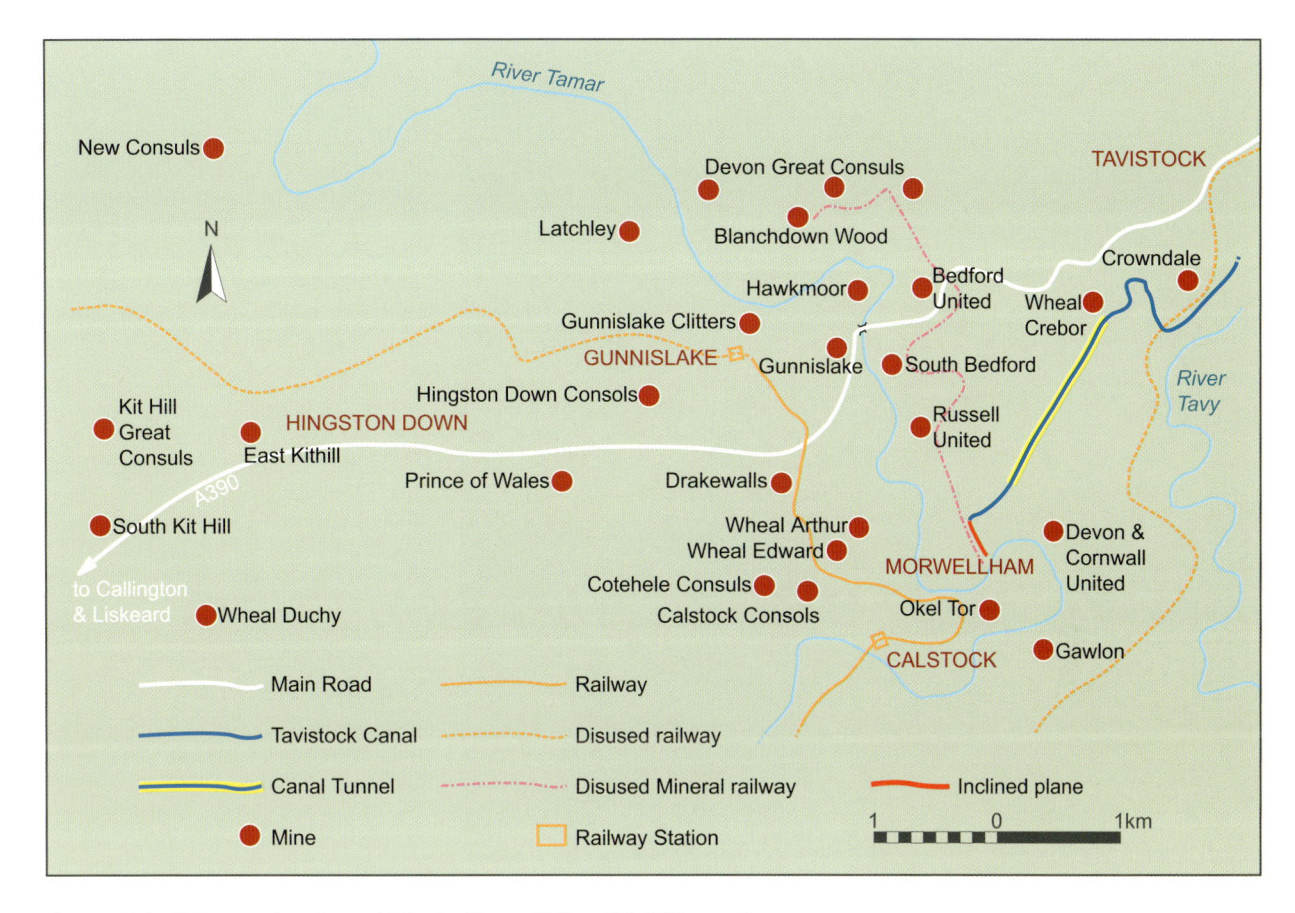

LANDSCAPES OF INDUSTRY

Fig. 8.23 Mines of the Tavistock–Gunnislake district.

almost 30 in St Just and perhaps 28 in the Tamar Valley–Kit Hill area. In addition to thousands of cottages that once accommodated miners and their families, many fine houses built for mine captains and pursers, both close to the mines themselves and in neighbouring towns, exist as a further important element of south-west England's industrial landscapes (Fig. 8.24).

Fig. 8.24 Botallack Mine, Cornwall, the Count House, restored by the National Trust. The original count house was sited beside the path down to the Crowns engine houses (see Fig. 8.19) but, when the ore-dressing floors were expanded in the 1860s, this new building was erected next to the track connecting Botallack and Levant. For a time after the mine's closure, the building was used by the Botallack School of Mines as a survey office.

147

SLATE AND STONE QUARRYING

Plentiful sources of good building stone exist in Devon and Cornwall. In consequence, the brick-making industry has been relatively modest in scale, although Lee Moor and Millbrook in Devon and The Lizard in south Cornwall became notable local centres. Pale-beige Beer limestone was quarried by the Romans and later used extensively for decorative work in churches and large houses. Harder Devonian limestone has been quarried from Plymouth to Torbay, and is still worked on a limited scale. Plymouth's Guildhall, Royal Citadel and old Dockyard walls are all built of this limestone. Though neither is worked today, trap (a basalt) and Heavitree stone (a breccia) were used by the Romans to construct Exeter's city walls; trap was used for the Norman castle and many of the city's medieval churches are built in Heavitree stone. The distinctive Hurdwick stone, though no longer worked, was used by the Benedictines in the construction of Tavistock Abbey and in the 19th-century redevelopment of the town centre. Good slate is also found at the nearby Mill Hill quarries.

Cornwall's Delabole slate has been quarried for more than six centuries. Today's quarry is 130m deep and more than 2.4km in circumference – the largest man-made pit in the country (Fig. 8.25). It produces slate of exceptional quality. In the mid-19th century, there were five separate businesses operating on the site, together employing more than 1,000 men. These companies were combined in 1898 as the Old Delabole Slate Company, which survived until 1977 and liquidation. Thereafter rescued, and operated as a corporate concern, the quarry was subject to a management buy-out in 1999; since then, the Delabole Slate Company has again been a private Cornish company employing 40 people and producing bespoke and specialist slate products. In 2005 just five men worked at the quarry face, using diamond-wire saws to remove 600-tonne blocks. These modern methods produce virtually no waste and thus add little to the debris once created as an unsightly by-product of this industry. The highly decorative serpentine rock that outcrops at The Lizard sustains local stone-carving activity that today focuses mainly on small domestic objects and souvenirs.

Granite has been used as a building material in the South West since antiquity. Its strength and durability are legendary. Merrivale, near Princetown, begun in 1875 by William Duke, is, however, Dartmoor's only working granite quarry (Fig. 8.26). Its stone is of the first quality and was used in the 1980s for the war memorial on the Falkland Islands. Granite was formerly quarried at King Tor and Foggintor, making use of the Dartmoor Railway for its transport, and the local landscape is still littered with the spoil heaps of these abandoned workings. However, it is the Haytor Quarry, developed on a large scale by William Templar in the early 19th century, which enjoys national fame. In 1825, Templar secured the contract to supply granite for London Bridge and Haytor stone was later

Fig. 8.25 Delabole slate quarry, Cornwall. Slate has been quarried here continuously since the early 17th century and activity probably dates back to the medieval period. The pit is more than 400 feet (122m) deep. Subjected to a management buy-out in 1999, the Delabole Slate Company Ltd is now a private Cornish company.

LANDSCAPES OF INDUSTRY

used for the British Museum Reading Room.

In addition to stone quarries, china clay and ball clay deposits have been worked on a large scale in the South West. Both materials are still commercially exploited. The firm of Watts, Blake and Bearne extract ball clay from Bovey Heathfield, thus continuing an industry begun more than two centuries ago. Three potteries were established in Bovey Tracey between 1760 and 1800 and the buildings of one of these still survive. In the second half of the 18th century a Plymouth chemist, William Cookworthy, discovered that kaolin was the main ingredient of Chinese porcelain and opened a factory at Coxside in 1768. Though this lasted only until 1773, it marks the beginning of porcelain manufacture in England. China clay (kaolin) extraction began in Cornwall and expanded rapidly in parallel with England's developing porcelain industry. In the late 18th century, both Josiah Wedgwood and Thomas Minton were major purchasers of clays quarried in the St Austell district. By the 1870s, 100,000 tons were produced annually for markets in Britain, Europe, India and the United States. Demand increased when china clay began to be used in the papermaking industry, a process pioneered by the Dutch. The English China Clays Company was formed early in the 20th century and quickly began to acquire smaller south-west producers including the West of England China Clay Company, the Martyn Brothers and North Cornwall China Clays. In 1932, English China Clays absorbed the company of John Lovering and H D Pochin. By then it was operating more than 50 pits and employed 2,700 workers. Today, English China Clays International, a subsidiary of the French company Imetal, dominates the industry in the South West. Output reached 3¼ million tonnes a year in 1988. Clay waste heaps in the St Austell area and across a swathe of southern Dartmoor have given the landscape a startling, 'other world' appearance that nature struggles to reclaim (Fig. 8.27). As in the tin and copper mining districts, disused pits and works have begun to feature as part of the 'heritage industry'; the Wheal Martyn China Clay Museum led the way in 1975 and 30 years later remains one of the leading attractions in the St Austell area.

Fig. 8.26 Merrivale granite quarry, Dartmoor. The Grimstone and Sortridge leat can be seen on the right of the picture.

Fig. 8.27 China-clay waste, St Austell area, Cornwall.

ENGINEERING AND FOUNDRIES

From the late 1770s the small-scale foundries that made tools for farming and domestic use were dwarfed by those making equipment and machinery for the south-west's mining industry. By far the most important early foundry was established by John Harvey of Hayle in 1779. Many famous steam engines were produced there, especially after James Watt's patent had expired in 1800 and the Cornish engineer Richard Trevithick had been able to incorporate improvements to their design. Both the home and the export market proved lucrative. For example, Harvey's made engines for the Dutch government to drain Haarlem Meer. The Perran Wharf Foundry, opened in 1791 between Truro and Falmouth, also sold engines to overseas customers. Nine were built for the Real del Monte silver mines in Mexico and three for the Burra copper mine in South Australia. The Tolgus Foundry was established in 1860 near Redruth and specialised in a range of smaller items required in the mining industry. Today, the site is another tourist attraction. In the 1820s, the Copperhouse smelting works at Hayle was converted into a foundry that soon rivalled Harvey's as the premier maker of steam engines in Cornwall.

Arguably the best-known foundry in Cornwall was that established in 1801 by the Holman brothers of Camborne. The company specialised in the production of rock drills, mining machinery, boilers and beam engines. Subsidiary foundries were subsequently added at Tregeseal in St Just, and in Penzance. Its customers ranged from Australian mines and the Sudan goldfields to Portsmouth's waterworks. In their day, south-west England's major foundries ranked in significance with the those of the Darbys of Coalbrookdale.

Explosives and fuses were required by the mining industry and both were manufactured in Cornwall. The earliest of several gunpowder factories was located in 1846 in an isolated valley at Herodsfoot, about 8km from Looe. William Bickford of Illogan patented the safety fuse in 1831 and established his factory at Tuckingmill, the first of half a dozen founded by competing producers in the Camborne area. Gunpowder-making began on Dartmoor in 1844 when George Frean opened his works near Postbridge. A proving mortar, used to test the powder, still exists by the lane leading to the remains of Powder Mills. Alfred Nobel's invention of dynamite gradually replaced gunpowder and production steadily declined. None of the Devon and Cornwall factories survived beyond the 1920s.

LANDSCAPES OF SHIPBUILDING AND SHIP-REPAIRING

The South West has a long history of shipbuilding, ship-fitting and repairing, but the industry has survived into the 21st century only on a drastically reduced scale (Fig. 8.28). Perhaps the most profitable activity today is the building of luxury yachts. Princess Yachts, established in Plymouth for nearly 40 years and formerly known as Marine Projects, has continued to flourish. The Pendennis Ship Yard at Falmouth, in business since 1989, builds motor yachts. However, the region's oldest commercial shipyard at Appledore was by 2005 precariously placed. The company, Appledore Shipbuilders, was founded in 1855 and has constructed more than 350 ships including trawlers, dredgers, bulk carriers, fishery-protection vessels and passenger-vehicle ferries (Fig. 8.29).

Devonport Dockyard, dating back to 1690, remains the largest and most important ship repairing and refitting facility in the region. The complex extends over 134ha and comprises 11 dry docks and 5km of deep-water berths. In the years after the Second World War, the dockyard employed more than 20,000 workers. Privatised in 1985, the new management company, DML,

LANDSCAPES OF INDUSTRY

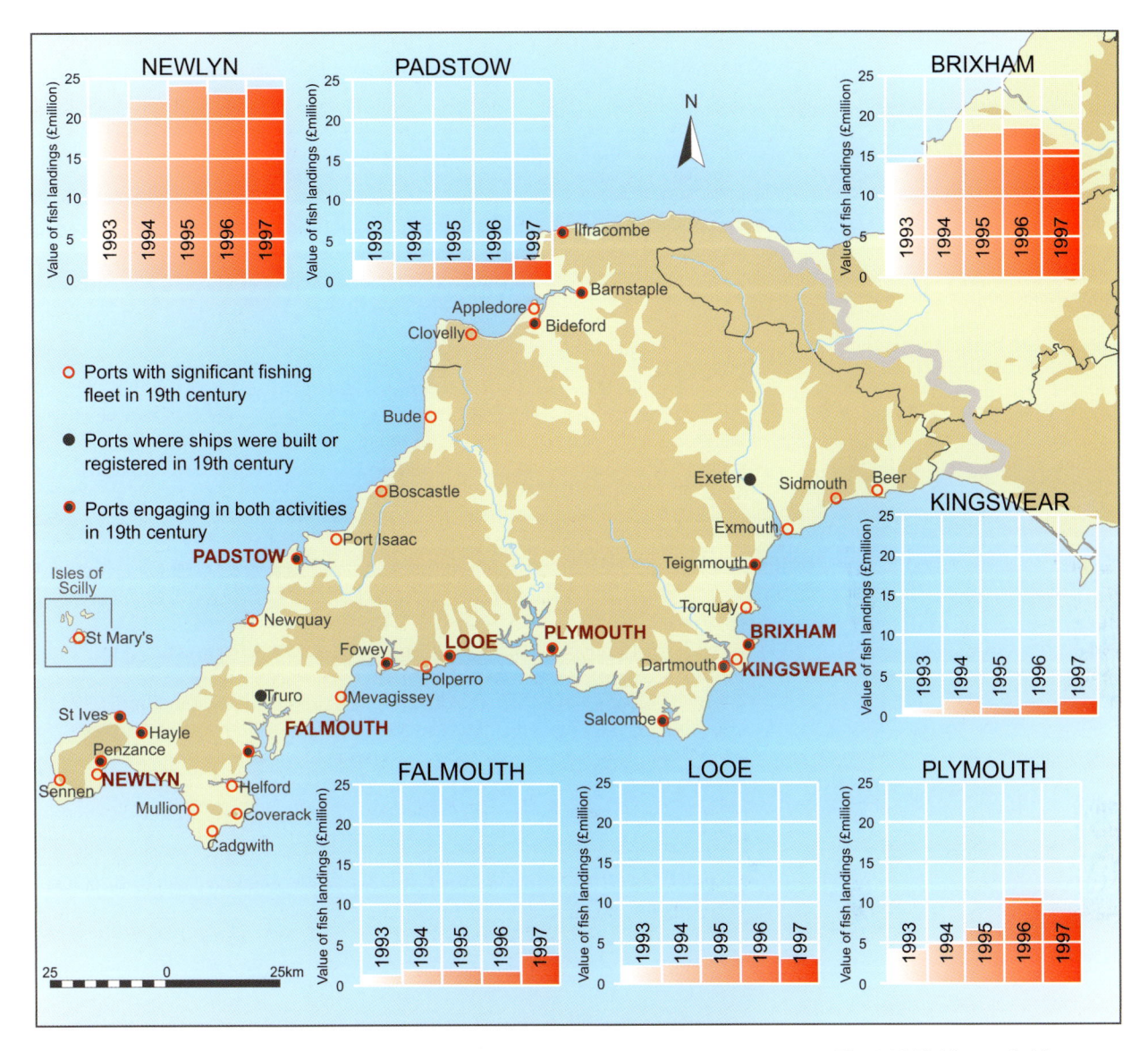

Fig. 8.28 Fishing and ship building in Devon and Cornwall by late-Victorian times.

Fig. 8.29 Appledore Shipbuilders, north Devon.

151

LANDSCAPES OF INDUSTRY

Fig. 8.30 Devonport Royal Dockyard, *owned since 1987 by the DML Group. The picture shows the frigate re-fit complex.*

Fig. 8.31 Wind farm, Cornwall, *a new element in the landscape of the power-generation industry in the South West.*

purchased the Yard in 1997 (Fig. 8.30). In 2005, the workforce of about 4,000 was building and refitting large yachts, modernising warships, and refitting and refuelling nuclear submarines.

LANDSCAPES OF NEW INDUSTRY

Harnessing the power of the wind and waves is hardly new in the South West. In the past, in addition to the hundreds of water mills that once operated in Devon and Cornwall, tide mills existed in certain locations such as Petherick Creek in St Issey, Antony Passage near Saltash, and at Stonehouse Creek near Plymouth. There were also many windmills; some 70 sites have been identified in Cornwall alone, though few traces survive today. The Edward VII Tower on the summit of St Mary's Buzza Hill in the Isles of Scilly is a rebuilt windmill, first erected in 1820. The ruin of another may be seen on Carlyon Hill in St Minver.

Since the mid-1990s natural energy has been employed in new ways in the region. Using wind energy to generate electricity has created startlingly new industrial landscapes. While only one 'wind farm' had been built in Devon by 2005 (at Bradworthy), two more had received approval and seven had been constructed in Cornwall. Their scale and obtrusiveness had led to strong local opposition. The region's first ten turbines were built at Delabole in 1991. By 2005 there were 103 Cornish turbines with a combined generating capacity sufficient to meet the annual supply needs of more than 26,000 homes (Fig. 8.31). These are located at (earliest first): Delabole, Carland Cross, Cold Northcott, Goonhilly Downs, St Breock, Four Burrows and Bears Down.

Early in the 21st century inward investment in hi-tech industries became prominent in the Devon and Cornwall economy. Lower costs and the quality of the environment have been cited as factors that have attracted companies to locate new factories in the peninsula. Moreover, when the GEC Plessey semiconductors plant was built at Roborough on the edge of Dartmoor, an important factor was said to be the availability of clean air for the production of advanced microchips. Buildings with uncompromising and stark designs have often been erected to accommodate these new industries, provoking a tension between the need to stimulate the local economy and the preservation of the region's attractive rural and urban scenery.

A number of hi-tech research and production businesses built plants in the region during the 1980s and 1990s. For example, Nortel, which manufactures electronic communications components, located factories in Paignton and Plymouth, while the American-owned Tyco Electronics Corporation established plants in Bideford and Torbay to make fibre-optic connectors for the electronics industry and rapidly became one of north Devon's biggest employers. From 2001, however, hammer blows began to be struck against all these businesses in the South West as demand for their products slumped. A seemingly relentless flow of redundancies ensued. In Cornwall, the engineering company CompAir, heir to the world-renowned firm of Holman Brothers of Camborne, encountered a fatal loss of business that prompted its demise. South-west England's industrial landscapes – new and old – are as volatile as ever.

A positive footnote to this survey is provided by the arrival of the UK Met Office, which moved from its Bracknell headquarters in Berkshire to a new centre in Exeter in September 2003. This occasioned the most complex relocation of computer and information technology ever attempted in Europe. Most of the existing Bracknell workforce transferred to Devon and few new jobs were created directly in the region, though building work and other benefits for the wider economy brought some fresh employment opportunities to east Devon.

MOVING ON

After more than three centuries as a mainstay of the local economy of Devon and parts of Cornwall, woollen-cloth manufacturing finally faltered in the mid-19th century and has now largely disappeared. The spectacular crash in Cornwall's and west Devon's copper-mining economy followed soon after. Tin mining in Cornwall, though much diminished, clung on until the late 1990s when the county's last surviving mine poignantly surrendered to market forces and closed. Stone and clay quarrying continues to flourish in both counties, but on a reduced scale. Time and nature have gradually healed the raw scars and softened the stark artefacts of much of Devon and Cornwall's former industrial activity, and landscapes that might once have seemed ugly and offensive are increasingly assuming a peculiar beauty and appeal. Paradoxically, places that formerly were the scene of unimaginably hard toil are now regarded as resources that can be 'commodified' and consumed for pleasure. Old industrial landscapes are finding new roles as the focus of heritage tourism (*see* Chapter 11).

In the early years of the 21st century employment in manufacturing industry in the South West had fallen well below the national average. Moreover, the growth in hi-tech and precision engineering businesses that occurred in the 1980s and 1990s had begun to reverse. Often owned by large outside conglomerates and multinational companies, these new industries at first held out the prospect of better-paid, more secure employment for a workforce that was used to neither. Later on, sharp falls in order books, many attributable to the world-wide downturn in the aerospace industry that followed the 11 September

2001 terrorist attacks in the USA, prompted a savage round of redundancies and closures in the South West. Orders for shipbuilding and repairing also dwindled and competition amongst Britain's remaining shipyards to secure the few contracts available had become intense. Devonport Dockyard was privatised in 1985, when its workforce was more 13,000. Ministry of Defence contracts subsequently became increasingly scarce and commercial ship and boat building even harder to sustain. Thousands of employees were made redundant. Though it remains locally important, south-west England's fishing industry has also struggled to survive within the constraints imposed by the European Union's common fisheries policy.

In keeping with the pattern in the rest of the country, employment in both Devon and Cornwall became dominated by the service sector. In 2005, almost three-quarters of Cornwall's working population were engaged in service occupations and the proportion was only slightly lower in Devon. Since the 1970s, the growth of tourism, as one of the region's major economic activities, has been especially significant. For example, in Devon, almost 10 per cent of the workforce had come to be employed in hotels and catering. Tourism, however, is a predominantly seasonal employer that tends to offer relatively low rates of pay. Both counties as a consequence have an above-average dependency on low-paid employment. By contrast, rates of unemployment in Devon fell significantly in the early years of the 21st century, although in Cornwall the unemployment total remained stubbornly high. In 2005, the county's jobless rate was double the national average. Indeed, winter unemployment in Newquay, Penwith and the Isles of Scilly was among the worst in England.

In both counties, part-time employment also tended to be much more common than elsewhere. In Cornwall, some 36 per cent of the occupied population worked part-time; in Devon the figure was 28 per cent. Although there were some notable large businesses, small firms with fewer than 25 workers predominated as employers in this region. Overall, the South West in 2005 was still a relatively poor region where traditional industries have either diminished or disappeared and where the range of job opportunities was far more limited than in many other parts of the country.

FURTHER READING

Though they were first written several decades ago, three outstanding surveys of the industrial archaeology of Cornwall, the Tamar valley and Dartmoor have not since been superseded. Thus, Todd and Laws 1972, Booker 1974 and Harris 1986 provide indispensable guides to the South West's industrial past.

A brief general survey of Cornwall's industrial landscapes is offered by Balchin 1983, 144–71.

For walkers interested in finding Dartmoor's best tin-working sites, Newman 1998 is highly worthwhile.

The studies of industry contained in Kain and Ravenhill (eds) 1999 are up-to-date, succinct and exceptionally rewarding. Among the best are Burt 1999, 345–9; Gerrard 1999, 330–7; and Havinden 1999, 338–44.

For a study of the heyday of south-west England's fishing industry *see* Northway 1994, 126–35.

Finally, two classic texts remain essential to any list of further reading on this region's industries and industrial landscapes: Rowe 1953 and Shorter 1971.

9

Urban Landscapes

MARK BRAYSHAY

Although south-west England is usually regarded as quintessentially rural in character, it possesses a surprisingly large and diverse range of towns. At the apex of the region's urban hierarchy stand Devon and Cornwall's county capitals: the cities of Exeter (2001 population: 111,076) and Truro (2001 population: 17,431). To these must be added the great port city of Plymouth, which, with a 2001 population of 240,720 is much the largest English metropolis to be found west of Bristol. Exeter and Plymouth are thus the leviathans, dominating south-west England's urban hierarchy in population size, geographical spread and socio-economic diversity. Yet for the richness and attractiveness that they contribute to the landscape, the array of smaller towns dispersed across Devon and Cornwall is perhaps more treasured. The evolution of south-west England's urban landscapes reflects in large measure the experience of England as a whole. However, past national trends have found local expression and identification, and have given rise to towns and cities in the region that have their own special personality and character.

England's urban landscapes are a complex physical embodiment of centuries of development and change and today's towns and cities reflect the decisions taken not only by those who now occupy them, but also by their inhabitants in the past. While each generation contributes something new to the urban landscape, only in exceptional circumstances, such as destruction by flood, fire or enemy action, is change sufficiently radical to erase completely the traces of what was there before. Towns and cities are dynamic entities, but they are also extraordinary palimpsests that encapsulate in their built environment elements of their own history. Making sense of urban landscapes is not easy, though an appreciation of the various factors that have helped to fashion them can help. Urban form and location, for example, are influenced by physical landscape considerations. In the earliest phases of town foundation, sites that were sheltered, well-drained and close to a secure supply of fresh water, where construction materials were to hand, and where protection from attack could be afforded, would be preferred. Positions that commanded important routeways, river crossings or coastal anchorages might be especially favoured. Above all, early towns depended on easy access to agriculturally productive land that not only assured a food supply, but also underpinned the trade and commerce that fuelled the urban engine.

In addition to the potential offered by the natural environment, urban landscapes have been shaped and determined by a range of human motivations and influences. Economic success might rely on the availability of resources in the natural environment, but the scale of profits to be made from trade or industrial activity in a town depended also on whether there were nearby competitors. Urban settlements located too close to an established rival might risk commercial failure and impaired prospects for growth. In the medieval period, market towns were not supposed to locate within 6⅔ miles (10.7km) of each other – the optimum round-trip distance that a trader might be expected to walk from his home in the countryside to sell his goods or animals. Some that ignored this rule were either absorbed by a larger neighbour, or lost their market function and reverted to village rank.

Towns and cities have always been focuses of social and political power. In the past, they might be places where a ruling elite built strongholds or powerful families had their homes. The built environment was also used to express social distinctions more generally, whereby those of greatest eminence would occupy the choicest parcels of land in the settlement. Cathedrals and churches, located prominently in the townscape, asserted the devotional role of urban settlements. The self-confidence and identity of a town and its people might be expressed by the splendour of its civic buildings, the might of the town walls and the imposing character of its gates. In England as a whole, by the 14th century, a circuit of walls was no longer necessary for the protection of a town and, where walls were retained, they served partly as customs barriers and partly as symbols of the 'otherness' and importance of places styled city or borough. However, in settlements located on England's south coast, vulnerable to foreign attack, physical defences remained a priority for much longer and continued to be important townscape elements.

Urban form is usually influenced by the pre-urban cadastre: the existing man-made property boundaries, highways and other public rights-of-way in the rural territory surrendered for town development. The shapes of fields, the alignment of hedges or the direction of lanes inherited from a pre-existing farm landscape may thus survive in the layout of the built environment that replaced them. Elongated crofts aligned along a village street can be preserved in the framework of a later borough's burgage plots and the lanes that once led out to the fields frequently survive as streets in a new town's layout. Rural cadastres often explain the otherwise baffling urban forms encountered in the 18th- and 19th-century suburbs that engirdle many of England's industrial towns and major cities, and many good examples of this phenomenon exist in the South West.

By the end of the medieval period, four categories of town may be identified in the English landscape and examples of all of them exist in Devon and Cornwall. First, there were towns of Roman origin. Second, there were the *burhs* or fortress towns founded from the 9th century as military bases with commercial functions (*see* Chapter 6). Third, there were towns that evolved organically as thriving villages grew to urban rank and were accorded market rights and maybe full borough status and functions. Finally, there were 'planted' towns, established at hitherto unoccupied locations from the late 11th century onwards as deliberate and planned operations by speculative seigneurs eager to share in the profits that could accrue from burgess rents, market tolls or the income from a fair or other urban commercial activity. While the South West possesses a city founded in Roman times, namely Exeter, and examples of Anglo-Saxon *burhs* (or their immediate heirs), it was in the medieval period that town foundation in the region peaked. Indeed, by the 14th century, Devon and Cornwall possessed an exceptionally close network of towns (Fig. 9.1). Depending on the inclusion or not of a small number of cases where the documentary evidence about borough status is doubtful, historians differ only slightly on the precise total. Thus Devon probably possessed 69 boroughs and perhaps another 20 places with the narrower legal right to hold a market. In Cornwall, there were some 37 boroughs. There was a particularly heavy concentration in south Devon and south-east Cornwall but few areas within the region were more than a few miles from the nearest market. Overall, Devon had the highest concentration of boroughs per 1,000 acres of any English county, while Cornwall ranked third. In his contribution to the *Historical Atlas of South-West England*, Harold Fox suggests three reasons for the proliferation of towns

URBAN LANDSCAPES

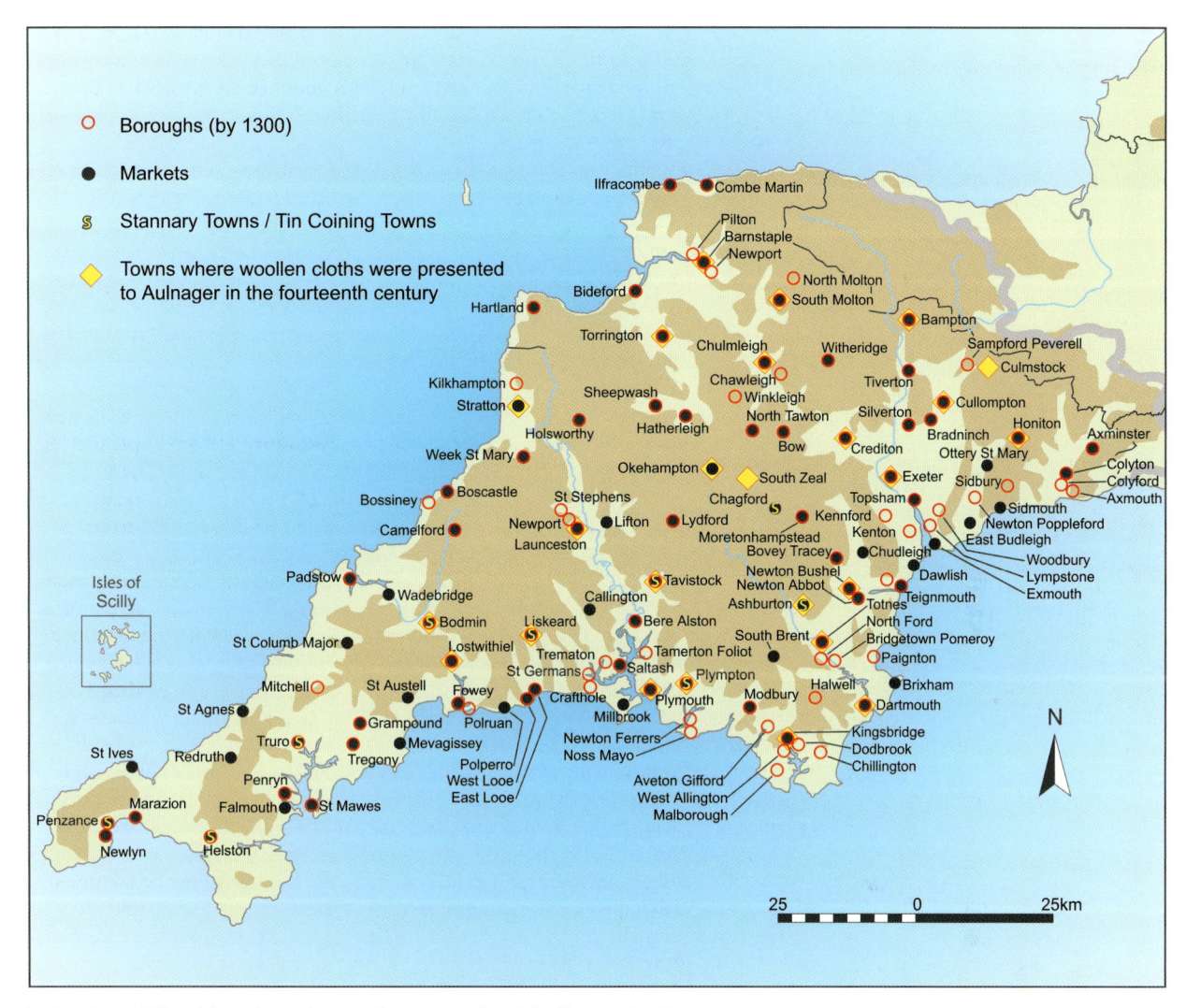

Fig. 9.1 Ancient boroughs and markets of Devon and Cornwall.

in the South West. First, he points to the unusually wide dispersal of landed estates amongst many different lords, which offered unusual scope for the establishment of boroughs. Second, south-west England's difficult topography made travel to a market more problematic than in other regions and towns therefore needed to be more closely spaced. Finally, the diversified medieval economy of Devon and Cornwall gave rise to towns founded to handle both the local flow of agricultural produce and longer-distance commerce in specialised commodities such as salted fish, tin or wool.

ROMAN EXETER

Discounting the claim that some Iron Age hillforts were classified by Roman invaders as *oppida*, and may therefore have had the characteristics of urban settlements, the establishment of a Roman fortress and later a city above the River Exe marks the real beginning of town life in the South West. Within a decade of the arrival of the Romans, the spur of land between the Longbrook and Shutebrook valleys that overlooks the Exe was chosen as the site of a 16ha fortress for the Second Augustan Legion, and this became their winter base for more than 20 years. Comprising 70 barrack blocks, stables, stores, workshops,

URBAN LANDSCAPES

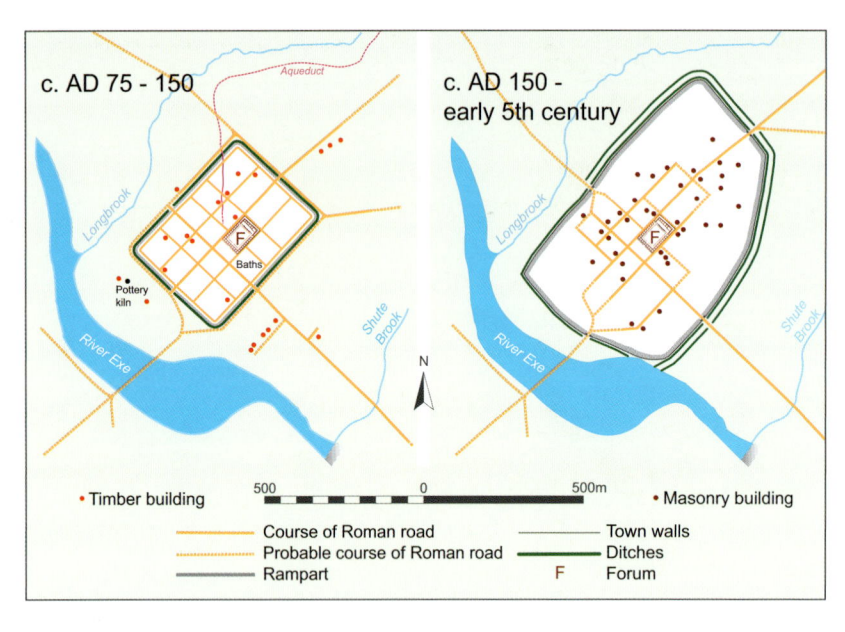

Fig. 9.2 Roman Exeter.

a stone-built bath-house, a legionary headquarters and a residence for the commander and other senior officers, the fort accommodated more than 6,000 soldiers and, in this period, was one of the largest settlements in the country. An aqueduct was constructed to bring fresh water from a spring located to the north-east. Around AD 75, the Second Augustan was redeployed to Wales and the base was dismantled and replaced by a civilian settlement, *Isca Dumnoniorum* (Fig. 9.2). The legionary bath-house was demolished and a forum and basilica complex was erected in its place. Civilian amenities, including a new bath-house, were provided and a grid of streets was laid out, but the town was not walled and simply spread over the in-filled ditch of the fort. However, in about AD 150, new earthwork defences, enclosing a much larger area of 37ha, were built but were only briefly in use. At the beginning of the 3rd century, a circuit of substantial stone walls, up to 3m wide at their base, was constructed. Though later rebuilding and repair makes interpretation difficult, much Roman masonry survives in Exeter's town walls and they are one of the region's most striking ancient architectural monuments. The most recent Roman coin found in Exeter dates to AD 388–392, indicating an imperial presence until a few years before the collapse of Roman rule in AD 410. Apart from the Roman coastal communities with port functions at Topsham and Seaton, there is no other evidence of an *urban* landscape in the South West in this period. For 350 years, therefore, Exeter was the only town in Devon and Cornwall; there was nothing else comparable in the entire peninsula.

THE SAXON *BURHS*

Exeter appears to have been deserted before the mid-5th century and thick organic deposits blanket the Roman archaeology, suggesting that little of the topography of *Isca Dumnoniorum* survived to shape medieval Exeter. Only the town walls and the alignment of the street running towards the north-east gate, dictating the course of the northern end of High Street, appear to have remained. A Christian cemetery built by the Saxons on the site of the Roman basilica might indicate a thread of continuity but, until the establishment of a minster within the town after Exeter was brought under the control of Wessex in the later 600s, evidence of urban life is extremely sparse. Indeed, a substantial re-emergence of the town occurred only during the late 9th century when King Alfred re-founded Exeter as one of his Devon strongholds or *burhs*, erected to protect this part of his realm from Danish invasion. The *burhs* are discussed in Chapter 6 in the context of landscapes of defence (but *see also* Figs 9.3 and 9.4). The impetus may have been military, but Alfred's burghal towns seem also to have been built with economic considerations in mind. By 895, Exeter was minting coins and making pottery. When Aethelraed became king in the early 11th century, there were more than 20 moneyers in Exeter and the town ranked fifth in the league of England's mints.

Evidence of settlements in Cornwall with nascent urban functions in the period before the Norman Conquest of 1066 is extremely sparse, although there

URBAN LANDSCAPES

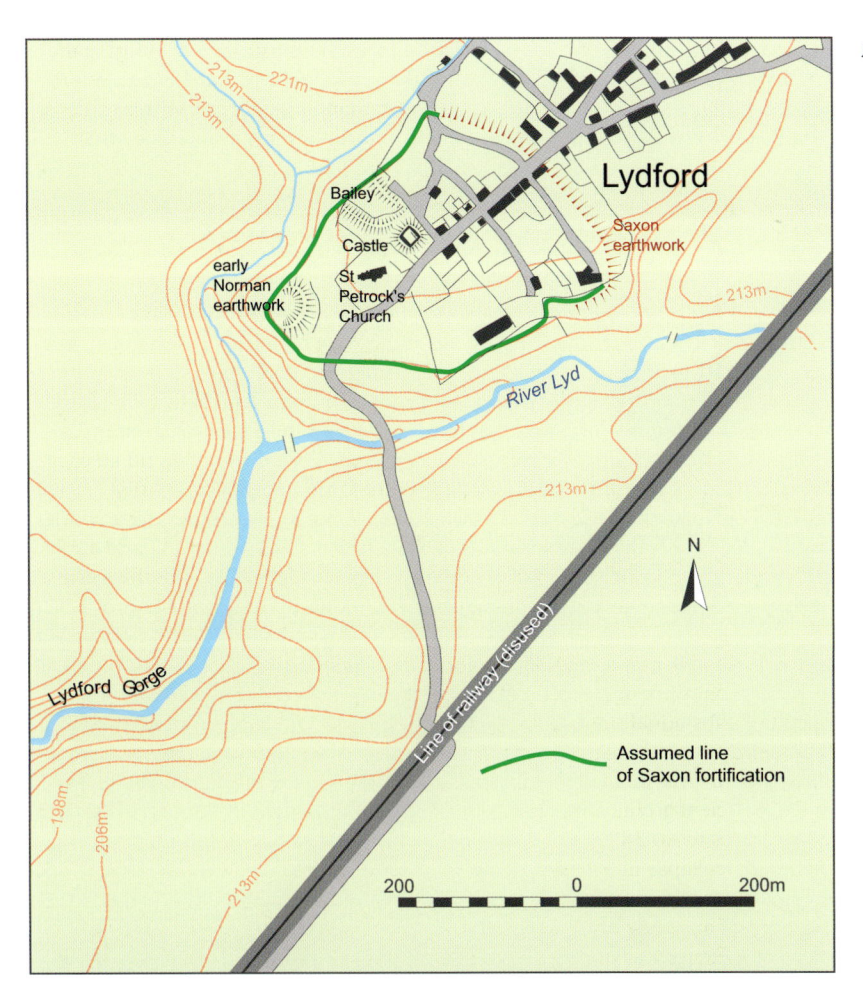

Fig. 9.3 Lydford, Devon, Saxon burh.

Fig. 9.4 Lydford (burghal hidage town), Devon, looking south-west. The earth bank built to protect the boundary of the town not defended by the steep slopes of the Lyd and its tributary is still clearly visible. Although the central, axial street now dominates the settlement, the lanes, which run at right angles, indicate the grid plan of the original Saxon town. Although there were other burhs, or fortified places, in Saxon Devon, only four were recorded in the burghal hidage document, signifying their urban status. Of these, only Lydford and Exeter remained as towns by the time of the Domesday survey; Pilton and Halwell were superseded by Barnstaple and Totnes.

159

URBAN LANDSCAPES

may have been a mint at St Stephens by Launceston in the reign of Edward the Confessor. A market near St Michael's Mount may indicate that Marazion also existed with urban functions. In addition, there were probably markets at Methleigh, Liskeard and St Germans.

POST-CONQUEST AND MEDIEVAL TOWNS

Domesday Book provides a valuable, though partial, record of Devon and Cornwall's late 11th-century urban landscape. Exeter's wider role as the administrative centre for the shires of the South West is clearly underlined: it was here in 1086 that the inquest evidence was brought and compiled in draft as the basis of the fair copy later despatched to the Exchequer in Winchester. The South West is extraordinarily fortunate that this draft copy – the so-called *Exon Domesday* – survives virtually complete in the archives of Exeter Cathedral. Mention of the burgage tenements in Exeter (referred to explicitly as a *city*), the building of Rougemont Castle, and the naming as boroughs of Barnstaple, Totnes and Lydford confirm the urban status of these places. Okehampton Castle is recorded with an associated market and four burgage tenements, indicating the birth of a Norman new town. For Cornwall, Domesday is less clear about the

Fig. 9.5 Launceston, Cornwall, Norman new town.

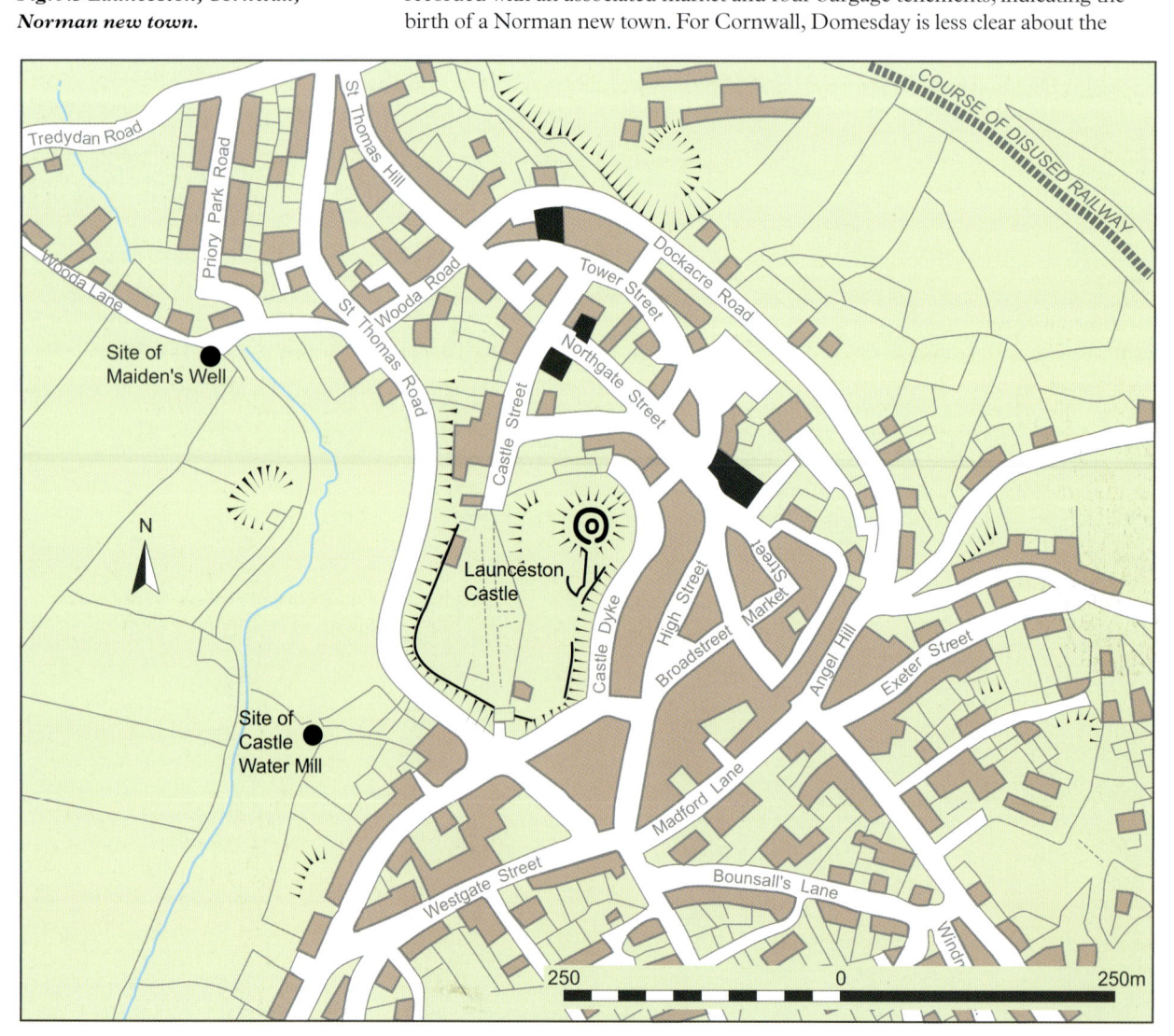

URBAN LANDSCAPES

existence of genuine town life. Thus, while the market or fair near St Michael's Mount is mentioned in earlier records, King William's survey makes no reference to it. However, in noting 68 houses at Bodmin and perhaps 40 at Helston, Domesday suggests that these were settlements of a size that also supported urban functions. As already noted, the markets at Liskeard, Methleigh and St Germans appear to indicate the existence of further small pre-Norman towns. Moreover, the transfer of St Stephens by Launceston's market to the Count of Mortain's new castle of Dunheved records the deliberate transplanting of an urban community by the Normans to support their new stronghold at Cornwall's 'gateway' (*see* Fig. 9.5). The building by Norman lords of new towns in the South West in association with imposing castles was both a symbolic expression of conquest and a deliberate strategy for developing the commercial potential of newly acquired estates. Certainly, by the end of the 12th century, there was no doubt about who held the reins of power. Castles in Exeter, Barnstaple, Okehampton, Totnes, Lydford, Launceston, Trematon and Restormel were military strongholds, the focus of new tenurial arrangements, and often the core of prominent boroughs within the region (Fig. 9.6 and *see* Chapter 6).

Fig. 9.6 Totnes, Devon. The oval form of the medieval town, dominated by the Norman castle with its motte and bailey, is still clearly visible at the heart of the modern settlement.

Building on these late 11th-century beginnings, the pace of town foundation in Devon and Cornwall quickened markedly. Prosperous, expanding villages, conveniently located to act as local nodes, sought the legal right (in the form of a charter) to hold markets and thereafter aspired to the privileges of burgesses enshrined in legally held borough status. Favoured coastal locations and crossing-points on estuaries prompted the growth of towns such as Bideford on the Torridge, Dartmouth on the Dart and Plymouth beside the tidal inlet near the mouth of the Plym. Positions on main highways, fishing activity, mining connections or links with the cloth industry were further key factors that encouraged the elevation of a village to the official status of town. In his *New Towns of the Middle Ages*, Professor Maurice Beresford calculates that three-quarters of Devon's medieval towns, and half of Cornwall's, originated in this 'organic' fashion. Significant numbers of 'planted' towns were also founded in both counties; activity peaked in the 13th century but was mostly spent two decades before the arrival in England of the Black Death.

A number of south-west towns, planted in the medieval period, still show clear evidence of deliberate planning whereby regularly spaced burgage plots were laid out along a road, where a market place was provided, and where land was reserved for a church. Examples include Grampound, Mitchell and East and West Looe in Cornwall. Although the earliest charter for Grampound is dated 1322, 28 burgesses were already paying rent to the lord of the manor by 1296. The new town was probably established soon after a bridge (the *Grandis Pons*), across the Fal on the road to Truro, was completed. There was never a church,

161

URBAN LANDSCAPES

Fig. 9.7 Grampound, Cornwall, *early medieval foundation.*

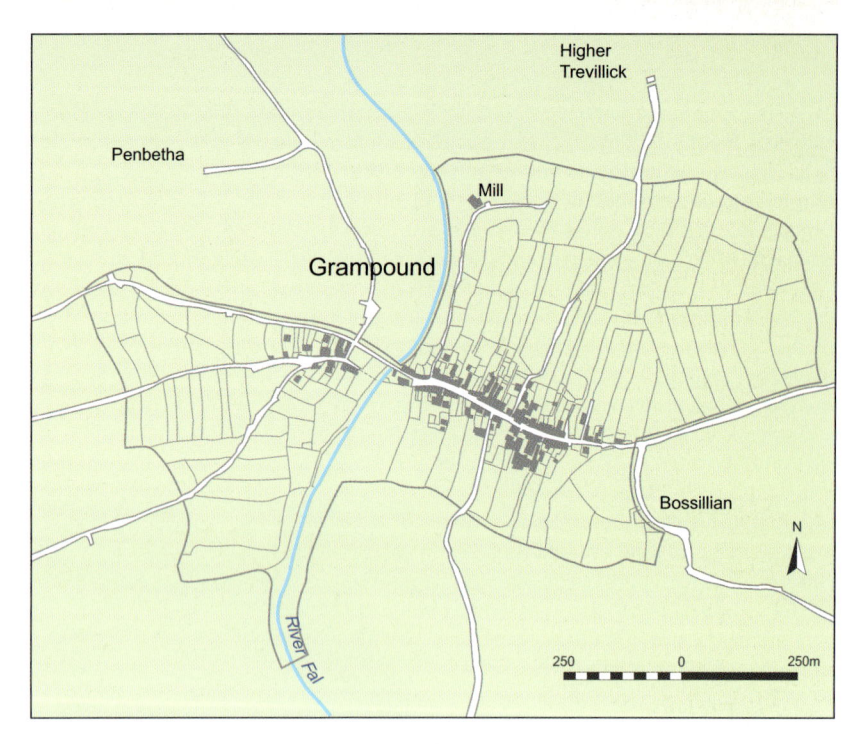

Fig. 9.8 South Zeal, Devon, *a medieval new town that failed to thrive partly because through traffic used the gentler, southern route to Okehampton via Ford Cross and Sticklepath, and therefore bypassed the settlement.*

but a chapel existed by 1370, although this was demolished in 1821. However, Grampound's 15th-century market cross does survive; it was erected outside the chapel where the medieval road broadened to accommodate traders. The original layout of the burgage plots is exceptionally well preserved in the shapes of the gardens of the houses on both sides of the main road (*see* Fig. 9.7). Today's bridge is not, however, the original *Grandis Pons* but a replacement built in the 18th century when the road was turnpiked and a new route was laid out on the west side of the Fal, just to the north of the old one.

In Devon, Newton Poppleford, Honiton, Bow and South Zeal also exhibit similar signs of conscious design (Fig. 9.8). Robert de Tony, lord of the manor of South Tawton, sought a charter for a new borough known as South Zeal in 1294 and rights to hold a weekly market and two annual fairs. While a small settlement at the edge of his estate on the London to Land's End highway may already have been developing, de Tony's planted town comprised regularly planned burgage plots that remain clearly discernible today (Fig. 9.9). South Zeal's small chapel survives at the point where the road widened out at the bottom of the hill, providing space for the market. But travellers found an easier route to Okehampton by going south, bypassing the borough, which then simply failed to thrive.

The prospect of either success or failure for a medieval planted town may now seem obvious, but would

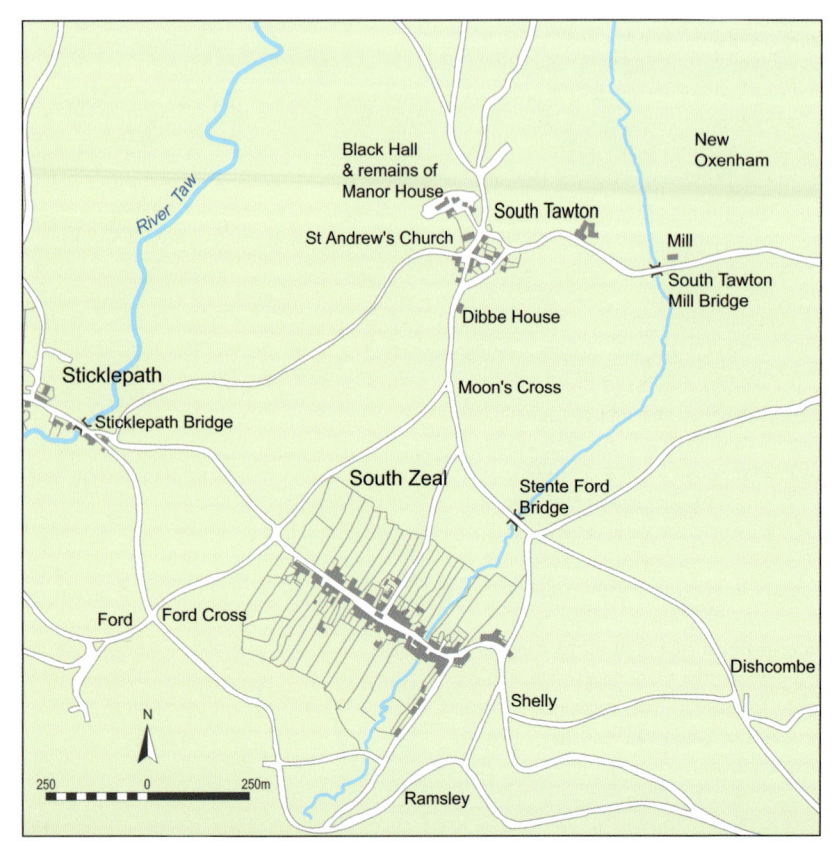

URBAN LANDSCAPES

Fig. 9.9 From the air, looking north, the medieval layout of South Zeal is clear in today's landscape. Narrow, regular burgages are arranged along the main street, each with a lengthy rear plot. Market traders would have laid out their stalls for trade where the main street widens, near to the chapel built at the centre of the settlement.

have been less clear to the founder and resident burgesses at the time. For example, those sited close to a larger neighbour might have expected to compete successfully for a share of the trade but in fact risked early extinction or absorption. Thus, West Alvington and Dodbrook were swallowed up by Kingsbridge, while Bridgetown Pomeroy became part of Totnes. Most remarkable was the founding in 1246 of the market town of Newton Bushel, immediately adjacent to Newton Abbot and separated only by the narrow channel of the River Lemon. The two markets ultimately coalesced, the stream was concealed beneath a culvert, and only the borough of Newton Abbot succeeded.

When Richard de Lucy, lord of the manor of Kenwyn, built his castle at Truro in about 1153 on a knoll above the confluence of the Kenwyn and Allen rivers and founded the settlement that was eventually destined to be Cornwall's 'capital', Devon's county town, Exeter, had existed for over a millennium (Fig. 9.10). Clearly south-west England's two principal cities have markedly different origins. The site chosen by de Lucy was at the tidal head of the Truro River, 5km above the Fal. The Earl of Cornwall conferred a borough charter in 1166. Nothing survives of the castle; the site was occupied by the city's cattle market until its redevelopment in 1988 as the new Crown Court complex (*see* Fig. 9.38). Although the modern city obliterates much of the evidence of the medieval town plan, vestiges of plot boundaries provide an occasional glimpse of its original urban form. Had silting not deprived it of access to the sea soon after it was founded, nearby Tregony might have seriously challenged Truro's fortunes as a port and borough. In fact Truro thrived and its prosperity was further bolstered in the early 14th century by its designation as one of Cornwall's coinage towns where tin was assayed and stamped before being sold.

163

URBAN LANDSCAPES

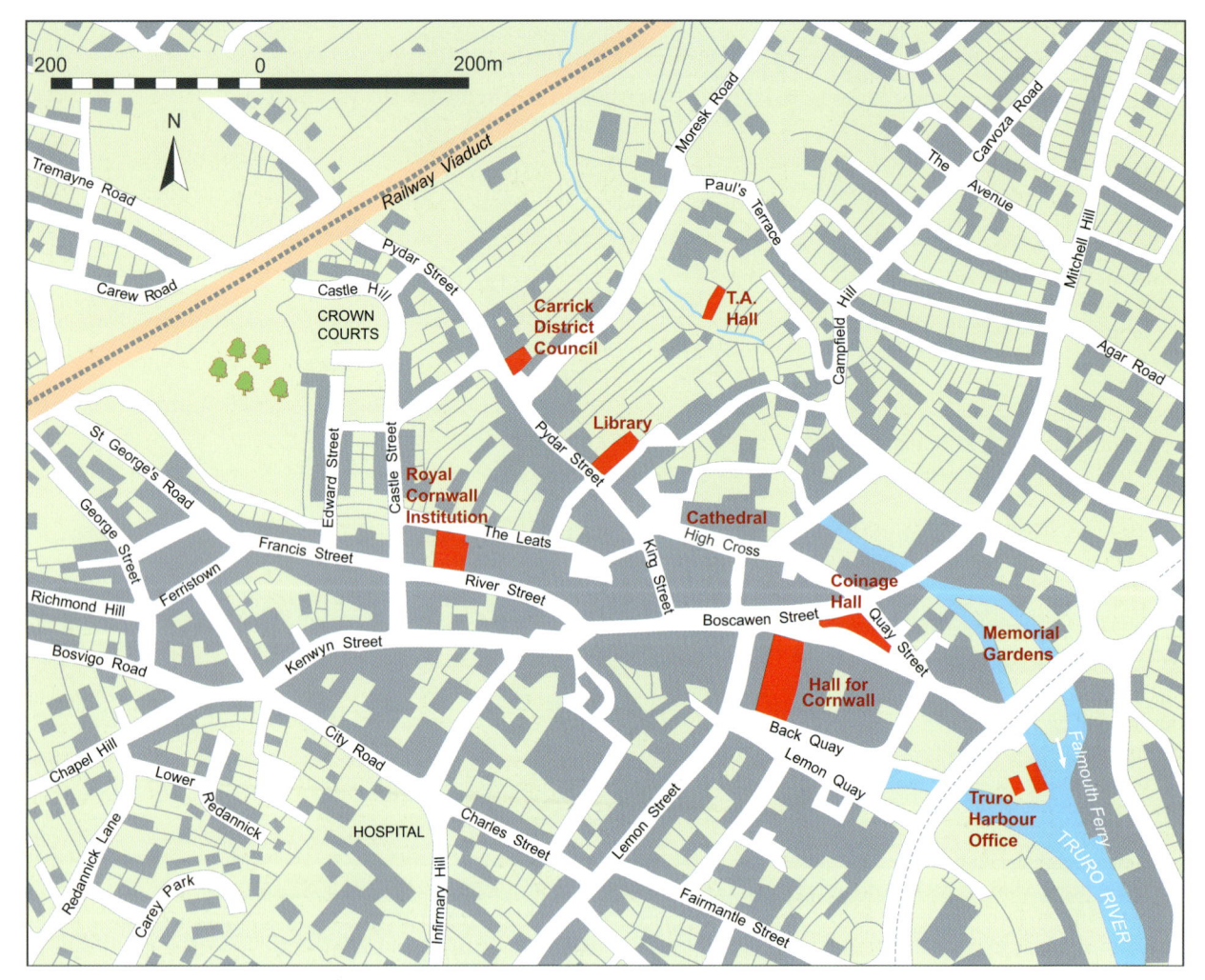

*Fig. 9.10 Central Truro, Cornwall.
The site of de Lucy's 12th-century castle is now occupied by the Crown Courts but its signature in the townscape remains discernible. Vestiges of the medieval town's layout of narrow burgage plots survive in the Castle Street and Pydar Street area.*

OPPOSITE PAGE:

TOP: *Fig. 9.11 Tudor House, Tudor Street in Exeter.*

BOTTOM: *Fig. 9.12 The Merchant's House, St Andrew's Street, Plymouth.*

EARLY MODERN AND RENAISSANCE URBAN LANDSCAPES

Following the catastrophic outbreak of plague in the mid-14th century, a return to prosperity and population increase in the towns of Devon and Cornwall came only slowly. Bodmin's population, for example, is reported to have fallen by 1,500 as a consequence of Black Death, while the Bishop of Exeter's boroughs of Crediton, St Germans and Penryn are said to have suffered desolation. Sea ports and inland towns alike were allowed a reduction in the assessment carried out for the lay subsidy of 1445. Devon's stannary towns of Tavistock, Ashburton and Plympton fared better than most, indicating that urban economies dependent upon the tin trade recovered more speedily than those involved in other sectors. But Exeter, Plymouth, Dartmouth, Kingsbridge, Crediton, Okehampton and Tiverton are examples of places that were still severely depressed. Thereafter, however, a corner seems to have been turned and the engine of urban growth restarted. For example, by the 1520s, Tavistock had not only recovered its pre-plague population of about 540, but had increased to more than 850 inhabitants. Between 1377 and the 1520s, Exeter's population increased from around 3,000 to a total of between 7,000 and 9,000. Two centuries of decay meant, however, that ruins were a conspicuous element in a number of the region's early Tudor towns. When John Leland saw Barnstaple in the 1540s, he noted that the town walls were almost 'clene faullen' and, apart from the keep, the castle was similarly decayed. But Barnstaple was already recovering strongly and the population numbered more than 2,000. Towns were outgrowing their walled areas and extramural 'suburbs' became an increasingly common feature of south-west England's urban landscapes. For example, the built-up area of 15th-century Totnes had probably doubled in size since the construction of the town walls; indeed almost two-thirds of the households assessed for tax in 1449 were located outside the walled area.

Growing urban wealth, confidence and importance encouraged more Devon and Cornwall towns to seek complete self-government as incorporated boroughs. Plymouth was incorporated by 1439, but another 14 Devon towns achieved this status in the 16th or 17th centuries. By 1700, perhaps aided by Duchy influence, all 21 Cornish boroughs were incorporated as full municipal boroughs. The enhanced independence and freedom bestowed by incorporation often found physical expression as civic authorities proclaimed their power and dignity by building or embellishing a town's common hall, courts, or market house. Thus the ornate forebuilding added to Exeter's Guildhall in the early 1590s is one of the region's best-surviving signs of the civic confidence and pride that characterised this era. The new façade completed a remodelling of the existing medieval building that had begun in 1468 and stands today as a resplendent adornment to the city's High Street scene. Exeter's wealthy merchants built their fabulous gabled houses in this street and those adjacent, and the few Tudor and Stuart buildings that remain offer a hint of the richly textured appearance of the townscape in this extraordinary period of brilliance (Figs 9.11 and 9.12).

Most towns associated with trade, tin mining or the woollen industry in Devon and Cornwall experienced considerable growth in the late 15th and early 16th centuries and this renewed vigour and prosperity was manifested in the redevelopment and further spread of their built-up areas. Though much has inevitably been lost, surviving evidence of early Tudor urban expansion in the South West is fairly plentiful, and is particularly abundant in Devon. New streets were laid out and new houses were constructed. Dartmouth provides an excellent example. Its large new quay was constructed on reclaimed land at the river's edge in 1585 and, thereafter, wealthy townsmen took up plots and erected timber-framed houses of great distinction. Enough survive to indicate the exuberance and optimism that must have then prevailed. The Butterwalk, a colonnaded walkway supporting overhanging upper storeys of houses built along its length,

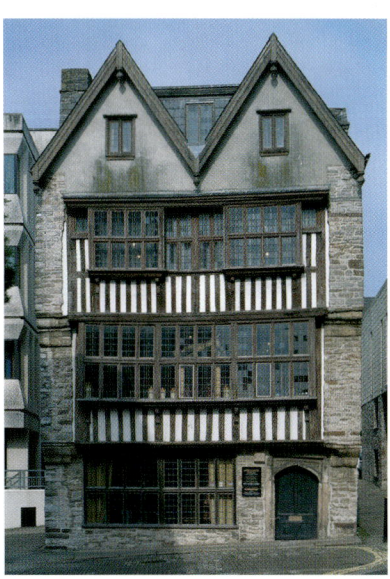

URBAN LANDSCAPES

was added in the early 17th century. Totnes is another Devon town, rich in Tudor and Stuart buildings, that possesses a similar high street arcade, but probably a century older than Dartmouth's Butterwalk. A similar, though less impressive feature exists in Plympton St Maurice's Fore Street. Butterwalks provided shelter for perishable goods traded on market days and protection from the elements for the occupants of the properties (Figs 9.13 and 9.14).

Fig. 9.13 Dartmouth, Devon, 'Butterwalk'.

Fig. 9.14 Totnes, Devon, 'Butterwalk'.

In Plymouth, though much has been lost, isolated glimpses of the Tudor and early Stuart expansion of the town survive. Thus Southside Street and New Street form the core of an Elizabethan addition on the southern side of Sutton Harbour (Fig. 9.15). Thereafter, building of quays below the site of the Carmelite friary on the harbour's north side in the early 1600s was quickly followed by the construction of slips and adjacent warehouses and homes. In north Devon, both Bideford and Barnstaple enjoyed a similar golden age, but rather less evidence survives conspicuously in their townscapes today.

Though there have been numerous losses in the stock of Tudor and Stuart domestic buildings, tangible evidence of this era of revival and prosperity is still detectable in lavish spending on churches in the region's towns. Among the most notable are St Peter's Church in Tiverton and St Andrew's in Cullompton where wealthy Devon cloth merchants spent generously and ostentatiously on embellishments to their local place of worship.

In Cornwall, the county's last 'planted' town, Falmouth, was founded in this era. Sir John Killigrew recognised the potential of the location for a town to rival the neighbouring boroughs of Truro, Tregony and Penryn, and building began some time after 1597. A charter was obtained in 1613 and the borough was incorporated in 1661. The church, dedicated to King Charles the Martyr, was added by 1664. The town was designated as the government's mail-packet station in the 1680s, a new harbour was built in 1705 and urban Falmouth developed quickly around the Market, Fish Strand Hill and Quay Hill. Although the mail-packet service ended in 1852, large-scale cargo handling sustained the town's continued growth and the ship-repairing business prompted the building of the 48ha dock, completed in 1861.

Although some of the principles of Italian Renaissance design filtered into the South West in the late 16th and early 17th centuries, the region did not share London's experience of pure Vitruvian and Palladian neoclassical architecture and town planning in the era before the Civil War. There is nothing of comparable date in Devon and Cornwall towns that competes with the elegant urban forms created by Inigo Jones in Covent Garden or Lincoln's Inn Fields, and certainly nothing to match the Whitehall Banqueting House or the Queen's House at Greenwich. Moreover, during the 17th century, a contraction of the cloth trade and the hiatus caused by warfare seriously interrupted the region's progress and prosperity. Following the Restoration in 1660, however, Renaissance townscape elements began to appear in Devon and, a little later, in Cornwall. Although the only notable piece of English Baroque architecture is the sumptuous gateway to Plymouth's Royal Citadel, completed in 1670, isolated but none the less important surviving 'Queen Anne' buildings embody the first stirrings of a lengthy love affair in the South West with classical design and form (Fig. 9.16). When the Renaissance proper arrived, it was Palladian classicism, rather than the florid 'Baroque' earlier popularised by Sir Christopher Wren and his adherents, that attracted the key architects who worked in Devon and Cornwall. John Wood's masterpieces and those of his son in Bath appear to have inspired the creation in 1772 of Robert Stribling's Bedford Circus in Exeter. Its site belonged to the Dukes of Bedford and the same vision that drove the development of their Bloomsbury estate may be detected in Stribling's commission. Tragically, the Circus was demolished after being damaged in the Exeter Blitz, but some of Matthew Nosworthy's work on other Bedford land in Exeter has been retained. Thus Barnfield

Fig. 9.15 Plymouth's 'south side' Tudor expansion is clearly visibly on the (left-hand) flank of the original inlet of Sutton harbour (at the centre of this picture). The sinuous course of Southside Street, which connected High Street with the Barbican, formed the main axis of this exuberant phase of urban expansion.

LEFT: 8*Fig. 9.16 Plymouth's Royal Citadel Baroque gateway was completed in 1670 in the reign of Charles II and is one of the few examples of the style in the South West.*

167

Fig. 9.17 Barnfield Crescent, Exeter, *survives as a glimpse of the once more-extensive Georgian domestic architecture that graced an area girdling the city centre.*

Crescent, Colleton Crescent, Southernhay and Dix's Field were built between 1790 and 1825 (Fig. 9.17). Three of these developments are reasonably intact, but only four heavily restored houses remain of the original two-dozen houses in Dix's Field as a hint of its former elegance; the rest fell victim to wartime air raids and post-war redevelopment, including the 1960s Civic Centre and a commercial development behind pastiche Georgian façades.

Surviving areas of coherently planned Georgian developments are thus unfortunately rather rare in Exeter. In any case, as elsewhere in the region, some of the city's best historic townscapes comprise an eclectic architectural mix of different periods and styles. Exeter's Cathedral Close is the outstanding exemplar. It contains the highest concentration of Grade I-listed buildings in the city with examples from the 16th to the 19th centuries. Facing the peerless medieval Gothic cathedral, the buildings of the Close blend miraculously as a composition of outstanding aesthetic quality, their diversity adding enormously to the quality of the urban scene (Fig. 9.18).

Fig. 9.18 Exeter's Cathedral Close *contains the highest concentration of Grade I-listed buildings in the city. Although this assemblage comprises a mix of styles and dates of building, it none the less blends as one of the most aesthetically pleasing prospects in Exeter.*

Georgian-period assemblages, as well as individual buildings, exist in many other Devon and Cornwall towns. While genteel neoclassical façades often provide a Georgian or Regency mask for medieval or early modern structures, entirely 18th-century builds are also to be found. Thus, central Truro is essentially late Georgian in date and style with some excellent ranges, such as the western side of Lemon Street, as well as individual buildings, such as the 1772 Bath-stone Assembly Rooms, the 1751 Mansion House, and the 1737 Prince's House. Launceston and Lostwithiel also contain some Georgian and Regency townscape elements and the same is true of Totnes, Dartmouth, Crediton, Honiton, Barnstaple and Bideford. While many fine Georgian buildings in

URBAN LANDSCAPES

Fig. 9.19 Surviving Officers' Houses in 'South Yard' (Devonport Dockyard) built in 1694. *Much of the glorious late 17th-century architecture was lost in the wartime attack that occurred in 1941, but these survive to hint at the splendours that have gone.*

Plymouth have been lost as a result of neglect, wartime bomb damage and insensitive redevelopment, some superb examples – both domestic and military – do remain. Among the finest are in Devonport's South Yard complex. The now stucco-rendered buildings, completed in 1694, are the only remnants of a group of three brick-built ranges of officers' houses designed with a 'palace' façade that echoed Wren's Royal Hospital at Chelsea (Fig. 9.19). Most of the Dockyard's Renaissance treasures, however, date to the Georgian period.

Elsewhere in Plymouth, the late 18th-century terraces in Stonehouse's Durnford Street provide a pleasing connection between the graceful elegance of the Royal Marine Barracks and the sublime Royal William Victualling Yard complex (Fig. 9.20). As more of these architectural treasures, increasingly

Fig. 9.20 The Royal William Victualling Yard, Stonehouse. *Completed in 1835 to the designs of Sir John Rennie, this complex occupies some 5.7ha (2.4ha of which comprise reclaimed land). With a brewery and cooperage, slaughterhouse, flour mill and bakery, and extensive storage facilities, its main task was to provision the fleet. The Yard finally closed on 26 August 1992 and has since been the subject of extensive development as a residential, retail and leisure facility.*

URBAN LANDSCAPES

redundant as military buildings, become accessible for the public to see and enjoy, it may be time to re-evaluate past assessments of Plymouth's townscape – so frequently condemned for the post-war drabness of the central shopping area. Some of the fine Regency stucco terraces of John Foulston and George Whitewick can still be seen in Athenaeum Street, Lockyer Street and Windsor Villas (Figs 9.21–9.24). There are also important survivals of Foulston's work in the planned developments focused on Stoke Damerel, which was fast becoming a fashionable suburb during the period of rapid growth in the early 19th century. A brief post-Napoleonic flirtation in England with Egyptian-inspired design produced a (now terribly forlorn) group of public buildings by John Foulston in Devonport and 'Egyptian Houses' in both Exeter and Penzance.

Some of Plymouth's fine Regency and Victorian stucco terraces.

TOP LEFT:
Fig. 9.21 Athenaeum Street.
TOP RIGHT:
9.22 Windsor Villas.
BOTTOM LEFT:
9.23 Durnford Street.
BOTTOM RIGHT:
9.24 Elliot Terrace.

Across the region as a whole, far more ubiquitous than surviving examples of Georgian townscapes are the streets of modest terraced houses laid out to accommodate a rapidly increasing urban population from the 1820s onwards. Many hectares of brick-built terraced houses, often erected at breakneck speed, surround the historic centres of the larger towns of Devon and Cornwall. The efforts of 19th-century speculative builders are prominently on display as an abundant element of south-west England's urban housing stock. The houses they constructed provide a monotonous, unmistakable 'guard of honour' for those arriving by car or train in Exeter, Plymouth, Truro, Newton Abbot, Totnes, Penzance and a number of other towns. Devon and Cornwall were largely spared the worst kind of jerry-built housing that characterised some of northern England's major cities; there were, for example, scarcely any back-to-back dwellings and the longevity of the region's Victorian terraces is a clear testament to their generally robust construction. Around the key centres of mining and quarrying such as Camborne, Redruth and St Austell, ranked battalions of terraced cottages document decades of soaring early-Victorian industrial expansion in the mining industries and have since stood sentinel as witnesses to its contraction.

Grander landscaped villas built for the wealthy middle classes, and imposing civic architecture in town centres, represent further, more distinguished, 19th-century contributions to the urban landscapes of the South West. Classical principles of design persisted and are perhaps best exemplified by the Higher Market in Exeter's Queen Street. Built in 1835 by Charles Fowler in honey-coloured Bath stone, with Doric fluted columns, this is one of the region's masterpieces. For many years it was disused and neglected, but is now incorporated as the frontage of the Guildhall Shopping Precinct, which was completed in the mid-1980s. Though restoration of Fowler's colonnade is greatly to be welcomed, the complex behind is a somewhat undignified appendage attached to so graceful and elegant a street frontage. The 1846 City Hall in Truro survives as an example of a good-quality Victorian public building in Cornwall. Built in Carn Brea granite to the Italian Renaissance designs of Christopher Eales, the hall originally accommodated not only the city council but also the market, the magistrates and the stannary courts, the police station and cells, and the fire brigade. It was damaged by fire in 1914 and not restored until 1925, when theatre facilities were installed. In recent decades the building gradually deteriorated and was at serious risk until its refurbishment and reopening in 1997 as the splendid Hall for Cornwall (Fig. 9.25).

Fig. 9.25 Truro City Hall, the Hall for Cornwall. The hall was originally built in 1846 to house the city's market, council offices, magistrates and stannary courts, police station and fire brigade. Its splendid granite façade in Italian Renaissance style was restored in the 1990s.

INDUSTRY, TRADE AND THE URBAN LANDSCAPE

Trade, fishing, mining and the cloth industry have fuelled the development of industrial townscapes in Devon and Cornwall since medieval times. In 1198, tin working in Devon was placed under the supervision of a Crown-appointed 'warden' who ensured that all newly smelted tin was assayed, stamped and taxed before its sale. This led to the development of 'stannary' or coinage towns where the function could be carried out and monitored. In Devon, tin produced from Dartmoor deposits was taken to be coined (a piece cut from the 'coign' or corner for assay) in Ashburton, Chagford, Plympton or Tavistock. Lydford Castle was used as a stannary gaol for the incarceration of those who offended against the elaborate code of stannary law. By 1305, comparable functions were provided for Cornish tinners in Bodmin, Lostwithiel, Truro and Helston. But coining activity in Bodmin and Lostwithiel had declined by the late 16th century and Liskeard had become Cornwall's fifth stannary town. Finally, in 1663 Penzance was made the county's sixth coinage town and rapidly grew as Cornwall's premier centre for this service. Towns such as Callington, St Austell, Camborne, Redruth, St Just-in-Penwith and Tavistock owe the development of much of their townscape to the expansion of mining and quarrying in the 18th and 19th centuries. Ports such as Charlestown, Falmouth, Fowey, Hayle, Looe, Lamorna, Padstow, Par, Penryn, Pentewan, Penzance, Porthlevan, St Agnes, St Ives, Teignmouth and Truro developed as a result of handling exports of mine and quarry products and imports of the industry's requirements.

Fishing and cargo-handling activities have stimulated the development of Devon and Cornwall coastal towns since medieval times. The boroughs of Polperro (1303), Port Isaac (1338) and Mevagissey (1410) are good examples of fishing ports where this specialised occupation provided a livelihood for the entire community. In addition to housing and fish cellars, such ports often required piers and breakwaters to protect their boats and provide mooring. In the 15th century, the building and rebuilding of such structures at Mousehole, Newlyn, Towan Blustry, Padstow, Bude and Clovelly stimulated urban growth as the fishing industry expanded (Fig. 9.26).

Communities of fishermen sometimes developed settlements separate from the core of an existing town. Brixham provides an example: two distinct elements developed in the townscape, one around the parish church on the hill, and another around the quay, harbour and strand. A second wave of pier or breakwater improvement during the 19th century

Fig. 9.26 Padstow harbour, Cornwall.
The sheltered harbour of Padstow, on the Camel estuary, was used by both Hawkins and Frobisher in the 16th century on their return from Atlantic expeditions. By the 17th century, exports of Cornish copper, slate and agricultural produce were sent from Padstow to Bristol and elsewhere. However, fishing was always the main commercial activity.

marks another major phase of growth as south-west England's fishing industry required enhanced port capacity and facilities. By then Plymouth, Newlyn, Brixham, Dartmouth, Looe, Falmouth and Padstow were the premier centres and they remain the region's major fishing ports.

Textile manufacturing and the cloth trade have also underpinned the region's urban development since the medieval period. The 14th-century accounts of the aulnager, who was required to inspect the quality of cloth offered for sale (and charged clothiers a fee for the service), list sales in 20 Devon towns and another seven in Cornwall. The building of fulling or tucking mills in Devon towns such as Honiton and Tiverton in the 13th century emphasises the importance of the woollen-cloth finishing process as a further direct stimulus to urban growth. Records of exports of cloth from Exeter as well as other Devon and Cornwall ports, including Dartmouth and Plymouth, underline the contribution of the trade to the wider prosperity of towns in the South West. From the 15th century, Exeter's clothiers controlled their industry from Tucker's Hall in Fore Street. The guild's 1471 chapel, converted after the Reformation into the two-storey secular hall, is all that survives today.

In Axminster, Thomas Whitty's carpet making began in 1755 and prompted growth in the town until the business transferred to Wilton in Wiltshire in 1835. However, in the 1940s, Axminster's carpet industry was revived. Lace making in Honiton remained important until the First World War but its impact on the town was not as significant as the introduction in 1816 of machine-made lace making by John Heathcoat in Tiverton. Along with Tavistock, where the Dukes of Bedford built 294 cottages for copper miners and quarrymen between 1845 and 1866, Heathcoat's workers' dwellings in Tiverton represent an otherwise fairly rare variety of 19th-century townscape in the South West: factory housing. The distinctive Bedford cottages accounted for around 25 per cent of Tavistock's total housing stock by 1871 and remain an unmistakable element in the town today (Fig. 9.27). Houses provided for Heathcoat employees were built to a variety of designs over the course of more than a century. At least 250 were constructed; the last ones were completed in 1936 (Fig. 9.28). They give the West-Exe district of Tiverton an authentic 'factory village' appearance, enhanced by the presence of the mill buildings, Heathcoat's 1843 school and the 1877 working men's institute.

Fig. 9.27 The Duke of Bedford's 'model' cottages, at Westbridge, Tavistock, in Devon, built in 1850. The ducal crest can be seen on the gable of the dormer at the end of the terrace.

Fig. 9.28 Heathcoat's factory housing, Westexe, Tiverton, Devon, built during the 19th and early 20th centuries.

URBAN LANDSCAPES

NATURAL DISASTERS, WARFARE AND THE URBAN LANDSCAPE

Writing his history of Devon in 1808, Richard Polwhele remarked that the destruction of town-centre property by fire 'has been the fate of more towns in the West than any other part of the kingdom' and that, in this regard, Crediton and Tiverton could boast 'a painful pre-eminence'. Indeed, frequent blazes and subsequent rebuilding in central Tiverton spared only one pre-18th-century building and this led Professor Hoskins to describe it as 'an undistinguished 19th-century town'. Nine major conflagrations in the period between 1598 and 1788 destroyed 1,500 houses and the 1625 floods wrecked another 53. In the period between 1679 and 1779, Crediton and Honiton each suffered four major fires, and serious blazes caused damage in Bradninch, Chudleigh, Ottery St Mary, Great Torrington and Cullompton. Although no Devon town can boast a rebuilt Georgian town centre to rival that created in Dorset's Blandford Forum following its destruction by fire in 1731, some of the more pleasing areas of Honiton and Crediton owe their existence to reconstruction after major blazes.

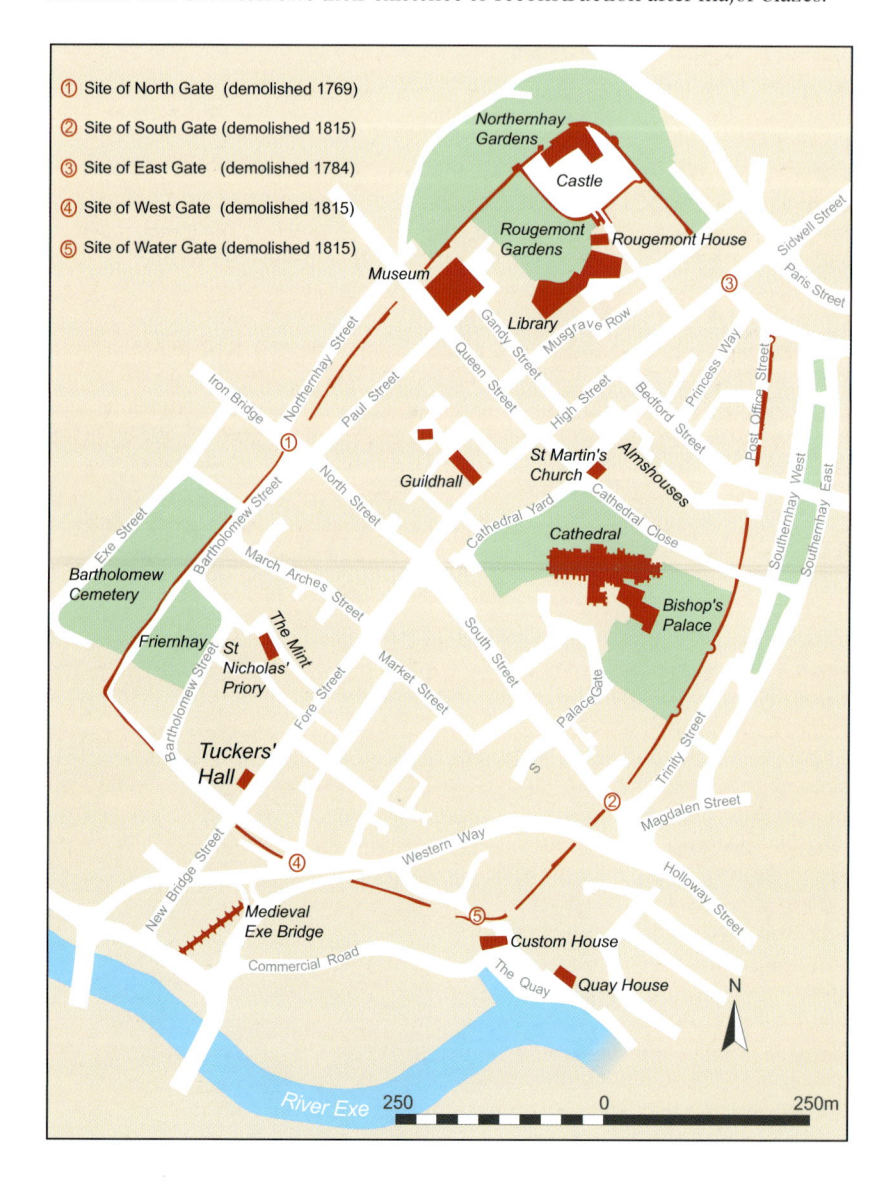

Fig. 9.29 Central Exeter.

Fire damage encouraged a switch from thatch to slate for roofing. This happened almost overnight in Chudleigh after 175 houses burned down in 1807 and, during the second half of the 18th century, brick and slate gradually replaced cob and thatch throughout the centre of Crediton.

Chapter 6 has reviewed examples where urban morphology in the South West has been tangibly influenced by the need for defence. Thus the city walls of Exeter, originally Roman, survive today as an indication of past imperatives to provide protection for urban populations against attack and to signify a boundary between town and country (Fig. 9.29). Elsewhere, though the structures themselves might long since have been demolished, the alignment of former town walls has exerted a lasting 'cadastral' influence on the pattern of streets and buildings in towns such as Totnes and Launceston.

Unprecedented and irrevocable change to the urban landscapes of the South West occurred during the Second World War. Stories of the bombing of both Plymouth and Exeter have been told and retold. But air raids were not confined to these two major south-west cities. Truro and Falmouth came under sustained attack on 24 September 1942, while the towns of Dartmouth, Saltash, Torpoint, Liskeard, Penzance, Camborne and St Austell were also the target of bombers and were damaged. Falmouth Dockyard and the St Eval airfield near Newquay were major strategic targets in Cornwall. None the less, the destruction in Exeter and Plymouth was far greater than anywhere else in the region. Air attacks on Exeter began in August 1940 and lasted until December 1942. Those on 24 April and 4 August 1942 were much the worst. A total of 59 separate raids on Plymouth began in July 1940 and continued until April 1944. In all, 72,102 homes were either destroyed or damaged in the city; 1,172 civilians were killed and another 3,269 were seriously injured. The guildhall and municipal offices, St Andrew's Church, Charles Church, the railway stations, other key public utilities, and the retail heart of both central Plymouth and Devonport were hit. Great damage was also caused to the dockyard. The worst episodes were in March and April 1941. Across five dates in late April, 1,140 high explosive bombs, 17 paramines and countless thousands of incendiaries rained down in attacks that lasted in all for 23 hours. More than a thousand people were killed or badly hurt. An estimated 2,000 separate fires raged across the cityscape; the reddish glow of Plymouth 'in flames' was easily visible from more than 30km away.

Both of Devon's great cities were brought low by these terrible attacks and both were subjects of famous post-war reconstruction plans. Thomas Sharp's landmark proposal for the redevelopment of bomb-damaged central Exeter was published in 1946. Evocatively entitled *Exeter Phoenix*, Sharp's plan envisaged an inner bypass and a protective green belt around the city centre. He designed bold new roads and large traffic islands at junctions in the central shopping centre. Mercifully, these were not fully adopted. The ring-road scheme was mostly realised, though Sharp could not have foreseen the current scale of Exeter's acute traffic-congestion problem. The ideas in *Exeter Phoenix* for major redevelopment in some of the bomb-damaged areas north and east of High Street were also implemented, but the resulting environment is somewhat bleak and a scheme to revitalise the Princesshay area is now under way. Refurbishment may improve the dreary 1960s appearance of this quadrant of central Exeter, which stands in such sharp contrast to the glories of the cathedral precincts and the rich architectural texture of some other parts of the city.

The blitz upon Plymouth caused damage on an almost unimaginable scale. But even before hostilities ended, schemes for the city's reconstruction were being devised. Viscount Astor, Plymouth's wartime mayor, invited Professor (later Sir) Patrick Abercrombie to help in the preparation of the *Plan for Plymouth*, which was published in 1943 as the blueprint for rebuilding the city. The *Plan* contained radical proposals on housing, shopping facilities, transport, population decentralisation, employment and recreation in post-war Plymouth,

URBAN LANDSCAPES

URBAN LANDSCAPES

but at its heart were sweeping designs for a completely new city centre. Working with the city engineer, James Paton Watson, Abercrombie and Lord Astor were determined to clear away Plymouth's complicated tangle of pre-war streets and to lay out a formal, grid-iron pattern of east–west boulevards, bisected by a grand north–south axis, Armada Way to link the railway station at North Cross with the Hoe. Work commenced in 1947 and resulted in the most comprehensively changed city centre in the South West (Figs 9.30 and 9.31). St Andrew's Church and the Victorian Guildhall were retained and restored, but the latter was drastically altered. Though regarded as a landmark of national significance for urban planning and reconstruction, the rigid geometry of the city centre layout devised in the *Plan for Plymouth*, and the rather mediocre standard of the architecture achieved by those who had the task of designing new buildings, resulted in a cheerless central townscape but redeemed of course by the undoubted magnificence of Plymouth's physical setting (Fig. 9.32).

Pedestrianisation and landscaping of the main shopping streets in 1988 did much to soften the bleak wilderness of straight lines that characterises Plymouth

OPPOSITE PAGE:
Fig. 9.30 Central Plymouth 1943.

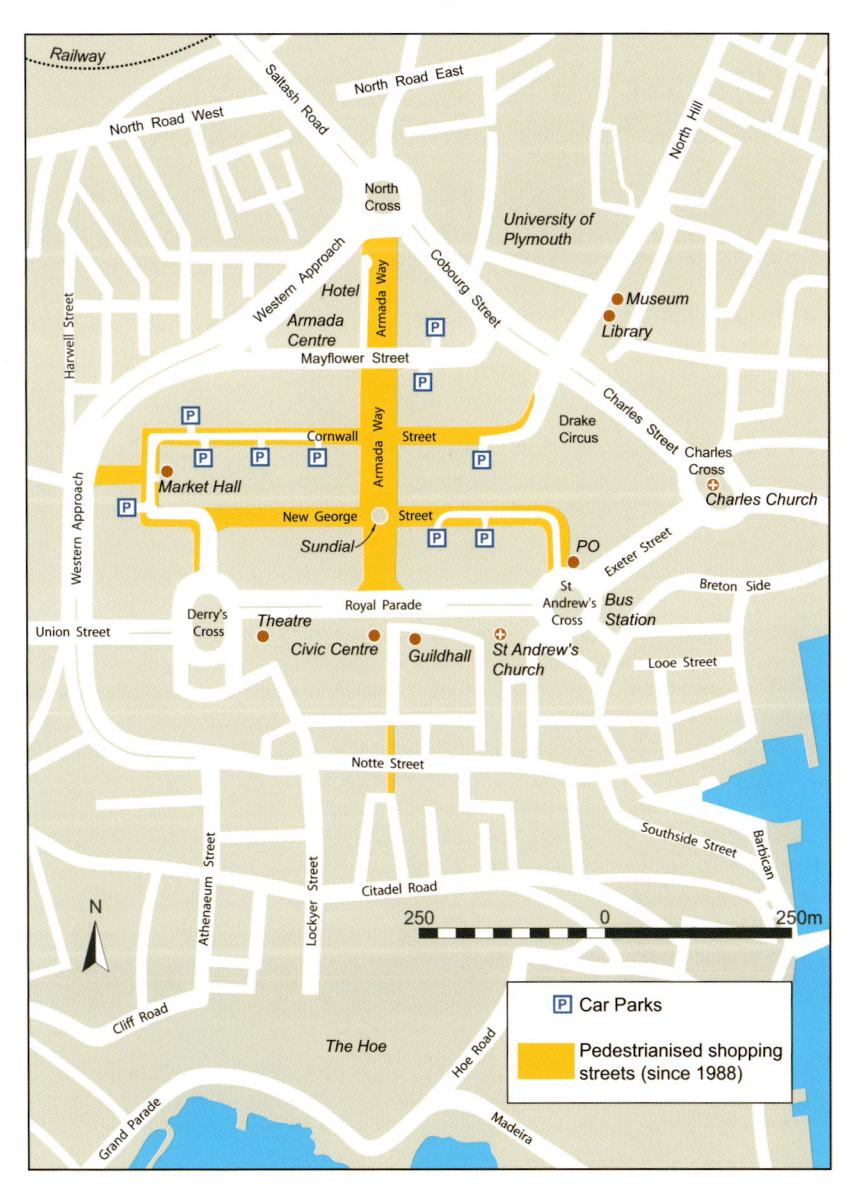

Fig. 9.31 Central Plymouth 2005.

URBAN LANDSCAPES

Fig. 9.32 Plymouth from the Sound, *looking north across the Hoe towards the regular geometry of the post-war city centre.*

and today there are further ambitious ideas for the revitalisation of the Abercrombie city centre. In addition, the somewhat neglected boulevard, Union Street, designed by John Foulston to link the three historic towns that comprise modern Plymouth, may at last be refurbished. Moreover, the local planners have now begun to recognise the enormous potential and unparalleled splendour of the city's 18km of waterfront and schemes are being implemented to improve access and amenities in this zone, and to integrate it effectively with the attractive narrow streets of the Barbican and Plymouth's central shopping areas. Comparisons drawn by the city's officials with the extraordinary revitalisation of Barcelona's waterfront might seem rather exaggerated, but signs of improvement in Plymouth are thus far encouraging. The Barbican area, with all its splendid historical associations, is now home to the National Marine Aquarium, made accessible by a bridge at the harbour entrance, a new visitor centre, hotels, restaurants and cafes. North Quay Marina and the comings and goings of fishing vessels bringing their catch to the new Fish Market add to the interest and liveliness of this part of the city. As a model of what might be achieved elsewhere on the waterfront, such improvements are an object lesson in reclaiming a patch of townscape and 're-inventing' it as a pleasant recreation space (*see* Chapter 11).

Beyond the reconstruction of the city centre, Abercrombie's *Plan for Plymouth* encompassed the entire 'greater Plymouth' area. He incorporated existing residential neighbourhoods, and planned others, where he hoped to engineer a local identity and community feeling. Population was to be 'decentralised' and attractive new housing was to be built. But Plymouth's resultant collection of more than a dozen bland and austere post-war inner suburbs is a rather disappointing response to thinking that, in the midst of war, had seemed so optimistic and visionary.

Wartime destruction clearly provided unique opportunities for Devon's two great cities. Plymouth's remodelling was far more comprehensive and has bequeathed a rather cumbersome legacy for today's planners as they face demands and expectations that are very different to those prevailing in the

1940s. The post-war planners were, on balance, less brutal in Exeter, though the rebuilt zones jar badly with the serene beauty of older parts of the townscape. Notwithstanding these criticisms, it may be noted that Exeter and Plymouth provide unrivalled laboratories of national importance for the study of the history of 20th-century town planning.

RECREATION, TOURISM AND THE URBAN LANDSCAPE

Mid-18th-century treatises on the medicinal benefits of sea air and sea-water bathing popularised Exmouth and Teignmouth as tourist towns, but lengthy and expensive stage-coach journeys limited visitor numbers and confined the delights of these two resorts to wealthy clients. In the same period, Torquay developed a lucrative trade in renting accommodation to families of naval officers. Demand ensured that new terraces and detached Gothic-style villas were being built long before the railway arrived in 1848. In all three cases, bathing beaches and bathing machines were advertised regularly during the Georgian era. Although Cornwall's resorts generally opened up much later than those in Devon, and depended critically on the arrival of the mainline railway, Penzance had developed a significant trade by the mid-1790s, describing itself as England's Montpellier. In fact, by then, war with France had closed off the Continent for tourism and other south-west resorts began to develop. A good example is Sidmouth, where town-centre lodging houses were built and 'summer cottages' set in parkland began to pepper the surrounding hillside (Fig. 9.33). Growth peaked in the 1840s but thereafter remained rather flat. Only a minor surge of expansion followed the building of Sidmouth's railway link in 1874. However, the resort experienced massive expansion in the final decades of the 20th century when areas of new housing were added, much of it to accommodate increasing numbers of retired residents.

Notwithstanding Sidmouth's experience – where the railway connection terminated well short of the resort itself – the construction of railways and the creation of urban landscapes devoted to recreation, leisure and tourism have elsewhere been intimately related. Thus a major new building boom began in Torquay in 1849 and its lasting pre-eminence, was thereby established. In the mid-Victorian period, restrained Italianate stucco architecture was in vogue. Much survives and parts of Torquay's townscape still resemble the Mediterranean Riviera. The resort has never lost its lead and in the early 21st century remains overwhelmingly the region's largest provider of holiday accommodation (Fig. 9.34).

There had been substantial development for tourism in Ilfracombe before the railway arrived in 1870. The resident population doubled between 1801 and 1851 and the resort marketed itself as the 'Brighton of north Devon'. But considerable further expansion occurred in late-Victorian times and

Fig. 9.33 Sidmouth, Devon, Fortfield and Coburg terraces.

URBAN LANDSCAPES

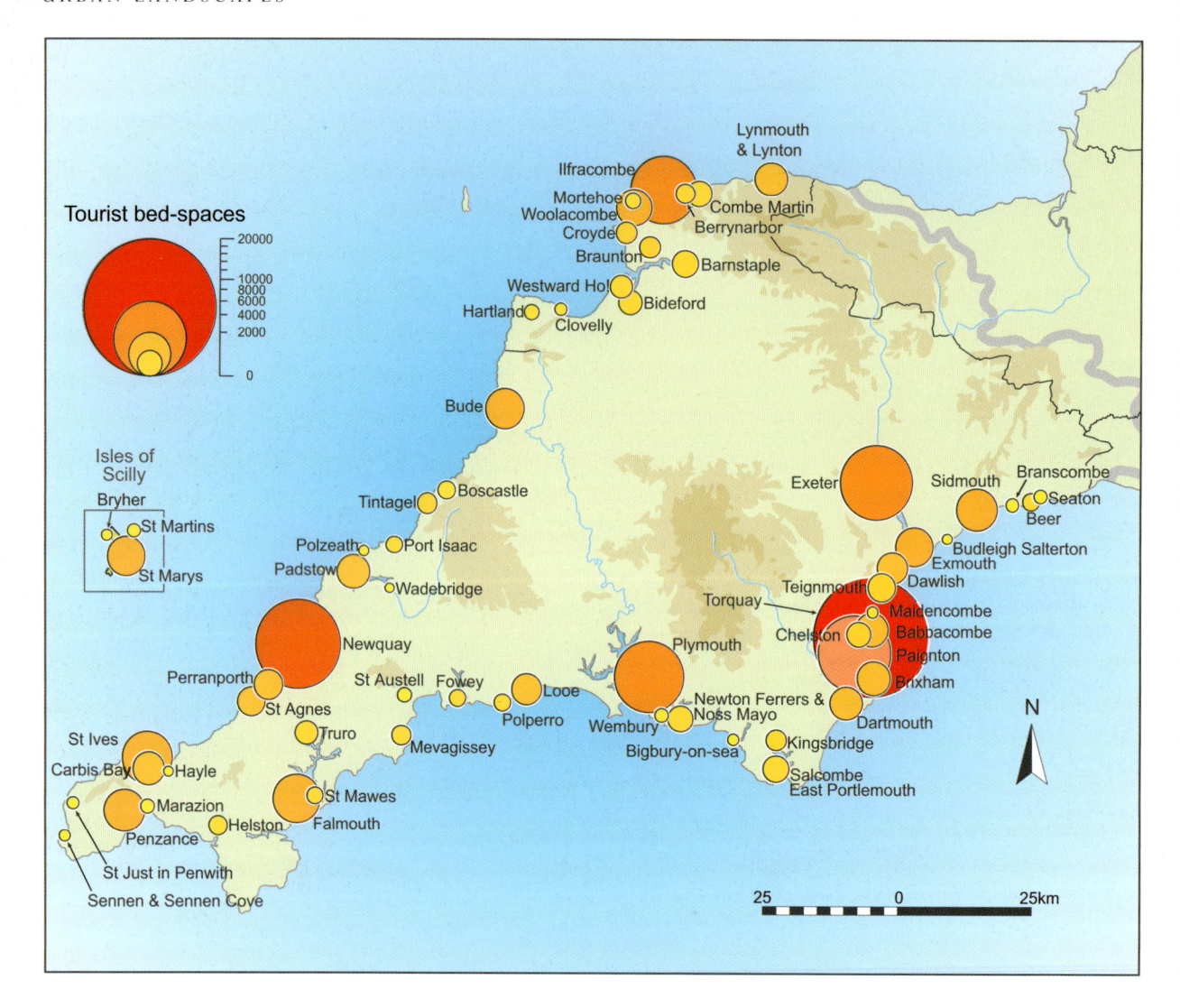

Fig. 9.34 Devon and Cornwall seaside towns (bed-space capacity).

Fig. 9.35 Westwell Hotel, Ilfracombe, typical of the extraordinary wealth of fine, late-Victorian architecture to be found in the north Devon seaside resort.

the population doubled again by 1901. Tangible evidence of Ilfracombe's rapid growth survives in the form of an exceptional array of outstandingly good late-Victorian buildings (Fig. 9.35). In Cornwall, the holiday resorts of Newquay and St Ives are essentially creations of the railway age. Both experienced economic problems that resulted from the faltering fishing and mining industries but, from the 1870s, tourism provided a rescue. The fishing village of Towan Blustry, clustered around the harbour, is the original settlement, but the new resort of Newquay within which it is now enveloped initially mushroomed next to the new railway terminus.

Tourist towns in Devon and Cornwall form a distinct urban genre. Coastal resorts exhibit an urban design aimed unmistakably at pleasure and recreation. Seaside promenades, ornamental gardens, parkland and generally low building densities are the morphological hallmarks. Having indulged the tastes of a particular era and class of clientele, today they are often townscapes constrained by their past, struggling to respond to fashion's changing whims. The setting of some has been scarred by areas of unsightly holiday chalets and caravans, while others possess awkward and outdated facilities that might have appealed to Victorian holidaymakers, but seem ill-at-ease as the setting for 21st-century tourism.

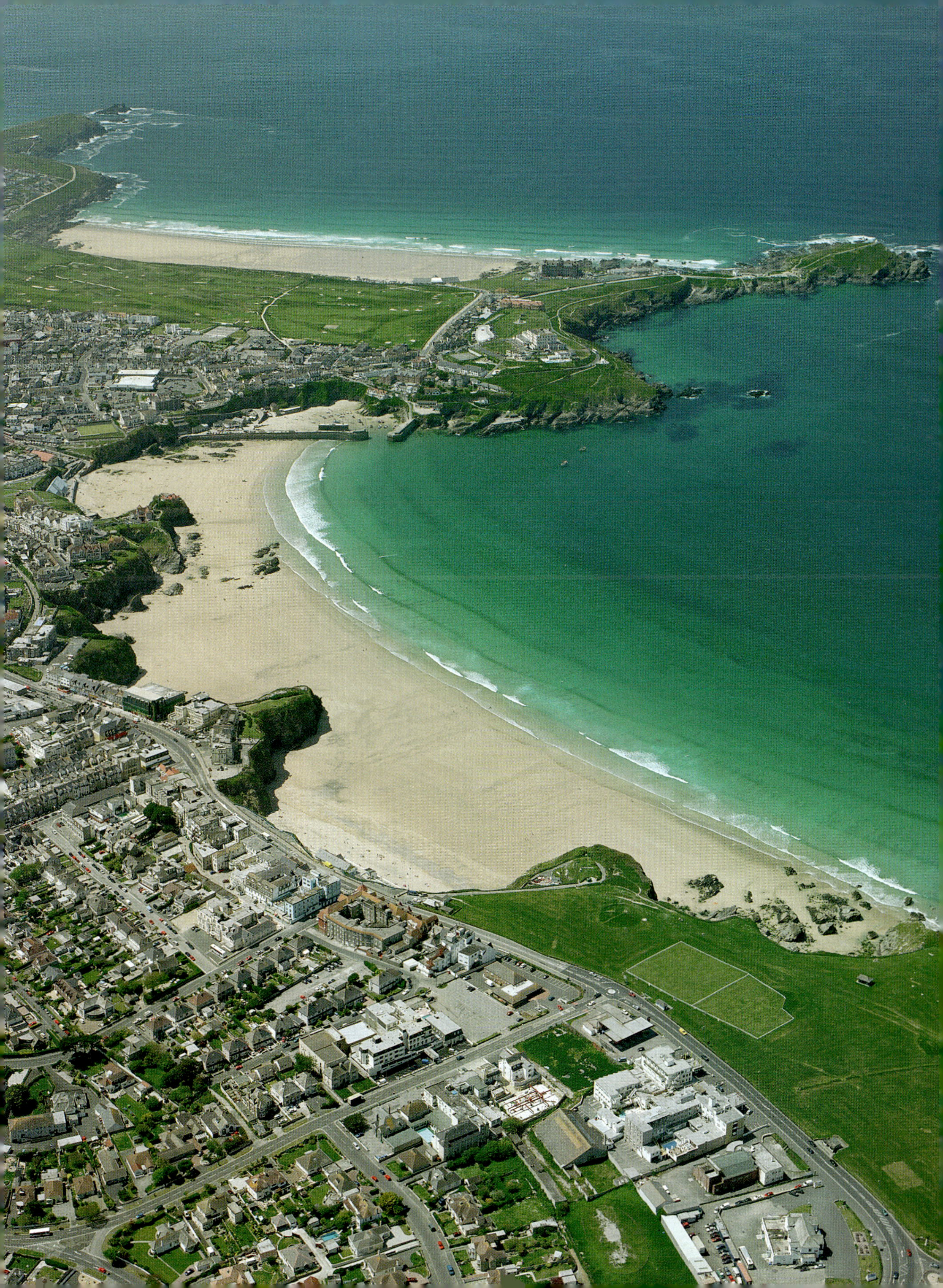

URBAN LANDSCAPES

PREVIOUS PAGE:
Fig. 9.36 Newquay, Cornwall. *The west-facing Fistral surfing beach can be seen in the background and is bordered by Towan Head. Towan (or 'Town') Beach is in the centre. Tolcarne Beach is in the foreground.*

Newquay's recent renewed growth in popularity amongst young holidaymakers is attributable largely to its reputation for surfing. In 2005 the town ranked second only to Torquay in its capacity to accommodate visitors (Fig. 9.36). Similarly, the rise in the fortunes of St Ives has been linked to the town's associations with painters and sculptors and the opening of the Tate St Ives in the town (Fig. 9.37). A generally benign climate and the beauty of the scenery remain the region's abiding advantages and the popularity of Devon and Cornwall as holiday destinations significantly outstrips other English regions. Tourism in the South West is currently estimated to be worth around £3 billion a year. Moreover, although provision for holidaymakers in the region's cities and inland villages and market towns has grown enormously in recent decades, holiday accommodation in coastal resorts still accounts for 65.8 per cent of the total.

Fig. 9.37 The Tate St Ives building, designed by the architects Evans and Shaleff, overlooks Porthmeor Beach on the outskirts of St Ives. Opened in 1993 it houses important works of the 'St Ives School' and a collection of Barbara Hepworth sculptures. A new 'creative centre' designed by Jamie Fobert is to be added to the gallery – a project that underlines the Tate's great success in this Cornish town, which is renowned for its long association with the work of notable artists.

URBAN LANDSCAPES AND ENCOUNTERS WITH MODERNITY

As elsewhere in England, the inexorable spread of the built environment has profoundly affected the landscape of Devon and Cornwall. Even the region's smaller, relatively remote market towns have 'modern' peripheral estates, sometimes gauche and intrusive, yet undeniably necessary additions to the accommodation stock. The region largely escaped the blight of the 1960s fashion for tower-block building and most residential development in the South West has comprised low-rise housing. Estates of bungalows, forming rather sterile outer cordons around Devonian and Cornish coastal resorts, are a further striking feature of south-west England's 20th-century urban landscapes.

Demand for housing in Exeter and Plymouth now outstrips the existing supply and both lack sufficient space to build enough accommodation inside their boundaries. Thus although Plymouth plans 9,000 new homes within the city by 2010, locating 90 per cent on 'brown-field' sites, a 'new town' of 3,500 homes is envisaged on grade II agricultural land in the Sherford valley in the

URBAN LANDSCAPES

South Hams near Brixton. A similar 3,000-home development has been mooted for the Clyst Valley near Exeter. Inevitably, the clamour of protest against further losses of rural scenery has been both loud and sustained. Paradoxically, access to affordable housing for the young in both counties has been denied as Devon and Cornwall's housing market is increasingly skewed by the purchasing power of second-home buyers and retirement migrants drawn in from more affluent areas of the country. Because young families with school-aged children are being 'priced out', the socio-economic and demographic balance of south-west urban communities is now being seriously damaged. The region's encounters with modernity have clearly not been easy.

TRURO, PLYMOUTH AND EXETER

This brief survey of Devon and Cornwall's urban landscapes ends, where it began, with the region's three cities: Truro, Plymouth and Exeter. The city of Truro has been Cornwall's capital since 1912. Lostwithiel and Bodmin, in turn, previously held the position. But as a major port, a key hub in the 18th-century turnpike network and later a node on the railway system, Truro was already the county's premier town (Fig. 9.38). The re-establishment of the diocese of Cornwall in 1876, separate from Exeter, and the enlargement of St Mary's to become Truro's cathedral, led to city status in 1877. Truro's pre-eminence might have been further underlined in the late 20th century if the Combined Universities for Cornwall development had been focused upon the city. However, the campus for the University of Exeter in Cornwall is at Tremough, near Falmouth.

Taking 30 years to complete, Truro Cathedral was the first to be built in England since London's St Paul's. The architect, John Pearson, was required to design for a cramped, central site where no space for a close existed. While its style contrasts markedly with church architecture elsewhere in Cornwall, Pearson's cathedral, dominated by spires soaring to 76m, is a building of immense power and grandeur. It is now Truro's foremost emblem, aptly symbolising Cornwall's spirit and independence.

During the boom years of Victorian expansion, the three towns of Plymouth, Stonehouse and Devonport physically coalesced and were united as a single local authority in 1914. City status was achieved in 1928. As the youngest, largest and brashest city in the South West, its senior cousins, Exeter and Truro, sometimes regard Plymouth with suspicion. The sprawling townscape can certainly seem raw and unsophisticated. In recent years, however, Plymouth's character has matured. The Theatre Royal, opened in 1982, the Pavilions Conference and Leisure Centre and the National Marine Aquarium, added in the 1990s, are not only considerable adornments to the townscape, but provide facilities of regional

Fig. 9.38 Central Truro. Truro developed around the confluence of two minor rivers, the Kenwyn and the Allen, which combine to form the Truro River, a tidal creek that drains into the Fal estuary. The medieval town was clustered around the castle, which stood on the site visible at the top left-hand corner of the picture. As the town grew, its centre migrated towards Lemon Quay, built at the highest tidal extent of the Truro River and, historically, the highest navigable point for sizeable vessels. Today's townscape is dominated by the cathedral, completed in 1910, the first to be built in Britain since the Reformation.

importance. On-going waterfront redevelopment and improvement, much aided by the relinquishing of buildings and land by the Ministry of Defence, has further transformed and enhanced the city. Although the University of Plymouth only received its charter in 1992, it is already a major asset. It has built on the former polytechnic, created in 1970 by expanding Plymouth's College of Technology, and has rapidly become one of the country's leading 'new' universities. Though its buildings possess no great architectural merit, and some are unremittingly ugly, the university's presence on its small campus adjacent to the shopping centre has injected considerable dynamism to the city in an era when the declining fortunes of Devonport Dockyard and Plymouth's traditional economic activities might have resulted in urban stagnation.

In his magisterial survey, *Devon*, Professor Hoskins wrote that Exeter before the Second World War was one of the most beautiful and appealing cities in England, 'full of colour, light and movement'. Exeter still possesses an appeal unlike any other town in the region. Urban sprawl during the 20th century has, however, greatly extended the city's built-up area. Development of housing on a massive scale in Exwick and Sylvania has come close to undermining one of Exeter's great assets, namely the ability to view from its centre the surrounding green hills. Industrial estates at Marsh Barton and Sowton are further 20th-century additions to the urban landscape. By contrast, the expansion on the city's northern edge of the University of Exeter has proved a considerable adornment. The institution's origins may be traced to the establishment of a School of Art in 1855 and the subsequent creation of the University College of the South West of England in 1920. But the acquisition in the 1930s of the greenfield Streatham Estate enabled the university to begin the creation of today's exceptionally fine campus.

With only a few high-rise blocks to spoil the prospect, Exeter's central townscape is still dominated by the majestic cathedral, where the main structure dates to the 14th century. No description can adequately convey its splendour; without doubt, it is one of the most beautiful of all English cathedrals. As it has been down the centuries, it remains the city's greatest treasure and attraction. Unrivalled and unequalled, Exeter is Devon's capital and the whole region's mother city.

FURTHER READING

Hoskins 1972, 104–23 and Balchin 1983, 120–43, provide useful introductions to the towns of Devon and Cornwall.

Pevsner and Cherry 1989, and Pevsner and Radcliffe 1970 offer indispensable guides to the region's architecture. For Exeter, these studies may be augmented by consulting Mellor 1989.

Beresford 1988, 399–414 and 417–26 is the classic study of medieval town foundation, but see also Fox in Kain and Ravenhill (eds) 1999, 400–7.

Early modern developments are discussed in Barry 1999, 413–25.

Useful material on Plymouth and Exeter may be found in Chalkley, *et al.* (eds) 1991, 62–81, and in Kain and Ravenhill (eds) 1999, 482–513.

For information about townscapes shaped by maritime activities, garrisons or the tourist trade the following are recommended: Kowaleski 1992, 52–71; Pye and Woodward 1996; Shaw *et al.* in Kain and Ravenhill (eds) 1999, 453–61; and Travis 1994, 136–44.

10

Landscapes of Transport

MARK BRAYSHAY

ROADS, TRACKS AND FOOTPATHS

As a long peninsula, with strong relief and a scattered population, the South West has developed a close mesh of roads, lanes and trackways. Devon has more than 13,197km of classified road, while Cornwall, with 7,708km, has the highest ratio of roads to area of any English county. The region's only motorway comprises a 38.6km stretch of the M5 in east Devon. Trunk roads account for 547km of the network, while there are another 1,411km of main road (Fig. 10.1). Almost three-quarters of the region's thoroughfares are therefore minor roads and lanes. The South West possesses an intricate web of footpaths, bridleways and byways that together amount to some 10,000km of public rights of way, representing about one-twentieth of England's entire network. These routes are increasingly valued as key recreational resources and those offering the highest scenic value are promoted as major rural tourism attractions. For example, the South-West Coastal Footpath, which runs for 1,014km around the peninsula from the Somerset border in the north to that with Dorset in the south, is an important asset that encourages holidaymakers to visit Devon and Cornwall. The Two Moors Way, connecting Ivybridge on Dartmoor's southern edge, with Lynmouth on Exmoor's Bristol Channel coast, extends 143km and passes through landscapes of huge variety and unsurpassed beauty. In Cornwall, the Saints Way links Padstow on the Camel estuary with Fowey on the south coast by a 42km footpath that follows a prehistoric itinerary probably used since the Bronze Age, though later associated with the peregrinations of Celtic saints. However, the countless local lanes and footpaths represent a more authentic transport heritage than the long-distance paths that have been 'invented' for modern consumption. Often omitted from discussions, rights of way survive as important relics of all those daily or weekly reasons for journeys on foot of half a mile, a mile or even five miles in times when travel in a vehicle was the exception rather than the norm. Collectively, they add up to a haunting, largely silent aspect of south-west England's transport landscapes that provides a glimpse of a land-based communications infrastructure that dominated in England for many centuries before the industrial revolution. Notwithstanding some completely new thoroughfares built since the 18th century, many of today's classified roads are, in reality, just the more successful, most heavily used footpath routes of the past.

Improvements to the 20th- and 21st-century road system build on those begun in Devon and Cornwall during the turnpike era of the 18th and 19th centuries. Until then, wheeled vehicles were uncommon outside the towns of the South West and the horse was still the main means of land-based transport – packhorses for freight and mares or geldings for riding. But the vast majority of journeys would have been made on foot. Ancient ridgeways and tracks that had

LANDSCAPES OF TRANSPORT

Fig. 10.1 Devon and Cornwall 'six-day motor coach cruise in 1939'. *Motor coach tours in Devon and Cornwall peaked in popularity in the inter-war years. The map reconstructs a holiday itinerary typically offered by the Midland Red Company. For an inclusive fare of 8 guineas, tourists enjoyed an extensive visit to the region. After the Second World War, with rising private car ownership and improvements to the road network that allowed for speedier travel, the popularity of such leisurely tours began to diminish.*

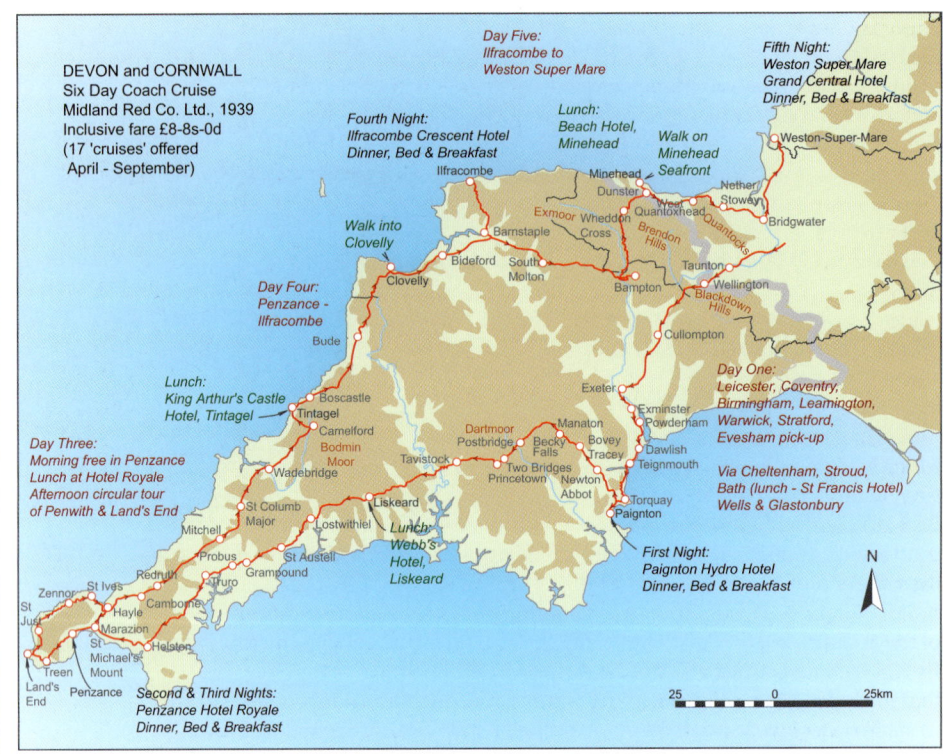

been used for millennia still formed the region's principal highways. Relics of these survive as minor roads in remoter districts and across the high moorland, where medieval stone crosses mark well-trodden routes. Some of England's earliest signposts survive on Dartmoor, for example the granite posts marking a route between Ashburton and Tavistock that were erected in the 1690s. Moorland rivers are still forded by distinctive stone 'clapper' bridges, several originally constructed in the 15th century or earlier, though most rebuilt many times since (Fig. 10.2). Indeed, the region's topography of steep valleys and fast-flowing streams has required that road bridges, ranging in date from medieval to modern, form a key element of the landscape. No original bridge chapels survive, but they certainly existed in more than a dozen locations in the medieval period. The bridge at Clyst St Mary dates from the early 14th century, and the remains of the medieval Exe Bridge are of similar age. Elsewhere, fine examples of medieval and early-modern bridges still in use include those at Bideford, Lostwithiel, Wadebridge and Gunnislake.

Post stages where horses could be hired, and where travellers could find accommodation and refreshment, existed on the main highways by the 1500s and were listed by Elizabethan authors such as William Harrison and Richard Grafton. At the end of the 16th century, posts from London to Plymouth, via Honiton, Exeter and Ashburton, provided a reliable means of conveyance for all state correspondence and a source of hired horses for ordinary travellers. By the 1620s, private letters could be 'posted' using the government's system. The wars in Ireland during the later years of Elizabeth's reign had prompted the extension of the service into Cornwall with routes running via Fowey to Penryn, and to Bodmin and Padstow, where one of England's earliest postal barques was engaged to convey the royal packet to and from Cork or Waterford.

Although it is a mistake to conclude that travel was rare before the era of privately operated turnpike roads, it was clearly far from easy. From the mid-1550s, a tightening of English laws obliged parishes to repair highways that passed through their jurisdiction, thereby recognising that serviceable thoroughfares were important for both commerce and the business of the state. But road maintenance was usually rudimentary and simply meant filling the deepest ruts with stone and rubble, cutting vegetation that encroached upon the thoroughfare and clearing ditches in order to assist drainage.

Writing in 1599, John Hooker described Devon as 'for the most parte wilde, full of wastes, hethes and mores, uphill and downhill amonge the rockes and stones'. Such difficult terrain meant that the county's thoroughfares were 'long, craggye and very paynfull for man or horse to travell'. Three years later, describing his native county, Richard Carew of Antony reported that the 'highwayes are … in the easterne part of Cornwall, uneasy, by reason either of their mires or stones, besides many up-hils and downe-hils'. Poor roads in the South West undoubtedly added to the region's sense of remoteness from the rest of the country. In addition, they were a mixed blessing when invasion threatened. In 1588, Devon's Lord Lieutenant, the Earl of Bath, informed the Privy Council that the county was quite 'unapt' for the use of carts or wains to transport victuals to soldiers deployed to defend the coasts against the Spanish Armada. But, as Hooker pointed out, the region was also 'so muche the lesse passable for the enemye with his troopes and impedimentes of warre'. Little appears to have changed when the indefatigable Celia Fiennes rode through the West Country on her 1698 tour, encountering roads and lanes 'exceeding narrow, and so covered up, you can see little about … so difficult that one could scarcely pass by each other, even the single horses, and so dirty in many places, and just a track for one horse's feet'. For observant travellers, interested in the landscapes through which they passed, the region's high hedgebanks thus obscured the view and frustrated their purpose. It was calculated in the 1840s that just 10 Exe Vale parishes still contained 2,657km of hedges. Though much reduced today, high hedges and sunken lanes remain a distinctive feature of the south-west landscape.

When William Marshall compiled his *Rural Economy of the West of England* in 1796, around 30 turnpike trusts were already established in Devon and Cornwall and conditions generally had begun to improve. Marshall nevertheless described west Devon landscapes as 'most remarkable for their steepness' and recalled the state of the highways a mere 50 years earlier when roads were still 'mere gullies, worn by torrents in the rocks; which appeared in steps, as staircases, with fragments lying loose in the indentures … there was not, then, a wheel carriage in the district; nor fortunately for the necks of travellers, any horses but those which were natives of the county'.

In fact, the establishment of turnpike trusts came relatively late to the South West. In England and Wales as a whole, 140 turnpikes were established by parliamentary act before 1750, but none was in Devon or Cornwall. Between 1750 and 1758, however, pre-existing roads around Exeter, Axminster, Honiton, Ashburton, Totnes, Plymouth and Tiverton were turnpiked, considerably improving local access to these nodal markets. In Cornwall, the first trust, established in 1754, linked Truro with Falmouth – the rapidly growing mail-packet port for Spain, Africa and the Americas. Within 15 years, however, all the principal highways in the two counties were operated by turnpike trusts and work was under way to form roads across both Dartmoor and Bodmin Moor, previously served only by rough tracks.

Fig. 10.2 Postbridge, Dartmoor 'clapper' bridge. *The bridge crosses the East Dart River, just 20m from the road bridge built as an element of the turnpike system in the 1780s. The clapper bridge comprises four large granite slabs supported on three granite piers. Each slab is more than 4m long by 2m wide and weighs approximately 8 tonnes. There are 30 clapper bridges on Dartmoor and many date from the medieval period, when tinners and farmers built them as a means of crossing the numerous small rivers that traverse the moors.*

LANDSCAPES OF TRANSPORT

The road engineer John Loudon McAdam moved to Falmouth in 1798 where he continued the experiments he had begun in this native Scotland into improved methods of road-construction, thereby bringing them to particular attention in the South West. After a lull in turnpike creation, the end of the Napoleonic Wars in 1815 saw a renewed impetus. Better roads were seen as a key means to revive the post-war economy. New stretches of highway were built to bypass difficult or steep sections of existing routes, or to provide better connections in areas such as the South Hams. By the 1820s, William McAdam (son of John) had been appointed surveyor to several Devon trusts and, using his father's famous building techniques, he re-routed some roads on more benign gradients across land hitherto regarded as too wet for highway building (Fig. 10.3). Interesting examples of early 18th-century realignment may be detected on the Exeter–Plymouth turnpike – near South Brent, for instance, the landscape itself clearly documents the history of roads in the area. South of the modern A38 'expressway', the ancient ridgeway survives on the edge of the South Hams as a

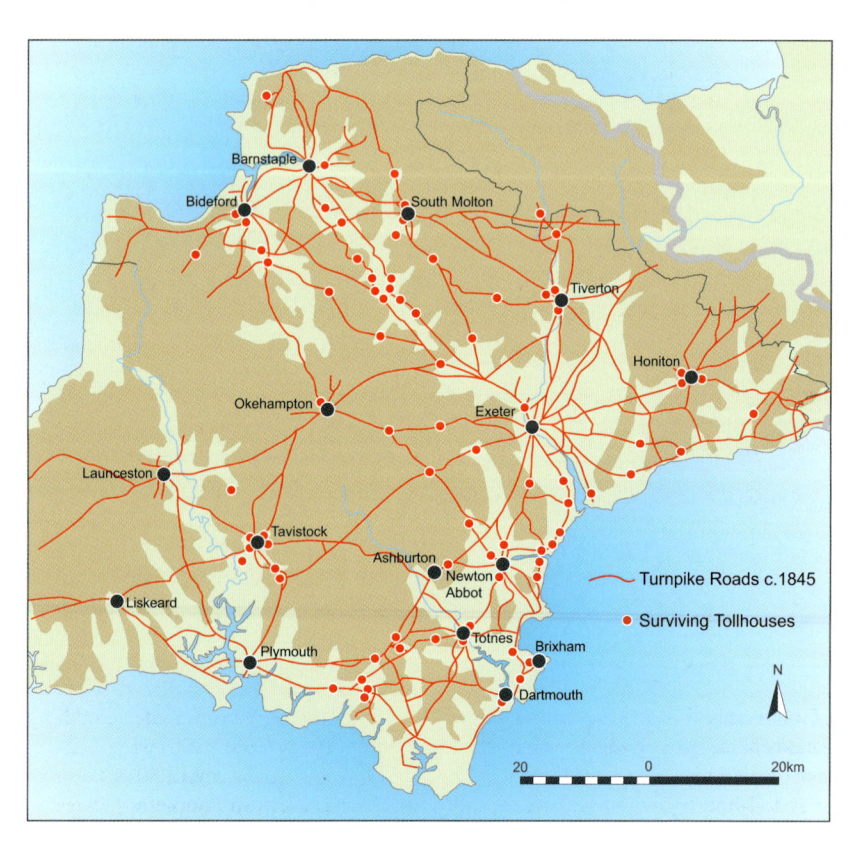

Fig. 10.3 Devon's turnpike road network c. 1845, and locations of surviving toll-houses.

minor road. The latter in part follows the improved turnpike route, completed in 1835, though further modifications were made in the 1970s. Earlier, the first turnpike had simply followed the undulating Exeter–Plymouth post-road, described by Harrison in 1587 and depicted by John Ogilby in his 1675 *Britannia*, passing through Ashburton and South Brent on its way towards Ivybridge and Plympton (Fig. 10.4).

Although there was no central controlling authority for the administration of England's roads, turnpike trusts usually maintained one or more thoroughfares by levying a toll on users, employing the revenues thereby raised to pay for the work and secure a profit. Charges were relatively high. One penny (0.4p) for a horse and one shilling (5p) for a coach added significantly to the cost of a journey. Pedestrians paid no toll, but animals driven to market were charged. The collection

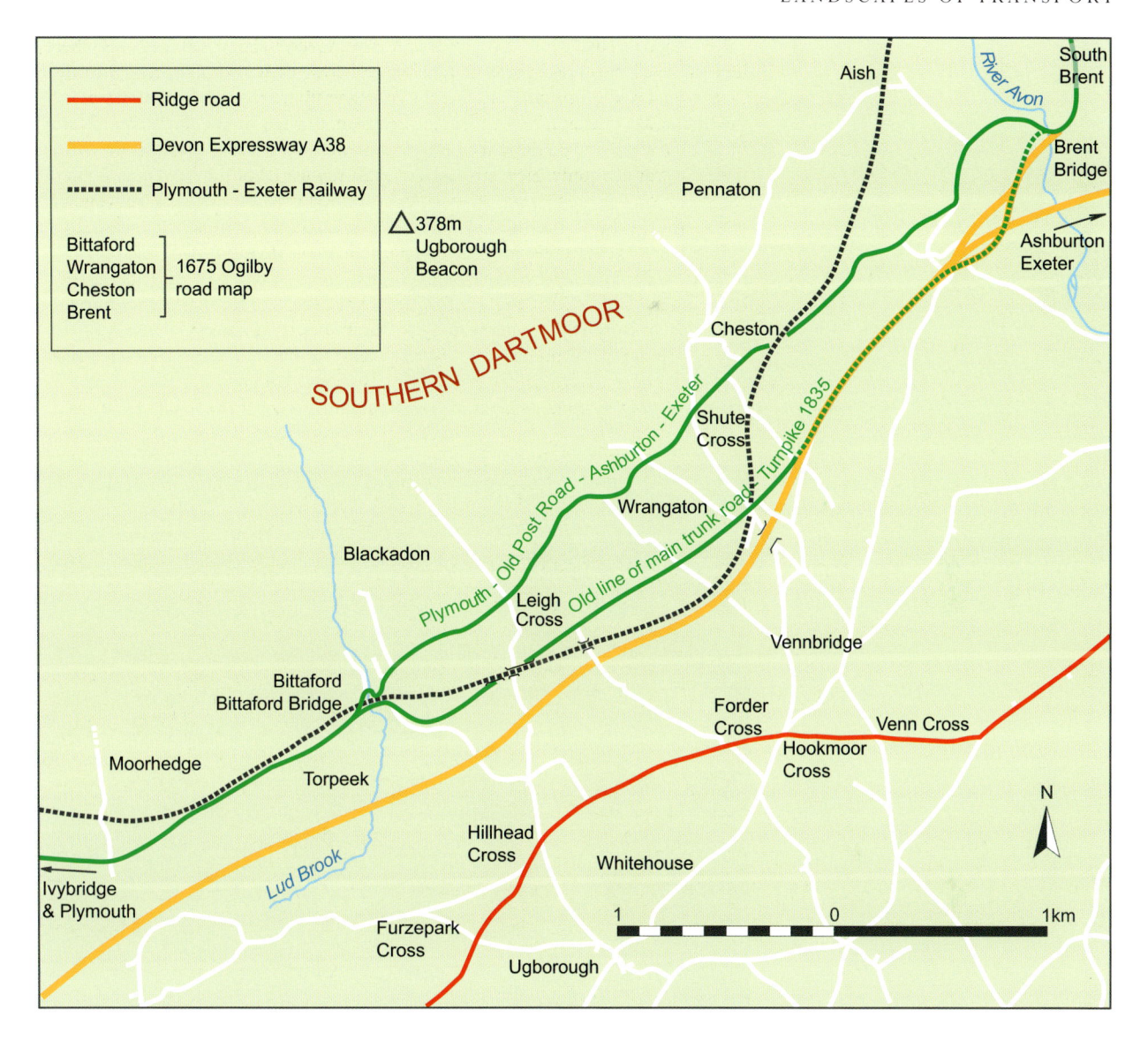

LANDSCAPES OF TRANSPORT

Fig. 10.4 Highway route changes between South Brent and Bittaford in Devon, c. 1500–2005: the legacy of past eras is indelibly marked in the landscapes of transport.

of tolls occasioned the building of hundreds of cottages to accommodate turnpike gatekeepers. Though their original purpose had decayed by the 1880s when the task of road maintenance passed to Victorian highways boards, about 80 of the 400 or so toll-houses built in Devon survive. The oldest, at Newton Poppleford, dates from 1758, but most were constructed between 1815 and 1845. Some were owned by independent trusts, such as the one that operated the bridge over the Teign at Shaldon. Typically two-storey cottages with a three-sided front, toll-houses had a door and porch facing the road and windows in the angled sides offering good views in both directions to enable the toll collector to look out for approaching traffic (Fig. 10.5). Charges were displayed on boards fixed to the external walls. Though functionally obsolete, the best of the survivors have become attractive homes that provide a tangible link with a former transport landscape.

The first motor vehicles appeared in Devon in 1897 and provision for them today dominates the transport landscapes of the SouthWest (Fig. 10.6). Drivers demand and receive the lion's share of transport planners' attention. In this region, a dispersed population increasingly dependent on goods and services provided only in distant centres, but poorly served by public transport, inevitably

LANDSCAPES OF TRANSPORT

means high dependence upon the private car. Not surprisingly, the rate of car ownership per household is greater in the South West than in England and Wales as a whole. Moreover, since the late 1950s, declining railway services, rising personal incomes and a growing desire to live in the countryside but to work in a town or city, have further contributed to huge increases in road traffic in Devon and Cornwall. There is no sign of a reduction in this growth. But away from the diurnally clogged commuting arteries feeding centres such as Exeter, Truro and Plymouth,

ABOVE: **Fig. 10.5 A turnpike trust toll-house.** This example is on the A379 near Yealmpton in Devon and displays a board showing the former scale of 'charges' for horse-drawn carriages, bullocks and so on.

Fig. 10.6 M5 motorway services and interchange near Exeter. The extraordinary scale of the demand for space imposed by the modern road network and the considerable dominance of motor transport in the landscape is underlined by this image.

serious road congestion in the South West is a peculiarly seasonal phenomenon. In Devon, for example, August traffic volumes are 50 per cent greater than the county's annual daily average. On summer Saturdays, the M5 near Exeter carries six times more vehicles than on mid-winter days. In Cornwall, traffic in August is more than 40 per cent above the daily average and twice the volume of winter flows. Throughout the last century, road improvements were made in response to inexorable increases in road traffic. The Exeter bypass, for example, was completed in the 1930s. The Tamar road bridge at Saltash was built between 1959 and 1961, thereby easing one of the region's worst summer bottlenecks – even before the Second World War, holiday traffic often faced a two-hour wait to cross the Hamoaze into Cornwall by means of the Torpoint Ferry (Fig. 10.7). After 1961, however, summer traffic jams built up beyond the new bridge as cars threaded their way through Saltash, a problem not significantly eased until the building of a tunnel beneath the town some 25 years after the bridge was completed. The 1960s bridge has itself recently been widened. By 1974, realignments and improvements, including the building of a continuous dual carriageway, were made on the A38 trunk road between Plymouth and Exeter. Within two years, the M5 motorway reached Exeter, but a good road linking its western end with north Devon opened only in 1987. The following year, after much controversy regarding its encroachment on National Park land, the Okehampton bypass at last improved traffic flows on the A30 running north of Dartmoor towards Launceston and Bodmin. Construction has just begun on another bypass on the A30, at Goss Moor in Cornwall, and a further bypass on the A38 at Dobwalls, also in Cornwall, now seems likely.

Fig. 10.7 The Tamar road bridge (opened 1961) and Brunel's Royal Albert railway bridge (opened 1859) at Saltash. The slipways on both the Plymouth and the Saltash sides of the river survive. Ferries operated between these before the road bridge was constructed.

CANAL LANDSCAPES

The River Exe was navigable for small craft as far inland as Exeter in Roman times but, by the 12th century, a majority of sea-going vessels unloaded at Topsham. Moreover, in the 13th century, three weirs were built below the city, making the river impassable. The first was constructed for Isabella, Countess of Devon, and is still known as 'Countess Weir'. Attempts in the 1540s to remove these obstacles were thwarted and, in 1563, the Welsh engineer, John Trew, was engaged to cut a canal to carry traffic between Exeter and Topsham and thence to the sea (Fig. 10.8). When work was completed two years later, the Exeter Canal,

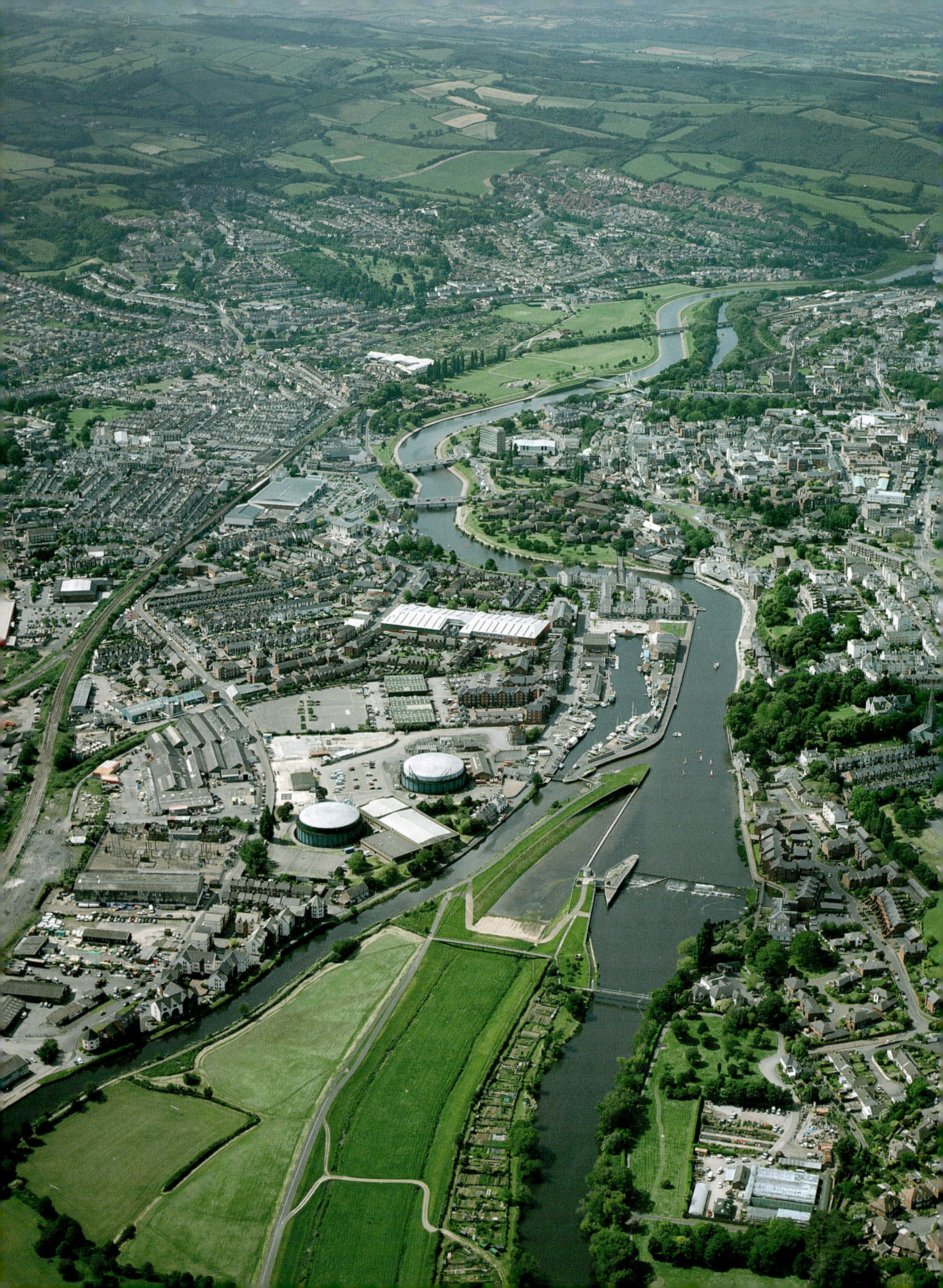

LANDSCAPES OF TRANSPORT

1m deep and 4.9m wide, ran for 2.8km and was capable of accommodating 10-ton lighters. It was the first English navigation to employ 'mitre gates' and pound locks. A quay was formed outside Exeter's Water Gate and, by 1574, the first warehouse, Crane House, was constructed. Rebuilt and enlarged in 1600, it was subsequently known as Quay House. The canal was extended to Lower Sluice in 1676 and, by 1700, the channel was enlarged to accommodate 200-ton vessels. An elegant Customs House, designed by Richard Allen, was completed in 1681 and survives as Exeter's oldest brick building (Fig. 10.9). Three splendid baroque plaster ceilings by John Abbott of Frithelstock add to the building's historical importance. In the 1820s, the engineer James Green was engaged to complete further deepening work and extend the canal beyond Topsham to Turf Lock. Capable of taking 500-ton ships and running for 8.4km, Exeter Canal was at that time Britain's second deepest inland waterway after Scotland's Caledonian Canal. While no longer used for commercial traffic, it survives today as the only fully operational canal in the South West (Fig. 10.10).

Though the far South West does not possess waterways on the scale of those built elsewhere in the country during the 'canal mania' of the 18th and early 19th centuries, small-scale navigation projects were undertaken in Devon and Cornwall. Thus, by 1794, James Templar of Teigngrace had built the 3km Stover Canal from Ventiford to Jetty Marsh on the Teign at Newton Abbot, thereby creating a direct link to carry pottery clay to Teignmouth. In 1843, Lord Clifford constructed the 1,000m Hackney Canal to provide another connection with the Teign on its eastern side. These operated until 1939 and 1928, respectively. Near Plymouth, John Parker commissioned the engineer, John Smeaton, to survey a canal route from his Cann slate quarries to Marsh Mills on the Plym in 1778. No work was undertaken until 1825 when Parker's son, the first Earl of Morley, built a 3.2km, narrow canal, connected in 1829 to a 0.8km tramroad crossing the Plym to link with the Plymouth and Dartmoor Railway at Crabtree. A decade later, however, Lord Morley's tramroad was extended to Cann Quarry and the canal was used thereafter simply as a mill leat.

The 9.7km Torrington Canal, enthusiastically supported by Lord Rolle, who was keen to improve farming on his north Devon estates, was opened after a long gestation in 1827. James Green had devised a scheme to link the River Torridge below Weare Giffard with New Manor Mill at Great Torrington, which included a double-track inclined plane, to conquer the steep gradient, and a stone aqueduct to ford the river from west to east at Beam. But Lord Rolle's canal operated for little more than 40 years, closing in 1871, largely because its freight business was taken over by the new railway. Rather more important in both engineering ambition and the value of the freight carried was the 7.2km Tavistock Canal, linking the Tavy below Tavistock with the Tamar port of Morwellham, which finally opened in 1817 having taken 14 years to build. The canal was the brainchild of the Norfolk-born surveyor and civil engineer, John Taylor, and ran for 3.2km of its length in a tunnel, 2.4m high and 1.8m wide, deep beneath Morwell Down. Boats going upstream were poled through the tunnel, against the current, and then re-hitched to horses for the journey's final stretch to Tavistock Quay. An aqueduct was built to conduct the canal across the River Lumburn near Crowndale. At its southern terminus above the Tamar, an inclined plane

Fig. 10.9 Customs House, Exeter.
Built in 1681, it is the city's earliest surviving brick building.

OPPOSITE PAGE:
Fig. 10.8 Exeter Ship Canal. Dating to the 1560s, this was the first English navigation to employ mitre gates and pound locks. A quay was built outside the city's Water Gate and, by 1700, the canal channel was large enough to take 200-tonne vessels. The entrance to the canal and the canal basin is visible above Trew's Weir.

193

LANDSCAPES OF TRANSPORT

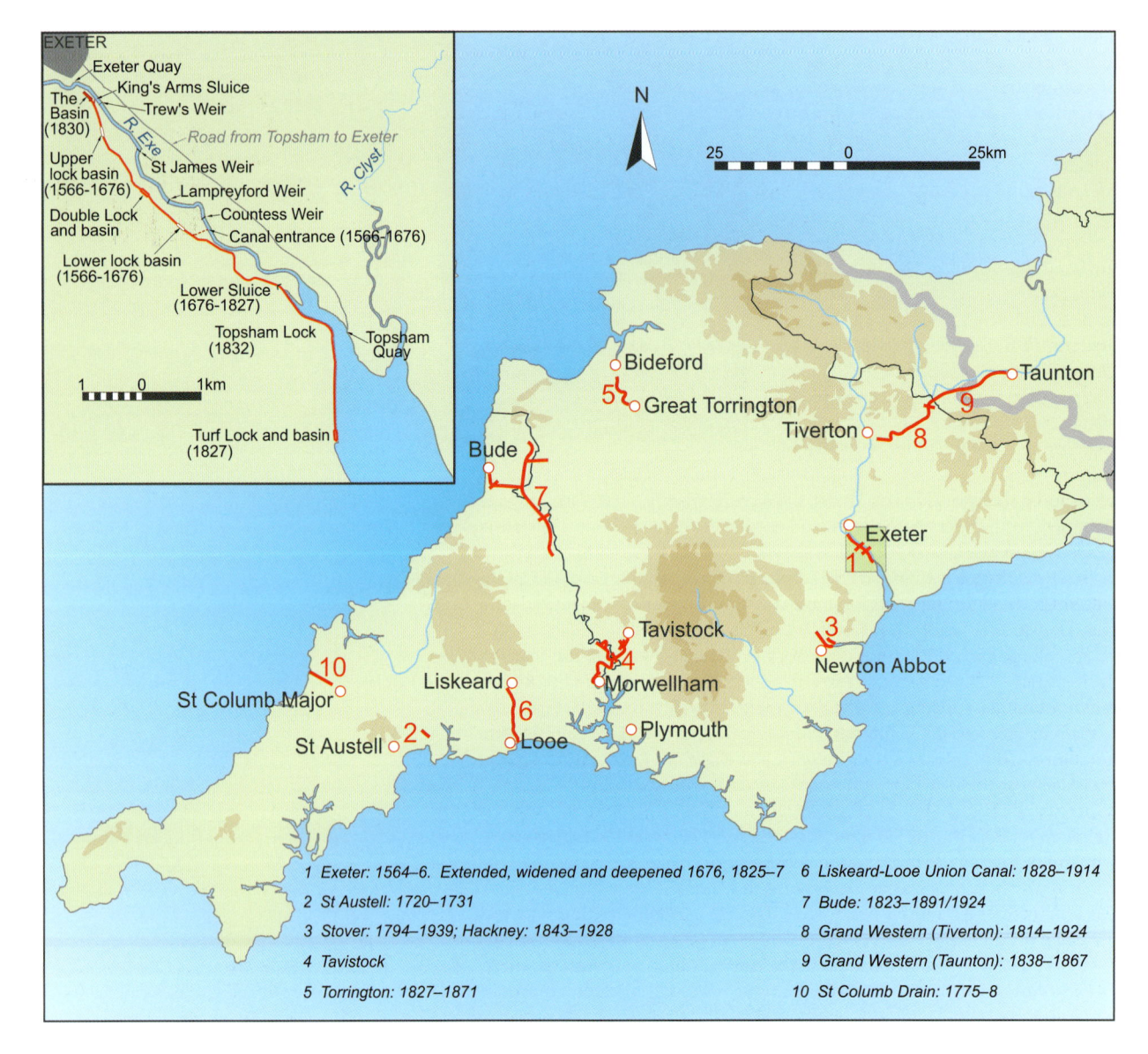

1. Exeter: 1564–6. Extended, widened and deepened 1676, 1825–7
2. St Austell: 1720–1731
3. Stover: 1794–1939; Hackney: 1843–1928
4. Tavistock
5. Torrington: 1827–1871
6. Liskeard-Looe Union Canal: 1828–1914
7. Bude: 1823–1891/1924
8. Grand Western (Tiverton): 1814–1924
9. Grand Western (Taunton): 1838–1867
10. St Columb Drain: 1775–8

Fig. 10.10 Canals in Devon and Cornwall.

descended 72m to connect it to Morwellham Quay on the river below. Power to raise and lower wagons over the double track installed on the plane was supplied by a waterwheel, 8.5m in diameter, fed by the canal's waste water. A branch linked the main canal with the Millhill slate quarries, north of Tavistock. When opened, shallow-draft iron barges, probably the first of their kind to operate on an English canal, carried copper ore, lead, granite, limestone and slates. In all, before its use declined at the end of the 19th century, perhaps a million tonnes of cargo had been transported along its short, but spectacular route.

The desire to establish a 48.3km canal link on the Tamar's Cornwall side between Morwellham and North Tamerton prompted the formation of a company in 1794, but no tangible progress was made until 1808. A 4.8km stretch of the canal was constructed from New Bridge near Gunnislake to Morwellham, where a substantial lock and basin gave access to the river. But the company was crippled financially by the unfavourable terms upon which its rights to create the navigation were agreed with the landowners – the Duchy of Cornwall and Lord Mount Edgcumbe – and no more of the canal was ever built.

LANDSCAPES OF TRANSPORT

The so-called Tamar Manure Navigation none the less operated successfully until the late 1920s carrying coal, sand, bricks, lime, granite and manure.

The only canal scheme in the South West devised to link the region with other long-distance networks, rather than merely serving a particular local need, was the Grand Western project to connect Taunton with Topsham and the Exe. Some of England's most noted engineers, including William Jessop and John Rennie, contributed to plans for the scheme. However, only a short stretch of the intended waterway was constructed – the 18km branch between Holcombe Rogus and Tiverton opened in 1814 – and this portion was finally linked to Taunton when a further 22km section was completed in 1837. Costly engineering problems were encountered, however, and construction of the Bristol and Exeter Railway, finished in 1844, was by then already under way. Four years later, the railway's branch to Tiverton opened. In 1867, the Bristol and Exeter Railway purchased the Grand Western Canal and immediately closed the Lowdwells to Taunton stretch. The western, Tiverton portion continued in commercial operation until its final abandonment by the British Transport Commission in 1962. A stretch has since been restored for use by pleasure barges (Fig. 10.11).

Befitting a county whose sons have been at the forefront of engineering innovation, Cornwall made a distinctive contribution to canal-building projects elsewhere in the country. For example, in 1777, John Edyvean of St Austell proposed a scheme for a canal to traverse the entire country. Rather more tangible results were achieved by William Praed of Lelant, a banker in Truro and Falmouth who later founded Praeds Bank in London and became MP for St Ives. He was one of England's greatest canal enthusiasts. In 1790, Praed promoted the Grand Junction Canal Bill in Parliament and subsequently formed the company that built it. Linking London with Birmingham, this great waterway is a monument to an extraordinary Cornishman.

With its long coastline and many ports, canals on the scale of the Grand Junction were not so necessary in Cornwall. Nevertheless, a short canal at Carclaze near St Austell, which ran in a tunnel, operated from 1720 until 1731, when a roof collapse entombed its barges and forced its closure. More significant, John Edyvean sought an Act in 1773 to build the St Columb Canal. Only two sections were ever constructed – a 7.2km stretch between an inclined plane at Trenance Point beach and Whitewater; and a 2km stretch from Lusty Glaze, south of St Columb Porth, to Rialton. By the early 19th century, however, the canal was already disused and it is hard to find any traces of it today.

Within a year of promoting the St Columb scheme, Edyvean proposed a 145km canal link between Bude Haven and the Tamar at Calstock. Although nothing came of the plan for several decades, there was a latent demand as considerable quantities of 'shelly-sand' were being hauled by packhorse from Bude to neighbouring acid soil districts of Devon and Cornwall to be used as a

Fig. 10.11 Tiverton Canal, a section of the Grand Western Canal scheme to link Taunton with Topsham, only part of which was built. This short stretch has been restored for recreational use.

soil conditioner and an alternative to lime. Renewed interest in the canal scheme, stimulated by the support of Earl Stanhope, who owned a farming estate at Holsworthy, led to the commencement in 1819 of a 56km channel, somewhat less than Edyvean's original intention. A sea-lock was constructed at Bude Haven to provide access to a basin accommodating 120-ton vessels. The lock and basin were enlarged between 1836 and 1856. In-bound cargoes comprised sand, coal, timber and salt, while agricultural produce was in turn exported. Bude Canal must rank as one of England's most remarkable engineering achievements. The scheme included an 886-million-litre reservoir built near Alfardisworthy, almost 137m above sea level and covering 28ha. When the canal closed in 1891, this reservoir, known as Tamar Lake, became a water-supply source for Bude and its neighbourhood. Steep gradients along the canal's length were conquered not by means of flights of locks, but by six inclined planes, the most ambitious being the hydraulic Hobbacott plane that rose 68m in height over a distance of 285m. Tub-boats, fitted with small iron wheels, were hauled up rails that dipped at each end into the waters of the canal, enabling the vessels to be floated on or off the incline. Should the hydraulic mechanism prove inadequate, a steam engine provided substitute power. Apart from the sea-lock and 'pound' behind it, little survives of the Bude Canal, though the alignment of the Hobbacott plane is still discernible. At its summit, the shell of the engine house and the incline-keeper's cottage also survive.

No other scheme in Cornwall matched the ambition of the Bude Canal, although the link between Looe and Liskeard is noteworthy. Indeed, it probably ranks as the county's most successful project and operated between 1828 and about 1914; again the railway ultimately deprived it of business. The 'Looe Union Canal' was proposed as early as 1770, but the project was not realised until 58 years later when a channel designed by Robert Coad was completed. Cargoes of agricultural produce, some copper ore, and stone from the Cheesewring quarries were carried down to the sea at Looe, while loads of coal, iron, timber and merchandise for Liskeard were carried up. Limestone was also transported for burning in the kilns at the canal's terminus at Moorswater, where remnants of two such structures are still visible. Few vestiges of the Looe Union itself survive apart from derelict locks and bridges. The last gasp of canal building in Cornwall is represented by the 3.2km cut, promoted by the mine owner Joseph Treffry of Fowey, which opened between Par and Pont's Mill near Tywardreath Highway in 1847. During its limited life this carried copper ore from the Fowey Consolidated Mines and some cargoes of china stone down to Par harbour.

RAILWAY LANDSCAPES

The construction of Devon and Cornwall's railways arguably wrought the most profound landscape changes ever experienced in the region. Though the network is now much diminished compared with its zenith in 1925, the 523km of railway that survive in the South West remain a crucial element in its transport infrastructure. The main line from London's Paddington station to Penzance is a vital link, while the routes to Exeter via Salisbury from London Waterloo, and from the Midlands via Bristol, are also of major importance. Seven short stretches of track exclusively used for freight account for 32km of the surviving network and another 207km comprise passenger branch lines. Indeed, south-west England's branch lines account for almost 40 per cent of the region's surviving railways. They occupy routes that pass through some of England's most beautiful scenery and, while daily passenger traffic provides their mainstay, they are also increasingly promoted as tourist attractions in their own right. In addition, privately owned steam railways, running on restored stretches of once-closed lines, account for another 40km in Devon and Cornwall, rising to 73km if

LANDSCAPES OF TRANSPORT

the magnificent West Somerset Steam Railway from Bishop's Lydeard to Dunster and Minehead is included (Fig. 10.12).

Both Devon and Cornwall can claim important associations with the story of Britain's railway development. The engineer Richard Trevithick, who was born at Illogan in Cornwall, built the first working steam railway locomotive, though Pen-y-daren in South Wales, rather than the South West, saw the earliest successful trials of his invention in 1804. In both counties, the work of one of the world's most important 19th-century civil engineers and inventors, Isambard Kingdom Brunel, survives in abundance. This is certainly a region rich in railway heritage. The story of the development of south-west England's railways is extraordinarily complex and no more than an outline can be provided here. However, a knowledge of when and why certain lines were built, how long they operated, and with what success is often a key to understanding other important processes of landscape change and development. Railways not only transformed landscapes physically, but also changed lives, and dramatically affected local economies and patterns of settlement. In a real sense, by providing a web of swift communication between disparate localities within Devon and Cornwall, the railways were an important agent in creating a shared regional identity for the south-west peninsula.

The network grew organically from seeds sown early in the 19th century when tramroads and railways in both counties were built to serve particular local mines and quarries. Among the first were horse-drawn lines connecting the mines of the

Fig. 10.12 Devon and Cornwall passenger railways, past and present. Only 523km survive of the formerly much more extensive network.

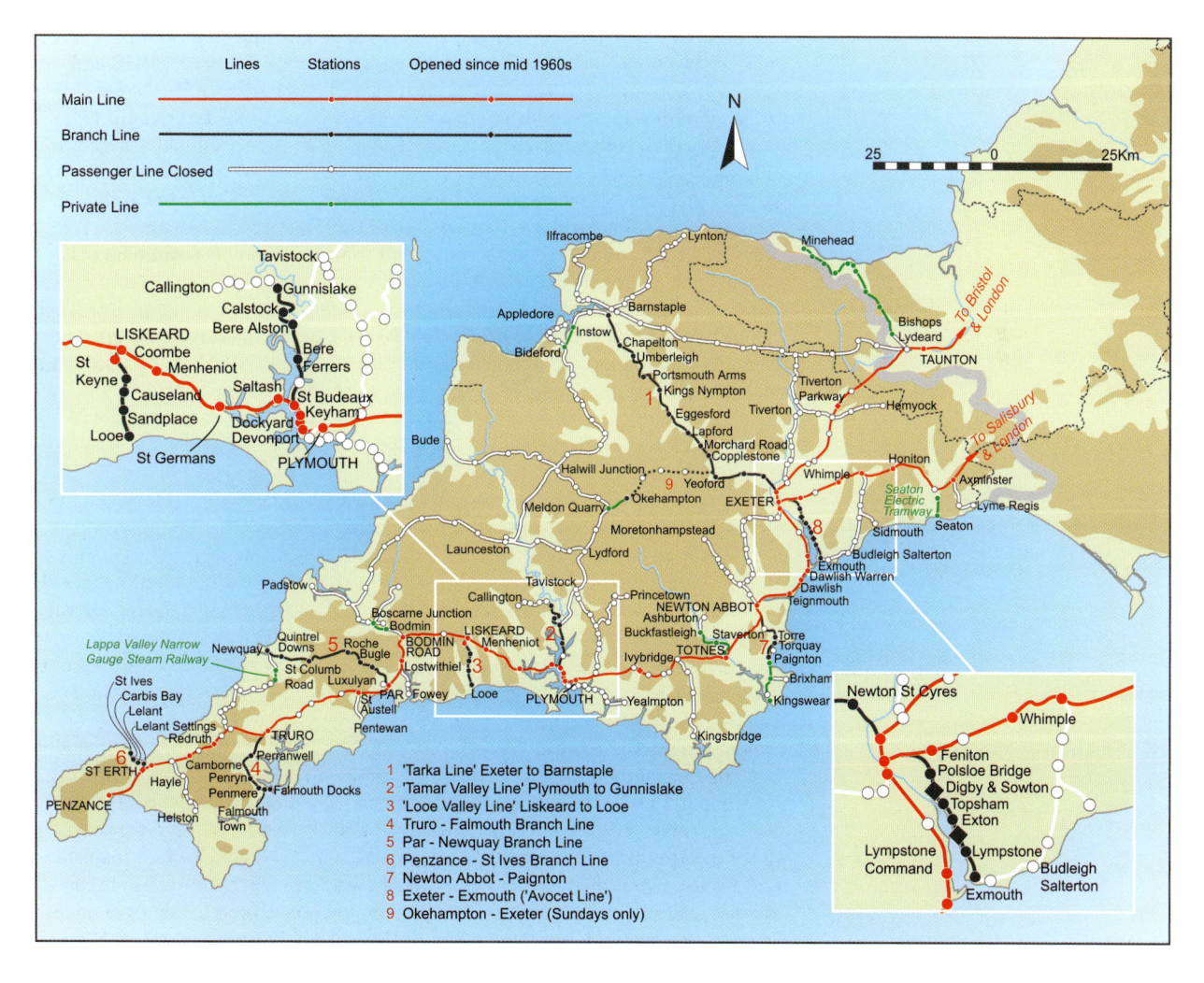

197

LANDSCAPES OF TRANSPORT

Fig. 10.13 Granite tramway, Haytor, Dartmoor, which was built in 1820 to bring quarry stone to Teigngrace on the Stover Canal.

Redruth–Gwennap district with the harbours of Hayle, Portreath and Devoran. The oldest was the Poldice railroad, opened in 1812, connecting Scorrier with Portreath. Cornwall's largest mineral line, the Hayle Railway, was begun in 1834 to link the harbour with the epicentre of the county's industrial activity and mines such as Dolcoath, Cook's Kitchen and Tin Croft. By 1838, branches to Portreath and Tresavean were added. Pioneering solutions to cope with steep gradients and the drop to Portreath harbour were devised by the engineer, William Sims.

A tramway built to a 4ft 3in (1.3m) gauge was opened in 1820 to carry granite from Dartmoor's Haytor quarries to Teigngrace on the Stover Canal, 16km away. Ingeniously, the track was made of the material it was intended to carry. Thus long blocks of granite, shaped with a 3-inch (80mm) flange on the inside, were used as rails (Fig. 10.13). This unique line flourished for more than 40 years. What survives of the track is now protected as an ancient monument. Thomas Tyrwhitt, the Essex-born secretary and friend of the Prince of Wales (later George IV), sought to develop industry and farming on the Duchy's land high up on Dartmoor by building Princetown. In 1818 he decided to connect his granite quarry and his new town with Plymouth by means of a 40km railway. Built to a 4ft 6inch (1.37m) gauge, this reached King Tor in 1823 and Princetown by 1827. By the 1840s, quarries and mines in south-east Cornwall were linked by mineral lines to the Looe Union Canal and, in 1859, the Devon Great Consols mines were linked to Morwellham by an 8km tramway. In 1872, the 3ft 6inch (1.1m) gauge East Cornwall Mineral Railway from Calstock to Callington was opened to serve mines, quarries and brickworks in the western Tamar Valley and Kit Hill districts. Lines serving the china-clay districts of Hensbarrow and St Austell in Cornwall and Lee Moor on south-western Dartmoor were also constructed in the 19th century. Foremost among these is Joseph Treffry's line from Par and St Blazey to Newquay harbour, commenced in 1839 and completed a decade later. Its most notable feature is the magnificent granite viaduct that conveyed the line across the Luxulyan Valley. Treffry's Viaduct is 201m long and accommodated both the railway track and an aqueduct on its 10 majestic arches, almost 30m above the valley floor (Fig. 10.14). The aqueduct's water provided power for turbines a mile away at Pont's Mill, used for crushing china stone. Between 1872 and 1874, the Par to Newquay line was rebuilt by Sir Moreton Peto as the Cornwall Mineral Railway and this included a new alignment south of Luxulyan that bypassed Treffry's viaduct. However, the latter survives as one of Cornwall's greatest and most graceful monuments to early Victorian civil engineering.

The Bristol & Exeter Railway Company was the first to establish a national rail connection with the region when its broad-gauge (7ft 0¼ in; 2.2m) line to Exeter was completed in 1844. The Great Western Railway Company's principal engineer, Brunel, was engaged to design the route. Five years later, the South Devon Railway Company extended the link to Plymouth. Brunel experimented with the 'atmospheric' system on the South Devon line in which stationary steam engines were used to pump the air out of large iron pipes laid between the tracks, thereby creating a vacuum (Fig. 10.15). A slot, sealed by a flap, ran along the top of the pipe and, as a train's leading carriage passed along, a special wheel opened the flap to allow a rod fixed to the underside of the carriage to draw a close-fitting piston though the pipe. The vacuum ahead of the piston enabled air re-entering the pipe from behind to propel it forward, thus driving the train. A small pressing wheel at the back of the train resealed the pipe to allow the steam engines to create a fresh vacuum. Immense engineering difficulties were encountered and

LANDSCAPES OF TRANSPORT

Fig. 10.14 *Treffry Viaduct, Luxulyan, Cornwall.*

while the track was laid to Newton Abbot by 1846, conventional locomotives were used until atmospheric trains began to run as far as Teignmouth in September 1847 and to Newton Abbot the following January. The track to Totnes was completed by the summer of 1848 and reached Laira, just outside Plymouth, later that year. But by then, the South Devon Railway Company had decided to abandon the atmospheric system and today little evidence of its brief existence remains. The pumping house at Starcross on the Exe is the most tangible memorial, while that at Torre (though never actually used) also

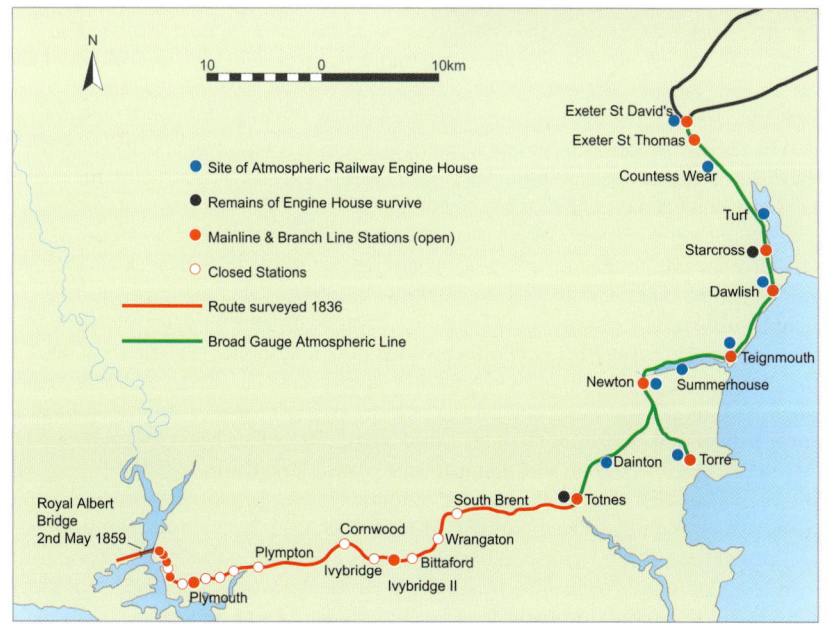

Fig. 10.15 *Brunel's contribution to the railways in south Devon.* The entire 84km route between Exeter and Plymouth was surveyed by Brunel (map left) who proposed running his atmospheric locomotives along it. In fact, the atmospheric railway only operated briefly from Exeter to Newton Abbot; engineering difficulties caused its abandonment in favour of conventional steam locomotives. However, for a brief period in the summer of 1848, atmospheric trains ran between Exeter and Teignmouth at average speeds of 64mph (103kph). One of Brunel's greatest engineering triumphs is undoubtedly the Royal Albert Bridge (above), which carries the railway across the River Tamar into Cornwall.

survives (Fig. 10.16). The lofty timber viaducts that carried the line over the deep valleys between South Brent and Ivybridge were later replaced with stone-built structures and, together with the Bristol and Exeter line, the South Devon was taken over by the Great Western Railway (GWR) in 1876. In 1906, the journey to London on the GWR was considerably shortened when a new line between Taunton and Castle Cary allowed Paddington trains to bypass Bristol.

In 1859, the mainline was finally carried across the River Tamar into Cornwall by means of Brunel's spectacular Royal Albert Bridge at Saltash (*see* Fig. 10.7). Cornwall was the last English county to be joined to the national railway network and the town clock in Penzance was the last to switch from local to London time. This connection nevertheless came 25 years after the inauguration in Cornwall of the county's first steam locomotive – on the Bodmin and Wadebridge Railway – in 1834. Until then, wagons had been mainly drawn by horses or hauled up inclines by fixed engines on Cornwall's network of tracks. The county's first locomotive, the *Camel*, though designed by a Cornishman, Henry Taylor, was built at the Neath Abbey Iron Works in South Wales. Locomotives were introduced in 1837 on the Hayle to Redruth Railway when the narrow-gauge mineral track was realigned and both passengers and goods were then carried. A year later, the Copperhouse Foundry, a mile to the east of Hayle harbour, built its first locomotive, the *Cornubia*, for service on the line. Within a decade, the Hayle Railway was taken over by the West Cornwall Railway and the track was re-routed to avoid inclines, passing over new viaducts instead.

Fig. 10.16 The Italianate-style atmospheric-railway pumping house at Starcross (visible beyond the platform on the right-hand side) is the most intact of those originally built, each housing two 41½hp (31kW) steam-powered vacuum pumping engines fed with steam from boilers at 40lbs per square inch (2.8 bar). Pumping engines were sited at intervals of approximately 3 miles from Exeter to Newton Abbot. The original chimney stack of the Starcross building was taken down some years ago for safety reasons.

The West Cornwall Company and the Cornwall Railway Company together participated in the construction of a through-route from Penzance to Saltash. Once again, a great West Country project was directed by Isambard Kingdom Brunel. Work lasted from 1847 until 1859 on a line that traversed some of the most difficult terrain in the country and that today provides the traveller with an unrivalled taste of Cornwall's richly varied landscape. Between Saltash and Truro, there are 34 embankments and 31 viaducts, the longest of which (405m) carries the line into Truro Station thereby offering an extraordinary bird's-eye view of the city and its cathedral (Fig. 10.17). It is the Royal Albert Bridge, however, that stands as the crowning achievement of a railway-building scheme that soared to new heights of engineering magnificence. To enter Cornwall by crossing the bridge remains one of England's best railway experiences. Brunel solved the problem of how to span the broad expanse of the lower Tamar, at a height sufficient to allow a 31m high-tide clearance for shipping, by means of an arched structure counteracted by the inward pull of suspension chains. Chains that had been manufactured by Cornwall's Copperhouse Foundry in the early 1850s for the Clifton Suspension Bridge, but were never used, were brought back from Bristol and, after modification, employed at Saltash. A key advantage of Brunel's ingenious design was that only one central pier was needed in the middle of the 21m-deep and 335m-wide river. This was sunk with immense difficulty through the silts and mud to the bedrock deep below, as a sole support for the bridge (*see* Fig. 10.7). All the other piers are built on the river's banks.

A rival company, the London & South-Western Railway, sought an Act in the mid-1850s to develop a standard-gauge (4 ft 8½ in; 1.43m) line connecting

Exeter with Salisbury and Waterloo; this was completed by 1860. The mix of gauges in the South West was already becoming an acute problem. For a time, attempts were made to share routes by means of inner rails fitted on broad-gauge track and outer rails on standard gauge, but operating problems ultimately led to the abandonment of broad gauge in 1892. In a single weekend that year, 212km of broad-gauge track in Cornwall were 'narrowed' – a feat of engineering never since matched.

Railway links to the coasts of Devon and Cornwall were crucial in stimulating the growth of the region's tourist resorts. The first of these branch lines reached Torre in 1848 thereby providing Torbay with an early advantage in the holiday trade, which it has never really lost. Bideford was linked in 1855 and, by the end of the 1860s, Exmouth, Falmouth and Seaton were also joined to the mainline. Lines where steeper gradients would be encountered were not tackled until later. Thus the lines to Ilfracombe, Sidmouth, Newquay and St Ives were not built until the 1870s and the branches to Kingsbridge and to Lynton were completed only in the 1890s. The latter was south-west England's only genuine narrow-gauge (1 ft 11½ inch; 0.60m) passenger railway. It closed in 1935 but some of its remains are now the focus of an active restoration project. Woody Bay Station was purchased in 1995 and in 1999 the Chelfham Viaduct and station were also acquired and restored.

Great railway viaducts, both used and disused, feature prominently in the transport landscapes of the South West. The Holsworthy Viaduct on the disused Bude to Halwill Junction line survives as the first of such size to be built in concrete. Still in use and one of the glories of the Tamar Valley branch line, is the immense railway viaduct that crosses the river from Devon into Cornwall at Calstock. Completed in 1907 and again constructed of concrete blocks, it extends for 305m and stands 36m high to provide breathtaking, sweeping views across the tidal river and surrounding valley landscape below (Fig. 10.18).

By the 1970s, the railway network in south-west England had drastically contracted. Dr Richard Beeching's 'axe' in the 1960s had cut deeply and the folly of his clumsy policy of closures, based on accounting procedures that separately condemned particular sections of a transport system that should instead have been judged as a whole, is now well known. Beeching sought to close all the lines in north and east Devon apart from the mainlines to Paddington and Waterloo. Cornwall was to lose its entire network except the principal artery to Penzance and the branches to Newquay and Falmouth. While much was thus destroyed, the Barnstaple, Exmouth, Paignton, Gunnislake, Looe and St Ives branch lines were reprieved. Given the need today to find an alternative to the car for commuters, it is a tragedy that the through line from Exeter to Plymouth via

Fig. 10.17 Truro railway viaduct and the city's station, Cornwall. Of the 31 viaducts between Saltash and Truro, this is the last and longest (405m) in a spectacular series of magnificent engineering feats.

Fig. 10.18 Calstock railway viaduct in Cornwall, completed in 1907. Built in concrete, it soars 36m above the tidal waters of the River Tamar and offers glorious views of the valley landscape.

Okehampton and Tavistock was lost. While the section from Exeter to Okehampton and beyond to Meldon Quarry has been revived and runs services at weekends, the prospects for installing track on the rest of the route seem distant. As elsewhere, a huge shift to motor transport has been experienced in Devon and Cornwall. Moreover, the absolute volume of travel has increased dramatically. In response to road congestion and environmental concerns, new or revitalised stations were provided from the mid-1970s at Bodmin Parkway, Tiverton Parkway, Ivybridge, Digby and Sowton, and Lympstone Commando to improve access to the railway and encourage increased usage. Though achieving some success, there seems little real prospect that these initiatives will significantly reduce the insatiable demand in the region for travel by private car.

COASTAL TRANSPORT LANDSCAPES

Historically, coastal transport has been a key feature of south-west England's transport landscapes. The Carrick Roads and Plymouth Sound are two of Europe's finest natural harbours, although both have in the past been obstacles for land-based transport. Many of the region's tidal estuaries are still crossed by ferries, as they have been for centuries. Today, some are operated only in summer, such as those on the Torridge and the Yealm. Ferries over the Camel, the Helford, the Fowey, the Carrick Roads, the Fal, the Dart and the Teign operate all year. The Cremyll and Torpoint ferries across the Hamoaze, and the Cattewater water taxi from Plymouth's Barbican, provide daily services, while the Starcross ferry to Exmouth and the Topsham service provide year-round crossings of the River Exe. Links by sea connect the mainland to Lundy and to St Mary's and other islands in the Scillies group (Fig. 10.19). Plymouth's car-ferry connections with France and Spain are a modern echo of the much more widespread network of international passenger shipping that operated from a number of the ports of the South West in the past.

In the 19th century, Plymouth was linked by regular steamer with Belfast, Dublin and Cork. There were also links with Newcastle, Hull, Liverpool, Southampton and London. Between 1840 and 1900, more than 430,000 emigrants left Plymouth; a majority travelled on assisted passages to Australia and New Zealand. Millbay Docks, designed by Brunel for the Great Western Dock Company, opened in 1857. Facilities were further improved in 1874 when a terminal was built for passengers and mail was brought ashore by tender from ocean liners. In the 1890s, seeking to win a share of the ocean-liner trade, the London & South-West Railway Company established a rival quay on the western side of Stonehouse Creek, which operated for several years until the Great Western's monopoly was reinstated. By then, cargo-handling services in the Cattewater had also been improved. Developments such as these set Plymouth apart from all other Devon and Cornwall ports. For example, by 1910 Plymouth handled 60 per cent of all the shipping movements in the South West. Its trade was 550 per cent greater than that of Dartmouth. Even though Falmouth's

LANDSCAPES OF TRANSPORT

Fig. 10.19 The 'Scillonian' ferry between Penzance and St Mary's, Isles of Scilly. The journey by sea takes 2 hours 40 minutes; by helicopter, the same trip requires just 20 minutes.

expansion in the 1860s significantly increased its capacity, Plymouth's activity was still more than four times greater. Among all the region's ports, coal was the major import. In terms of exports, however, some specialist trade existed, such as the former china-clay shipments from Charlestown and Pentewan in Cornwall, and the ball-clay cargoes that are still handled today at Teignmouth. Passenger and cargo-shipping services connected Bideford, Padstow, Penzance, Falmouth, Plymouth, Dartmouth, Torbay and Exmouth. In 1881, there were 67 operational ports handling significant cargoes in the South West, but by the Second World War coal transport had transferred to the railways and the remaining minor coastal trade mostly came to an end in the 1980s. Nevertheless, clay cargoes are shipped from Teignmouth, Par and Fowey.

Activity at the Ocean Passenger Terminal at Millbay flourished in the first half of the 20th century. The Great Western Railway's 'ocean liner specials' provided a direct connection from the quayside to London's Paddington Station. More than 30,000 passengers arrived or left Plymouth via Millbay in 1913 and upwards of 500 liners called at the port. Emigration, which had dipped before and during the First World War, resumed in the 1920s and many departed from Millbay. But the luxury-liner trade was both larger and more lucrative. More than a dozen passenger lines were using Plymouth, including P&O, the White Star Line and Hamburg American and the business peaked in the interwar period. By the 1950s air competition had caused a decline in the ocean-liner market and the terminal closed in 1963. Ten years later Millbay's fortunes were revived when Brittany Ferries started a freight-vehicle service between Roscoff in France and Plymouth, adding a passenger service in 1974. By 1978, a service to Santander in northern Spain had been introduced.

South-west England's coastline is subdivided into specified stretches administered by 'customs head ports'. In the early 1880s, there were 13 (Fig. 10.20). Shipowners

Fig. 10.20 Major ports of Devon and Cornwall and the jurisdiction of the 'head' ports.

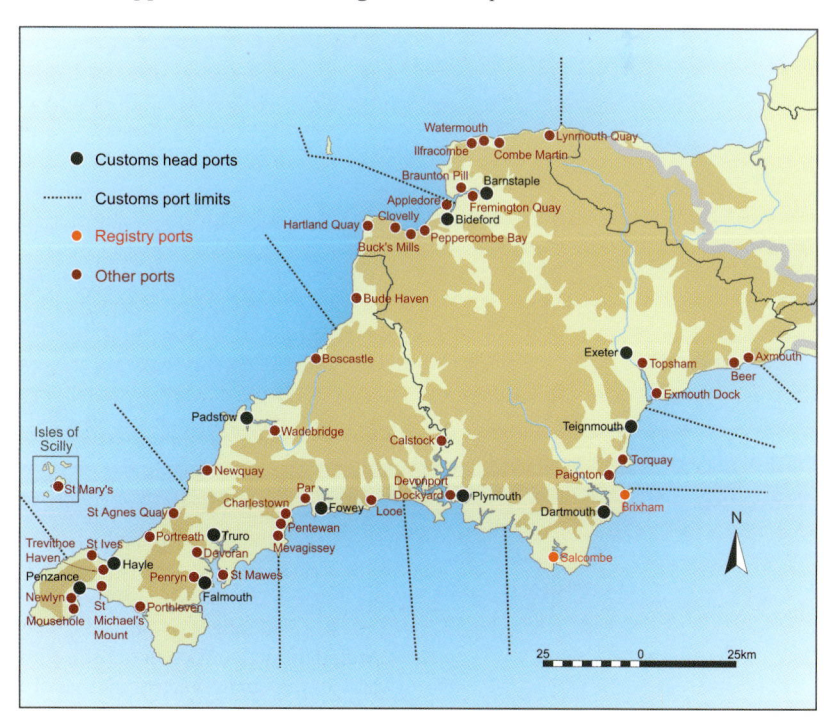

203

LANDSCAPES OF TRANSPORT

operating out of the ports and harbours within each jurisdiction are required to register their vessel at the designated head port or the nearest registry port. The arrangement of head ports has not remained static, however, and today there are only seven jurisdictions: the head ports of Exeter, Teignmouth, Plymouth, Fowey, Par, Penzance and the Isles of Scilly control shipping movements for the entire coastline of Devon and Cornwall.

Although the estuaries and inshore waters of south-west England have long been used for recreational sailing, this activity has greatly expanded since the 1950s and has brought considerable change to the character of the region's ports. Yachts, motor cruisers and dinghies dominate anchorages, moorings and specially constructed marinas where merchant ships, passenger steamers and fishing vessels once held sway.

LANDSCAPES OF AIR TRANSPORT

A surprisingly large number of past and current airfield sites exists in the South West (Fig. 10.21). Although the history of aviation in the region dates back before 1914, it was the need for aircraft to patrol the English Channel for enemy

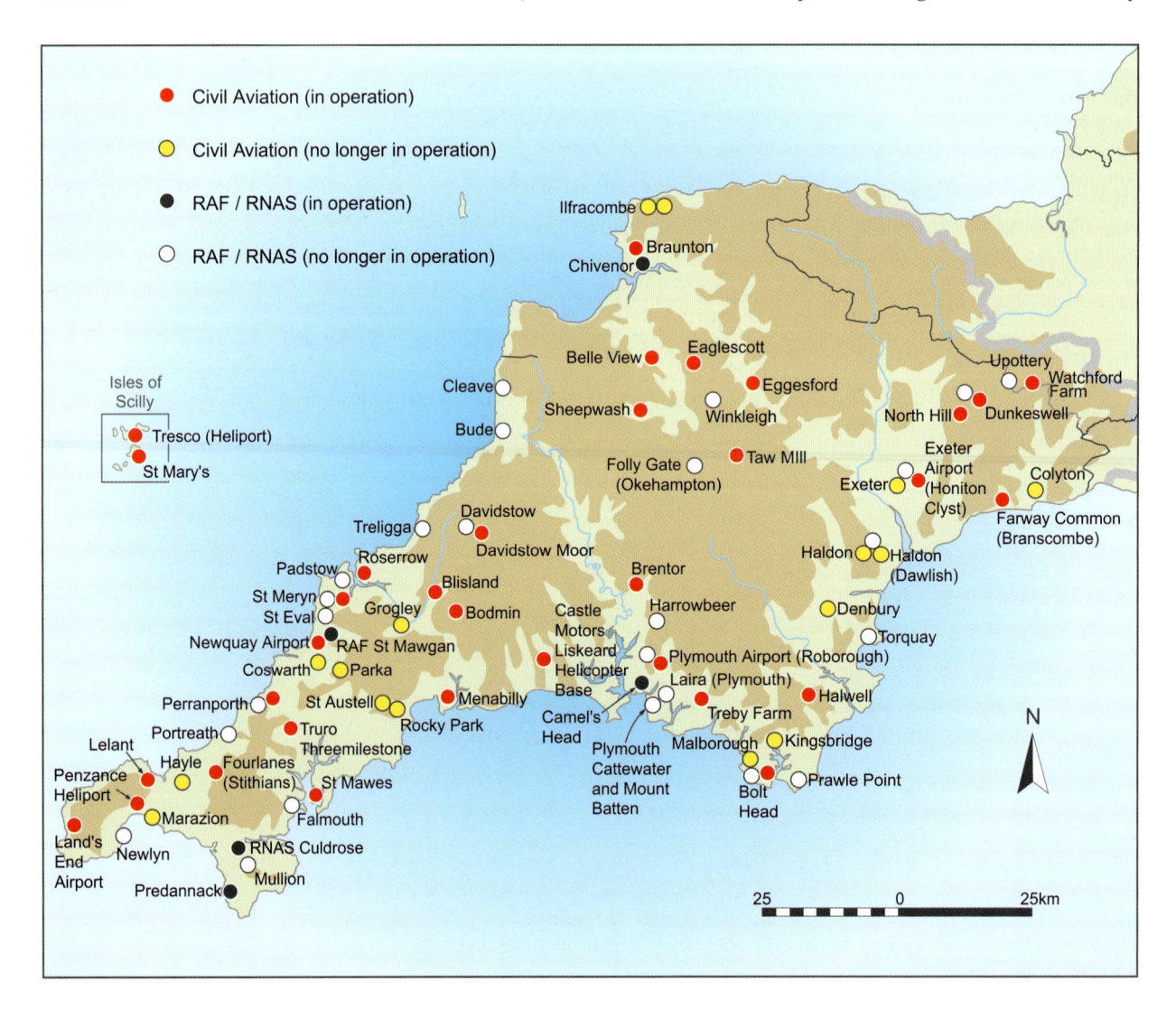

Fig. 10.21 Airfields of Devon and Cornwall.

submarines during the First World War that led to the establishment of Royal Naval air stations in Cornwall. Most of these bases were taken over by the Royal Air Force in 1918. Civil flying began in the interwar years when the Great Western Railway Company operated air services to the Isles of Scilly, Lundy and other holiday resorts. By 1939, regular scheduled services were offered throughout the region from airports built in the Isles of Scilly, St Just, Plymouth and Barnstaple. In the Second World War, Coastal Command bases at St Eval and St Mawgan were built to counter the threat of submarine attacks, and Fighter Command airfields were established to protect the ports of the Bristol Channel, Devonport Dockyard and the aircraft factory at Yeovil. Later, their aircraft provided escorts for bombers and carried out raids on enemy installations in France. By 1944, the number of civil and military airfields in the South West had reached its peak. After the war, several Devon and Cornwall airfields took on new roles. For example, until its closure in 1969, St Eval, between Newquay and Padstow, was the home of operational training squadrons of Coastal Command. Nearby St Mawgan is a base now responsible for Sea King helicopter maintenance, search-and-rescue services, and participation in air-training exercises for the defence of the South-West Approaches. It is also the civil airport for Newquay, which provides Cornwall with connections to international airports at Stansted and Gatwick, as well as to the Isles of Scilly. RNAS Culdrose, between Helston and The Lizard, remains a search-and-rescue helicopter base and a training centre for Royal Navy aircrew. In Devon, Chivenor near Barnstaple was originally a civil airfield but was taken over by the RAF in 1940 and became the county's premier airbase. It combined a military and civil role in the early post-war years and today serves as a search-and-rescue helicopter base and gliding school.

Compared with other regions, air-travel services in the South West have been modest in scale. Moreover, the pattern of links both within and beyond the region has been subject to radical changes over short periods of time. The story of the airports at Exeter, Plymouth, Newquay and Land's End, is both remarkable and complex. For Plymouth, the failure in 1961 to gain approval to develop the wartime Harrowbeer aerodrome near Yelverton as a replacement for the geographically constrained civil airport at Roborough, has meant serious limitations on prospects for developing air services appropriate for south-west England's largest urban agglomeration. Searches for a new 'greenfield' airport site seem destined to encounter fierce local opposition. Paradoxically, therefore, the newly renamed Exeter International Airport offers south-west England's widest range of services and has the greatest potential for further expansion (Fig. 10.22). At the time of writing in 2005, Exeter was focused on charter and low-cost flights to Mediterranean resorts, but scheduled services by budget airlines seem likely to be developed in future. In addition, there are air links by helicopter and fixed-wing aircraft between west Cornwall and the Isles of Scilly. Less prominent, but no less a feature of the region's transport landscapes, are the numerous small private airfields, helipads and, of course, many disused aerodromes.

Fig. 10.22 Exeter Airport. This began as a 36ha airfield on 31 May 1937. Civil schedules were suspended during the Second World War and the airfield was used until 1946 by the RAF. Civil aviation resumed in 1947. Devon County Council became sole owners of the airport in 1974 and its growth was boosted when Jersey European Airways chose to locate its headquarters there in 1985. It was renamed Exeter International Airport on 15 July 2000.

TRANSPORT AND LANDSCAPE

The transport landscapes of Devon and Cornwall embody the story of the region's attempts to build a communications infrastructure across a peninsular terrain fashioned and fractured in the Pleistocene era (*see* Chapter 2). The long coastline, high moorland, steeply incised valleys and broad estuaries have all exerted an exceptional influence on south-west England's transport geography. Local needs to connect the coast with the interior, and regional requirements to link the peninsula as whole with the country beyond, have bequeathed an unusually high density and great diversity of transport routes. Canal locks, tunnels, inclined planes and embankments, railway cuttings, bridges, viaducts, embankments and tunnels, road bridges, turnpikes and modern highway alignments all add up to an extraordinary legacy. Over the centuries, remarkable, sometimes literally breathtaking, solutions have been found to overcome the acute difficulties of the Devon and Cornwall landscape.

In the past, those who built roads, canals, railways and even airports, operated in a more liberal environment. Their feats were made possible by a freedom to construct and an access to finance that are unimaginable today. By contrast, the planning and environmental controls that now prevail reflect a much greater resistance to transport development of any kind – whether by road, rail or air. Transport landscapes are thus a manifestation of a former cultural and economic milieu and thereby encode rather more about the past than the physical structures might at first suggest.

Of all forms of transport, it was undoubtedly the railway that created a shared regional identity for the South West. Via long-distance connections, the South West was also bound more closely into the nation as a whole. But the building of main-line railways may also be seen as a form of 'colonisation' of Devon and Cornwall by companies, such as the Great Western Railway and the London & South-West Railway, whose headquarters, interests and sources of finance were based elsewhere. Moreover, past solutions to overcoming the difficulties of south-west England's terrain have left some awkward legacies. For example, Brunel's route for the South Devon railway between Newton Abbot and Plymouth, designed in anticipation of the superior motive power of an atmospheric system, contains gradients and curves that make it slow and inefficient as a modern line. It is an extraordinary fact that the prospects today for achieving a much-desired under-three-hour regular rail connection between London and Plymouth are now constrained by the choices made by Isambard Kingdom Brunel well over 150 years ago.

FURTHER READING

Duffy *et al.* (eds) 1994 and Kain and Ravenhill (eds) 1999, contain a considerable quantity of up-to-date information about the development of south-west England's transport landscapes.

Studies of the region's canals include Clew 1984 and Hadfield 1985.

Useful background to the evolution of Dartmoor's road and track network is provided by Groves 1983, 182–203.

A huge corpus of literature exists on the railways of Devon and Cornwall. Among the most useful are Booker 1977, St John Thomas 1981, Hadfield 1984 and Whitehouse and St John Thomas 1984.

By contrast, studies of aviation in the region are rather scarce, but the chapter by Charlton 1998, 265–82, is useful and a gazetteer of sites is offered in Teague and White (nd).

Maritime transport landscapes are covered in Starkey 1994, 32–47 and Gill 1994, 226–34.

11

Landscape as Heritage and a Recreational Resource

DAVID HARVEY

PART III

LANDSCAPES AS SYMBOL AND INSPIRATION

Fig. 11.1 Grimspound, Dartmoor. *The open expanse of Dartmoor from the air reveals many layers of human occupation, stretching over many thousands of years.*

BELOW: ***Fig. 11.2 Location map of places mentioned in the text.***

Cornwall and Devon have an extraordinarily rich legacy of past patterns and practices that are 'writ large' in the present-day landscape. Although this landscape resource reflects closely the story of human occupation over the last few centuries, the form and pattern of the landscape also recall the history of human endeavour in the South West over several millennia (Fig. 11.1). In addition to their record of human occupation, Devon and Cornwall also contain one of the richest assemblages of natural heritage in these islands, with their long coastline and upland ecosystems of international significance for wildlife, sea-life and plant-life (Fig. 11.2).

The landscape is commonly viewed as one of the most important factors in

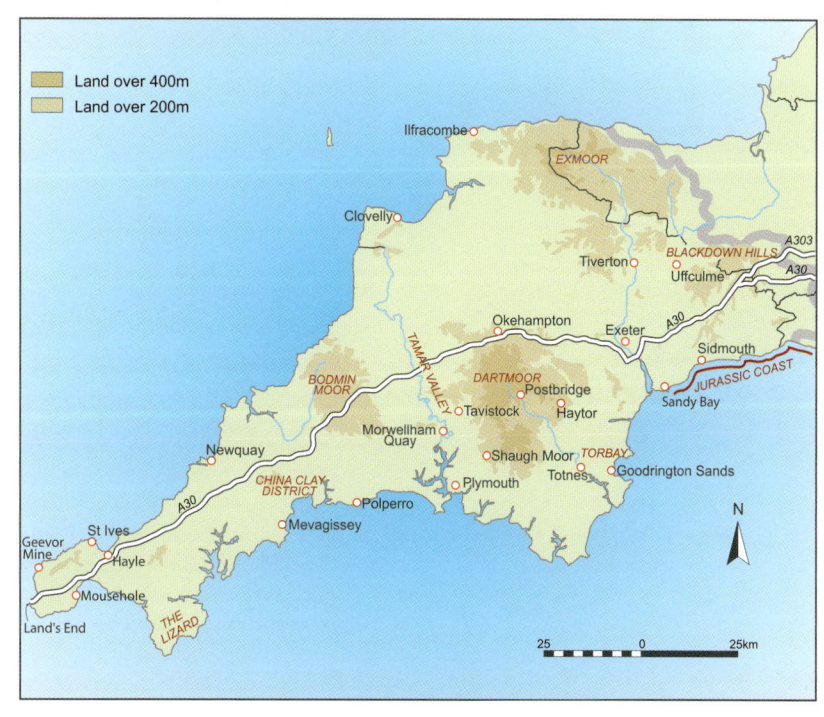

Fig. 11.3 Land's End. *Contrary to popular opinion, Land's End is not the most westerly point of mainland Britain. It is, however, a landscape of national significance, being recognised almost as instantly as the white cliffs of Dover.*

Devon and Cornwall's popularity among both visitors and residents. But it is this very popularity that is often cited as a most serious risk to the continuing integrity of that rich landscape legacy. The heritage resource is therefore seen as far more important than its power to attract tourists would suggest. Indeed, the variety of distinct landscapes throughout the South West can be seen as crucial elements in the way that identities are constructed at a number of scales: from the national and regional significance of Dartmoor or Land's End (Figs 11.1 and 11.3) through the local identity of the clay districts of Cornwall (Fig. 11.4), to the myriad landscape elements to which a sense of personal identity and heritage may be attached. It is this complexity and ambiguity of ownership, value and use of the landscape-heritage resource in the South West that this chapter explores, concentrating on what can be termed 'cultural' heritage (as opposed to 'natural' heritage). It examines the landscape heritage at a range of scales, drawing on the idea that for every aspect of it there are a number of 'stakeholders', a number of different uses and a number of agendas, sometimes complementary, sometimes competing.

Fig. 11.4 The clay districts of Cornwall. *The unique landscape of Cornwall's 'clay district' has become a potent symbol of regional identity, and is reflected, for example, in the work of the local poet, Alan M Kent.*

First of all, however, it is necessary to examine the idea of 'heritage' itself: what it is and what it is not. What does heritage mean to the society that defines it? And, crucially, it is important to analyse the *when* around which heritage revolves. It is very easy to talk about the fabric of the present-day landscape as being 'produced in the past', but it is defined and given meaning only in the present. Whenever it was that certain elements in that landscape were initially produced, their meaning will since have changed; the assemblage will have been added to, and a large number of other sites and patterns that would have been familiar centuries ago will have been forgotten or destroyed. In short, it is necessary to recognise that what we see today is a 21st-century landscape, viewed with 21st-century eyes – one that has developed both piecemeal and wholesale, and that has been altered in a planned and a haphazard fashion over many centuries.

HERITAGE DEFINED IN THE HERE AND NOW

There is a tendency in popular, journalistic and guidebook circles to attach a period of time to a landscape or townscape in order to add a mystical veneer or popular appeal and thus to give them supposed 'heritage value'. To be fair, the idea that one might be entering 'medieval' Totnes, taking a seaside dip at the 'Regency' resort of Sidmouth, or walking through the 'prehistoric' landscape of Dartmoor is a very immediate and compelling method of conveying certain messages about the conservation value or even the history of development of such landscapes. However, this simple period-tagging of landscapes ignores the essential truth of the physical landscape as an evolving entity that has been created, manipulated and interpreted over many centuries. More importantly, the idea that these landscapes exist in any other time than the present is misleading. Heritage, by definition, purports to be about the past, but in reality its value and meaning lies entirely within the present – it can never reside in any other time period. The 'creation of heritage' through the act of attributing a 'heritage' label to an object or landscape, always involves a process of human decision-making in the present. Indeed, the existence of the past as an objective reality is not even a precondition for the creation of heritage. In this sense, therefore, heritage can only ever be seen as a contemporary product shaped from a perceived impression of the past.

Rather than being a physical relic, artefact or particular landscape, heritage may perhaps more properly be seen as an attribute that may be attached to any object or any landscape. This process of heritage attribution, or labelling, occurs within the social and political present and is subject to all the whims of fashion and subjective choice that this suggests. Early in the 21st century, the china-clay tips of St Austell (Fig. 11.4) are deemed to represent an important strand of 'Cornish heritage': one day, the caravan park at Sandy Bay, near Exmouth will perhaps take its place as a heritage landscape that similarly merits preservation. In short, as a society, we conserve that which we would like to see rather than that which is actually there. The process of 'heritage-making' provides buildings and landscapes with a particular contemporary meaning and serves to convey present-day attitudes and values into the future. Whether the people of the future will thank us for conserving, managing, restoring and destroying what we have in our own turn inherited from the past is another matter!

The case of Dartmoor is instructive here (*see* Fig. 11.1). The landscape that is revered as essential heritage and supposedly 'natural wilderness' today, has actually been carefully nurtured and managed over many years to look the way it does. Without human intervention, these artificial moors would change immensely. People fight hard to protect this landscape from development, seeking to prevent the spread of china-clay workings or an 'inappropriate' expansion of housing, while carefully preserving the more picturesque aspects of past development, such as the mining remains of previous centuries, or the prehistoric landscape division of reaves that must once have transformed Bronze-Age Dartmoor in as dramatic and long-lasting a manner as any planned road or new town of today. It is ironic that many of the same people who petitioned *against* the Okehampton bypass, would petition *for* the re-establishment of rail connections (the motorways of their day) between Crediton/Okehampton and Tavistock/Plymouth in order to ease the pressure on Dartmoor's over-used road network. Whether today's dual carriageway will become a heritage object of tomorrow is the decision of future generations, but it is up to present-day stakeholders to define, preserve, interpret and display today's heritage landscape of Dartmoor. It is we, therefore, who need to decide what today's society is going to be remembered for – whether we want to be remembered for concrete dual carriageways or sustainable public transport is perhaps a very good illustration of this point!

It is not the intention of this chapter to make an apologist's case for untrammelled development and unchecked alteration of the landscape. On the contrary, its aim is to bring to the fore both the importance of heritage management and the complexity of its subject matter. Despite the pretence of heritage lying 'in the past', it is the future that heritage managers and stakeholders should be thinking of. What we, as a society, choose to preserve, develop and otherwise manipulate will inform our descendants about the sort of ancestors they had. What message do we want them to receive? This process of heritage 'tagging' and management is neatly shown in Peter Howard's 'Heritage Cycle' diagram (Fig. 11.5) in which each segment represents a complex arena of decision-making and negotiation between interested parties – or stakeholders.

Fig. 11.5 The 'heritage cycle', *after Peter Howard (2003).*

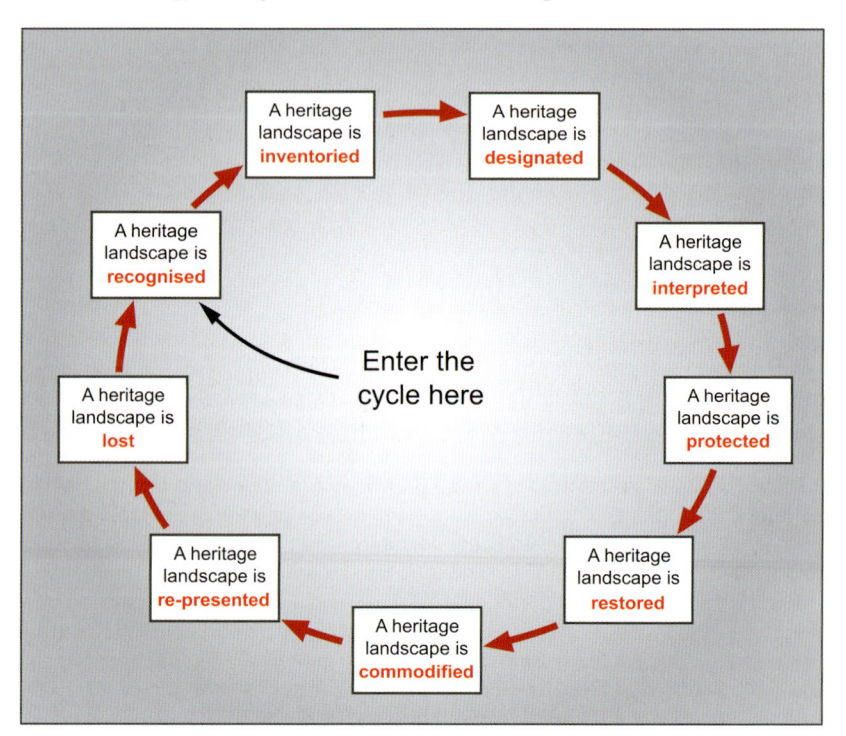

THE SOCIAL CONTEXT OF HERITAGE IN THE SOUTH WEST

Since heritage is something we define for ourselves, then it follows that the heritage 'resource' in the South West is inexhaustible in terms of quantity and unlimited in terms of typology. Literally anything – any landscape attribute, pattern or form – can be given a 'heritage' tag. This is not to say that all of the landscape types and forms in the South West are inexhaustible and therefore do not require management. Indeed, a social definition of heritage demands that attention be paid to its up-keep – we have 'chosen' the landscape that we would like to present to the world, and to future generations, and considerable effort is thus required to maintain it the way we want it to be. Of course, the idea of there being an 'us', who make such 'choices' over the landscape is far too simplistic.

Rather, the landscape around us has been arrived at through a process of complex negotiation and compromise between stakeholders: alteration and development of the new, alongside the endurance and survival of the old, all within the context of the competing agendas and cultural baggage that human society cannot do without. In order to flesh out the idea of there being heritage 'stakeholders', it might help to look first at the myriad different groups, individuals and institutions that *use* heritage landscapes in the South West (Fig. 11.6).

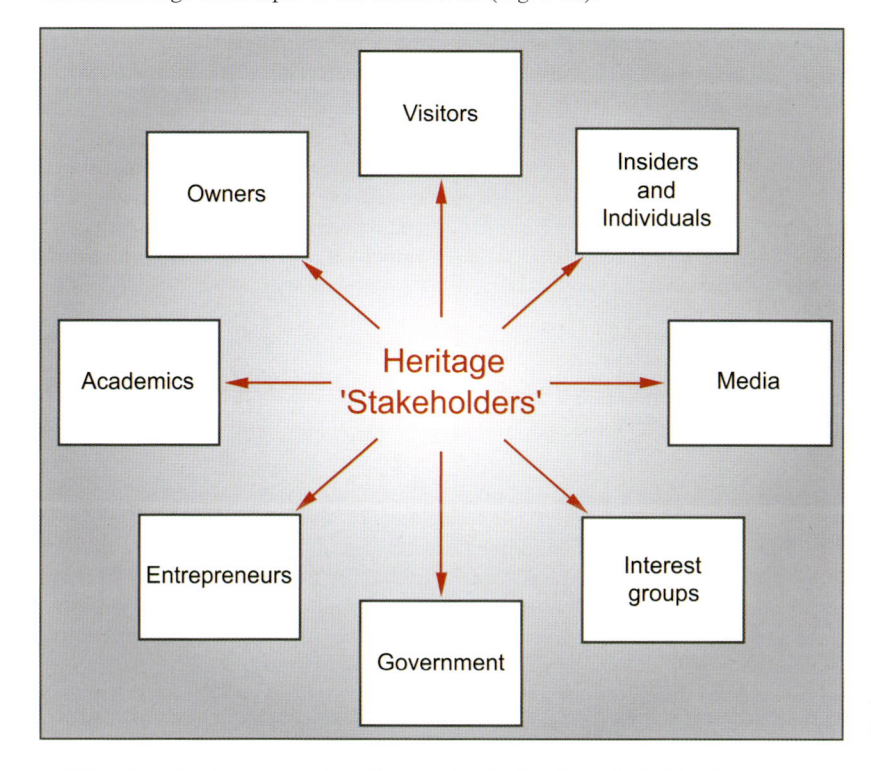

Fig. 11.6 Heritage stakeholders, *after Peter Howard (2003).*

All heritage landscapes are legally *owned*, whether by an individual, group or institution. In terms of their heritage *use*, these groups often pursue ideals of privacy, of security, economy and exclusive access. In addition to this use of the heritage, the question of liability and public responsibility also looms large for its owners, who often have to weigh up the 'rights' of access that other groups might expect to have, with their own liability for accidents that, as legally defined *owners*, they have to acknowledge. In addition, the owners of heritage landscapes may not recognise or desire the heritage value being attributed to their land. This may often be seen in the case of National Parks and Areas of Outstanding Natural Beauty, where statutory orders to preserve and manage attributed heritage in a particular way can conflict with the desires of the actual owners of the land. In the case of the Shaugh Moor china-clay workings on Dartmoor, for instance, the landowner's desire to extend quarrying conflicts with the perceived heritage value that others have given the landscape. In this case, the force of statutory bodies, together with input from other stakeholders (such as the local population, visitors, the media and independent interest groups, for example the Dartmoor Preservation Association), has outweighed the desires of the landowner, thereby showing how the owners of a particular heritage landscape may not have total control over its management. A similar conflict over rights of access to Dartmoor's Vixen Tor, where the landowner's concern for privacy has led to her attempt to exclude all other groups, has yet to be resolved (Fig. 11.7).

This group of heritage owners often overlaps with another group of heritage 'entrepreneurs', who seek economic gain from their interest in heritage, normally

LANDSCAPE AS HERITAGE AND A RECREATIONAL RESOURCE

Fig. 11.7 Vixen Tor, Dartmoor. *The issue of access to Vixen Tor has still to be resolved. Signs like this 'no public access' sign were painted on bare rocks in 2003, attracting widespread criticism.*

through tourism. For heritage entrepreneurs, the protection of the heritage value is imperative, but this often needs to be weighed against the commercial need to make a profit. This search for profit may sometimes lead to destruction of the heritage asset itself, either physically through its over-use, or through the degrading of its perceived heritage value through over-commercialisation. Heritage entrepreneurs also need to recognise the rights of heritage visitors who have desires for access, value for money and education. The landscape of Dartmoor, for instance, is appreciated by huge numbers of visitors – so much so, that many would argue that the heritage *value* of Dartmoor itself is being eroded through over-use (Fig. 11.8). The heritage landscapes of Cornwall and Devon are among the most widely recognised resources in the region, and careful management is required in order to balance the interests of heritage definition, protection and access.

Overlapping with the heritage visitors, are the heritage 'insiders'. In Devon and Cornwall, these insiders are most obviously the local residents, who feel that they have a particular right of control over 'their' heritage resource, as well as a right of access to it. Other insiders include the members of specialist clubs and societies, from hunt followers to birdwatchers, who all feel that their insider status deserves particular regard when it comes to heritage access and management. Although insiders rarely seek to exclude 'outsiders', their use of the landscape-heritage resource is subtly different from that of outside groups. In the South West, many local residents feel that 'their' landscape heritage is imbued with a particular regional expression that gives them both spiritual succour and a sense of communal identity.

Fig. 11.8 Postbridge, Dartmoor. *'Honeypot' sites such as the clapper bridge at Postbridge reveal the tensions between preservation and tourism within the heritage debate.*

Perhaps the most important class of insider, and by far the most difficult to generalise about, is the individual person, whoever he or she may be. Some of us might be heritage visitors, locals or even owners, but all of us have our own unique perspective of what constitutes a heritage landscape. Although we might express our concern through wider umbrella groups, the reasons *why* we view any landscape element in the way we do is always, ultimately, personal. An illustration of this point can be seen in Fig. 11.9, an image that may reflect many people's views of a typical (though certainly not outstanding) piece of south-west coast. Although most people would acknowledge that the beach at Mousehole is worthy of some measure of protection, few would claim it to be a unique example of coast that requires more protection than (say) nearby St Michael's Mount.

As well as these groups of heritage stakeholder that appear 'on the ground' there are a number of wider groups and institutions that have a genuine stake in heritage-landscape management, although often from a more remote position. Most obvious in this class are the various organisations that are involved, directly or indirectly, in heritage management for reasons that are ostensibly higher than simple local, or regional interest. Whether it is English Heritage, The National Trust, English Nature or the Royal Society for the Protection of Birds, each has a strong foothold in heritage-landscape management throughout the South West, but in pursuit of an agenda of its own that is formulated and driven by wider heritage concerns. The most important of these more remote stakeholders is the Government. The input and leverage of local or national government, often through their position as funders, is impossible to ignore. While acting on behalf of wider democratic interests, whether national or local, they also accrue legitimacy, prestige and credence for themselves through heritage. Their democratic mandate would, meanwhile, seem to provide them with almost ultimate authority over use and value of heritage. Even here, however, there is conflict, in which Westminster's authority to act on behalf of the nation may be questioned by some people in Cornwall. The recent destruction of landscape elements along the A30 near Honiton (not to mention the infamous Okehampton bypass) similarly left many people questioning the commitment of government to any effective protection of their landscape heritage.

Often going unnoticed, but none the less essential to the wider assortment of heritage stakeholders, are two particular interest groups that are so often vital when conflict emerges – the media and the academic sector. First, the media must be recognised as important consumers of heritage. Through writing, filming and otherwise communicating certain ideas and aspects of heritage to a mass audience, they play a critical role in helping to form wider views of heritage, both within public and private realms. Their concern for newsworthiness often means that heritage conflicts are choice arenas for media interest, while their power in advertising (intentional or otherwise) can make or break heritage entrepreneurs.

Fig. 11.9 Mousehole beach, Cornwall.
Although I have no legal claim to it, I think of Mousehole beach as somehow being 'mine'!

SCALE, IDENTITY AND THE USE OF HERITAGE IN THE SOUTH WEST

Academics constitute a final group of heritage stakeholders. As an author, I consume heritage by writing about it – I am informing readers' views of heritage simply by writing this chapter! Academics are often key players in the discovery of heritage and are certainly important in the interpretation and management of heritage landscapes, often with a particular concern for aspects of their 'authenticity'.

The South West contains landscapes that have had a heritage appellation attached to them on grounds of their significance at all levels of society. Certain landscapes, such as the Jurassic Coast of Dorset and east Devon, have been given the status of World Heritage Sites, while many other areas, particularly of a coastal and moorland nature, have long been regarded as containing heritage of international significance. In addition to these international accolades, a number of landscapes in Cornwall and Devon have been recognised as being of national importance, often through an association with a sense of national identity. Dartmoor and Exmoor, as National Parks, are obvious examples, while the rolling hills, village and farmstead settlements and deep green valleys of Devon are often described as being somehow 'quintessentially English'. Similar motifs are also often used to define a sense of regional landscape heritage. Devon's red soil for instance, while covering only a small portion of the county, is often associated with an overall sense of Devon heritage (Fig. 11.10). In Cornwall, a sense of distinct identity is similarly expressed through heritage

ABOVE: **Fig. 11.10 Devon red soil**. *From representation in picture postcards to the need for vigilance in car washing during the winter, red Devon soils have become synonymous with the county.*

Fig. 11.11 Bodmin Moor's ancient landscape *has a beauty all of its own and is often associated with a sense of Cornish distinctiveness.*

LANDSCAPE AS HERITAGE AND A RECREATIONAL RESOURCE

Fig. 11.12 Perranporth beach, Cornwall. In recent years, the popularity of surfing has led to an alignment of 'surf culture' with a sense of 'Cornishness'; some parts of Cornwall possess a quintessential surfscape.

landscapes ranging from the windswept plateaux of The Lizard and Bodmin Moor (Fig. 11.11), through the industrial heritage of the china-clay or tin-mining areas, to the surfscape of Newquay (Fig. 11.12).

At a smaller scale still, a myriad local identities are often presented and acknowledged through specific landscapes of heritage – for instance, the Royal Dockyard (*see* Fig. 9.20), Charles Church and (particularly) the Hoe are each representative of a particular aspect of Plymouth's sense of heritage and distinct local identity (Fig 11.13). There are as many uses as there are users of these landscapes, from recreation to profit-making.

Fig. 11.13 Icon of Plymouth's identity: Smeaton's Tower, the Hoe.

A SOUTH-WEST HERITAGE LANDSCAPE? DISSONANCE AND OPPORTUNITY

To offer a simple definition of a typical south-west England landscape would seem to be an impossible task. Certain settlement forms, such as the dispersed farmsteads and small villages that cover much of both Devon and Cornwall, perhaps hold a strong claim to be the characteristic landscape of the South West (Fig. 11.14). Although we cannot escape the fact that a vast majority of Cornwall and Devon's population do *not* live in thatched cottages or granite farmhouses, a certain range of buildings and landscape elements seem almost to pick themselves as representative of the region. These images have emerged as a result of a

LANDSCAPE AS HERITAGE AND A RECREATIONAL RESOURCE

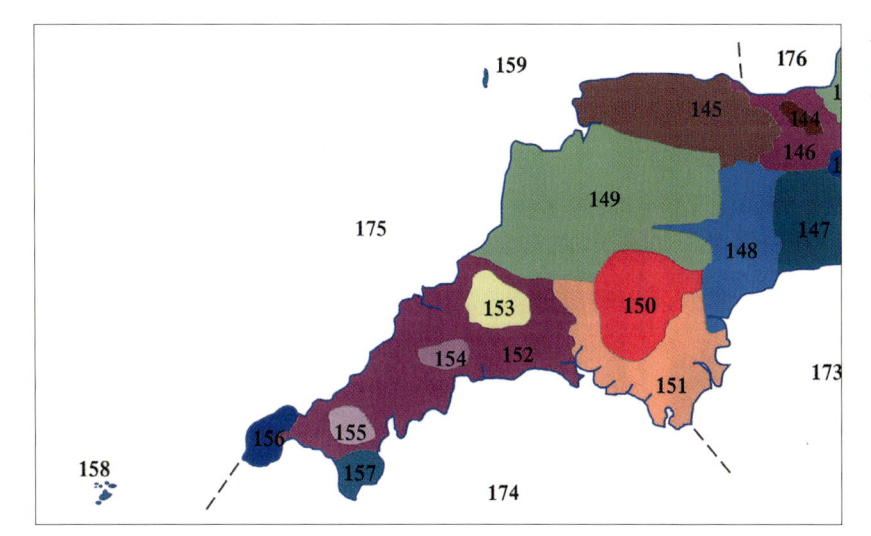

Fig. 11.15 An extract from the Countryside Agency's 'landscape characterisation' map.

protracted negotiation between a range of heritage stakeholders – they have been chosen to represent the South West, chosen as somehow particularly significant. Although they may be false (or at least misleading) images of what life and landscape in Devon and Cornwall were once really like, they are what we want to preserve and pass on to future generations. Whatever the ethics of choosing and maintaining a particular landscape, the landscape that we pass on to the future is a negotiated representation of our world, with all its conflicts and compromises.

In an attempt to try to make sense of landscape heritage at a general level, the Cornwall Archaeology Unit undertook pioneering work during the 1990s on the characterisation of the county's historic landscape. Although the categorisations used in this historic-landscape assessment scheme have an obvious archaeological slant, its county-wide perspective of the heritage resource at a landscape level (rather than at the levels of individual buildings, sites or artefacts) has proved very useful for the purpose of heritage planning and management. More recently, a similar approach has been taken up nationally by the Countryside Agency, in their *Countryside Character Initiative*. This survey includes systematic descriptions of the features and characteristics that make the landscape special and distinctive, together with guidance on how to undertake more detailed local landscape character assessments. Fourteen of England's 159 'characteristic landscapes' lie in Devon and Cornwall (Fig. 11.15), each being categorised according to 'what gives a locality its own sense of place, what makes it different from its neighbouring area, and what conditions should be set for any new development and change'. Although the subjectivity and present-centred circumstance of the Countryside Agency's survey is perhaps underplayed, such a uniform coverage of what the landscape represents, together with a concerted and comprehensive strategy for future management is surely a positive step.

LANDSCAPES OF INDUSTRIAL HERITAGE IN THE SOUTH WEST

The South West is perhaps not the first region in Britain that springs to mind when considering the role of industry in shaping the landscape (*see* Chapter 8). There are no coal mines, car plants or steel works, and precious few large cities. Nevertheless, the role of industry in shaping the landscape of both Devon and Cornwall still has to be fully acknowledged, partly because it has so often been written out of the normal heritage story, particularly in Devon.

OPPOSITE PAGE:

Fig. 11.14 Typical rural Devon and Cornwall. Although by no means ubiquitous, the pattern of dispersed farmsteads and small hamlets is seen by many as somehow typical of Cornwall and Devon.

LANDSCAPE AS HERITAGE AND A RECREATIONAL RESOURCE

Figs 11.16–11.19 South-west industry.
TOP LEFT:
Fig. 11.16 Spoil heaps near Pendeen.
TOP RIGHT:
Fig. 11.17 The Geevor Mine heritage attraction in West Penwith.
BOTTOM LEFT:
Fig. 11.18 Coldharbour Mill, Uffculme, belying the image of a Devon countryside lacking 'heavy industry'.
BOTTOM RIGHT:
Fig. 11.19 Polperro – a 'typical' Cornish fishing village.

Today, for instance, Tavistock appears as a small market town in the heart of 'rural' west Devon. A look beyond such postcard images, however, would reveal Tavistock's previous role as one of the world's foremost copper- and arsenic-mining centres (*see also* Chapter 8). The nearby outdoor heritage museum of Morwellham Quay allows the visitor an entrance point into this long-gone world of large-scale industrial development, but can only touch the surface of what the actual copper-mining landscape, with its vast areas of contaminated land, spoil heaps and social hardship, really looked like. The valley sides of the Tamar, once scorched with poison from arsenic manufacture, are now green and tranquil. This is a landscape of industrial heritage *par excellence*, but surely no one would demand the preservation of misery and blight in the name of heritage?

On a larger scale, vast areas of the South West, particularly in Cornwall, have been touched (or torn apart) over many centuries by the mineral-extraction industry. Recent years have seen an upsurge of interest in these landscapes, both as examples of industrial ingenuity and also as touchstones of local identity (Figs 11.16–11.19). One of the major problems of industrial-heritage management is the question of how to deal with such vast areas of poor or even contaminated land. In short, there is an over-supply of industrial-heritage landscapes in the South West, and a very real problem of meaningful presentation. These areas once employed thousands of workers, and were among the most advanced industrial regions of their day. The challenge to present a socially truthful heritage product from such vast areas of dereliction is being tackled at such sites as Morwellham Quay on the Devon side of the Tamar valley, Wheal Martyn near St Austell, and at Geevor in Penwith (Fig. 11.17), where a much more recent industrial past (the tin mine closed for the last time in 1990) has led to a very different mode of heritage presentation.

An industrial-heritage landscape of a very different type is found across vast areas of rural Devon in the form of small towns and villages in which the textile industry once thrived. Today, only Tiverton maintains its past associations with textiles to any great extent, but three centuries ago, the South West was further advanced in the textile industry than Lancashire or Yorkshire. The heritage of the industrial landscape that never developed any further is still to be found, for example in the picturesque mills of small towns such as Uffculme, where Coldharbour Mill has been redeveloped as a heritage attraction (Fig. 11.18).

In terms of its importance to the image and self-identity of the South West, the fishing industry far exceeds its actual importance in terms of employment and its lasting impact on the landscape. For very obvious reasons, fishing is concentrated around particular coastal havens and has left very little mark on the rest of the landscape. Despite the fact that there were probably more shopkeepers than fishermen across the region, fishing is an industry with a deeply felt and widely acknowledged link to the regional identity of Devon and Cornwall. The landscapes of small harbours, brightly painted boats and occasional larger fish markets are among the most distinctive of the region, and perhaps the most popular image for postcard buyers (Fig. 11.19). No caption is required – the image *is* the typical landscape of Cornwall and Devon. As with the tin mines, however, there is still a heritage dilemma here. In the case of the tin mines, there is an over-supply of a resource, much of which many people would describe as being fairly ugly. In the case of fishing, there are a very few honey-pot villages, the prettiness of which belies the hard lives and terrible working conditions that were associated with their pasts. In both cases, there is a real problem of how to represent these landscapes in any honest way. No one would choose to tear down the pretty village of Polperro, for instance, but its preservation in aspic has arguably led to its transformation from a working village to a tourist 'museum' without deeper significance. In the case of places such as Polperro, Mousehole and St Ives, conservation in the name of heritage has wrung out much of the meaning that they once held – they have literally been loved to death.

LANDSCAPES OF RURAL HERITAGE IN THE SOUTH WEST

In terms of the physical form of the landscape, farming is the industry that has had by far the largest impact. Beyond the built-up areas and narrow coastal fringes, almost the entire face of the peninsula bears the imprint of agricultural activity, from the rich arable fields in the fertile valleys of east Devon, to the highest of the granite moors (*see* Chapter 7). A very strong sense of heritage is invoked through the traditional farmlands of both Devon and Cornwall, with

LANDSCAPE AS HERITAGE AND A RECREATIONAL RESOURCE

pastures and hay meadows, hedgerows and field patterns, lanes and pathways all seemingly timeless and certainly worthy of protection (Fig. 11.20). The pressure for the heritage of rural life and landscape to be conserved is reflected in renewed interest in active conservation work, as well as through lobbying groups as diverse as the Rambler's Association and The Countryside Alliance. There has been considerable official support for much of this work, through well-financed schemes to support 'traditional' farming methods in Environmentally Sensitive Areas, alongside existing arrangements to protect Areas of Outstanding Natural Beauty. An outcome of this heritage-led interest in the traditional countryside, however, is that conflict arises over its use and very meaning (Fig. 11.21).

For instance, the levels of funding for hedgerow protection and replanting can seem to fly in the face of a wider agricultural policy geared to the encouragement of increased production on all fronts (Fig. 11.22). A fundamental tension thus arises between the mechanisation and intensification of agriculture of the last 50 years, and the protection of a traditional landscape that is valued for

New features in the landscape of The Blackdown Hills, east Devon, an *environmentally sensitive area with many restrictions on development.*

ABOVE:
Fig. 11.20 The yellow of rape in flower.
RIGHT:
Fig. 11.21 The black plastic sacks of silage.
BELOW:
Fig. 11.22 Grubbed-up hedges.

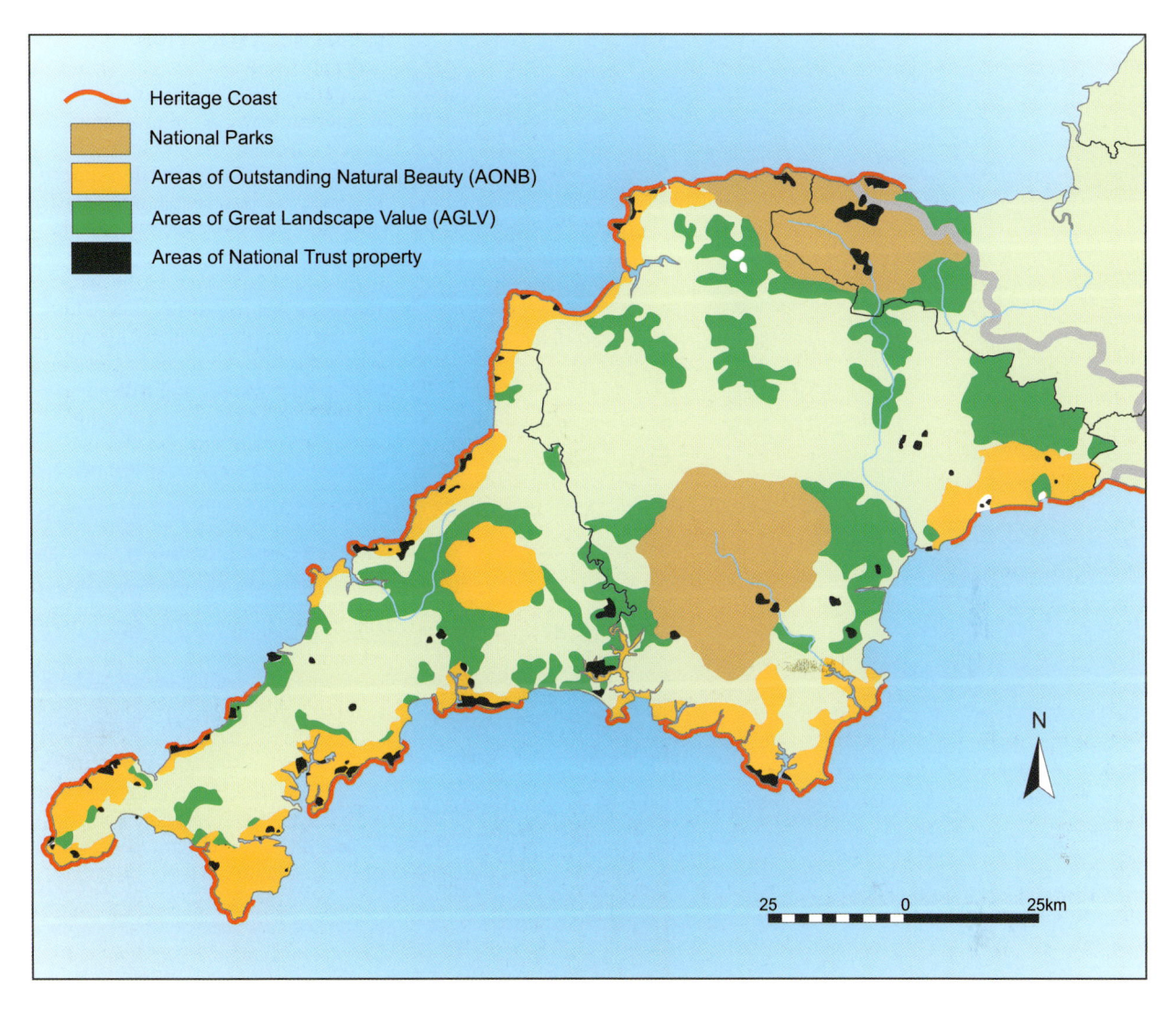

aesthetic, spiritual, educational and conservational reasons. Difficult decisions have to be made over what we would like our agricultural countryside to look like in the future, and yet many stakeholders appear to be standing in slightly ambiguous positions. On the one hand, there are pressures to further intensify arable production through the use of improved (and maybe even genetically modified) varieties of crops, or to increase yields through methods of animal husbandry that bear a closer resemblance to high-tech science than traditional ways of farming life. On the other hand, especially in view of the importance of the tourist industry in Devon and Cornwall, there are pressures to protect public rights of way and to improve public access. From a heritage point of view, even if aspects of the traditional landscape such as hedgerows and field boundaries are protected, the diversification of crops, and even the move away from hay to silage, will still lead to a 'new' landscape (*see* Fig. 11.20). The heritage value of the agricultural landscape of the South West is agreed by almost everyone, and the need for its continued management is undeniable. But if the landscape we pass on to future generations is to be one of which we can be proud, we need first to question its fundamental meaning in an open debate (Fig. 11.23).

Fig. 11.23 Map of National Parks, Areas of Outstanding Natural Beauty and other designated areas in the South West.

ABOVE: **Fig. 11.24 Haytor, Dartmoor.** *The 'honeypot' site of Haytor requires sensitive management in order to satisfy both tourist needs and conservation concerns.*

Fig. 11.28 Guide Book to touring north Devon (1885). *This guide book to north Devon and Cornwall reflects the great upsurge in domestic tourist activity that occurred during the late 19th and early 20th centuries. Increasing leisure time and expenditure, together with improved transport infrastructure, allowed new sections of society to take annual holidays.*

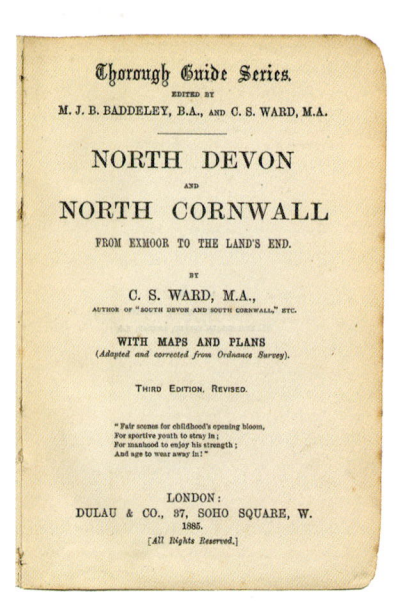

LANDSCAPES OF TOURISM

In physical terms, the industry with the largest impact on the South West is agriculture. Economically speaking, however, it is tourism that is the most important industry today. On the one hand, the landscape is itself the tourist industry's biggest asset; on the other, it is tourism that perhaps poses the greatest threat to that landscape. In addition, it must be accepted that the tourist industry produces a distinct landscape of its own that has become an important additional part of the landscape heritage of the South West. Large areas of Cornwall and Devon have been affected by tourism, from the trampling of green swards around Haytor (Fig. 11.24) to the massive seaside development around Torbay (Figs 11.25 and 11.26). Concerns about the homogenisation of the landscape through the pressures of tourism appear, however, to have subsided in recent years – not least because the tourism industry itself has become so diverse. This short survey of the impacts of tourism, therefore, focuses on the newer heritage of tourist landscapes rather than the impacts of tourism on the pre-existing landscape.

Tourism has a very long history in Devon and Cornwall (*see* Chapter 9). Early tourists soon spread out from the cathedral city of Exeter to towns such as Sidmouth, which sprang from a wave of aristocratic tourist interest in the seaside during the Regency period (Fig. 11.27). In the 19th century, the guidebooks that were produced specifically for the popular market increasingly began to advertise Cornwall and Devon on the basis of their heritage appeal (Fig. 11.28). The lineal descendants of those guidebooks can be found today among the mass of promotional and travel literature about the region, together with their embodiment in carefully preserved heritage villages such as Chagford, Clovelly, Cockington or Cadgwith (Fig. 11.29).

More recently, the 'bucket-and-spade' English seaside resort, so popular during the first three-quarters of the 20th century, has been remodelled and augmented by the diversity of present-day tourism landscapes. From the caravan parks of Sandy Bay to the surfscape of Newquay, the modern tourist landscape purveys a plethora of overlapping heritages, often mediated through a multitude of different personal memories and remembrances of childhood holidays.

Tourism. *The South West contains a myriad tourist landscapes. Even 'seafronts' come in a number of guises – and display a great variety of both attractions and tourists.*

TOP:
Fig. 11.25 Torquay.
CENTRE:
Fig. 11.26 Goodrington Sands.
ABOVE:
Fig. 11.27 Sidmouth.
LEFT:
Fig. 11.29 Clovelly.

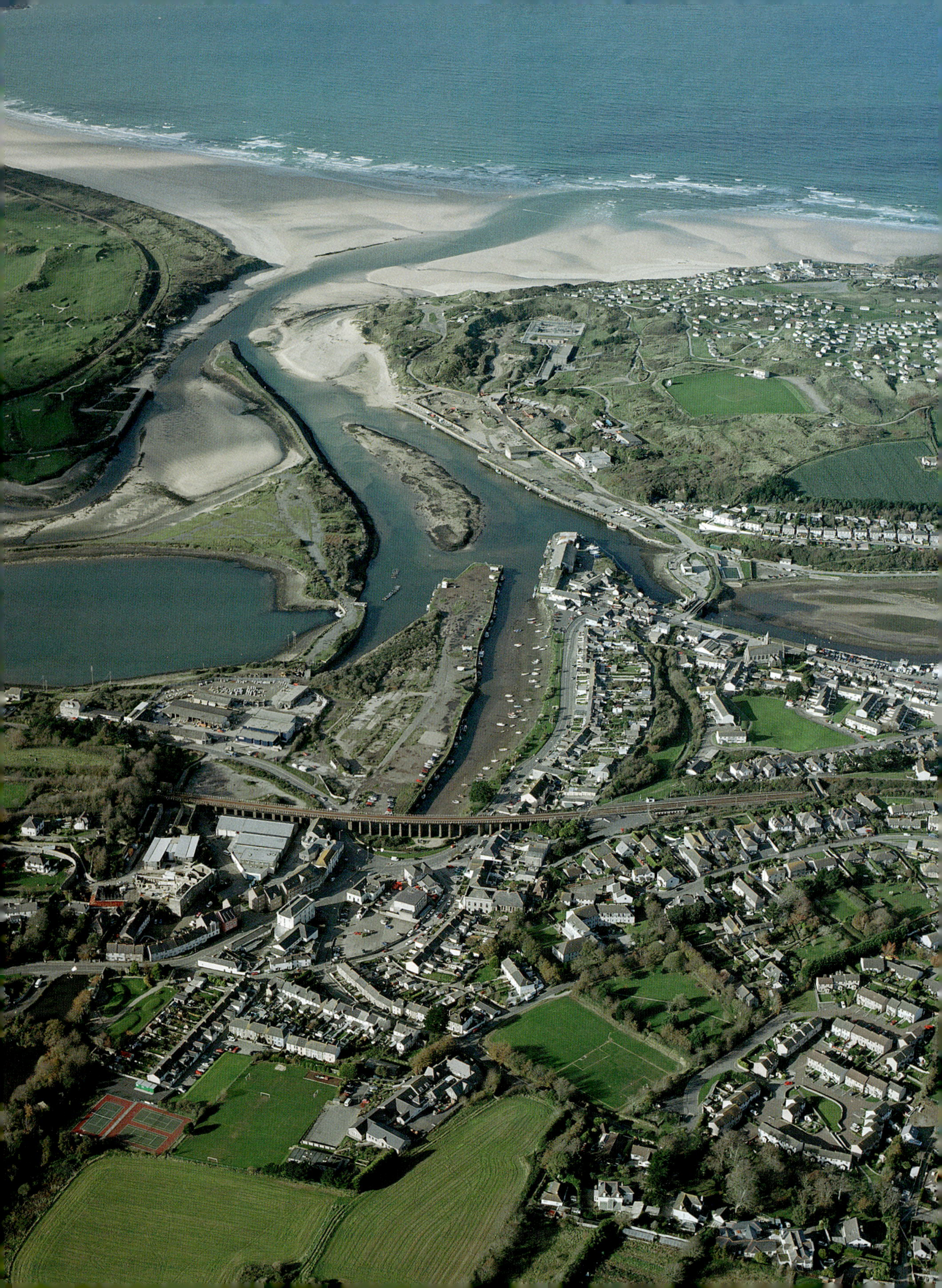

HERITAGE INERTIA AND THE QUESTION OF DEVELOPMENT

While to many people's eyes, the South West is characterised by its rural landscape, we should not ignore the heritage landscape of Devon and Cornwall's built-up areas. Newquay's surfscape and Torbay's seaside resorts have already been mentioned, but the two largest cities of Exeter and Plymouth also require attention (*see also* Chapter 9). Plymouth's contemporary urban heritage derives largely from the city's destruction during the Second World War. Its city-centre landscape of 1950s planning represents Sir Patrick Abercrombie's ideal of a 'brave new world' and is one of the best examples of its type. Exeter contains its own heritage of wartime destruction, and also has its own post-war plan in the form of Thomas Sharpe's *Exeter Phoenix*. Today, however, Exeter focuses on the heritage of the preserved parts of its ancient city centre, mostly within the remains of its Roman walls. In both cities, heritage conflicts are clearly visible, as arguments about development, inertia and blight are added to debate about what heritage itself means for the present and future. These challenging issues can be explored a little further through two case studies, of very different character and at opposite ends of the south-west peninsula: Hayle docks in west Cornwall, and Princesshay in Exeter.

By the mid-19th century, Hayle was one of the most important industrial centres in Cornwall; with foundries for both copper and iron, it was a major centre of the tin and copper-exporting trade, as well as the world's leading centre for the manufacture of industrial pumps (Fig. 11.30). Even today, Hayle people proudly boast that many of Holland's polders were claimed from the sea with the help of Hayle pumping engines, while Foundry Square saw the birth of the *Great Eastern* ship among other industrial milestones (*see* Chapter 9). After a century of decline, Hayle stands today as a small town greatly in need of more investment, but with a heritage asset that may sometimes seem a millstone. Hundreds of hectares of former docks and rambling foundry buildings make up an industrial-heritage landscape of some value. The cost of maintaining the buildings, together with the stringent planning guidelines that cover such a heavily protected zone, has nevertheless led to a situation of what we might call 'heritage blight'. The people of Hayle want employment and prosperity and no one wants to see a continuance of the empty and derelict land that exists at present. The problems associated with the regeneration of such a heritage-sensitive area, however, has led to a number of botched plans and broken dreams (Fig. 11.31). In 2006, 20 years after the first large-scale scheme was proposed, the site still stood empty and the differences between the need for development and the protection of a valuable heritage resource (not to mention the value of the estuary for bird life) were still not reconciled. Again, this example raises the issue of what heritage actually means – of how it is defined and used. There are some who would argue that the physical protection of buildings and dock frontages has been raised to a higher level of importance than the value of a thriving local community. While the untrammelled expansion of monotonous 'identikit' housing and holiday homes cannot be justified, the stasis of the present must be broken. Hayle ought not be turned into a characterless holiday dormitory, but neither can it be preserved purely as a museum.

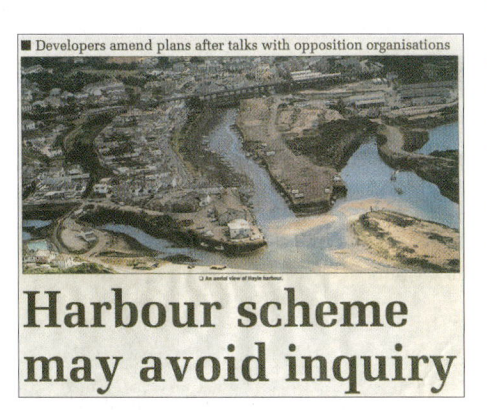

OPPOSITE PAGE & INSET:

Figs 11.30–11.31 Conflict. Hayle Docks and a piece in the Cornishman relating to Hayle (November 2001). Hayle is a small working town in west Cornwall. The historic importance of its now largely redundant dock and foundry area sometimes appears to be an unwanted encumbrance to further development that might bring with it some badly needed jobs.

LANDSCAPE AS HERITAGE AND A RECREATIONAL RESOURCE

Fig. 11.32 Conflict. Princesshay, Exeter. Close to Exeter's historic city centre, Princesshay was torn down in 2005, despite the objections of some protesters who saw a heritage value in its status as England's first concrete shopping arcade.

Although there seems to be a large measure of agreement that much of the rural landscape of Devon and Cornwall contains heritage value and should be protected, the heritage of urban landscapes is often more ambiguous. Princesshay in Exeter is a case in point (Fig. 11.32). Supporters of its preservation claimed it as the first concrete pedestrian shopping arcade of the post-war period, and a masterpiece of its genre. Detractors saw it as an ugly concrete blot in Exeter's historic urban core. Plans for its wholesale redevelopment were held up and calls for a public enquiry supported by, among others, English Heritage, who noted its architectural importance. Both sides in the argument welcomed investment, but whether one believes that this investment should have been in demolition and rebuilding or in further preservation and enhancement of what existed, a stalemate was good for no one.

Fig. 11.33 'Experience the difference'. This postcard image is typical of a long-established tradition that seeks to invoke a sense of separateness and 'foreignness' in Cornwall.

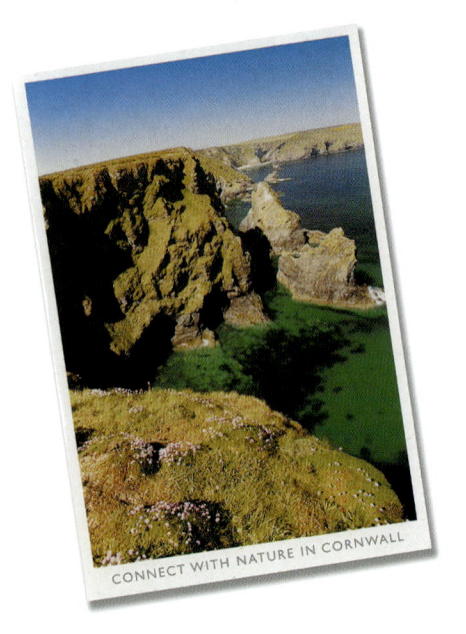

CORNISH HERITAGE: DISTINCTION AND RESISTANCE

Earlier in this chapter, mention was made of how certain heritage landscapes have come to be associated with deeper spiritual meaning or given the power to frame identity. The contentious issue of historic sites in Cornwall is indicative of how divisive and problematic the definition and interpretation of the heritage can become. A particular sense of heritage – even a particular 'type' of landscape – is invoked by the idea of Cornishness (Fig. 11.33). The labelling of such heritage as 'English', particularly when the sites concerned are owned and managed by the non-governmental agency, English Heritage, has led to a great deal of conflict in recent years. The focus of this dispute has been a campaign by Cornish nationalists to deliberately deface the English Heritage and English Tourist Board signposts that advertise these heritage attractions and landscapes, a practice that has even led to prosecutions (Figs 11.34 and 11.35). Whatever the rights and wrongs of such direct action, it raises once more the issue of how stakeholders in heritage define themselves and seek to impose their agendas on others: in this case, some individuals claim that English Heritage should not have *any* stake in defining and managing a distinctly *Cornish* heritage.

The job of outlining an alternative mechanism for managing and presenting the heritage of Cornwall is often ignored by these self-elected protesters, whose reification of an homogenous and uniform sense of Cornishness deserves to be questioned. The apparent 'claiming' of aspects of heritage in Cornwall as expressions of Englishness, however, is equally open to question. In addition, most authorities (both unofficial *and* official) are regularly seen to be keen to

LANDSCAPE AS HERITAGE AND A RECREATIONAL RESOURCE

Cornish conflict.

LEFT:

Fig. 11.34 *Vandalised English Heritage sign.*

BELOW LEFT:

Fig. 11.35 *Piece in the* Guardian *newspaper (19 January 2002).*

BELOW:

Fig. 11.36 *Ginster's lorry.*

BOTTOM:

Fig. 11.37 *The* Atlantic Edge.

The black-and-white flag of St Piran daubed on signposts in Cornwall is a common sight and English Heritage has had a particular problem with such graffiti artists. On the other hand, the invocation of a sense of difference and 'non-Englishness' is often used as an icon of prestige that may add economic and cultural value – as seen here in the service of a local commercial interest.

push their own agenda by using a distinctive local heritage to invoke a sense of Cornish *difference*. An image of difference, and even of isolation from the modern world, can often be seen as a valuable marketing tool, both in terms of the placing of a product in a distinct marketing category in which 'heritage' adds value, and also in terms of tapping into the expanding and lucrative market for 'Celtic' goods and lifestyles (Fig. 11.36).

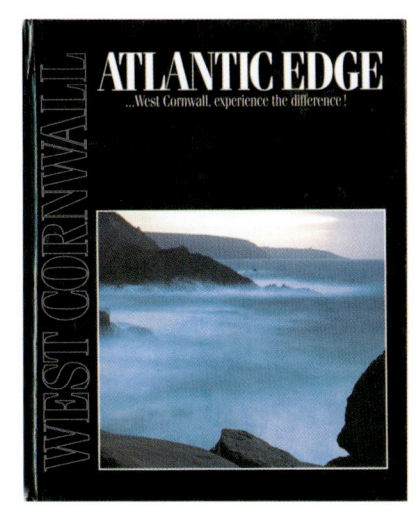

The invocation of a sense of Cornish difference, and even 'foreign-ness' has a long history, and Penwith District Council's publication *Atlantic Edge – West Cornwall, Experience the Difference* (1995), supported by the Countryside Commission and the Rural Development Commission, is an excellent example of the continuing trend to invoke Cornwall's landscape heritage as somehow different and ostensibly non-English (Fig. 11.37). The step between such efforts to conjure up a sense of distinction through marketing and media management, and the more direct efforts of some Cornish graffiti artists at English Heritage sites, is a short one. It is at the same time an important one, which brings us back once again to the crucial question of how heritage is negotiated between democratic and accountable stakeholders.

HERITAGE FUTURES IN THE SOUTH WEST

A question with which to conclude: which is it that better represents the essential 'heritage landscape' of Devon and Cornwall – a seaside village such as Mousehole or Clovelly, or the A30 trunk road? If we try to be honest about the aspects of the present-day landscape that the people of the future will remember us for, then the A30 would be a very good example. Today, the road provides an axis and backbone to the region, and is a symbol of the region to the outside world (surely one of the most persistent and common memories of holidaymakers and childhood memories of Cornwall and Devon is sitting in a traffic jam on the A30). Perhaps, therefore, this is a far more meaningful memory to preserve than the typical picture-postcard images. In terms of 'our achievements' in the landscape, the road network (love it or hate it) is surely among the most enduring symbols of early 21st-century life in Devon and Cornwall – the protests over the upgrading of the A30 near Honiton and the more recent debates over road noise are surely perfect examples for us to present to the people of the future of the hot issues of development and conservation that we are facing today. The value and purpose of heritage and its conservation are normally taken for granted and not questioned. In reality, heritage and conservation are very complex issues that involve a great many stakeholders. Heritage is *not* about the past – it is *everything* to do with the future!

FURTHER READING

The Countryside Agency *Countryside Character Initiative*: http://www.countryside.gov.uk/LivingLandscapes/countryside_character/index.asp Fourteen of England's 159 'characteristic landscapes' are found in Devon and Cornwall. This website offers an overview, both of the scheme and of each landscape, in terms of its heritage value and meaning.

Graham *et al*. 2000. For those interested in studying the meaning and construction of heritage to a deeper level, this textbook gives a clear overview of the issues.

Herring 1998. A clear and locally oriented guide for people interested in investigating how ideas of landscape heritage are formed.

Howard 2003. This is an important book for anyone interested in heritage issues, but it is also much more than that. This book is a personal and sometimes provocative account by a respected heritage author and activist. Peter Howard lives in Devon and many of his case studies are from the South West.

Kain and Ravenhill (eds) 1999. A number of chapters in this atlas will be of interest to people who would like to find out more about the development of the landscape in Devon and Cornwall with a heritage and recreational perspective.

12

Landscapes and Senses of Place

CATHERINE BRACE

In 1976 a geographer named Ted Relph wrote that 'to be human is to live in a world that is filled with significant places'. He was trying to call attention to the ways in which human beings identify what he called 'sense of place'. At the most basic level this refers to the ability to recognise different places and different identities of a place or the unique combination of architecture, topography, flora and fauna, culture, social life and landscape that makes places different from each other and gives them an inimitable character. Relph recognised the profoundly human emotional attachments that people form with places and attempted to show how very personal and individual factors make a difference to people's sense of place.

Senses of place can be very fluid, sometimes almost intangible or ephemeral and sometimes felt very powerfully. They can work across many scales, from a set of meanings associated with a particular group of stones, such as Lanyon Quoit, right up to a general and popularly held understanding of the character of south-west England despite the diverse landscapes, traditions and people found in Devon and Cornwall. Senses of place can be shared between individuals and human groups but sometimes they are contested. They can also be contradictory or inconsistent. People who live in south-west England might, for example, identify something called 'the West Country' and agree in very broad terms about what distinguishes it from the West Riding of Yorkshire or the Midlands, but then find it difficult to articulate that difference and would disagree on the precise nature of the West Country character. It is important to remember that people who live in south-west England are not the only ones constructing its senses of place. The thousands of tourists who visit every year, as well as those who have never visited but have only seen Devon and Cornwall on the television or read about them in books, will still imagine it, if only to define more clearly a sense of place for where they live.

It is tempting to think that people who live in south-west England necessarily have a more truthful, more accurate or more authentic sense of place than people who live elsewhere. We should be cautious about such claims, however. While close proximity to a place might engender a sense of emotional 'ownership', much work by geographers and others has shown that a sense of place hardly ever has a final, objective, stable meaning. This is not to devalue the meanings that people give to places – in fact, these meanings can be terribly important and have real material consequences. For instance, strong feelings about what Dartmoor should look like and what kinds of activity should go on there have prevented the encroachment of new buildings, roads and industry in the National Park.

Because of the capricious, somewhat unpredictable way in which people give meaning to places, it is often said that senses of place are 'constructed'. Using the word 'constructed' helps us to remember that a sense of place is not innate – it is not something we are born with and it is not something that we automatically absorb when we visit a place. Rather, a sense of place is constructed or made through all kinds of social process like visiting, talking about a place, seeing it on television, writing about it, painting it, filming it or just living there. Some geographers would argue that defining a sense of place is more about finding our own identities than anything else. The geographer Nigel Thrift has argued that places 'form a reservoir of meanings which people can draw upon to tell stories about and thereby define themselves'. In other words, our sense of place helps us to define who we are and what we think is important. The continuous process of creating and re-creating a sense of place is crucial, for it is the steady *accumulation* of ideas and images about a place that is really important to the creation of place identity.

One of the most important ways in which a sense of place is created and communicated is through landscape and its representation in words (through poetry, and imaginative and topographic writing), visual art of all kinds (from fine art, through postcards, prints, book jackets or posters) and the media (including television, film and radio). The word 'landscape' is used rather glibly in the English language in a way that ignores its very specific meanings. It often gets conflated with words like region, area, nature, place, scenery (particularly rural countryside), topography or environment. Landscape more properly refers to a portion of the earth visible by an observer from a particular position or location, and especially that which can be seen in a single view. But landscape is much more than this. The word also suggests the active engagement of a human subject with a material object through which the material object is appropriated visually and modified through imaginative processes. As Denis Cosgrove puts it, 'landscape denotes the external world mediated through subjective human experience'. It is not merely *what* we see but a *way* of seeing; not just an object but an imaginative construction of an object. Seeing a landscape always involves having an imaginative response to it – whether we are standing in an art gallery, looking at something on television or gazing out over the countryside from a hilltop. This imaginative factor helps to explain why different people have such different responses to places and landscapes.

In this chapter about the relationship between landscape and sense of place in the South West, representations of regional landscapes in art and literature will be used to show how senses of place and regional identities in south-west England are articulated. It is important to note from the outset, however, that there is no one single landscape or sense of place that sums up south-west England. Whilst several iconic landscapes, pieces of landscape art, novels or poems might seem to capture something quintessential about the region, a final, definitive sense of place is impossible to capture for a region as large and diverse as the South West (*see* Chapter 11). Rather, several different senses of place can be identified – sometimes these have similarities and sometimes they are quite different.

DISCOVERING THE SOUTH WEST

Probably one of the key factors underpinning the creation of powerful and enduring place images for Devon and Cornwall was the growth of their enormous popularity as tourist destinations from the 18th century onwards. Travellers, tourists and trippers who actually visited the region were joined, especially in the 20th century, by armchair explorers, who consumed the large quantity of countryside writing produced in the years between about 1920 and 1950. Much of this contained descriptions of topography, sites of antiquarian, historical and architectural interest, traditions, rural customs and local culture on a region-by-region basis. Tourism in the 20th century also stimulated new kinds of advertising, such as railway-carriage-panel art.

In the late 18th and early 19th centuries, Devon's and Cornwall's coastal towns were considered ideal venues to indulge the fashion for sea-bathing stimulated by George III. Resort towns grew rapidly, especially in south Devon. Cornwall was 'discovered' by holidaymakers much later, mainly because of its distance from main centres of population. Only by the late 19th century were places like Bude and Newquay enjoying rates of growth that the south Devon resorts had been experiencing since the early years of the 19th century and before. The development of tourism has an effect on the construction of a sense of place in two main ways. First, and most obviously, tourists visit and take home an impression of a place, which is fixed in the memory by talking about the holiday, reminiscing and, in more recent years, looking at holiday photos. Second, the development of tourism also encourages the growth of a particular arm of publishing – especially guidebooks, holiday brochures, souvenir books containing photographic or pen portraits of a place and lastly, the great icon of the seaside holiday, the picture postcard. Such items continually recycle certain images – sandy beaches, blue skies, inviting sea, picturesque fishing villages, dramatic coastal scenery and beautiful countryside – until these things become synonymous with Devon and Cornwall in the popular imagination. Of course, the other crucial thing about holidays is that they are often a feature of our childhood and we start to build up a repertoire of place images from our holidays at an early age. Later in life, these are often tinted with nostalgia and we sometimes become quite sentimental about a place in which we enjoyed happy family holidays as a child. The tourist 'discovery' of south-west England is, then, extremely significant to the development of the region's sense of place.

The popular discovery of south-west England through the late 19th and into the 20th centuries has a great deal to do with the growth of railways (*see also* Chapter 10). Simon Trezise has noted that the expansion of the railways enabled more people of more classes to visit than had been possible when long-distance travel entailed an expensive, uncomfortable, and sometimes dangerous coach ride. Between 1846 and 1848, 4,000km of railway were built nationally, rising to 11,265km by 1851. In 1844 the rail link was completed between Bristol and Exeter. Lines reached as far as the south Devon coast in 1846. In 1855 Barnstaple was linked to Exeter and in 1860 the rail link between Exeter and London was improved with a new route via Yeovil that was quicker than travelling via Bristol. Through the 1860s, rail routes into Cornwall also improved markedly. Indeed, Thomas Cook organised the first 'package' tour to Cornwall using a specially chartered train from Bristol. But the railways did more than bring passengers to the area. Through clever marketing, branding and advertising, the Great Western Railway (GWR) in particular was instrumental in creating some of the most enduring images of Devon and Cornwall.

Shaw, Greenwood and Williams have argued that the GWR helped to shape a lasting image of Cornwall as well as build up resorts like Newquay and St Ives. The GWR encouraged the development of hotels – some, like the Atlantic Hotel in Newquay, of considerable luxury – and at St Ives actually took a lease on Tregenna Castle and opened it as a hotel in 1878. Of greater importance, however, was their rebranding of an area of Cornwall as the 'Cornish Riviera' as part of their Cornish Riviera Express service. In 1928 the GWR published a specially commissioned guidebook by the popular writer and broadcaster, S P B Mais, entitled *The Cornish Riviera*, that combined Mais's anecdotal style with asides on architecture, traditions, crafts, local lore and descriptive tours of the principal sights. The use of 'riviera' as a way to describe West-Country resorts is a brand concept that still resonates through promotional literature today and refers to the appeal of a warm climate and sandy beaches. A GWR promotional poster that announced 'there is a great similarity between Cornwall and Italy in shape, climate and natural beauties' might have been stretching a point somewhat, but the concept has stuck. Unlike Cornwall, Devon already had well-established

LANDSCAPES AND SENSES OF PLACE

Fig. 12.1 Dartmouth, Devon, by Frank H Mason, 1954.

Fig. 12.2 Widecombe-in-the-Moor, near Ashburton, Devon, by Jack Merriott RI, 1954.

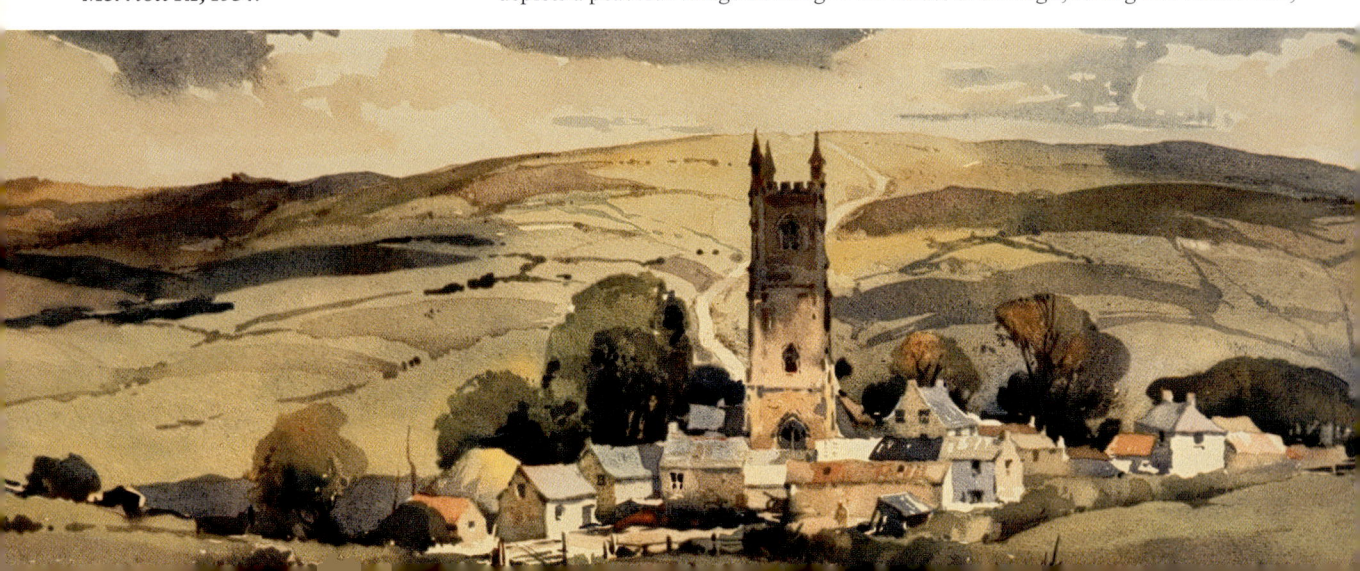

resort towns such as Exmouth before the arrival of the railway. However, some towns, like Torquay, were transformed from fashionable watering places to popular tourist resorts by more frequent and faster train services that delivered more and more tourists to the town. The GWR also joined other rail companies in promoting tourism through the innovative use of carriage panels. Carriage panels were the frames or recesses above the seats inside railway carriages that allowed the insertion of photographs, maps, prints or advertisements. Greg Norden has remarked that between the late 1930s and the mid-1960s, 'railway publicity departments moved into colour reproduction and commissioned some of the leading watercolour artists of the day to paint scenes from all around Britain, [and] the trains became travelling art galleries'. The carriage panels commissioned by the GWR brought Devon and Cornwall into the carriages of thousands of commuters. In 1954 it was possible to sit in a train at Paddington Station on a cold, rainy, Monday morning and gaze across the seats to a lovely watercolour of Mousehole, St Mawes, Dartmouth (Fig. 12.1) or Widecombe-in-the-Moor (Fig. 12.2). Frank Mason's watercolour view up the River Dart evokes a bygone age of sail with a majestic, fully rigged, tall ship dominating the scene, dwarfing the smaller more modern yachts in the background. Meanwhile, Jack Merriott's watercolour of Widecombe-in-the-Moor, near Ashburton in Devon, depicts a peaceful village nestling in the midst of the high, rolling Dartmoor hills, distant from the march of progress and the vicissitudes of modern life. The idea of the South West as distant from and different to a modern, metropolitan England has considerable weight in literary representations of the region. In the two carriage panels reproduced here, the GWR offers up the South West in general, and Devon in particular, as an idyllic rural retreat from the hustle and bustle of everyday life. The carriage panels make explicit use of landscape (or seascape) to invoke a sense of place, omitting references to modern buildings, pylons, new roads or urban sprawl. The context in which they are viewed – that chilly GWR carriage sitting at Paddington – is also important for their impact. These carriage panels are part of an advertising strategy built on 'getting away from it all' and as such they make an appeal to a landscape of peace, quietude and tranquillity yearned for in the imagination of thousands of GWR passengers.

Through the later decades of the 19th century and the first half of the 20th century, tourism as an industry was fundamentally altered by, first, the growing number of lower-middle-class and working-class families who were able to take holidays and day trips and, second, the growth of car-ownership. By the 1870s, bank holidays and half-day holidays on Saturday were becoming formalised and it was possible, with improvements in the rail network, to use this free time to travel into the countryside from large industrial cities, especially with the advent of cheaper fares and special excursion services. Likewise, the growing popularity and affordability of the motor car had a tremendous impact on countryside recreation. In 1911 there were 132,000 privately owned cars in Britain. By 1939 this figure had risen to more than 2 million. New pastimes such as motor touring and motor picnicking gained popularity. As Shaw and his collaborators have noted, 'this reduced the dominance of railheads and allowed increasing numbers to seek out remoter coastal villages and the countryside'.

In addition to these newly mobile visitors discovering Devon and Cornwall in cars and charabancs, there were more and more armchair explorers reading the vast quantities of non-fictional rural writing that were published in the interwar years. The term 'non-fictional rural writing' covers everything from the personal memoir to full-blown topography, and the diversity of the genre is characterised by a heady combination of historical proselytising, humorous anecdote, polemical ranting, patronising pomposity, sentimentality and nostalgia. B T Batsford Ltd was among the largest producers of these books, publishing 113 countryside books in seven series; more than half of them appeared between 1934 and 1940. Although Devon and Cornwall featured throughout Batsford series such as *The Legacy of England* and *English Villages and Hamlets*, the region in its own right was the subject of a volume called *The West Country* by C Henry Warren, which was published as part of the *Face of Britain* series. Its dust jacket sets the tone of the book:

> *West Country! The words call up a vivid and unique picture – one unlike that suggested by any other part of England … It is Mr Henry Warren's purpose in this book to analyse the varying qualities which together make up this charm … The geology, the landscape, the architecture, the history, and literary associations of the West Country* [are woven] *into an account which tells the reader the concrete reasons for his hitherto perhaps ill-defined love for these three counties* [Cornwall, Devon and Somerset].

Like many other examples of non-fictional rural writing, *The West Country* presented an essentially conservative vision of rural life. Written in 1938, the book is in part a product of its times, countering the problems of the depression, the General Strike and the threat from Nazi Germany with images of the South West as timeless, tranquil and unchanged. Although the political circumstances have changed, these sorts of images continue to inform a sense of place in south-west England. They are present not only in non-fictional writing, but also novels and poems.

LITERARY LANDSCAPES OF THE SOUTH WEST

South-west England has a rich literary tradition and we must limit ourselves here to a discussion of the work of the well-known novelists R D Blackmore and Daphne du Maurier and the work of a poet less well known nationally but with a vigorous local reputation that has outlasted him: Arthur Caddick.

When some people think of south-west England they call to mind the heady, bodice-ripping, swashbuckling romanticism of novels like the *Poldark* series by Winston Graham. Such highly romanticised, 20th-century images were already circulating in literary culture in the South West in the 19th century and were in part a product of the English imagination of Cornwall as a primitive 'Celtic' land of myth and romance. These images drew in turn on much older traditions, characters and fragments of folklore. Ultimately this continual reworking of local themes contributes to a sense of place that has become embodied in figures like Ross Poldark, Joss Merlyn, and John Ridd.

John, or Jan, Ridd is the hero of R D Blackmore's famous Exmoor novel, *Lorna Doone* (1869). The Doones are the scourge of Exmoor, burning farms, attacking men and carrying off women. The storyteller, John Ridd, meets the captivating Lorna Doone at the black pool that marks the entrance to the Doone's lair in a hidden wooded valley. John, whose father was killed by the Doones, has promised revenge upon them but he falls in love with Lorna who is promised to Carver Doone, her cousin. John Ridd eventually wins Lorna and has his revenge, but only

Fig. 12.3 Exmoor, Lorna Doone Country.

after many adventures and mishaps. On the surface, the tale contains all the classic elements of a 19th-century romance but a closer look reveals a novel rooted in the stories and legends associated with a particular part of north Devon.

Simon Trezise shows that Blackmore's novel was a product of no fewer than three inter-related Exmoor legends: those of Jennifred de Wichehalse, Tom Faggus the Highwayman, and the sinister outlaws – the Doones. Several versions of these legends, which were part of an oral tradition, were collected and written down by different clergymen with antiquarian interests in the 19th century. Each dating from the 17th century, these stories passed through assorted versions told in fisherman's cottages, clergymen's studies and travellers' inns, and gradually migrated from oral tradition to manuscript form and eventually printed publications with local and national circulation. It was these that Blackmore drew upon to weave his Exmoor romance. Trezise argues that this engagement with existing myths, oral traditions, guidebooks and serialisations informed only part of Blackmore's creative effort. For, 'as Blackmore read the written versions of the talks, he recognised his own origins and landscape' from his boyhood schooling in South Molton. Blackmore immersed himself in local topography, artfully using place-names, dialect and topographical knowledge in *Lorna Doone* to capture the flavour of Exmoor. Trezise has also noted how Blackmore was sent 'back to the land of his Exmoor boyhood, his own direct access to the atmosphere and characters underlying the printed serial [of the Doone story in *The Leisure Hour*]'. It is not surprising that a tale of intrigue, revenge and villainy is set in an inhospitable landscape. As Helen Hughes notes, 'Blackmore's Exmoor is portrayed as a wild, fearful place, with its dark heaths and marshes, cliffs and secret valleys, made even more fearful by traditional tales of the devil and witchcraft' (Fig. 12.3). In Blackmore's novel, myth, half-history and remembered and imagined topographies are combined in a compelling formula that has made the book, in the words of Trezise, 'an inseparable part of Exmoor's tradition and the public perception of the West Country'.

Many of the themes that help to construct a sense of place for Exmoor also run through Daphne du Maurier's representation of Cornwall and in particular Bodmin Moor. Daphne du Maurier (Fig. 12.4) moved to Cornwall in the late 1920s after spending many family holidays there. The move was in part a response to a weariness with London and in part a reflection of the rather complex relationship she had with her father, who holidayed in Cornwall but frequently returned home early because he loathed country life. Du Maurier stayed on, seeking solitude in what Alison Light in her *Forever England* … calls 'the right kind of periphery, a place from which she could reject modernity, without having, entirely to leave home'. Cornwall's peace and stillness was in direct contrast to the restlessness of London. Like many writers before and since, du Maurier identified with a Cornwall located in a distant, unspecified past in direct opposition to a feverishly contemporary London. Light notes that 'by making Cornwall her home, du Maurier was indeed dwelling in an imagined past: the past of smugglers and legend, of peasants and gentry'. To a certain extent du Maurier embodied the things she valued about Cornwall by roughing it in a cold house by the sea, wearing trousers, chopping wood, camping on the moors, sailing, riding and exploring.

Alison Light has argued that a romance with the past informs much of Daphne du Maurier's work. 'To enter the world of Daphne du Maurier's fiction' she writes, 'is to breathe an entirely different air.' She goes on: 'It is the wide open spaces of hill and sea which dominate her novels: the howling winds around *Jamaica Inn*, starkly isolate on Bodmin Moor, the crashing Cornish breakers and precipitate cliffs of *Rebecca*.'

Jamaica Inn was du Maurier's fourth novel, published in 1936. It tells the story of an orphan, Mary Yellan, who is sent to live with her Aunt Patience and Uncle Joss Merlyn, the landlord of Jamaica Inn on Bodmin Moor. Joss has gathered a disreputable band of smugglers and wreckers around him and Mary witnesses

Fig. 12.4 Dame Daphne du Maurier, by Dorothy Wilding, 1949.

smuggled goods arriving at the inn, a hanging, and the gang deliberately luring a ship on to the rocks with a false light. Much of the adventure focuses on Mary's attempt to bring Joss and his gang to justice, with suspense provided by the uncertainty about whom she can trust. There are dramatic scenes on Bodmin Moor, in particular a chase that ensues when the real leader of the wreckers, the vicar of Altarnun, kidnaps Mary. Joss's brother Jem, whose complicity in the wrecking and smuggling remains uncertain in much of the book, rescues Mary after shooting the vicar dead.

As Helen Hughes has pointed out, the enduring image of Cornwall in *Jamaica Inn* is of an ancient, wild and marginal land, despite the fact that Helston is depicted as a pretty town full of good-natured, sociable, civilised folk. This lasting impression is conveyed early on with descriptions of Mary's journey towards Jamaica Inn across the moor:

> [the rain] *spat against the windows with … venom … No trees, no lanes, no cluster of cottages or hamlet, but mile after mile of bleak moorland, dark and untraversed, rolling like a desert land to some unseen horizon.*

The dark, brooding landscape, black sky, sinister tors, austere rocks and eternal wind all work to heighten the malice and treachery present in the plot. The landscape is invested with a frightening power and its people are seen to be closer to nature, shaped by their landscape and afraid of it. Such narrative devices are common throughout romantic literature of this kind. Crucially, part of the power of du Maurier's bleak moorland landscapes lies in their difference to the pretty, pastoral landscapes associated with other parts of England. Being able to identify and mark out the differences between England and Cornwall is important to the creation of a unique place-identity for Cornwall: a sense of place is not only constructed through ideas about what a place is like, but also what it is not like.

In her novels, du Maurier represented Cornwall as on the border of Englishness – distant physically from metropolitan centres but also distant in time, temperament and tradition. This is part of a literary tradition that has long envisioned Cornwall as a romanticised periphery by utilising ideas about the past, tradition, history and continuity. Du Maurier manages this in part through representing the landscape of Bodmin Moor in *Jamaica Inn* as bleak, windswept, unforgiving, somehow more primitive and less civilised than the cosy rurality frequently associated with representations of England. Anyone who has driven over Bodmin Moor in inclement weather will appreciate her descriptions of 'granite sky' and 'lashing, pitiless rain'. In and of themselves, such descriptions only go part way to create the sense of place that du Maurier achieves. They draw at least some of their power from being set into a romantic tale of smuggling, murder and double-dealing in a novel populated with the colourful figures of myth – a motley gang of wreckers and smugglers, an untrustworthy tavern-keeper, a wicked vicar, a daring hero and a brave heroine. Additional credibility is given to the sense of place created in *Jamaica Inn* because it is a real place, a tavern that has perched on the edge of Bodmin Moor for about 400 years. This boundary between fact and fantasy in the novel becomes so blurred that people associate the real place with its literary characteristics. Such factors help a novel like *Jamaica Inn* make a strong appeal to the popular imagination, building up an association between Cornwall and a distant, romantic past.

What is important about Daphne du Maurier and R D Blackmore is that they and their work have become so intimately associated with a place – the town of Fowey and the Fowey estuary (Fig. 12.5) and Exmoor, respectively – that it is now possible to speak of 'du Maurier Country' or 'Lorna Doone Country' in the same way as the term 'Shakespeare Country' identifies Stratford-on-Avon and parts of Warwickshire. A yearly du Maurier Festival held in and around Fowey attracts more than 20,000 people and entered its tenth year in 2006. It features

Fig. 12.5 Fowey.

talks, tours and dramatisations based on du Maurier's work as well as art and flower exhibitions and historic walks, all of which focus on Cornish arts, crafts and traditions. All this contributes to the construction of a sense of place that draws powerfully upon the representation of Cornish landscapes and people depicted in du Maurier's popular novels. Yearly festivals and celebrations of du Maurier make these connections stronger year on year, until other representations become less significant in the popular imagination. Similarly, the evocation of Lorna Doone Country in Exmoor books and guides continually reasserts the connection between place and a particularly vivid literary imagining, which seems to have crystallised the essence of the landscape into a book or set of books and struck a chord with a reading public.

Like Daphne du Maurier, the poet Arthur Caddick moved from London to Cornwall in search of a different way of life distant from the clamour of the city. Caddick, who was born in 1911, lived and worked in Nancledra, near St Ives, in

Fig. 12.6 Arthur Caddick.

Cornwall, between 1945 and 1981 and had a colourful local reputation as an inveterate drinker but also as a man of great and at times incisive wit (Fig. 12.6). He counted among his friends many of the West Penwith artistic community. Although Caddick was not Cornish, his writing made explicit the link between Cornish landscape and a sense of place.

Arthur Caddick arrived in west Cornwall at a time when Cornish language, identity, culture and nationalism were topics of widespread debate. Caddick participated in these debates through his poetry and prose, in which he frequently insisted that Cornishness was not a matter of birth but a state of mind realised through contact with the culture and landscape of Cornwall. In his work Caddick argued that the unique qualities of the Cornish landscape inspired creative effort and invoked a particular sense of place. This, in his view, was the explanation for the attraction that the area held for the many artists who made Penwith their home, including internationally famous painters, sculptors, engravers, printers, potters and writers. As a Yorkshireman by birth, Caddick satirised those who insisted that only people born in Cornwall could feel or evoke the spirit of the place. In this he was at odds with the Cornish Gorsedd, a group of bards who supported the revival of the Cornish language and ways of life. Here we start to see some of the complexity that surrounded the articulation of Cornish identity in the post-war period, for while Caddick set his face against England and celebrated Cornwall's marginality, the Gorsedd attempted to shift the focus from a metropolitan vision of England that positioned Cornwall on the margins to a sense of Celtic nationhood that positioned Cornwall as one of the six Celtic nations (Scotland, Ireland, Wales, Brittany, Cornwall, Man), with England on the margins of this Celtic world. The Cornish nationalist movement, Mebyon Kernow (Sons of Cornwall), goes further, seeking political independence from England. Caddick satirised the efforts of both organisations mercilessly, because he believed that they were irrelevant to the problems of high unemployment and industrial and economic decline in post-war Cornwall.

Caddick's corpus of written work, which includes both satirical and lyrical poems, is interesting for three main reasons. First, he thought the Cornish landscape was more important to a sense of place than the Cornish language. Second, he recognised that an attachment to place is made and not given. Third, Caddick's work shows us that a sense of place is created by both 'insiders' and 'outsiders' – in this case, Caddick actively contested the right of the Cornish Gorsedd to claim that only pure-bred Cornish could come to know the essence of the place.

Despite satirising the effort to revive the Cornish language and traditions, Caddick himself in his lyrical poetry still drew on well-understood imagery of an ancient, timeless landscape with deep historical roots and a distant mystical past. He reflected on the way the landscape inspired creative effort in the poignant poem 'Lesson Learnt on Cornwall's Hills':

> *Through having passed half my life among them*
> *I have become one with giant outcrops*
> *Of gaunt granite at extraordinary angles,*
> *Hieroglyphics which record the ravages*
> *Of time's unsentimental journey.*
>
> *One, also, with the subtle delights*
> *Of high places, the scent of heath, furze, bracken,*
> *The flowering from gale-bent blackthorn branches*
> *Of delicate white sprays*
> *Before green leaves break open*
> *And the omens sea-gulls cry aloud*
> *As they follow the plough on inland fields*

That a hurricane has crossed the horizon
To shroud the blue bay in a pall of cloud
And scrounge the shore with whip-lashed squalls of rain
I have stood in a luminous silence
Where no one who stands alone is lonely…

In this poem, the configuration of soil, rock, plants, animals, sea, wind and rain make up Cornwall's particular character for Caddick. The idea of a place 'where no one who stands alone is lonely' speaks to a profound connection between people and landscape that re-animated him. He was attached elementally in more ways than one, reflecting that 'a man comes here from a metropolis and finds himself face to face with the silent, unrelenting scrutiny of the eternal elements'.

For Caddick, the intangible creative force that Cornwall exercised was given material form by artists of all kinds in paint, clay, verse, prose, wood, iron and stone. The creative possibilities were endless in what he called the 'clearing house' for the spirit, where life was lived closer to the elements and distant from the ceaseless buzz of metropolitan England. Cornwall is seen to be set apart and different from the rest of England, and, most particularly, from metropolitan England. To feel and understand something of Cornwall depended not on being able to trace your Cornish ancestry or speak the language but in the sense of being connected to a place unlike any other capable of inspiring creative effort. In arguing this, Caddick resisted the exclusionary practices of the Cornish Gorsedd and Mebyon Kernow, which he saw as marginalising both 'un-Cornish' with a strong attachment to the county and ordinary Cornish people themselves. Where the Gorsedd and Mebyon Kernow insisted that Cornish identity was constructed around language, Caddick instead highlighted the significance of landscape and climate, and his personal connection with the land.

ENVISIONING LANDSCAPES

The artist Peter Lanyon, born in 1918, was a key member of the St Ives school of modern art until he broke away from this group after a disagreement (Fig. 12.7). David Crouch has argued that Lanyon's art forms 'a distinctive cultural understanding of place which incorporates the politics of Cornish culture, work

Fig. 12.7 St Ives.

and dissension; about everyday knowledge of what was around him; and of mythic meanings of land and sea'. Crucial to Lanyon's artistic philosophy was the rejection of the landscape tradition that attempts the depiction of three-dimensional actual space through perspective. The static viewpoint only served to constrain the creative mind. Instead, Lanyon deliberately attempted a multi-dimensional engagement with place, pointing out that:

> I wasn't satisfied with the tradition of painting landscape from one position only. I wanted to bring together all my feelings about the landscape, and this meant breaking away from the usual method of representing space in a landscape painting – receding like a cone to a vanishing point. I wanted to find another way of organising the space in the picture. For me, this is not a flat surface. I've always believed that a painting gives an illusion of depth – things in it move backwards and forwards.

After Lanyon broke away from the St Ives school in 1950, he started a new phase in his work in which he became more immersed in Penwith, the area of west Cornwall that was his home. Crouch argues that there is a certain amount of ambivalence in Lanyon's sense of Cornishness. On the one hand, in attempting to record and resist the post-war exploitation and cultural appropriation of Cornwall, he was capable of essentialising place. On the other, his work undermined the idea that places have fixed and stable essences and meanings that never alter and are the same for everybody. Instead he tried to show how place is encountered in lots of different ways, at different speeds (walking, cycling, in a car, flying in a glider) and from different positions (in the sky, at ground level, from a nearby hill, from the sea). He managed this in part by incorporating into one canvas numerous places and times encountered from different positions and different speeds. In this he departed radically from the convention of painting a particular tract of land at one particular time from one fixed, static and often elevated viewpoint. All these features of Lanyon's work are evident in his painting *Porthleven* (1951) (Fig. 12.8), in which a point of reference is provided by the town's iconic clock tower, part of the Bickford-Smith Institute building.

Incorporating speed, movement, feelings, knowledge, history and memory into a painting allowed Lanyon to arrive at a much more richly contextual understanding of the Cornish landscape and also to enter into the social issues that were on-going in his part of Cornwall, about which he felt strongly. This is demonstrated in his painting *St Just* (1951–3). Lanyon was angry that the tin-mining district, at the centre of which lay the town of St Just, had been exploited and its wealth removed by mine owners who were indifferent to the area, its people or the great loss of life from mining accidents caused by negligence. As Crouch argues, 'Lanyon's anger is made explicit in the painting in the form of a crucifix which runs down the centre of the painting like a black mineshaft' with landscapes and mourners on either side.

Lanyon's art emphasises the highly complex, multifaceted encounter with place that we all have but which is difficult to express within traditional conventions of landscape art. Lanyon tells us something about the politics of identity-formation in Cornwall in the post-war period and illustrates the larger point that sense of place is fluid and on the move, contingent, and partial. These themes are also reflected in the work of the contemporary artist, Kurt Jackson, for whom a daily encounter with the ever-changing weather, colours, sea conditions and landscapes of Land's End forms a crucial part of his construction of a sense of place.

Kurt Jackson was born in 1961 in Dorset. He now lives near Land's End and works in the *plein-air* tradition of painting outdoors directly on a canvas rather than in a studio from sketches. Jackson works in watercolours, oils and acrylic

Fig. 12.8 **Porthleven,** *by Peter Lanyon, 1951.*

and often uses a technique that involves sweeping the brush across the canvas without touching it to 'throw' the paint across the surface. He also scrapes away layers of paint, peels a layer of paper away or includes collage to create added texture. He paints for most of the time with the canvas flat on the ground to prevent the paint from running, sometimes deliberately propping the canvas up to achieve unusual effects with dripping paint.

Jackson is important to this discussion of sense of place because of the intimacy he achieves with the locality in which he lives and works. Jackson constantly revisits the same coves, cliff tops and valleys of Land's End, painting them in all weathers and moods. He notes that 'when you paint the same location repeatedly, there's a deep affinity that develops between you and that place'. In one project, he walked the length of the Kenidjack Valley from source to sea, painting an image every 20 paces, producing 110 watercolour sketches in all. Jackson's capacity to be inspired by the familiar is constantly renewed by capturing the subtle variations in sites visited over and over again. In another example, Jackson has been painting Priest Cove and Cape Cornwall for the last 15 years and notes that three factors are important to his painting:

> [First] *the experience of being there, of what I am hearing and seeing. Secondly, there is the matter of trying to achieve a likeness, some resemblance to what I'm looking at. And finally, there is the use of the paint, the painterly enjoyment of using the medium – what is often referred to as 'mark making'.*

In attempting to communicate the experience of being there, Jackson includes on the canvas notes, reflections, musings and scribblings about the weather, the mood and the work of the artist. His painting *Priest Cove 27.12.98* (Fig. 12.9) includes these words written across the sky: 'strong winds, more rain on its way.

***Fig. 12.9* Priest Cove 27.12.98**, *'strong winds, more rain on its way. Tide ebbing, a woman is looking for driftwood amongst the foam-covered forshore. I'm getting too cold to continue', by Kurt Jackson, 1998.*

Tide ebbing, a woman is looking for driftwood among the foam-covered foreshore. I'm getting too cold to continue.' The arrangement of the words on the canvas resembles a piece of poetry in which each sentence forms a line of verse. Whereas Lanyon called to mind the presence of the artist in the creative effort of making the art by combining the different viewpoints and speeds in one painting, Jackson inserts himself into the picture through these textual interventions.

Jackson's own personal and political predilections also influence his painting. His strong environmental ethic and ambivalence about landownership are reflected in paintings that include text from local signs such as 'dangerous cliff' and 'stone row 1km'. He notes how the juxtaposition of the open sea with a 'no parking' sign in the foreground highlights the occasional inappropriateness and intrusiveness of organisations like the National Trust. *Priest Cove 27.12.98* includes the words 'Cape Cornwall' and 'Caution Slippery Surface' on the landward side of the painting, hinting at the juxtaposition between the land on which ownership is inscribed through such signage, and the open sea, which defies attempts to impose ownership upon it.

Fig. 12.10 **Endless February '00,** *by Kurt Jackson, 2000.*

Some of Jackson's best-known works are his seascapes, which are deceptively simple compositions of shore, sea and sky which form horizontal bands (Fig. 12.9). These bands are one of the two principal compositional forms in Jackson's work, the other being the v-shape of the deep valleys that run down to the sea, known as zawns. His painting *Endless February '00* demonstrates the use of horizontal bands to produce great depth to the painting (Fig. 12.10). Starting at the dark foreshore, here occupying only a small proportion of the canvas compared to other works (*see* Fig. 12.9), the sea stretches away with the eerie calm that characterises some cold, still, cloudy winter days. The horizon is barely visible through the gloom and the sky bleaches out into a misty white. The painting and the title *Endless February '00* evokes the sense of longing for the dynamism of spring and summer while capturing something of the suspended animation that winter brings. Using naturalistic colours as his starting point, Jackson makes colours more muted or vibrant for effect as the work develops. The colours are an important component in the sense of place that Jackson constructs:

> You become very aware of the unique colours here if you go away and compare it with somewhere else. There's an earthiness about the colours, very subdued. My father lives in Suffolk and whenever I go there I do a painting in the fields opposite his house. It's a typical monoculture field and the greens are just so acid because of all that fertiliser in the soil. In Cornwall the greens have more blue in them than yellow; the reverse is true when you go upcountry. When I bring those paintings back here and look at them they seem totally surreal! But

that's the joy of Cornwall – the lack of intensive land use. Its allowed to become overgrown – they call them Devil's Gardens here – with little pockets of wildflowers that have always been part of the landscape.

By suggesting that Cornwall has avoided the vicissitudes of modern agriculture, Jackson draws on and contributes to a popular understanding of Cornwall as distant from modernity and the damaging march of progress. For Jackson, the landscape of West Penwith is the product of Neolithic and Iron Age human activity, not modern agricultural or industrial effort. It is possible to glimpse this respect for a distant, unknowable past in his seascapes in which evidence of contemporary life, such as tankers, liners, yachts and trawlers, are absent (Figs 12.9 and 12.10). This sits neatly with Jackson's environmental ethic through which he also imagines the sea as a last wilderness:

That's why I often do paintings of the open sea with no land visible: the last wilderness here is the sea. You can look out there to the Atlantic and there is no visible sign that we have done anything to it, although we know we have. That's the fascination I have with it and why I paint it over and over again – big expanses of open sea and open sky… When I'm painting I often try to get myself in a place where I'm totally surrounded by rocks on a beach or cocooned by gorse.

The work of Peter Lanyon and Kurt Jackson shows that place can be powerfully envisioned through landscape art. Both these artists draw on, reproduce and contribute to the accumulation of images about Cornwall through which a specific sense of place is constructed for the county.

A UNIFIED SENSE OF PLACE FOR THE SOUTH WEST?

To what extent, if at all, can a sense of place be identified for south-west England as a whole, rather than for Devon or Cornwall, or even individual towns and landscapes in these counties? Sense of place operates at many scales and any attempt to define it for the region as a whole will ultimately fail because of the inconsistencies and contradictions that will be exposed. Nevertheless, very powerful and enduring senses of place operate throughout the region at specific locations such as Bodmin Moor, Doone Valley and West Penwith. For this reason, the region offers fascinating case studies as its landscapes have inspired very different responses from authors, poets and painters among others.

Notwithstanding the fact that it is impossible to identify a singular, all-encompassing sense of place for the South West, several general points about the construction of place identities in the region can be made. First, it is clear from the examples used here that senses of place are cumulative, often gathering around particular place-based histories, myths, legends, traditions or folklore. Sometimes a particular artist or writer will crystallise all those things into a single piece of work, which becomes an icon of place, landscape and identity. Second, a sense of place often accumulates around an intimacy with a particular landscape or location. This can be developed over many visits, perhaps by holidaymakers, or by the daily encounter between an artist or writer and the chosen spots to which he or she is drawn over and over again, as in the case of Kurt Jackson. Third, many representations of the South West in art, novels and poetry imagine the region as distant to and different from the rest of England. Timelessness, historical continuity, a mythic past and a land of supernatural potential are frequently recurring motifs in the creative work of writers and artists from Devon and Cornwall. Perhaps this is the only really unifying feature of all the sense of places that are created in the South West.

LANDSCAPES AND SENSES OF PLACE

LANDSCAPES AND SENSES OF PLACE

Fig. 12.11 Textile map, Uffculme, 2001.

Although this chapter has concentrated on what might be termed 'elite' aspects of the creative arts – fine art and literature – it is important to remember the ways in which other forms of creative effort express a sense of place. A good example of this is the textile map stitched by people in the parishes of the Culm Valley in Devon (Fig. 12.11). In its keenly observed, lovingly recreated detail this map expresses a profound sense of attachment to a particular place and local landscape. It is always tempting to imply that something like a well-known book or piece of art has more to say about sense of place than an object like this material map, but this is to underplay the sense of belonging to a community engendered by the very act of creating the map.

All the forms of representation discussed here, whether in print, on paper, canvas or fabric are vitally important to the way the imagined landscapes of the South West contribute to popular understandings of place and identity. While a quintessential south-west England landscape may elude us, Devon and Cornwall are characterised by a rich literary and artistic history in which different senses of place are articulated. Future generations encountering Devon and Cornwall will continue to contribute to the rich repository of meanings already laid down in the landscapes of south-west England.

FURTHER READING

Brace 1999, 130–46. An accessible account of a talented local poet possessed of an acerbic wit.

Crouch 1999, 72–89. A sophisticated analysis of Peter Lanyon's work from a geographical perspective.

Cosgrove 1998. A scholarly work of considerable importance, in which the idea of landscape is examined from a number of different perspectives.

du Maurier 1992. Daphne du Maurier's highly evocative novel that captured the spirit of Bodmin Moor and immortalised the famous inn on the road between Launceston and Bodmin.

Hughes 1997, 68–76. A very readable analysis of the role of landscape in *Jamaica Inn*.

Light 1991. An in-depth, scholarly analysis of Daphne du Maurier's novels.

Jackson 1999. Kurt Jackson's marvellous collection of paintings opens with a detailed interview with the artist.

Norden 2001. A richly illustrated book that traces the history of carriage panels on British railways.

Shaw *et al.* 1999, 453–61. A fascinating insight into the history of tourism in the South West.

Trezise 2000. A closely researched, engaging history of the Lorna Doone tales.

Bibliography

Balaam, N D, Smith, K and Wainwright, G 1982. 'The Shaugh Moor Project: fourth report'. *Proc Prehist Soc* 48, 203–78

Balchin, W G V 1983. *The Cornish Landscape*. London: Hodder and Stoughton

Barlow, F (ed.) 1969. *Exeter and its Region*. Exeter: Exeter University Press

Barry, J 1999. 'Towns and processes of urbanization in the early modern period', *in* R J P Kain and W Ravenhill (eds), *Historical Atlas of South-West England*. Exeter: University of Exeter Press, 413–25

Beresford, M 1988. *New Towns of the Middle Ages: Town Plantation in England, Wales and Gascony* (2nd edn). Gloucester: Alan Sutton

Binding, H 1995. *The Changing Face of Exmoor*. Minehead: Exmoor Books

Booker, F 1974. *The Industrial Archaeology of the Tamar Valley*. Newton Abbot: David and Charles

Booker, F 1977. *The Great Western Railway*. Newton Abbot: David and Charles

Brace, C 1999. 'Cornish identity and landscape in the work of Arthur Caddick'. *Cornish Studies* 7, 130–46

Bryant, D 1971. 'Demographic trends in South Devon in the mid-nineteenth century', *in* K J Gregory and W L D Ravenhill (eds), *Exeter Essays in Geography*. Exeter: Exeter University Press, 125–42

Burnham, C P *et al.* 1980. 'The soils of England and Wales'. *Field Studies* 5, 349–63

Burt, R 1999. 'Metal-mining since the eighteenth century', *in* R J P Kain and W Ravenhill (eds), *Historical Atlas of South-West England*. Exeter: University of Exeter Press, 345–9

Campbell, S, Hunt, C O, Scourse, J D, Keen, D H and Stephens, N 1998. *Quaternary of South-West England*. London: Chapman and Hall

Chalkley, B, Dunkerley, D and Gripaios, P (eds) 1991. *Plymouth: Maritime City in Transition*. Newton Abbot: David and Charles, 62–81

Charlton, C 1998. 'Flying against the odds? The evolution of Plymouth's air transport services and airport', *in* M Blacksell, J Matthews and P Sims (eds), *Environmental Management and Change in Plymouth and the South West*. Plymouth: University of Plymouth, 265–82.

Clew, K R 1984. *The Exeter Canal*. Chichester: Phillimore

Cosgrove, D 1998. *Social Formation and Symbolic Landscape*. Madison: University of Wisconsin Press

Countryside Agency 1999. *Countryside Character*, Vol 8: *South West*. Cheltenham: Countryside Agency

Creighton, O H 2002. *Castles and Landscapes* (reprinted 2004). London: Continuum Press

Crouch, D 1999. 'Everyday abstraction: geographical knowledge in the art of Peter Lanyon'. *Ecumene* 6, 72–89

Darby, H C and Welldon Finn, R (eds) 1967. *The Domesday Geography of South-Western England*. Cambridge: Cambridge University Press

du Maurier, D 1992. *Jamaica Inn* (1st edn 1936). London: Arrow

Duffy, M *et al.* (eds) 1992. *The New Maritime History of Devon*. Vol I. London: Conway Maritime Press

Duffy, M *et al.* (eds) 1994. *The New Maritime History of Devon*. Vol II. London: Conway Maritime Press

Durrance, E M, Selwood, E B and Laming, D J C (eds) in press, 2007. *The Geology of Devon* (2nd edn). Exeter: University of Exeter Press

Findlay, D C *et al.* 1984. *Soils and their Use in South West England*. Harpenden: Soil Survey of England and Wales

Fleming, A 1988. *The Dartmoor Reaves*. London: Batsford

Fox, H 1999. 'Medieval urban development', *in* R J P Kain and W Ravenhill (eds), *Historical Atlas of South-West England*. Exeter: University of Exeter Press, 400–7

Fyfe, R M and Rippon, S J 2004. 'A landscape in transition? Palaeoenvironmental evidence for the end of the "Romano-British" period in South West England', *in* R Collins and J Gerrard (eds), *Debating Late Antiquity*. Oxford: British Archaeological Reports, 33–40

Gent, H and Quinnell, H 1999. 'Excavations of a causewayed enclosure and hillfort at Raddon Hill, Stockleigh Pomeroy'. *Proc Devon Archaeol Soc* 57, 1–76

Gerrard, S 1997. *Dartmoor*. London: Batsford

Gerrard, S 1999. 'The tin industry in sixteenth- and seventeenth-century Cornwall', *in* R J P Kain and W Ravenhill (eds), *Historical Atlas of South-West England*. Exeter: University of Exeter Press, 330–7

Gerrard, S 2000. *The Early British Tin Industry*. Stroud: Tempus

BIBLIOGRAPHY

Gilg, A 1999. 'Population changes in the twentieth century', *in* R J P Kain and W Ravenhill (eds), *Historical Atlas of South-West England*. Exeter: University of Exeter Press, 125–35

Gill, C 1994. 'Ocean liners at Plymouth', *in* M Duffy *et al.* (eds), *The New Maritime History of Devon*, Vol II. London: Conway Maritime Press, 226–34

Graham, B J, Ashworth, G J and Tunbridge, J E 2000. *A Geography of Heritage: Power, Culture and Economy*. London: Arnold

Gregory, K J, Shorter, A H and Ravenhill, W L D (eds) 1969 *Southwest England*. London: Nelson

Griffith, F 1988. *Devon's Past: An Aerial View*. Exeter: Devon County Council and Devon Books

Griffith, F and Weddell, P 1996. 'Ironworking in the Blackdown Hills: results of recent survey', *in* P Newman (ed.), *The Archaeology of Mining and Metallurgy in South West Britain*. Matlock: Historical Metallurgy Society, 27–34

Grigg, D B 1989. *English Agriculture: An Historical Perspective*. Oxford: Basil Blackwell

Groves, R 1983. 'Roads and tracks', *in* C Gill (ed), *Dartmoor: A New History*. Newton Abbot: David and Charles, 182–203

Hadfield, C 1984. *Atmospheric Railways: A Victorian Venture in Silent Speed*. Stroud: Alan Sutton

Hadfield, C 1985. *The Canals of South West England* (2nd edn). Newton Abbot: David and Charles

Harris, H 1986. *Industrial Archaeology of Dartmoor* (2nd edn). Newton Abbot: David and Charles

Hatcher, J 1977. *Plague, Population and the English Economy 1348–1530*. London: Macmillan

Havinden, M 1999. 'The woollen, lime, tanning and leather working, and paper-making industries, *c*1500– *c*1800', *in* R J P Kain and W Ravenhill (eds), *Historical Atlas of South-West England*. Exeter: University of Exeter Press, 338–44

Herring, P 1993. 'Examining a Romano-British boundary at Foage, Zennor'. *Cornish Archaeol* 32, 17–28

Herring, P 1994. 'The cliff castles and hillforts of West Penwith in the light of recent work at Maen Castle and Treryn Dinas'. *Cornish Archaeol* 33, 40–56

Herring, P C 1998. *Cornwall's Historic Landscape: Presenting a Method of Historic Landscape Character Assessment*. Truro: Cornwall Archaeological Unit, Cornwall County Council, in association with English Heritage

Higham, R (ed.) 1987. *Security and Defence in South West England before 1800*. Exeter Studies in History No. 19. Exeter: University of Exeter Press

Holbrook, N 2001. 'Coastal trade around the South-West peninsula of Britain in the later Roman period'. *Proc Devon Archaeol Soc* 59, 149–58

Hooke, D 1994. *The Pre-Conquest Charter-Bounds of Devon and Cornwall*. Woodbridge: Boydell

Hoskins, W G 1952. 'The making of the agrarian landscape', *in* W G Hoskins and H P R Finberg (eds), *Devonshire Studies*. London: Jonathan Cape, 289–333

Hoskins, W G 1954. *Devon*. London: Collins

Hoskins, W G 1972. *Devon* (2nd edn). Newton Abbot: David and Charles

Howard, P 2003. *Heritage: Management, Interpretation, Identity*. London: Continuum Press

Hughes H 1997. 'A silent, desolate country: images of Cornwall in Daphne du Maurier's *Jamaica Inn*', *in* E Westland (ed.), *Cornwall: The Cultural Construction of Place*. Penzance: Patten Press in association with Institute of Cornish Studies

Jackson, K 1999. *Paintings of Cornwall and the Scillies*. Plymouth: White Lane Press

Johnson, N and Rose, P 1994. *Bodmin Moor: An Archaeological Survey*, Vol 1. London: Royal Commission on the Historical Monuments of England

Kain, R J P 1980. *The Shell Book of English Villages*. London: Michael Joseph

Kain, R J P and Ravenhill, W (eds) 1999. *Historical Atlas of South-West England*. Exeter: University of Exeter Press

Keene, P 1996. *Classic Landforms of the North Devon Coast*. London: Geographical Association

Kowaleski, M 1992. 'The port towns of fourteenth-century Devon', *in* M Duffy *et al.* (eds), *The New Maritime History of Devon*, Vol I. London: Conway Maritime Press, 52–71

Landscape Design Associates 1994. *The Cornwall Landscape Assessment 1994*. Truro: Cornwall County Council

Light, A 1991. *Forever England: Femininity, Literature and Conservatism between the Wars*. London: Routledge

Mellor, H 1989. *Exeter Architecture*. Chichester: Phillimore

Miller, E and Hatcher, J 1978. *Medieval England: Rural Society and Economic Change 1086–1348*. London: Longman

Mottershead, D 1996. *Classic Landforms of the South Devon Coast*. London: Geographical Association

Needham, S 1996. 'Chronology and periodisation in the British Bronze Age'. *Acta Archaeologica* 67, 121–40

Newman, P 1998. *The Dartmoor Tin Industry, A Field Guide*. Exeter: Short Run Press

Norden, G 2001. *Landscapes Under the Luggage Rack*. Northampton: Great Northern Railway Publications

Northway, A 1994. 'The Devon fishing industry in the eighteenth and nineteenth centuries', *in* M Duffy *et al.* (eds), *The New Maritime History of Devon*, Vol II. London: Conway Maritime Press, 126–35

Olson, L 1989. *Early Monasteries in Cornwall*. Woodbridge: Boydell

Orme, N (ed.) 1991. *Unity and Variety: A History of the Church in Devon and Cornwall*. Exeter: University of Exeter Press

Overton, M 1996. *Agricultural Revolution in England: The Transformation of the Agrarian Economy 1500–1850*. Cambridge: Cambridge University Press

Padel, O 1985. *Cornish Place-Name Elements*. Nottingham: English Place-Name Society, vols 56–7

Parry, A 1997. 'South-West England and the Channel Islands', *in* D Wheeler and J Mayes (eds), *Regional Climates of the British Isles*. London: Routledge, 47–66

BIBLIOGRAPHY

Pearce, S M 1999. 'Bronze Age metalwork', *in* R J P Kain and W Ravenhill (eds), *Historical Atlas of South-West England*. Exeter: University of Exeter Press, 69–73

Penhallurick, R D 1986. *Tin in Antiquity*. London: Institute of Metals

Pevsner, N and Cherry, B 1989. *The Buildings of England: Devon* (2nd edn). Harmondsworth: Penguin Books

Pevsner, N and Radcliffe, E 1970. *The Buildings of England: Cornwall*. Harmondsworth: Penguin Books

Pye, A and Woodward, F 1996. *The Historic Defences of Plymouth*. Truro: Cornwall County Council

Quinnell, H 1986 'Cornwall during the late Iron Age and the Roman period'. *Cornish Archaeol* 25, 111–34

Quinnell, H 1994. 'Becoming marginal? Dartmoor in later prehistory'. *Proc Devon Archaeol Soc* 52, 75–83

Riley, H and Wilson-North, R 2001. *The Field Archaeology of Exmoor*. London: English Heritage

Rippon, S 2004. *Historic Landscape Analysis: Deciphering the Countryside*. York: Council for British Archaeology

Roberts, A 1999. 'Later Upper Palaeolithic and Mesolithic hunting-gathering communities 13,000–5,500 BP', *in* R J P Kain and W Ravenhill (eds), *Historical Atlas of South-West England*. Exeter: University of Exeter Press, 47–54

Roberts, B and Wrathmell, S 2000. *An Atlas of Rural Settlement in England*. London: English Heritage

Rose, P and Preston-Jones, A 1995. 'Changes in the Cornish countryside AD 400–1100', *in* D Hooke and S Burnell (eds), *Landscape and Settlement in Britain AD 400–1066*. Exeter: Exeter University Press, 51–68

Rowe, J 1953. *Cornwall in the Age of the Industrial Revolution*. Liverpool: University of Liverpool Press

Saunders, A D 1989. *Fortress Britain: Artillery Fortification in the British Isles and Ireland*. Liphook: Beaufort

Selwood, E B, Durrance, E M and Bristow, C M (eds) 1998. *The Geology of Cornwall*. Exeter: University of Exeter Press

Shaw, G, Greenwood, J and Williams, A 1999. 'The growth of tourism in the nineteenth and twentieth centuries', *in* R J P Kain and W Ravenhill (eds), *Historical Atlas of South-West England*. Exeter: University of Exeter Press, 453–61

Shorter, A H 1971. *Paper Making in the British Isles*. Newton Abbot: David and Charles

Shorter, A H, Ravenhill, W L D and Gregory, K J 1969. *Southwest England*. London: Nelson

St John Thomas, D 1981. *A Regional History of the Railways of Great Britain*, Vol 1: *The West Country* (5th revised edn). Newton Abbot: David and Charles

Starkey, D J 1994. 'The ports, seaborne trade and shipping industry of South Devon, 1786–1914', *in* M Duffy *et al.* (eds), *The New Maritime History of Devon*, Vol II. London: Conway Maritime Press, 32–47

Teague, D C and White, P R nd. *A Guide to the Airfields of South Western England*. Plymouth: Baron Jay Publishers

Thomas, C 1994. *And Shall These Mute Stones Speak? Post-Roman Inscriptions in Western Britain*. Cardiff: University of Wales Press

Todd, A C and Laws, P 1972. *The Industrial Archaeology of Cornwall*. Newton Abbot: David and Charles

Todd, M 1987. *The South-West to AD 1000*. London: Longman

Travis, J 1994 'The rise of the Devon seaside resorts, 1750–1900', *in* M Duffy *et al.* (eds), *The New Maritime History of Devon*, Vol II. London: Conway Maritime Press, 136–44

Trezise, S 2000. *The West Country as Literary Invention*. Exeter: University of Exeter Press

Watts, M A and Quinnell, H 2001. 'A Bronze Age cemetery at Elburton, Plymouth'. *Proc Devon Archaeol Soc* 59, 11–43

Whitehouse, P and St John Thomas, D 1984. *The Great Western Railway*. Newton Abbot: David and Charles

Wilson-North, R (ed) 2003. *The Lie of the Land: aspects of the archaeology and history of the designed landscape in the South West of England*. Exeter: The Mint Press and Devon Gardens Trust

Wrigley, E A and Schofield, R S 1981. *The Population History of England 1541–1871: A Reconstruction*. London: Edward Arnold

Index

Abercrombie, Sir Patrick 175, 177, 178
Agricultural Marketing Acts, 1930s 123
Agricultural Revolution 117–19
Agriculture Act 1947 125
agriculture:
   Bronze Age 49, 51–5, 66
   decline of 72
   'Great Depression' 120–1
   intensive 220–1
   Iron Age 58–60, 66
   medieval 110–13, 116
   Neolithic 46
   postwar growth 125–7
air transport 204–5
airforce bases 205
Alfred, King 158
Aller Farm, Stockland 58
Amalveor 113, *113*
Appledore 150, *151*
arable farming 116–17, 118–24
art and landscape 230–43
Ashburton 69, 137, 140, 164, 172
Astor, Lord 175, 177
Axe valley 25, 45
Axminster 61, 78, 138, *139*, 173

Baggy Point 26
Bagley, Exmoor 64
Bampton 91, 97
Bantham 62–3
Barnstaple 59, 68, 80, 90, 93, 136, 137, 160, 161, 165, 168, 205
Bats Castle, Dunster 56
Bayard's Cove Castle *104*
Bears Down 152
Beeching, Dr Richard 201
Beer 20, 21, 138
Beer Head 60
Bere peninsula 139
Berry Head, Brixham *17*, 90, 106–7, *106*

Berry Pomeroy castle 97–8, *98*
Bickford, William 150
Bickleigh 98
Bideford 137, 153, 161, 168, *186*, 201, 203
Birch Tor, Dartmoor 142
Bittaford 53
Black Death 69–70, 113, 164
Black Tor, Dartmoor 140
Blackdown Hills 61, 62, 115, *220*
Blackmore, R D 234–5
Blanchdown Woods, Tavistock 142
Bodmin 68, 77, 80, 161, 164, 172, 186
Bodmin and Wadebridge Railway 200
Bodmin Moor 23, 91, 113, 128, 187, *214*, 215
   prehistoric times 45, 46, 48, 50, 52–3, 54, 55, 58
   soil types 33, 34
bomb damage, World War II 175–6
boroughs, growth of 156–7
Boscarne 62
Boscastle floods 38–9, *39*
Bossiney 98
Botallack tin mine 144, *145*, *147*
Bovey river 20, 33
Bovey Heathfield 149
Bovey Tracey 149
Bow 58, 162
Bradinch 174
Bratton Down 50
Braunton Great Field 111–12, *112*
Braunton Burrows *25*, 36
Brayford 61
breweries 132
brick making 148
Bridgerule 132
bridges, medieval 186, *187*, *212*
Bristol and Exeter Railway 195, 198
Brisworthy 140
Brixham 103, 106, 119, 128, 172–3
Bronze Age 43, 44, 49, 51–5, 66

monuments 48–50, 66
Broom 45
Brown, Capability 115
Brunel, Isambard Kingdom 197, 200, 202
Buckfastleigh 137, 138, 140
Buckton Hill *23*
Bude 172, 230
Bude Canal 195–6
Budleigh Salterton cliffs *20*
Budleigh Salterton Pebble Beds 19
building, speculative, 1930s 123
building materials 21
Burhs 89, 90, 91, 92–5, 156, 158–60

Caddick, Arthur 234, 237–9, *238*
Cadgwith *133*, 222
Calstock 135
Calstock Viaduct 201, *201*
Camborne 83, 139, *146*, 150, 153, 171, 175
Camel (steam locomotive) 200
Camel river and valley 132, 202
Camelford 38
canals 191–6
Cann Slate Quarries 193
Caraclaze Canal 195
Caradon 139
caravan parks 130, *130*, 180, 223
Carboniferous Period 16, 18–19, 33
Cardinan family 99
Cardinham 98
Carland Cross 152
Carleen *84*
Carn Brea 46
Carnmenelis 33
carpet making 138, 173
Carrick Roads, The 202
Carvossa 59
castles and fortified towns 89–108, 161
Cataclews Stone 21
Catterwater river 202

INDEX

cattle farming 116, 119, 120, 121, 126
Chagford 140, 172, 222
chalk 20
Charles, Prince of Wales 12
Charlestown 172, 203
Chefham viaduct 201
china clay 19, *19*, 29, *29*, 50, 149, 198, 203, *208*, 209, 215
Chivenor, RAF 205
Chudleigh 174, 175
churches and places of worship 75–81, 84–5
  alternative 87
  Celtic 77
  dissenting 81–4
  minsters 78
cider making 132
Civil War 81, 90, 103, 142
clapper bridges 186, *187, 212*
Clayhanger 61
Clifford, Lord 193
climate 11, 15, 30–3
Clovelly 172, 222, *223*
Clyst St Mary 186
Coad, Robert 196
coastal raids 70
coastal transport 202–4
Cob 21
Cockington 222
Codsend Moor 53, 58
Coke, Thomas 119
Cold Northcott 152
Colliford Reservoir 128, *128*
Colyton 136, 138
Combe Martin 60
Compton Manor 97
Cook, Thomas 231
Cookworthy, William 149
Coombe Martin 139
copper industry 72, 139, 142–3, 153, 196, 218
Copperhouse Foundry 200
Corn Laws, repeal of, 1846 119, 123
Cornish identity 226–8, 238, 239
Cornish Riviera 231
Cornubia 16, 18–21
Cornubia (steam locomotive) 200
Cornwall Railway Company 200
Cornwall, Richard, Earl of 99
Cornwell, Edmund, Earl of 100–1
Cotehele, St Dominick 132
Countisbury, Exmoor *63*
Countryside Character Initiative 217
Courtenay family 103
Cox Tor *23*, 25
Coxside 149

Crackington Formation 37
Craddock Moor *47*
creameries 132
Crediton 38, 68, 78, 136, 164, 168, 174, 175
Cremyll ferry 202
Cretaceous Period 20
Cromwell, Oliver 117
crop marks 43, 59–60
Crowndale aqueduct 193
Crows-an-Wra *85*
Culdrose, RNAS 205
Cullompton 61, 136, 137, 166, 174
Culm 33, 37
Culm Measures 18, 50, 65
Culm river and valley 48, 136, *244–5*
cultural periods, pre-Conquest 44

dairy production 132
'Dark ages' 61–5
Dart estuary 104, *104*
Dart river and valley 45, 132, 202
Dartington 138
Dartmoor 20, 23, 58, 62, 91, 113, 186, 187, 209–10, 211
  clapper bridges 186, *187, 212*
  mining 139, 140–2, 172
  prehistoric times 45, 46, 48, 50, 51–3
  reaves 51–3, 63
  soil types 33, 34
  weather 11, 30, 32–3, 38, 55
Dartmoor, Forest of 94
Dartmouth 81, 91, 103, 104, *104*, 164, 165–6, *166*, 168, 173, 175, 203, 232, *232*
Dartmouth Castle *104*
Dawlish Warren 28, *28*
De Lucy, Richard 162
De Tony, Robert 162
deer parks 96, 108
defence, coastal 90–3, 103–8
Defoe, Daniel 136
de-industrialisation 72
Delabole 21, 152
Delabole Slate Quarry 148, *148*
Devonian Period 16–18, 33
Devonport 29, 150, *152*, 152, 154, 169, *169*, 170
Diptford 118
Dissolution of the monasteries 80–1
Dobwalls 191
Domesday Book 67, 94, 110, 116, 160
Drizzlecombe *49*
Du Maurier, Daphne 234, 235–7, *235*
Duckpool 60, 62

Dumnonia and Dumnonii 59, 63, 65
Dunkery Beacon 22
Dutfield 138

Eales, Christopher 171
Earthquakes 37
East Cornwall Mineral Railway 198
East India Company 137
East Moor 46
East Pool tin mine 144
East Portlemouth 80
Eddystone Lighthouse 131
Edyvean, John 195
EEC entry 125
elm 46
enclosure, Parliamentary 113–15
English Heritage 226
Eocene Epoch 20
Erme estuary 63
Exe estuary 28
Exe river and valley 33, 45, 46, 48, 49, 50, 101, 110, *118*, 136, 191
Exeter 21, 38, *38*, 55, 69, 72, 73, 80–1, 83, 90, 93, 94, 136, 137, 135, 158, 160, 164, 165, 167–8, 170, 173, *174*, 175, 182–3, 184, 225
  airport 205, *205*
  Belmont Chapel *86*
  blitz 175, 201, 202
  Bypass 191
  castle 97, 161
  cathedral 21, *85*, 160, 184
  cathedral close 168, *168*
  city walls 148
  Customs House 193, *193*
  Guildhall 165
  Higher Market 171
  Jewish graveyard *86*
  Met Office 153
  Mosque *86*
  postwar redevelopment 175, 179, 225
  Princesshay 205, 206, *206*
  Roman 59, 93, 157–8, *158*
  Royal Albert Memorial Museum *21*
  St Michael's church 85
  Tuckers' Hall 137, *137*
  University 74, 183, 184
Exeter Canal 191–3, *192*
Exminster 102
Exmoor 20, 23, 91, 115
  legends 234–5
  prehistoric times 46, 49, 53, 54, 55, 57, 58
  Roman 61, 62
  soil types 33, 34

INDEX

topography 41
Exmouth 38, 179, 201, 203, 232
Exon Domesday 160
Explosives manufacture 150
Eylesbarrow, Dartmoor 142

Fal river 40, 101, 150, 162, 166–7, 202
Fal estuary 122
Falmouth 74, 91, 105, 129, 131, 150, 166–7, 172, 175, 187, 201, 202
Fernworthy Forest, Dartmoor 123, *124*
ferries 202
field systems:
    infield-outfield 113
    Iron Age 59–60
    medieval 110–13
Fiennes, Celia 187
fire damage, of towns 174–5
fishing industry 116, 119, 128–9, 132, 154, 172–3, 219
floods 38–9
flower and bulb production 126
Fogginter, Dartmoor 148
footpaths and tracks 185–6
forestry 123, 127–8
Forestry Commission 123, 127
Foulston, John 170, 178
foundries and forges 135, 150
Four Burrows 152
Fowey 91, 103, 172, 196, 203, 236–7, *237*
Fowey river 99, 100, 202
Fowler, Charles 171
Frearn, George 150
Fremington-Hele 23
fulling mills 137, 173

Garrow Tor 54
Gault 20
Geevor Mine 143, *143*, 144, *218*, 219
glaciation 15, 23
global warming 33, 39
Gold Park, Shapley Common 54
Goodrington Sands 223
Goonhilly Downs 152
Goss Moor 191
Grampound 161–2, *162*
Grand Western Canal 195
granite 18, 20, 21, 22, 23, 41, 142, 148–9
Great Staple Tor 24
Great Torrington 91, 97, 174
Great Western Railway 199, 231
Grimspound 52, *207*

guide books 231
Gulval 122
Gunnislake 186, 194
Gunwalloe 80
Gwennap mines *83*, *146*
Gwinear Churchtown 80
Gwithian 123

Hackney Canal 193
Harvey, John 150
Haldon Hill 20, 46
Hamoaze river 191, 202
Harbertonford 38
Hares Down, Exmoor 58
Hartland *18*, 78
Hawkcombe Head 45
Hayle 172
    foundries 150
Hayle Docks *224*, *225*
Hayle Railway 198, 199
Haytor 198, *198*, *222*, *222*
Haytor quarry 148
Hazard Hill 46
Heathcoat, John 138–9
Hedgebanks 114, *114*
Hele, Devon Valley Mill *136*
Helford 40, 129
Helford, river 202
Helman Tor 46
Helston 132, 161, 172
Hembury 46, 61
Hemyock 98
Henry VIII 105, 106
Heritage 149, 153 207–28
    development issues 225
    'Heritage Cycle' 210
    industrial 217–19
    meaning 209–10
    rural 219–21
    social context 210–14
    statutory bodies 211–12, 213
    tourism 222–3
Herodsfoot 150
High Peak 46
High Week 97
High Willhays 22
Higher Holworthy, Parracombe 58
Higher Trenoweth, Scilly 132
Highland Zone, features of 15
hillforts and cliff forts 55–6, 62
hillslope enclosures 57–8
hi-tech industries 153
Hoar Moor, Exmoor 58
Holcombe 58
Holman Brothers 150, 153
Holne Moor *51*

Holocene Epoch 26, 28, 34, 35
Holsworthy Viaduct 201
Honiton 138, 162, 168, 173, 174, 213
Hooken landslip *35*
Hooker, John 187
Hound Tor 113, *114*
housing demand, modern 182–3
Hughes, Helen 235, 236
hunter-gatherers 43, 45
Hurlers, The *48*

ice sheets 24–6
Ilfracombe 179–80, *180*, 201
Illogen 197
Indian Queens 29
Iron age 43, 44
    agriculture 58–60, 66
    monuments 87
    settlements 55–8

Jackson, Kurt 240–3
    Priest Cove 27.12.98 241, 241–2
    Endless February '00 242, *242*
Jamaica Inn 235–6
Jurassic Period 19

Kenidjack valley 241
Kenn river 69, 103
Kensey river 96
Kents Cavern 45
Kilkhampton 98
Killerton estate 120
Killigrew, Sir John 166
Kilworthy model farm 120, *120*
King's Tor, Dartmoor 148
Kingsbridge 162, 164, 201
Kingsbridge estuary *28*
Kingswear Castle *104*
Knight family 115

lacemaking 138, 173
Lamorna Cove 122, 172
land capability map *37*
land improvement 117
land, ownership of 62, 211–12
Landewednack 80
Lands End 205, 208, *208*
landslides 37–8
Langland Lane 58
Lanhydrock 21
Lanyon Quoit 229
Lanyon, Peter 239–*40*
    Porthleven 240, *240*
    St Just 240
Launceston 91, 95–6, *96*, 97, 102, 108, 135, 160, 161, 168, 175

252

INDEX

lead mining 139
leather industry 135–6
Lee Moor 19, 148
Leland, John 165
Lemon river 162
Leskernick 50
Levant tin mine 144, *144*
Light, Alison 235
lime quarrying and processing 132–5, 148, 196
limestone 16, 20, 21
Liskeard 56, 136, 161, 172, 175
literature 234–9
Littleham Mudstone *20*
Lizard, geology of 18
Lobbs Bog, Exmoor 58
Loddiswell 98
Loe Pool 28
London & South Western Railway 200–1
Long Range 58
Looe 123, 161, 172
Looe Union Canal 196, 198
Lorna Doone 234–5, 237
Lostwithiel 96, 99–100, 168, 172, 186
Loughwood Baptist Chapel *82*
Lumburn river 193
Lundy 20, 202, 205
Luxulyan valley viaduct 198, *199*
Lydford 68, 91, *93*, 93–5, 108, *108*, *159*, 160, 161, 172
Lyn river 38
Lynmouth flood disaster 38
Lynton 201

Magor Roman villa 59
Mamhead 115
manganese extraction 139–40
market gardening 122–3
Marshall, William 187
Martinhoe 61
McAdam, John Loudon and William 188
Mebyon Kernow 238, 239
medieval field systems 63–5
medieval settlements 110–13
Men-an-Tol *88*
Mendip 61
Meneague 78
Mercia Mudstone 22
Merrivale, Dartmoor *52*, 58, 62, 148, *149*
Mesolithic society 43, 45
metal extraction 18–19, 60–1, 139–47
 maps 145–7
Methleigh 161

Methodism 82–4
Mevagissey 116, 172
Meyn Mamvro 87
Milk Marketing Board 123
Milton Abbot 140
mining related industries 150
Miocene Epoch 20
Millbrook 148
Mitchell 161
model farms 119–20
Moles Chamber, Exmoor 58
monastic life 80–1
Moretonhampstead 123, 136
Mortain, Robert of 95
Morte Bay 23
Morvah Churchtown 79
Morwellham 193, 194, 198
Morwellham Quay museum *135*, 218, 219
Mothecombe 63
Mount Batten, Plymouth Sound 60
Mount's Bay 122
Mousehole 86, 122, 172, 213, *213*, 219

Nancledra 237
Nanstallon 61
Natsley *64*
Neolithic society 43, 44
 agriculture 46–7
 monuments 47–9
Nether Exe 48
New Red Sandstone 16, 19, *20*, 21
Newlyn 60, 128, 172
Newquay 73, 74, 111, 154, 175, 180, *181*, 198, 201, 205, 215, 223, 225, 231
Newton Abbot 59, 97, 162, 170, 199
Newton Bushel 97, 162
Newton Poppleford 162, 189
Newton St Cyres 140
Normans 68, 95
North Tawton 132

Okehampton 68, 91, 94, 97, 98, *98*, 108, 160, 161, 164
 bypass 191, 209, 213
Old Burrow 61
orchards 125–6
Otterton Mill, Budleigh Salterton 132
Ottery St Mary 138, 174

Padstow 172, *172*, 186, 203, 77, 137
Padstow estuary 123
Paignton 153
Palaeocene Epoch 20

paper mills 136
Par 172, 203
parks, landscaped 115–16
Parracombe 98
Paton Watson, James 175
Pawton 68
Payhembury, Tuck Mill 138
Pearson, John 183
peat 33, 34
Pendeen *218*
Pendennis 104–5, *105*
Pendower, Gerrans Bay 26, *26*
Penkneth 99
Penryn 103, 105, 135, 172
Pentewan 172, 203
Penwith 50, 113, 154, 240, 243
Penzance 85, 86, 122, 150, 170, 172, 175, 179, 200, 203
Permian Period 19
Perranporth 215
Perran Wharf Foundry 150
Petrockstowe river 20
pewter industry 60–1, 140
pilgrim centres 78, 81
Pleistocene Epoch 23–6, 34
Pliocene Epoch 20
Plym river 108, 140
Plymouth 152, 153
Plymouth 59, 71, 73, 74, 81, 86, *86*, 91, 103, 107–8, *107*, 123, 136, 137, 155, 164, *164*, 166, 167, *167*, 169–70, *170*, 173, *178*, 182, 183, 201, 225
 airport 205
 Barbican 178, 202
 blitz 175–6
 Charles Church 85, 175, 215
 fishing industry 119, 129
 Guildhall 148, 175, 177
 Millbank Docks 202, 203
 National Marine Aquarium 178, 183
 Old Dockyard 148
 postwar development 175–9, 225
 Royal citadel 148
 Royal Dockyard *169*, 215
 shipping 202–3
 Smeaton's Tower 215
 University 184
Plymouth Princess Yachts 150
Plymouth Sound *60*, 108, 202
Plympton 90, 91, 97, 101–2, *101*, 132, 140, 164, 172
podzols 33
Poldice railroad 198
Polperro 38, 116, 172, *218*, 219
Polwhele, Richard 174

253

INDEX

population distribution 68–74
Porlock 45
Port Eliot 115
Port Isaac 116, 172
Porthleven 123, 172
Portreath 198
Postbridge 150, *212*
pottery:
  early 44, 48, 54
  Roman 59, 60
Poundstock 80
Powderham Castle 97, 102–3, *102*
Praa Sands 62
Praed, William 195
Princesshay 225
Princetown 30, 198
Probus 77

Quarrying 148–9, 153
Quartly, James and Francis 119

Raddon 42, 56
Raddon Hills 46, 48, 114
radon radiation 38
railways 122, 180, 183, 196–202, 206, 231
  'atmospheric' 198–9, *199*
  closures 201–2
  earliest 197–8
  gauges 201
  images of South West 231–3
  new stations 202
  on Dartmoor 198
  restored 196–7, 201
  routes to London 196
  and tourism 201–2
rain and snowfall 31–2, 38–9
Rainsbury 61
raised beaches 26
reave system 51–3, 63
Rebecca 235
Redruth 136, 139, *146*, 150, 171
religious dissent 81–4
Repton, Joseph 115
resorts 73–4
Restormel 91, 96, 99, *99*, 100, 108, 161
retirement 73, 74
Rheic Ocean 18
rias 28, *28*
roads 185–91
Roborough 153
Rolle, Lord 193
Roman settlement 59
Romano-British period 43–5, 55–61, 66

Rougemont Castle 160
Rough Tor 46, 53, *53*, 54, 58, 62
Royal Albert Bridge 199, 200

sailing, leisure 204
St Agnes 135, 140, 172
St Agnes formation 20
St Austell 19, 29, 140, 149, *149*, 171, 175, 209
  brewery 132
St Breock 152
St Buryan 77, 80, *81*
St Cleer parish *47*, 48
St Columb Canal 195
St Day 80, 81
St Erth Beds 20
St Eval 205
St Germans 80, 161, 164
St Issey 152
St Ives 103, 172, 180, 201, 219, 231, *239*
  School 239–40
  The Tate 181, *181*
St Just *83*, *84*, 205, *146*, 205
St Just in Penwith 72, 119
St Keverne 77, 80
St Mabyn 80
St Mary's Buzza Hill 152
St Mawes 11, 104, 105
St Mawgan 31, 59, 205
St Michael's Mount 60, 62, 63, 81, 161, 213
St Minver 152
St Piran *80*
St Teath 80
St Tudy 80
St Winnow 80
saints, Celtic 77, 79–80
Saints Way 185
Salcombe 103
salt extraction 61
Saltash 98, 135, 152, 175
Saltram House 138, *138*
Sanders Farmhouse, Lettaford 21
sandstones 16, 19, *20*, 21, 34
Saunton Down 26
schists 19
Scilly, Isles of 23, 26, *27*, 39, 132, 154, 202, *203*, 205
seaside resorts, development of 222–3
Seaton 138, 201
sense of place 229–30
service occupations 154
'set-aside' land 125
Shaugh Moor 50, 56, 211
sheep farming 116, 120, 121, 126

Sherracombe Ford 61
ship/boat building 150–2, 154
Sidmouth 20, 73, 138, 179, *179*, 201, 222, *223*
Simonsbath 115
Slapton Lea 28, *29*
slate 21, 148, 193
Smeaston, John 131
soils 33–7
Sourton Down 58
South Crofty tin mine 143, *143*, 144
South Devon Railway 198–9
South Hallsands 28
South Hams 56, 183, 188
South Zeal 162, *162*, 163
South-West Coastal Footpath 185
Stanhope, Earl of 196
stannary laws 94
stannary towns 172
Stannon Moor 54
Starcross ferry 202
Starcross pumping house 199, *200*
Start Bay 28
Start Point 19
Sticklepath, Finch Foundry 135, *135*
Sticklepath Fault 20
Stockleigh English 76
Stockleigh Pomeroy *42*
Stoke Damerel 170
stone circles 87
Stover Canal 193, 198
Stripple Stones, Bodmin Moor 48
subsidence 38
Sweetworthy, Luccombe *57*, 64

Tamar, River and Valley 108, 122, 126, 139, 200, 218
Tamar Lake 196
Tamar Manure Navigation 195
Tamar road bridge 73, 191
Taunton 195
Tavistock 69, 94 136, *147*, 164, 172, 218
  Abbey 80
  Westbridge 173, *173*
Tavistock Canal 193–4
Taw Torridge estuary *25*
Taw river 110
Teign river and valley 139, 189, 202
Teignmouth 30, 129, 172, 179, 193, 203
Templar, James 193
Templar, William 148
Tertiary Period 20, 23
textile industry 173, 219 *see also* woollen industry

254

INDEX

Thorverton 114
Three Holes Cavern 45
tide mills 152
tin mining 50, 60, 70, 72, 95, 139, 140–47, 153, 172, 219
   engine houses 144–5
   maps *145–7*
Tintagel 60, 62, 63, 78, *79*, 90, 98
Tiverton 61, 69, 137, 138, 140, 164, 167, 173, *173*, 174, 219
   Manor 101
   West Exe Mills 138–9, *139*
Tiverton Canal 195, *195*
Tolgus Foundry 150
toll-houses 189, *190*
Topsham 59
Topsham ferry 20
Tor Royal, Dartmoor 58, 62
Torbay 38, 73, 153, 201, 203, 222, 225
Tornewton 45
Torpoint 175
Torpoint Ferry 191, 202
Torquay 73, 129, 179, *223*, 232
Torridge river 202
Torridge estuary 50
Torrington Canal 193
tors, formation of 24–5
Totnes 59, 68, 80, 90, 93, 137, 160, 161, *161*, 162, 165, 166, *166*, 168, 170, 175, 199
   Town Mill 132
   Wineries 132
tourism 130, 154, 179–82, 201, 222–3, 230–3
Towan Blustry 172, 180
Towednack 80, 113
trade, early 60–2
Trebartha Barton model farm 119
Trebetherick Point 23

Treffry, Joseph 196, 198
Treffry Viaduct 198, *199*
Tregenna castle 231
Tregeseal 150
Tregony 90, 91, 97, *100*, 105, 166
Tremaine 80
Trematon 98, 168
Trencreek 111
Tresellern Marsh, Bodmin Moor 58, 62
Trethellen Farm archaeological site 54
Trethevy Quoit 47
Trevillett Mill, Tintagel 132
Trevithick, Richard 150, 197
Trewellard 86
Trezise, Simon 235
Triassic Period 19
Truro 85, 105, 137, 155, 162, *163*, 166, 168, 170, 172, 175, 183, *183*
   Cathedral 183
   City Hall 171, *171*
Truro river 163
Truro viaduct 200, *201*
turnpike roads 185, 187–9
Two Moors Way 185
Tyrwhitt, Thomas 198

Uffculme *244*–5, 246
Uffculme, Coldharbour Mill 138, *138*, *218*, 219
Ugbrooke Park 115–16, *115*
universities 74, 183, 184
Upper Greensand 20, 22, 38
Upton Pyne 140
uranium 140

Variscian Orogeny 18, 19
vegetation, human impact on 35–5
Venford 113
Vermuyden, Conrad 131

Veryan, Melinsey Mill 132
viaducts 198, 199, 200, 201, *201*
Vitifer 142
Vixen Tor, Dartmoor 212, *212*

Wadebridge 135, 186
Warren, C Henry 233
water mills 131–2, 152
Week St Mary 91, 99, *99*
Werrington Park 115
West Cornwall Railway 200
West Penwith 63
West Somerset Steam Railway 197
Westward Ho! 25, 45
Wheal Martyn China Clay Museum 149, 219
Wheat Act, 1932 123
White Downs 22
Whitty, Thomas 138
Widecombe-in-the-Moor 38, *75*, 232
wind farms 152
wineries 132
Winkleigh 97, 132
Winsford Hill, The Punchbowl 24
Wistman's Wood 36, *36*
Wiveliscombe 61
wolfram extraction 140
Woodbury Common 35
woodland and forest clearance 46, 49, 55, 58, 110, 123, 127
wool and textile production 72, 136–8, 153
World War II 123, 175–6
Wotter Common, Dartmoor 58

Yealmpton toll-house *190*
Yealm ferry 202

Zennor, Trewey Water Mill 132

255

Picture Credits

Images on the following pages © Crown copyright.NMR or © English Heritage: 17 (DP017011); 18 (DP017021); 19 (NMR 23512/11); 20 (DP017036); 21t (DP017043); 21b (DP017050); 23t (DP017056); 23b (DP0170165); 24t (DP017071); 24b (DP017078); 25 (NMR 23597/21); 27 (NMR 23893/12); 28t (NMR 23589/34); 28b (NMR 23443/10); 29t (NMR 23557/17); 29b (NMR 23464/37); 35t (DP017087); 35b (NMR 23444/04); 36b (DP017076); 56t (NMR 15864/27); 57 (NMR 15856/04); 64 (NMR 23649/05); 75 (NMR 23520/23); 76 (NMR 23599/24);79t (NMR 23511/07); 81 (NMR 23681/05); 83 (AA98 10218); 85b (AA99 04993); 93 (NMR 21581/10); 95 (NMR 23516/14); 98 (NMR 23700/14); 99t (NMR 23650/16); 99b (NMR 23651/01); 100 (NMR 23517/15); 101 (NMR 23589/28); 102 (NMR 23555/17); 104 (NMR 23557/06); 105 (NMR 18513/19); 106 (NMR 23556/17); 112t (NMR 23679/24); 112b (NMR 23598/06); 113 (NMR 23681/24); 114t (NMR 15423/28); 115 (NMR 23701/17); 118 (NMR 23653/19); 122b (NMR 23757/20); 124 (NMR 23701/15); 128 (NMR 23589/00A); 130 (NMR 23754/23); 133 (NMR 23512/23); 136 (NMR 23442/18); 139 (NMR 23753/15); 140 (AA99 04965); 143t (AA98 17938); 143b (BB95 09768); 144tl (AA98 10573); 144tr (AA98 10572); 144b (AA98 10337); 145t (AA98 10390); 148 (NMR 23516/04); 149b (NMR 23512/07); 151b (NMR 23508/22); 159 (NMR 23449/16); 161 (NMR 4882/21); 163 (NMR 23449/08); 166l (AA041956); 167 (NMR 23651/07); 173b (NMR 23753/17); 178 (NMR 23651/12); 181 (NMR 23517/09); 182 (AA052729); 183 (NMR 23755/14); 190b (NMR 23474/14); 191 (NMR 23513/08); 192 (NMR 23554/21); 201 (NMR 23680/03); 202 (NMR 21892/07); 207 (NMR 23468/11); 208t (NMR 23680/30); 208b (BB97 09567); 215b (MF99 0718/04); 216 (NMR 23700/19); 218tl (BB92 14688); 218tr (BB92 14594); 218bl (AA024520); 218br (MF99 0666/35); 222 (NMR 23521/12); 223 (BB98 21600); 224 (NMR 23755/24); 224 (AA024600).

English Heritage ground photography was taken by Alun Bull, Derek Kendall and Peter Williams. Additional English Heritage photography by Steve Cole, Patricia Payne and Bob Skingle.

Additional photographs: Apexnewspix.com, photo Nick Gregory: 39; © Mark Brayshay: 138b, 147, 152t, 168, 187, 190, 199t; CORBIS: © Angelo Hornak: 85t; © David Cornforth: 226tl,tc,tr; Cornish Picture Library © Paul Watts: 122t; Devon County Council, photo F.M. Griffith. Copyright Reserved Stockleigh Pomeroy: 42b, 56b; Pictures courtesy of the *Express & Echo*: 38; FLPA: Holt/Nigel Cattlin 114b, Holt/Angela Hampton 129b; © *The Guardian*: 227cl; © Peter Goodrum: 227br; © David Harvey: 80b; © Kurt Jackson: 241, 242; National Portrait Gallery, London/copyright Tom Hustler: 235; courtesy of the Greg Norden Collection as reproduced in 'Landscapes under the Luggage Rack': 232t,b; © Tate, London 2006: 240; *Historical Atlas of South-West England* Editors Roger Kain and William Ravenhill, ISBN 0859894347/University of Exeter Press/ photo: Mr. Andrew Teed: 21t; *Western Morning News*, Courtesy of Exeter University Library (Special Collections): 238.

Aerial survey acknowledgements
New English Heritage aerial photographs were taken by Damian Grady. The Aerial Reconnaissance team would like to thank the following people for their help: a special note of thanks must go to the skills and patience of the pilots Mick Webb and Marten White; the aircraft owner David Sanders; the NMR cataloguing team Rose Ogle, Katy Groves, Catherine Runciman, Cinzia Bacilieri, Philip Daniels, Geoff Hall; Jon Proudman for all the publication scanning; and Sarah Prince for laser copying thousands of aerial photographs to send to the authors.